CUMBIA!

EDITED BY
HÉCTOR FERNÁNDEZ L'HOESTE
AND PABLO VILA

CUMBIA!

Scenes of a Migrant Latin American Music Genre

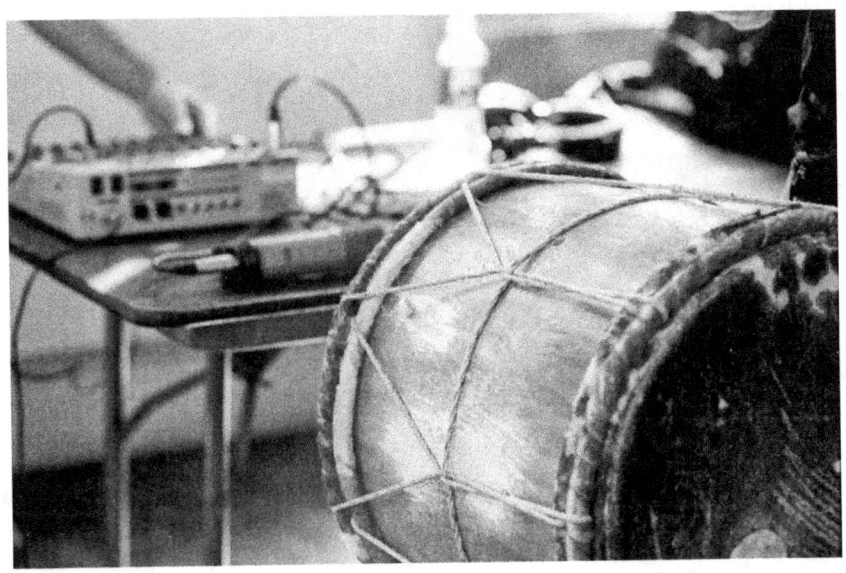

DUKE UNIVERSITY PRESS   DURHAM AND LONDON   2013

© 2013 Duke University Press
All rights reserved

Designed by C. H. Westmoreland
Typeset in Whitman with Gill Sans display
by Tseng Information Systems, Inc.

Library of Congress Cataloging-in-Publication Data
Cumbia! : scenes of a migrant Latin American music genre /
Héctor Fernández L'Hoeste and Pablo Vila, eds.
pages cm
Includes bibliographical references and index.
ISBN 978-0-8223-5414-7 (cloth : alk. paper)
ISBN 978-0-8223-5433-8 (pbk. : alk. paper)
1. Cumbia (Music)—America—History and criticism.
2. Working class—America—Songs and music—History and criticism.
I. Fernández l'Hoeste, Héctor D., 1962– II. Vila, Pablo, 1952–
ML3475.C86 2013
781.64098—dc23
2013004645

frontispiece: Photograph © Donald Martinez.

Duke University Press gratefully acknowledges the support of Georgia State University, which provided funds toward the publication of this book.

Para Elena Cogollo y Beatriz Escorcia,
for the love of culture.
Para Juan Enrique "Chango" Farías Gómez
and Luis Alberto "El Flaco" Spinetta,
two "turning-point" characters in the history of
Argentine popular music, for the love of culture,
Argentine-style.

Contents

Acknowledgments ix

Introduction
HÉCTOR FERNÁNDEZ L'HOESTE AND PABLO VILA 1

CHAPTER 1. Cumbia Music in Colombia: Origins, Transformations, and Evolution of a Coastal Music Genre
LEONARDO D'AMICO 29

CHAPTER 2. ¿Pa' dónde vas Marioneta? ¿Pa' dónde va la gaita? La Cumbiamba Eneyé Returns to San Jacinto
JORGE ARÉVALO MATEUS WITH MARTÍN VEJARANO 49

CHAPTER 3. Cumbia in Mexico's Northeastern Region
JOSÉ JUAN OLVERA GUDIÑO 87

CHAPTER 4. Rigo Tovar, Cumbia, and the Transnational *Grupero* Boom
ALEJANDRO L. MADRID 105

CHAPTER 5. Communicating the Collective Imagination: The Sociospatial World of the Mexican *Sonidero* in Puebla, New York, and New Jersey
CATHY RAGLAND 119

CHAPTER 6. From *The World of the Poor* to the Beaches of Eisha: Chicha, *Cumbia*, and the Search for a Popular Subject in Peru
JOSHUA TUCKER 138

CHAPTER 7. *Pandillar* in the Jungle: Regionalism and *Tecno-cumbia* in Amazonian Peru
KATHRYN METZ 168

CHAPTER 8. Gender Tensions in *Cumbia Villera*'s Lyrics
PABLO SEMÁN AND PABLO VILA 188

CHAPTER 9. *Feliz, feliz*
CRISTIAN ALARCÓN 213

CHAPTER 10. *El "Tú" Tropical, el "Vos" Villero*, and Places in Between: Language, Ideology, Music, and the Spatialization of Difference in Uruguayan Tropical Music
MATTHEW J. VAN HOOSE   226

CHAPTER 11. On Music and Colombianness: Toward a Critique of the History of Cumbia
HÉCTOR FERNÁNDEZ L'HOESTE   248

References   269
Contributors   285
Index   289

Acknowledgments

Héctor

Aside from Elena and Beatriz, who inspired this entire project, I'd like to thank Pablo Vila for his support and input throughout the journey. Due to personal circumstances, this was not an easy ride, but Pablo managed everything quite gracefully. Special thanks go to the Center for Latin American and Latino/a Studies and the College of Arts and Sciences at Georgia State University for their solid assistance and encouragement. In addition, special credit goes to my son, Sebastián, and my sisters in Miami and Bogotá during a challenging period of my life. Last but not least, a big shout-out goes to Liliana Saumet, who reminds me daily how important music can be.

Pablo

First of all, I have to thank Héctor Fernández L'Hoeste for inviting me to participate in this wonderful project. It was a very generous offer that I really appreciate. Numerous people helped to make this book possible. Special thanks go to Malvina Silba, not only for her outstanding fieldwork in the *bailes* and her superb interviews in the neighborhoods but also for the intense dialogue we have maintained over the years, which helped me to better understand the complex world of Argentine cumbia. Finally, I must acknowledge my children, Juanchi, Paloma, and Malena, and my wife, Julia Chindemi Vila, for all their support.

Our gratitude goes to the staff at Duke University Press. Four anonymous reviewers offered important criticisms that greatly improved the final product. Valerie Millholland and Gisela Fosado, handling our numerous doubts and inquiries pertaining to the text, and Judith Hoover, who copyedited the manuscript, were a pleasure to work with. Their dedicated efforts are greatly appreciated.

Map 1. The Americas and pertinent locations.

HÉCTOR FERNÁNDEZ L'HOESTE
AND PABLO VILA

Introduction

Héctor

Like intelligence, education comes in many packages. Growing up middle class in Latin America, I was educated not only at home, in school, and at church but in the most unexpected ways and locations. At home, aside from what I may have learned from my relatives, a good chunk of my education took place in the kitchen, where I worked on my homework while women like Elena Cogollo and Beatriz Escorcia prepared our family meals. Always on in the background, tuned to their preferences, clearly indicating who ruled in the kitchen—most definitely, it wasn't my mother—was the radio. Those radio stations, in most cases, led me into a world despised by some of my more snobby acquaintances, but I found them strangely gratifying. In a world populated by characters like Arandú, Prince of the Jungle, and Toloamba, his black companion, and Kalimán, the Incredible Man, and Solín, his Egyptian sidekick, the soundtrack was incontestably *cumbia* and *vallenato*. While my instructors at school Anglicized me and revealed the complexities and joys of Led Zeppelin, Pink Floyd, and Supertramp, at home Elena and Beatriz reminded me how to be a "true" *costeño* (a coastal person), that is, an inhabitant of the Colombian Caribbean. And being *costeño* was, without a doubt, linked to more than the nasally Caribbean accent of my Spanish, quite different from what is habitually identified as Colombian Spanish: the various dialects of Andean provinces. In this sense, my culture was closer to Cuba's or Puerto Rico's than to those from the inner provinces of the country.

Like most cultures, food and music incarnated sizable factors in the operation of *costeñidad* (coastalness). Food incarnated a liking for *arepas con huevo*, *bollo*, *mote de ñame*, and *alegría*. In terms of music, though, Elena and Beatriz made sure that I knew what being a *costeño* was all about. Instead of the fancy, middle-class diet of U.S. and U.K. tunes played by some local radio stations, the radio in the kitchen was invariably tuned to frequencies that blasted the latest in tropical music, appealing to the working-class sensibilities of my kitchen educators, who were bent on making me more than the spoiled brat that so many of my school acquaintances represented. In the eyes of Elena and Beatriz, this task involved making sure that, just as I could enjoy the sagas of many radio series, I could distinguish between the various versions of "La creciente" (The Swell), a local vallenato hit, and that I could judiciously discriminate between the contributions of Pacho Galán (a local hero) and Lucho Bermúdez (a *costeño* who had sold out to the *cachacos*, the inhabitants from the interior of the country). Being musically literate—in particular, with respect to anything related to *música costeña*—was a big part of this facet of my education. Genotypically speaking, as the darkest member of my family, I felt a certain kindred for the cultural products that both of these women defended with such fervor. While they ironed clothing, the radio would play *radionovelas* and music from all over the Caribbean, teaching me to distinguish between Dominican *merengue*, Cuban *son*, and *cumbia soledeña*. One thing, though: beyond Elena's and Beatriz's coaching, I still treasure rock. (Lately my son has learned about the complexities of *Breakfast in America*; so much for siding with music of the subaltern.) In fact, true to my generation, I see very little contradiction in this eclectic disposition. I'm quite sure that my love for tropical music nourishes my appreciation for rock and vice versa. In the end, it's a matter of acknowledging and embracing multiple identities and hoping they will contribute to a more enlightened reading of experiences.

Many years later, the memory of Elena and Beatriz still haunts me. To them I owe—I can see clearly now—my ability to consume and enjoy Latin American cultural products with a relatively open mind, paying close attention to the social, racial, and gender aspects explored in their content, though never forgetting that their ultimate object is, most surely, to entertain, to lighten one's heart, soul, and mind. As I grew in Barranquilla during the 1960s and 1970s, how was I to know that I was witnessing the evolution of a music that would come to define national identity? If I knew anything as a child, it was that people from elsewhere in Colombia talked funny and couldn't dance. A quick exposure to Bogotá during my years of college took care of these prejudices. Nevertheless, how was I to understand that my *costeñidad*, challenged by the crisp sound of Spanish from the interior, would eventually debunk preconceived notions of what it meant to be Colombian? And that, even in Bogotá, while I attended college, I would witness the displacement of *música ranchera* by vallenato, a genre that, according to many inhabitants of the interior, so unaccustomed to the problematization of racial difference, embodies a far better vehicle for national identity than cumbia? I listened to this shift take place before my ears. In 1980, when I landed in Bogotá, the airwaves ruling the public transportation system were owned by Mexican music (yes, some Bogotá buses do play music); by the time I left the capital a decade later, vallenato reigned uncontested.

However, aside from these two experiences, my adolescence as a *barranquillero* brought me into close contact with a cultural tradition that negotiates class, racial, and gender barriers in fashions unknown in Anglo latitudes. Endless sessions of practice for carnival *comparsas* at the local social club—a tedious, mind-numbing experience, at best—and many dances hosted by the local ensemble, the Orquesta de Pedro Movilla, which shifted easily from merengue to *merecumbé* to *porro* to cumbia, taught me quite well. This was all long before I even heard of political correctness. In Caribbean culture, quite clearly, there was no room for such Anglo distractions. Men were men, being white was better than being black, the rich tolerated the poor, and women knew their place, even if things were changing. In the music, however, aside from the beats, riffs, melodies, and harmonies, I recognized unexpected ways to deal with issues that were omitted in other circles. And cumbia, being so local, so close to my battered sense of *costeñidad*, served as a suitable vehicle to settle many differences. That is why, nowadays, when I listen to the lilting beat of Mexican cumbia played by a pickup that passes by, a smile lightens up my face, because in this music I recognize a distant though solid connection with my past and origin. It says volumes about how many of us have made the journey from cities by a warmer ocean, in the mountains, and by muddy rivers and eventually found homes in places harnessed by the winds of winter and twirling tornadoes. And this journey, I think, has taught many of us about difference and how to deal with it, how class, race, and gender are culturally determined and ethnocentrically appraised constructs with significant impact on our relation with modernity.

Not that this journey came without its travails. For the most part, amid a culture that, though generally tolerant, has grown increasingly uncomfortable with Latin(o) American presence, many of us ended up incarnating the Other and were left to embody difference, never mind issues of subjectivity. So, in a sense, I guess that I like to trace the evolution of cumbia because, to a certain extent, the evolution of my identity mimics its ways. As a child, without being aware of it (my ethnocentrism would not allow this), I incarnated a cultural norm that operated within the periphery of a national construct.

Once I moved to Bogotá and New York—and eventually to Atlanta—this peripheral quality remained, though it then operated closer to the interests of a hegemonic construct. In terms of class, I've replaced many of my Colombian ways with a more pragmatic U.S. middle-class mind-set, which, to be sincere, hasn't embodied much of a sacrifice. Genderwise, the intricacies of life have imposed single fatherhood on me, an aspect I also cherish. Thus, as I've lived, I've had to "recalculate" my ways. The journey of cumbia has followed a similar path. As a regional construct, it thrived as a Caribbean cultural practice. Traveling to the interior of the country, it turned self-conscious and assumed a more agreeable form, ornamented with hints of U.S. modernity. Eventually it left the country, adopting practical ways, adapting its makeup to local preferences, giving birth to multiple forms of the national kind.

Pablo

Growing up in Argentina seems to be a very peculiar way of growing up in Latin America. On the one hand, being middle class seems to be very different from the way Héctor experienced his middle-classness: when I was growing up, my family didn't have money to hire someone to prepare our meals. After all, Argentina is more socially equitable than Colombia. I am the typical product of the particularly amazing process of social mobility that characterized Argentina until, let's say, the late 1960s and early 1970s. Not only were my grandparents immigrants (some of them illiterates in any language, the others literate only in their original one), working-class folks who literally died at work, but my mother was an immigrant as well. Both my mother and my father worked from a very early age; my father from the age of six, my mother since she was twelve. Following family tradition, I started working at the age of fourteen.

But Argentina offered people with *inquietudes* (roughly speaking, people who wanted to better their lives, both intellectually and materially) the possibility of a free education all the way to college and even graduate school. My parents, with great effort, followed that route and became professionals. Trying not to forget their origins, they actually became "leftist professionals," lower middle class but highly educated, in Bourdieu's terms, people with low economic and social capital but with an enormous cultural capital. (We had a 10,000-volume library at home!) We had little money but lots of books. And some music.

As heirs of the Enlightenment (after all, they were Marxists, and Adorno was on their reading list), they loved classical music, and during my childhood that was the music we listened to the most. But we also listened to some popular music, above all music with social content, either Argentine folk à la Yupanqui and Horacio Guaraní, or African American leftist singers like Marian Anderson and Paul Robeson. (When I came to the United States, I was surprised that so few people knew as much as I did about these singers.) Like others my age, I was highly influenced by the folk music boom that characterized Buenos Aires in the early 1960s. I played guitar and sang in many school combos a very sophisticated type of folklore, the one leftists like my parents and I enjoyed, a folklore highly influenced by either American jazz or the classical chorus tradition (or both). That was my musical environment when cumbia arrived to Argentina in the 1960s, and my reaction to it was linked to my well-learned "enlightened" musical education: I didn't like it! Honoring Argentina's penchant for its European roots, given the scant visibility of mestizo or mulatto presence in our culture (despite the New Song and tango's African descent), cumbia seemed unacceptable.

To me, cumbia was *música mersa* (music for uneducated people). In my case (being a leftist), it didn't mean "working-class music" but unpretentious music that appealed to people (of any class) who did not know what "good" music was all about. But it was irksome to me to acknowledge that, for some reason, cumbia was a type of music that especially appealed to working-class folks. Something similar happened with other types of "bad music," and, as a matter of fact, my attempt to understand such an attachment was one of the reasons that, many years later, I decided to follow a career in the sociology of music.

In the 1960s what I (and many other "enlightened" people like me) considered "bad" music was epitomized by a television program called *El Club del Clan*, in which well-prepared musical characters deployed different popular musical styles. For instance, Johnny Tedesco played the role of "rocker" (Elvis style); Palito Ortega (a future governor) was the poor immigrant from the countryside; Jolly Land was the Doris Day character; and Nicky Jones played the part of the *cumbiero*. That Jones was the most clownish of this troupe didn't contribute to my appreciation for cumbia at the time, or that he always appeared on the program with absurdly colorful Hawaiian shirts. Later on, I discovered that he was a very good jazz bass player who shifted his career to cumbia to survive, as did the more "sophisticated" cumbia singer of the period, Chico Novarro, a very well-known drum player in the jazz scene of the late 1950s. That Novarro's most popular cumbia was "El Orangután" ("Estaba el orangután, meciéndose en una rama y llegó la orangutana, comiéndose una banana" / There once was a male orangutan swinging from the branch of a tree, when a female orangutan arrived, eating a banana) did not contribute to my appreciation for the genre either.

My love for the type of folk music that characterized the folk boom of the 1960s (what can be called "projection" or "fusion" folk because it mixed very modern musical elements: Los Fronterizos, Los Trovadores, Mercedes Sosa, Los Huanca Hua, El Grupo Vocal Argentino, El Cuarteto Zupay, and, above all, Miguel Saravia) was separating me from the musical taste of my parents and guiding me into a different political direction as well, because, through my contact with folk music, a process of nationalization started to grow within me that, eventually, led me to become what my parents hated the most: a Peronist! In other words, folk music, the music of the Argentine countryside and mestizo immigrants, made me aware that there were some elitist elements in the enlightened culture of my parents that did not allow them to understand how important Peronism was to the process by which those despised immigrants acquired political and social citizenship. Quite clearly, through their move from working class to lower middle class via a learned culture devoid of self-criticism, they had inadvertently internalized several elements of the Argentine elite's imaginary. Weirdly enough, having lived in extreme poverty, they couldn't really understand the reasons for the political preferences of other poor people (for instance, people like my own maternal grandfather, who, not knowing a word of Spanish, disappeared for two days from his household without further notice because he wanted to go to Evita's funeral). Becoming a Peronist allowed me to appreciate the musical choices of Argentine popular sectors in a different light and moved me away from the "false consciousness" hypothesis endorsed by my parents to explain why working-class folks liked cumbia.

Thus, while Héctor's ability to consume and enjoy cumbia and vallenato (that is, Colombian popular music) with a relatively open mind, paying attention to the social, racial, and gender aspects explored in their content, resulted from a sensible exposure to working-class cultural codes, my ability to understand the musical choices of Argentine popular sectors without conventional prejudices came after my conversion to Peronism (to the horror of my enlightened parents and friends, who, not surprisingly, rapidly became my ex-friends). In this way, deep in the southern part of the continent, the way I came into close contact with a cultural tradition that negotiates class, gender, racial, regional, and ethnic barriers was not my participation in a particular popular culture device like Héctor's carnival *comparsas*, but my participation in a political movement that, historically speaking, had tried to incorporate not only working-class folks into the national project but also mestizos from the countryside and women as well. (Not only did Peronism institute women's right to vote for the first time in Argentine history, but it required women to be represented in the legislature as well.) Instead of moving from music to politics, as Héctor did, I made the opposite move: from politics to music. I didn't learn to appreciate, through music, that other, more egalitarian forms of human relationships were possible. Instead, through politics, I learned that social actors historically linked to Peronism used particular types of music (clearly cumbia since the 1970s) to advance their identitarian claims (which are always political).

All this came full circle in the early 1980s, when I started doing my research on rock *nacional* for my bachelor's thesis. At that time, discovering that rock was mostly a middle-class movement, I realized that, in a clear move toward "distinction" that Bourdieu would have loved, many *cumbieros* where portraying themselves as the "others" regarding rock nacional, that is, as the representatives of the Argentine popular sectors, not their middle classes. That was quite prominent in the work of one of the most popular cumbia combos of the period, Los Caú, who were called the "Kings of Chamamé Tropical," the cumbia-*chamamé* hybrid that was the most popular incarnation of cumbia at that time.

Even though the cumbia of the late 1960s and 1970s continued to be popular among Argentine popular sectors, it was so because it underwent a process of blending itself with native Argentine rhythms—prominently, the most danceable of them: chamamé. Out of this blend, "chamamé tropical" was born, a rhythm that reigned through the 1970s and early 1980s. Los Caú (the Drunk Ones), mimicking Kiss, painted their faces in black and white. Humor was their main characteristic, and they made fun of everything, especially the most important musical genre of the period, rock nacional and the middle-class culture it represented. When the epitome of popularity for *rockeros* was to perform on the "temple of rock," the Obras Stadium in Buenos Aires, Los Caú titled a record *Los Caú en Obras*, imitating the LP titles of many rock nacional bands recorded live in that stadium. Obviously, Los Caú never performed in Obras, and the photos on the cover make fun of the celebrity aspiration of rockers; they also evince class differences that separate cumbia musicians and rock nacional's audience. This is so because, on the cover, Los

Caú were portrayed with all the attire and tools of masons, a working-class occupation, literally *in obras*, that is, building a house. They were playing with the name of the stadium, whose complete name is Obras Sanitarias de La Nacion (Argentine Sanitary Works).

My appreciation of cumbia grew exponentially in the late 1980s, when I was finishing my course work at the University of Texas at Austin, and I decided to write my dissertation on the *bailanta* phenomenon that was starting to grow in Buenos Aires at that time. I was really preoccupied by the neoliberal turn that the Peronist movement was experiencing under the leadership of Carlos Menem. If Peronism was turning neoliberal, who was going to defend the interests of its historical constituency, the *negros* from the countryside who, by that time, were the bulk of the working class? My hypothesis was that, considering that Peronism, in its Menem incarnation, was abandoning the representation of working-class interests given the neoliberal project embraced by the new president, somebody or something was going to occupy the representation of Argentine *negros*. Given what was going on in the bailanta scene, I thought that tropical music was going to offer identifications that Peronism was abandoning. For a variety of reasons, that dissertation never happened, and I ended up writing one on identification processes on the U.S.-Mexican border. But my respect for cumbia was already there, and, as soon as I had the opportunity, I returned to the subject with my research on gender issues in cumbia *villera* (coauthored with Pablo Semán).

In this regard, I see Argentine cumbia as cumbia from the "Deep South," in the double meaning of the term. On the one hand, because Argentine cumbia is the southernmost incarnation of the Colombian style, it shows that the tropics can somehow be reproduced in much more temperate climates. But, on the other, Argentine cumbia is music of the "Deep South" because it's *negro* music, music that Argentine *negros* (the mestizos who were baptized as *negros* by chauvinist Euro-Argentines in the 1940s) have been using since the 1960s to advance some of their most important identitarian projects.

And talking about identitarian projects, if I want to be consistent with my claim that we have multiple identifications and all of them have the traces of each other as the condition of possibility of their own existence, I have to identify those that have the possibility of undermining my analytical lens to comprehend cumbia (because I am assuming that my political identification is helping me to do so; I am sure the readers of this book will identify many other identifications I am completely unaware of). We are talking about the dark side of the moon here.

First of all, cumbia is not the music I listen to for pleasure. That music is jazz. Second, I don't dance! When roles were distributed in childhood and adolescence, I decided to play instead of dance; I played guitar. There is an old Argentine saying: "El que toca, nunca baila." At the same time, I am a sound freak. I have been involved in audio since the late 1960s, and over the years I was able to build a very good audio system. I have an acoustic-treated listening room at home and plenty of tube equipment: one preamplifier, one pre-preamplifier, three amplifiers, a tuner, a cassette player, two turntables, a CD player, a computer-based server, four speakers, and two subwoofers. There is nothing more distant from Argentine *cumbieros* than my meticulousness about sound equipment.

In terms of more "traditional" identifications that probably are affecting my capacity to understand the cumbia villera world, I have to mention that I am in my late fifties, and the audience of this genre is, in many cases, forty years younger than I. In terms of class, even though most of my life I considered myself lower middle class or marginal working class, I did much better than 99 percent of cumbia followers. And in terms of gender, even though for a while I tasted some of the roles women usually perform (I was the single parent of two very young children for more than ten years), that does not transform my subject position into a female one. Therefore, only the readers of this book can gauge how this other side of the moon has influenced my (mis)understanding of cumbia.

Both

Unlike human beings, music has the uncanny capability of crossing borders freely—even if it's occasionally persecuted and outlawed by authoritarian governments—settling in new places and, thanks to its malleability, eventually evolving into more culturally diverse forms. This is, most definitely, the case of cumbia during its travels throughout the Americas. Like many Colombian bands, the Corraleros de Majagual might have traveled to Mexico and popularized their music long ago, but it also helped that Colombian drug cartels developed links with Mexican organizations. Along the way, in the same planes that transported illicit substances, a few cassette tapes made the trip, sharing a common appreciation for Caribbean, accordion-based melodies. If northern Mexico bears a healthy tradition of regional music, so does the smuggling culture of the Colombian Caribbean, appropriated by many of the reckless travelers who landed in Aztec latitudes with precious cargo. In turn, when Mexican laborers journeyed north, once they made a few dollars, music was a main staple, bringing much needed relief, given the distance from the homeland. With its happy lilting beat, so different from the melancholy of *corridos* and related genres, which encourage sorrowful nostalgia and hard drinking, cumbia was the ideal companion for a long day at work or a festive night at the local dance club. Hence in any of its Mexican incarnations, cumbia would travel back to the towns in the Michoacán, Guerrero, or Nuevo León countryside, completing a full circle and granting greater presence to the previously ignored inhabitants of working-class *barrios*.

Generally speaking, unlike other cultural exports, cumbia arrived lacking any hegemonic pretense. Colombia was—is?—conceived as a backwater eternally affected by internecine conflict, so who could imagine that one of its products would signify such an identitarian challenge to well-established national musical genres? Unlike Mexican or Brazilian music, which arrived with the support of an established nationalist scheme and a relatively efficient distribution network, or Argentine music, which cloaked itself with airs of superiority, given the profile of a Eurocentric project of culture, cumbia usually arrived through the back door and in the hands of the dispossessed. In the case of Mexico, aside from the Colombian bands that visited and toured working-class circuits, it was its very citizens, who, returning from the United States, contributed to and accelerated a massive diffusion of the music. For Argentina, internal immigrants from the countryside and recent Bolivian and Paraguayan migrants, usually despised as *bolitas* and *paraguas*, performed a crucial role in the development of the bailanta circuit in Buenos Aires. In Peru, it was *serranos*, the recent arrivals from the Andes, who developed an appetite for cumbia in the mid-1960s. In short, cumbia's initial arrival was so insignificant—by and large, it was consumed by people who didn't seem to matter and who, as a rule, were not even visible to the state—that cultural establishments barely registered its presence. By the time the music advanced, cornered the market—usually in bootlegged versions—and evolved in the hands of the corresponding social outcasts, it was too late. The scale of sales and events was usually beyond the control of members of the establishment. Even when cumbia came in through the front door—when Colombian orchestras like Bermúdez's or Galán's embarked on successful journeys to play abroad at high-society clubs—who could imagine that such happily infectious music would some day conceal a socially militant, culturally resistant agenda?

However, what happened to this music once it landed abroad was an entirely different story. In Mexico, cumbia evolved into a number of versions, allowing greater visibility for the lower classes, though occasionally operating in the same way as other middle- and upper-class products, effectively concealing issues of race. In other words, in terms of class difference, cumbia performed swimmingly. When it came to race, though, it seemed as inept as other alternatives. Though cumbia was perceived as coming from a nation with a greater Afro presence, its Mexican variants made clear that the blackness of its content was purely a matter of imitation and not of an affirmative protagonism. After all, Mexican negritude had been effectively erased from the many narratives tracing national origin, and not by chance, most of the narrative identities of the people who liked cumbia had much more room for articulating class interpellations than for articulating race-based ways of addressing them (both of which were available in cumbia lyrics, sound, and performances).

In Peru, on the other hand, cumbia became a vehicle for the new immigrants from the Andes, who, according to most scholarship on the topic, wanted to celebrate their arrival to the capital. Along the way, its popularity mushroomed with such vigor that the more privileged classes were forced to contend with its presence. That is to say, the millions who crowded the *pueblos jóvenes* (the young towns, or slums) on the outskirts of the capital could be ignored, but their diabolically strident music, with a monotonous beat that drilled the mind, could not. Nevertheless once cumbia evolved into its *selvática* or *elegante* varieties, the approach was similar to Mexico's: a rehashing of autochthonous origin through the appropriation of traces of U.S. culture (cowboy gear in Peru, hip-hop bling in Mexico, just as Colombians had done decades earlier with big-band jazz) or the internalization of a condition of class, ethnic, and regional inferiority by way of Caribbean emulation (evidenced by a propensity for "fine" salsa-like arrangements in bands from provincial Peru, who argued for the technical superiority of less Andean-sounding arrangements).

And in Argentina, just as in Mexico (only in a different way), cumbia became the music of choice of *negros*—mind you, not the literally black ones; after all, it is Argentina. In this case, despite the presence of some Afro communities in the greater Buenos Aires area (Cape Verdean, Uruguayan, a few locals), in Argentina the label *negro* does not necessarily refer only to skin color or phenotypic features (which are a given trait); these characteristics also form part of a larger imaginary construction encompassing not only geographic, class, and political implications but moral ones as well. The end result is that Argentina is characterized by a very complex construction of racial and ethnic identities, a complexity that is behind the paradox that people who are phenotypically mestizos are nonetheless addressed as *negros*, where the label is used to name people of Native American heritage and people of African ancestry as well, depending on the situation. In a nutshell, the process behind this paradox started in the late 1930s and early 1940s, when a number of different demographic and political issues (the huge migration of people of Native American ancestry from the countryside to Buenos Aires, their political mobilization by the Peronist movement, and the animosity—personal and political—that such a migration generated among the mostly white population of Argentina's capital city) resulted in the labels *cabecita negra* (little black-headed one) and *negros* being (pejoratively) applied to the internal immigrants who became one of the most important groups of political actors in the Peronist project. In the last two decades or so, the increasing immigration from Bolivia and Paraguay added complexity to the picture, because the pejorative stance spread to the members of these communities as well, where racist connotations were combined with chauvinistic undertones. All of these *negros* (internal mestizo immigrants, Bolivians, and Paraguayans) adopted cumbia as their danceable music of choice, but, of course, the proto-racial discourse of cumbia lyrics, sounds, and performances (alongside the class, gender, age, and ethnic discourses also present in cumbia) entered the variegated narrative identities of Argentine internal migrants, Bolivians, and Paraguayans in quite different and complex ways.

In same fashion, other neighboring countries also fell to the spell of cumbia (Ecuador, Panama, and Venezuela, out of sheer proximity; Chile and Uruguay, by way of coziness with greater *mestizaje* and a penchant for tropical beats among working-class sectors), which lent itself to dealing with issues of a national social nature through a cultural practice of unpretentious disposition. In addition, one must consider cross-fertilization between many of these varieties, as in the case of Argentine villera and Peruvian cumbia, as well as Mexican and Uruguayan varieties and villera. Thus it is not just a matter of tracing direct linkages between Colombian imports and local kinds, but of contemplating the multiple ways in which these many national varieties interact with each other. Brazil, with its distinct linguistic and racial context, stands as an eminent exception to this Latin(o) American phenomenon, although, within the Amazonian basin, a very interesting variety of cumbia has flourished as well. Cuba, with its eminent role as cultural actor, is another exception, given the rejection of tropical genres—music traditionally associated with larger ensembles and oriented toward dance—embodied by the initial phase of the revolutionary regime. (By the time it embraced tropical varieties—witness the Buena Vista Social Club boom—cumbia was already thriving elsewhere.)

As a result, the general hypothesis of this volume is that the focused examination of cumbia as perhaps the most widespread musical genre of Latin American origin evinces some of the mechanisms through which eminent forms of identity, like nation, region, class, race, ethnicity, and gender (and all their articulations) are achieved, negotiated, and provisionally and locally enacted by its followers. Each of the different national cases examined in this book illuminates a particular way in which cumbia assists those different identification processes. Having said this, however, we want to clarify that we are not advocating any sort of "homology thesis" in this book, that is, that there is a strict correspondence between particular cultural practices (like cumbia) and determined social identities. Neither are we straightforwardly proposing the competing hypothesis, which claims that music by itself has the capacity to construct social identities instead of only reflecting them (like the homology thesis claims). The various contributors to this collection address this dichotomy in different ways and, linked to their own theoretical predispositions, tilt the balance between both differently, even though the tension still exists in most of the essays. This, we believe, is part of the healthy exercise of differing viewpoints in any academic collection.

Nevertheless we also want to add our own twist to this tension, introducing into the readings of the different essays—voilà—another tension. And we want readers to challenge themselves and read the essays beyond what the respective authors explicitly claim or implicitly state about their positions in the constructing/reflecting debate. We want readers to take into account that most debates between the reflection and construction theories that relate to music and identity do not take fully into account the fragmentary character of the processes through which people end up identifying themselves in terms of nation, gender, class, race, ethnicity, or age. At the same time, many of those theories also neglect the complex articulations that habitually occur within these different identifications. And finally, there always is the possibility that certain types of music "reflect" some of the narrative identifications people "use" to understand who they are, while others help (to different degrees) in the construction of such identifications. For this reason, we propose the term *to articulate* rather than *to reflect* or *to construct* because it encompasses both possibilities at once.

The fact that the reflecting/constructing debate tends to homogenize musical practice in the same way that it homogenizes identities does not contribute to the advancement of our understanding of the complex relationships people establish with music. Thus, more often than not, the attempted relationship is not only between wholly formed identitarian groups but also between these groups and musical practices in toto. If we change the focus of attention to the components of the musical practice instead of its end result, the analysis changes as well. In this regard, if we consider a musical practice as a complex combination of (at least) sound, lyrics, performance, and commentary about the music being performed, and we link this complexity to the fragmentary process of identity construction, we end up with the possibility of different identification processes being helped by different components of the musical performance, sometimes in a very contradictory way. We think that most of the essays in this collection open themselves up to a second reading, taking into account these different possibilities.

People do not encounter cumbia as a unified entity (youth, migrant, *sonidero*, *cumbiero*, *chichero*, working-class, male, etc.) in the different venues they attend and allow it to interpellate them as something that they accept because it either reflects who they believe they are or helps them in the construction of who they believe they will be from now on. When people engage in these encounters with cumbia, they bring along myriad narrative identities about who they are in terms of their different subject positions. If these encounters occurred before, certainly some of these different narratives are already influenced by cumbia itself, and the new encounter challenges the connection previously accomplished between the narrative identities and the cumbia performance being enacted at the current event. In any case, the multiple possible identifications of our fictitious ~~cumbier@~~ (using this term "under erasure" à la Derrida, to signify that we don't agree with the term because it unifies and materializes an actor out of what is, *sensu stricto*, a social practice) enter into a process of negotiation with the multiple messages of the cumbia event (the sound, the lyrics, the performance of the musicians, the performance of other ~~cumbier@~~s at the scene, what is said about the performance on the venue, what is written about the music in magazines and on YouTube, websites, Facebook, and the like). Out of that negotiation, situationally and provisionally, a process of identification (or disidentification, for that matter) takes place.

As Vila has written elsewhere (Vila 2001), music performance is part of privileged practical activities that, while condensing basic significations, construct identities through the production of an imaginary effect of having an "essential" (which, of course, is a fiction) identity inscribed on the body (as an ethnicity, race, region, class, nationality, gender, or age). Thus musical performativity would be among the types of discourses that, through repetition and its inscription on the body, have the capacity to produce what it names. However, to finally move from the capacity (the realm of discursive offers) to the actual production of identity in specific actors, we have to reformulate the previous statement as follows: musical practices construct identifications anchored on the body through the different alliances we establish between our diversely imagined, diversely narrated identities and the imaginary "essential" identities that various musical practices materialize through their (often contradictory) different components (sound, lyrics, performances, etc.). In other words, we believe that, quite often, a particular musical practice helps to articulate (a word that, as mentioned before, we prefer over either *reflect* or *construct*) particular imaginary, narrative identifications when performers or listeners of this very music feel that it (complexly) resonates with (obviously following a complex process of negotiation between musical interpellation and argumentative storyline) the narrative plots that organize their variegated narrative identities.

In this regard, matters of regional, national, and transnational identifications are center stage in chapter 2, showing how cumbia, as a musical practice, allows musicians to negotiate their engagements with different geographical spaces simultaneously. Jorge Arévalo Mateus shows that those negotiations are highly contested by the different reactions of the public and the "guardians of tradition" regarding those complex musical performances.

The complex relationship between regional, national, and transnational forms of identification is brought back into the picture in chapter 4. But this time Alejandro L. Madrid, writing about the cumbia-based *onda grupera*, emphasizes their overlapping with issues of class and migration status as lived by Central American and Mexican immigrants, prominent actors in the Latin American diaspora. Considering that he is also writing about Mexican cumbia in Monterrey, it is not surprising that José Juan Olvera Gudiño's essay (chapter 3) deals with the way cumbia helped in the articulation of regional, class, and migration forms of identification, but he also illuminates the way cumbia provided symbolic resources to internal immigrants in Mexico as well.

The construction of a Mexican immigrant identity in the United States and how cumbia helps in that regard is the topic of Cathy Ragland's essay (chapter 5), in which issues of nationality (being Mexican), migration status (many immigrants are illegally working in New York and New Jersey), and class (most Mexican immigrants are working class) are complexly intertwined. Identifications linked to migration processes are also central in Joshua Tucker's essay on Peru (chapter 6), where they complexly mix with ethnic identifications (most migrants from the Andes are Native Peruvians) that, in turn, impinge upon national identification processes by the way such immigration deeply questions the meaning of being a "Peruvian." That cumbia mixed with Andean rhythms played a crucial role in this broadening of the idea of Peruvianness, shows, in general, how music is central in many processes of identity construction, in particular, the ubiquity of Colombian cumbia in that regard. While Tucker shows how people who move from one part of Peru to another use cumbia to navigate their migration process, Kathryn Metz (chapter 7) shows how Peruvians who decide *not* to migrate and remain in their Amazon enclave still use cumbia to carve out a legitimate and valued place in Peruvian society. Again issues of regional, ethnic, and national identifications are worked out using cumbia.

Gender identification topics are center stage in Pablo Semán and Pablo Vila's essay (chapter 8), as they show how cumbia villera complexly addresses the newly acquired sexuality of many young women belonging to the popular sectors. But those gender issues are intertwined with class (most cumbia villera fans and musicians are working class), age (they are young people), and region and ethnicity (they are also immigrants from the countryside and mestizos). Matthew Van Hoose's essay (chapter 10) moves us back to regional (living in the River Plate basin) and national (being Uruguayan) identification processes, showing how pronominal meaning—the use of *tú* and *vos*—is closely connected with spatialized forms of social identity. At this point, that cumbia plays a very important role in this regard shouldn't surprise the reader. National identification processes appear again in Héctor Fernández L'Hoeste's essay (chapter 11), but this time intersecting with regional (how a *costeño* genre, cumbia, displaced a mountain genre, *bambuco*, as the epitome of Colombian music) and class issues (showing how *tropipop* is an upper-middle-class offspring of cumbia).

That these contributors analyze particular sets of articulations (nation, region, and class; class and gender; migration status, class, and nation; etc.) and not others does not mean that the other possible articulations are absent in the phenomena they study. It means that they consider the ones they explore to be in the forefront and the others operating only in the background. In fact, more than operating in the background, all the other possible identifications are present through the echoes of their absences. That is, none of the main articulating identifications analyzed in these essays is present in the actual lives of the actors involved in and of themselves, referring only to themselves. Following Derrida, we can say that all of them have the traces of many of the other possible intersecting identifications as the condition of possibility of their own existence. If, as we mentioned earlier, gender issues are clearly intertwined with class, age, region, and ethnicity, in the case of Argentine cumbia villera this is so because they are part of a system of syntheses and referrals in which political identifications (being a follower of Peronism), educational subject positions (being mostly uneducated), and even moral considerations (being a *negro de alma*, that is, having a "black soul," regardless of the color of one's skin) are present (in their absence) as echoes that add thickness to the articulations that do appear. The same can be said about any of the other national cases, in which, for instance, issues of gender and class are the subject positions that, in their absence, make possible, as a trace, the clear appearance of regional, national, and ethnic identifications propelled by cumbia (in the two Peruvian cases) or the appearance of migration-based identities (in the case of Mexican cumbia). In most of the cases addressed in this book, age is the "invisible" and "unmarked" identification that plays in the shadows of the way people relate to cumbia, because it is usually the case that the audiences of this music are young.

An important aspect of the processes of identification that cumbia allows and is part of is that those processes are part and parcel of important symbolic struggles for recognition. This is so because most of the identifications cumbia propels are linked to social actors who, in different locales, are positioned in subordinated arrangements of different kinds in terms of class, region, migration status, gender, and the like. Of course, cumbia also offers identifications and participates in symbolic struggles in which its practitioners have the lion's share regarding other subordinated groups. (Gender is a particularly ominous example of this possibility, as Semán and Vila show.) But that does not deny its importance for empowering particular actors, regardless of its role in disempowering others.

A very interesting characteristic of the popularization of cumbia all across the Americas is its role in buttressing some national projects. In some usages, cumbia allows people to embrace and use it for the advancement of national interest, regardless of its degree of geographical determination — or perhaps precisely because of cumbia's fondness for it. Throughout this process, a beneficial feature of cumbia is its propensity to transgress social and geopolitical boundaries, its marked mobility. Few national genres display such flexibility when it comes to engendering homegrown versions, blatantly ignoring historical, cultural determination. The context of tango, for example, is too particular to be reproduced effectively in other latitudes and serve as a vehicle of resistance or hegemony. Samba (even bossa) and ranchera, though imitated in other countries, ultimately fail to represent anything other than a Brazilian or Mexican cultural practice, never mind the actual nationality of its performers. The Orquesta de la Luz may play excellent salsa, but we doubt that, as an expression of cultural difference, it means much to mainstream Japanese. Even more contemporary forms like merengue and *reggaetón*, though vastly popular and reproduced in other places of the Americas—such as Colombia and Argentina—fail to engender alternate national conditions, speaking to a wider audience and thus achieving mainstream status. With the exception of Argentina, even rock, with its middle-class appeal, has failed to engender national varieties. Then again, it is true that Argentines can talk about rock nacional, but very few in Latin America can describe their rock production in monolithic terms as rock *mexicano*, *colombiano*, or *venezolano*, even if they actually exist. The failure of these productions to act as units has rendered futile any efforts dedicated to the further exploration of national identity.

Cumbia, on the other hand, has given way to forms that, though they proudly retain the name *cumbia*, are undeniable versions of national orientation: cumbia *peruana*, *ecuatoriana*, *chilena*, *argentina*, *mexicana*, and so forth, each one confidently different from its forebear, operating under distinct, locally determined circumstances, full of regional varieties and with a wider appeal to a home audience. That cumbia mexicana is a complex cultural artifact with plenty of regional variations is well described in Madrid's and Olvera's essays. Something similar occurs with cumbia peruana, covered by Tucker and Metz, and the cumbia followed by Mexican immigrants in the United States, described by Ragland. Cumbia in Argentina follows a similar path, in which regional varieties (*norteña*, *santafesina*, villera) are, paradoxically, showing the national complexity of the way Colombian cumbia became "Argentinized."

In a nutshell, cumbia is a fortunate example of transnationalism at work, mutating at will to engage its followers in a more effective manner. Generally speaking, what serves as an established vehicle of nationality and regional or ethnic identity in one place, once culturally determined and fixed, seldom works as the basis for a massive exercise of these types of identifications in another setting. In the case of cumbia, this axiom does not work. The essays in this book have been closely vetted to highlight issues of this nature. In his contribution to this collection, "Cumbia Music in Colombia: Origins, Transformations, and Evolution of a Coastal Music Genre" (chapter 1), the Italian musicologist Leonardo D'Amico supplies the reader with a remarkable quantity of information, from a detailed description of the geopolitical context of cumbia to a summary of the various versions of the term's etymological origin. D'Amico accounts for the difficulties associated with establishing periodization for a cultural construct as unstable and fragmentary as a musical genre, shying away from an actual endorsement of a theory in argumentative terms. Instead he chooses to review the multiple aspects of cumbia as cultural practice: its instruments, a formal analysis, the genres associated with its evolution and dissemination, and, ultimately, its relation to other relevant national and transnational genres. D'Amico's informative style is motivated by the hope of providing a sensible context for cumbia as a seminal practice, so new genres and variants may be assessed in the greater light of their ancestry, that is, not only with the specific national context in mind but in relation to the actual shifts experienced in Colombia before and during the music's transition to another latitude. In this way, he facilitates the tracing of an evolution for the genre in strict terms of positivist musicology, leaving the considerations of identity and nation to more culturally oriented approaches. From this perspective, though cognizant of the value of interdisciplinary schemes, D'Amico plays the role of a scholar predominantly interested in the actual circumstances of the musical practice, slightly detached from theoretical considerations more associated with a cultural studies agenda.

In chapter 2, "¿Pa' dónde vas Marioneta? ¿Pa' dónde va la gaita? La Cumbiamba Eneyé Returns to San Jacinto," Jorge Arévalo Mateus chronicles his trip to the town of San Jacinto, epicenter of the world of *gaita* and home to the renowned *gaiteros*. Arévalo skillfully uses the journey to explore what happens to a musical practice when its followers and performers come from corners of the world that challenge habitual constructs of practice, in this case, the fact that Martín Vejarano and his ensemble, Marioneta, come from places like Bogotá and New York, which, nationally and transnationally, challenge the conventions of gaita music. Cosmopolitanism meets nationalism meets regionalism. For the judges at San Jacinto, it appears contradictory that Vejarano, who lives in New York but comes from the interior of Colombia (and thus qualifies as *cachaco*), excels at playing the gaita. But to followers of gaita, more accustomed to the eccentricities and vagaries of the music market, Vejarano and his friends make all the sense in the world. As cumbia evolves, it is only sensible that the practice of gaita begins to reflect contacts beyond its habitual milieu. Arévalo describes the journey in detail and ponders what it means that Marioneta has landed the second prize at the Festival Nacional de Gaitas for two consecutive years. In the end, his essay helps us understand how is it that cumbia has managed to travel across the Americas and appeal to so many people, regardless of nationality or place of origin.

From cumbia in its country of origin, the collection then moves abroad to those countries in which, for different reasons, cumbia became popular. In chapter 4, "Rigo Tovar, Cumbia, and the Transnational *Grupero* Boom," the Mexican scholar Alejandro Madrid reviews the story of the Tamaulipas native Rigo Tovar and describes his importance in terms of the ascent of cumbia as a Mexican American cultural practice and its contribution to the visibility of previously ignored segments of national society. Most important, Madrid points outs clearly how the Mexican cultural industry has enacted this "invisibility," in which the cultural offer of media exhibits acts that differ markedly from national reality (i.e., portraying versions of events that contradict, ethnically, socially, and in terms of gender, what is immediately apparent in daily life). Tovar's embrace of his condition of *naco* (a vulgar, uneducated person) speaks volumes about changes in Mexican culture. Within this context, the rise of the *onda grupera* embodies a first wave of change for the Mexican regional music market. It also describes how working-class acts have accumulated significant cultural capital amid challenging economic circumstances: the end of the so-called Mexican miracle and the collapse of the national economy during the 1980s. Madrid integrates the concepts of cultural citizenship and dialectic soundings to discuss the inner workings of this process of freshly gained visibility, in which migrants and their communities "negotiate sites of identification that ultimately allow for the recognition of their difference while still recognizing their rights to belong locally and transnationally." Overall, Rigo Tovar is proposed as the precursor of a wave of music that, using cumbia as its foundation, allowed Mexicans and Central Americans to establish a prominent position in a new map of the Latin American diaspora.

Continuing with the impact of cumbia in Mexico, in chapter 3, "Cumbia in Mexico's Northeastern Region," José Juan Olvera Gudiño describes the different cumbia styles that are popular in northeastern Mexico nowadays: *norteña, grupera, colombiana de Monterrey,* and *villera*. In the first part of the chapter, Olvera offers a historical explanation of the reasons Monterrey eventually became the "music center" par excellence of the entire northeastern Mexican region. Then he reviews a brief history of the introduction and eventual success of cumbia in the region and explores the various ways different audiences appropriate diverse cumbia styles. Olvera delves into issues of identity construction, relevance, and legitimacy concerning cumbia, as well as the peculiar dialogue that takes place between cumbia and other popular music genres of the region, above all *música norteña*. He aims to show that the most enduring and successful cumbia styles in northeastern Mexico are those that result from a hybridization that takes into account the elements that are peculiar to a specific group, be it rural, regional, or transnational. Furthermore he demonstrates that cumbia creates a space of dialogue and encounter between diverse audiences, turning the genre into one of the most popular expressions of music in northeastern Mexico.

Continuing with cumbia's route north, and closely associated with the migration of millions of Mexicans to the United States, Cathy Ragland addresses the popularity of cumbia among Mexican immigrants currently living in the United States. In chapter 5, "Communicating the Collective Imagination: The Sociospatial World of the Mexican *Sonidero* in Puebla, New York, and New Jersey," she discusses a social dance event that has become increasingly popular among the Mexican migrant and immigrant communities in New York City and nearby northern New Jersey. In those dances, *sonideros* (deejays) play the latest cumbia hits and, through voice manipulation, smoke, lights, and a variety of sounds, including music, create a "sociospatial environment" that is neither the United States nor Mexico but somewhere in between. Among the most powerful components of the cumbia sonidera experience studied by Ragland is the personal connection between the Mexican immigrants in the club and their friends and family back in Mexico. As the cumbias are played, the deejay reads into the microphone the personal salutations and dedications scribbled by the immigrants. These messages are recorded over the cumbia music, and at the end of the set, the dancers line up to purchase a recording of the cumbia with their dedications. The dancers then mail the music (initially, cassettes; more recently, CDs and, most likely, data files via phone or computer) to family and friends in Mexico.

According to Ragland, through the space-age travel sounds played by the deejay, the juxtaposition of American and Mexican musics, and the dedications of those present to those in Mexico, the experiential foreground and background of the *baile* shifts constantly between New York and Mexico. Ragland claims that by manipulating music and simultaneously reconfiguring time and place, the deejays and their public in New York and New Jersey turn feelings of displacement and marginalization into a collective sense of identity and connectedness, generating a "diasporic public sphere." Those attending sonidero bailes, having varying degrees of actual memories of Mexico, develop a new sense of personal and national history, both imagined and real, based upon Mexican and American myths, their own experiences, and those of relatives and friends. The sonidero bailes accommodate, dramatize, and legitimize this sort of ambiguous existence and memories, with its sense of presence and absence and its simultaneous investments in both the United States and Mexico. Baile attendees are able to imagine the presence of those who are physically absent. They can speak to them and bring them into the local public space, while also addressing those at the dance who overhear the dialogue. In this way, those dances and the music that is played there present yet another idiosyncratic fusion of tradition and modernity, in which the roots-oriented sounds of a rural vallenato-style cumbia are combined with the sonidero's space-age sound effects. The creative appropriation and cultivation of the Colombian cumbia to suit a specifically Mexican sensibility is another good example of the complex way cumbia has spread across the Americas.

Cumbia not only traveled north from Colombia. It also went south. One of the countries in which cumbia became quite popular was Peru, and what happened with cumbia there is chronicled by Joshua Tucker and Kathryn Metz. In a way, Tucker's text on the rise of the *chicha* star Lorenzo Palacios Quispe, better known as Chacalón (Big Jackal), reproduces many of the tropes suggested by Madrid. In chapter 6, "From *The World of the Poor* to the Beaches of Eisha: *Chicha, Cumbia,* and the Search for a Popular Subject in Peru," Tucker's detailed review of Lima's music scene provides great context for future and present scholars of music and popular culture in Peru. However, just as Madrid describes a musical phenomenon intimately related to a process of migration (from Mexico and Central America to the United States), Tucker relates strongly to the cultural milieu resulting from the migration of people from the Andes to the outskirts of Lima, in a virtual redefinition of Peruvianness. From this perspective, Tucker draws a tighter connection with a critique of the history of a national music genre and its relationship with an alternative idea of nation. Despite all evidence to the contrary, certain sectors of Peruvian society still do not warm up to the fact that the majority of Lima's population embraces cultural forms that speak about a wider, more racially mixed national reality, an aspect that Tucker covers intelligently in the latter part of his essay. In plain terms, chicha embodies a discourse that challenges and revamps the idea of nation supported by the Iberocentric center of gravity located in Lima. Thus, to discuss chicha in a greater context, Tucker centers on Chacalón, suggesting him as an alternative to Los Shapis, which dates from a later period (the 1980s). By tracing Chacalón's influence on the evolution of chicha, he promotes a rehashing of national memory, clarifying how the origins of the music are closely tied to the popular masses and their willingness to establish a presence in the national scene.

Tucker is also ingenious enough to quote the scholars Peter Wade and Thomas Turino when it comes to deliberately discussing a matter that is essential to this volume and was addressed earlier: the relation between expressive culture and processes of social identification. Music may express "a shift in the collective subjectivity of its listenership" just as easily as it can signify a "process of collective consumption and mutual recognition." Thus, just because music evolves in a particular fashion—in this case, cumbia—does not mean that it necessarily reflects certain intentionality as a measure of cultural resistance or hegemony.

With chapter 7, "*Pandillar* in the Jungle: Regionalism and *Tecno-cumbia* in Amazonian Peru," by Kathryn Metz, we move from Lima to the Peruvian Amazon. Her contribution is about *pandilla*, a folkloric genre of the Peruvian Amazon whose performance was generally reserved for carnival but that, in recent years, under the form of electrified pandillas (a mix of Amazon folk rhythms and *tecno-cumbia*) has become common year-round thanks to Explosión, a tecno-cumbia ensemble from Iquitos. Electrified pandillas have incited regional pride and also a desire to attain a more prominent place in the Peruvian imagination. Although Peru boasts three distinct geographic regions (highlands, jungle, and coast), the jungle has often been disregarded, relegated to "backwoods" culture good for little beyond interesting flora and fauna.

Metz claims that tecno-cumbia's current incarnation in and around Iquitos, in northeastern Amazonian Peru, has firmly represented and even propelled forward the area's difficult dialogue with cosmopolitanism as people in the city negotiate the forces of global modernity, attempting to maintain an Amazonian identity while also gaining more comprehensive entrée into the nation's imagination. She describes how pandilla represents a quest for regional cultural autonomy within an integrated national vision. In the first section, she discusses the basic character of the pandilla, examining its history, its musical and poetic character, the context of its consumption, and the importance of indexing indigenous Amazonianness in performance. In the second section, she frames this understanding of contemporary pandilla in conjunction with its development in the tecno-cumbia sphere with a consideration of Iquitos's complex history and cultural identity that has been shaped by transnational influences. She concludes by showing how the pandilla serves as a key connection between a region's past, molded by colonial dominance, and the present, which is steeped in cosmopolitanism and regional pride as the area seeks integration into the greater body politic.

Moving still farther south, cumbia reached the Rio de la Plata shores and became one of the most popular musical genres in both Argentina and Uruguay. For the Argentine case we have two contributions, one by Pablo Semán and Pablo Vila, and the other by Cristian Alarcón. In chapter 8, "Gender Tensions in *Cumbia Villera*'s Lyrics," Semán and Vila analyze one of the most important incarnations of cumbia in Argentina, *cumbia villera* (cumbia from the shanty town). Cumbia villera started in the late 1990s, its emergence closely related to the economic disaster in which Argentina defaulted on its foreign debt in 2002. While the songs typically depict the vicissitudes of poor people in the country (above all in Buenos Aires), a very important portion of those songs refer, in very sexist terms, to women's sexuality. Semán and Vila contrast their interpretation of cumbia villera to the dominant interpretations that have underlined the misogynist character of its lyrics (very similar to certain kinds of rap). Without denying the sexist character of the lyrics, the authors prefer to analyze the tensions that are at play in the context of the emission of the songs. Semán and Vila claim that these tensions derive from and simultaneously fuel the transformation of women's roles in both the imaginary and everyday life of the Argentine popular sectors.

The chapter starts with a brief history of cumbia in Argentina and then moves to a classic textual analysis underscoring the misogynistic character of most lyrics. From there the authors consider the peculiar conditions of emission of the lyrics, the context in which what the lyrics so graphically express is often clearly contradicted. By *emission*, the authors mean all the social performances (understood as linguistic and nonlinguistic discourses) that accompany, in different ways, the artistic presentation of a particular song. Semán and Vila claim that some of the dimensions of emission of the songs are pretty close to the musical performances themselves, such as the way of singing, the corporeal movements of the singers, their facial expressions, the comments of the announcers before and after the song, and the expressions of the public who go to the shows in which those songs are performed. Some other dimensions of emission are a little more distant from the actual performance of the song, acting as a general cultural background against which those songs are performed. In the case of the highly sexualized songs that characterize cumbia villera as a genre, Semán and Vila take into account the way that sex is publicly discussed in the television, radio, and magazines that cumbia villera fans usually consume, the way sex is talked about in the everyday conversations of these youths, and so forth. At the same time the authors illustrate how the lyrics themselves show internal contradictions, reflecting an unsettled dispute about gender relationships among the poor people who are both singers and the public.

In chapter 9, "*Feliz, feliz*," Cristian Alarcón interviews Pablo Lescano, the so-called inventor of cumbia villera, the last incarnation of a long tradition of Argentine cumbia and perhaps the one that has acquired the most international exposure. In a piece that moves back and forth from Lescano to Alberto Sánchez Campuzano (a Colombian artist and filmmaker who went to Buenos Aires to make a film on Lescano), Alarcón discusses the development of new cumbia styles (much more mixed with electronic sounds) that Lescano is developing for a more modern ("eccentric" is the word used by Lescano) audience that congregates in the trendy Buenos Aires nightclub Žižek (named, of course, after the noted philosopher Slavoj Žižek). From there, the interview moves to Campuzano, who, now living in Mexico, cannot understand why the cumbia that people dance in Buenos Aires ended up being a very peculiar mixing of quite distinct North and South American traditions, such as Argentine chamamé, Mexican cumbia sonidera (Colombian cumbia recycled in Monterrey), and Andean rhythms brought by Peruvian, Bolivian, and northern Argentine immigrants to Buenos Aires.

Lescano tells Alarcón the origin of his passion for Colombian cumbia: at the age of ten, he went to the "Cathedral of cumbia," Tropitango, for the first time. He also discusses with Alarcón how chamamé was an important part of his musical upbringing. Lescano describes the musical traits that differentiate various styles of cumbia that are popular in Argentina nowadays, such as *cumbia santafesina* and *cumbia colombiana*. In the last part of the interview, Lescano tells Alarcón about his musical origins with the group Amar Azul, his struggles to abandon drugs, and how he sees the current cumbia scene, in which cumbia villera (his invention) seems to have lost its unquestionable leading role.

In his essay on cumbia in Uruguay, chapter 10, "*El 'Tú' Tropical, el 'Vos' Villero*, and Places in Between: Language Ideology, Music, and the Spatialization of Difference in Uruguay," Matthew Van Hoose explores the theorization of pronominal meaning—the use of *tú* and *vos*—and its connection with spatialized forms of social alterity. By way of a balanced discussion on the evolution of language and music along the River Plate, Van Hoose analyzes the way cumbia, as a cultural practice, operates as a site for the production and enactment of language ideology. His critique of cumbia includes a brief review of the arrival of the musical genre to Uruguay and the relevance of the contrast in pronominal usage between the local form, in which the *tú* form is employed to tropicalize musical production, and Argentine villera, in which the *vos* is more dominant, drawing a line between nationalities. Van Hoose quotes a very early essay by David William Foster to clarify how pronominal usage is utilized to mark a difference in terms of geocultural context. In the end, Van Hoose details how, by way of language and music, this region—the River Plate's basin—has tended to accentuate its own geographical, social, and cultural distance from the rest of Latin America, even to the point that, because of their denial of a relationship with the rest of the continent, Uruguayans and Argentines are generally unaware of the fact that Salvadorans, Nicaraguans, Costa Ricans, Colombians, and other nationalities in Latin America also use the *vos* as part of their daily language. Along the way, cumbia substantiates once again its role as champion of musical and identitarian difference.

Closing the volume, in chapter 11, "On Music and Colombianness: Toward a Critique of the History of Cumbia," Héctor Fernández L'Hoeste proposes a more critical, flexible view of the historical narrative of cumbia, clarifying how different theories on the origins and evolution of the genre have interacted and been accepted or rejected to benefit a particular view of the nation. He makes explicit the intent behind the adoption of specific narratives that serve the interests of a cultural or political establishment, eager to impose its version of events on a general society. In broad strokes, the history of cumbia is the story of its replacement of bambuco as the preferential Colombian national genre (despite criticism from conservative sectors in the interior of the country) and, eventually, its transformation into a feasible cultural export. However, in his analysis of cumbia's more modern phase—the period from the 1990s until today—Fernández L'Hoeste discusses very recent events, prior to their moment of integration into the musical historiography of Colombia. While part of the chapter reviews the rise of cumbia throughout the twentieth century and its eventual journey to other parts of the hemisphere, the discussion also involves the development of tropipop—as followers have called a more contemporary offspring of cumbia—and points out how its evolution from cumbia (and vallenato) simultaneously serves as an example of hegemonization by the upper classes and alleged defenses of purism substantiated by class prejudice. Vallenato and tropipop also deal with how cumbia is being consumed and assimilated by current generations of Colombians and might even be displaced from its privileged position as the quintessentially national musical form. Given its proximity to pop, this latter stage of this musical genre's history, yet unwritten and unanalyzed by many academics, promises to be fertile ground for a debate on the evolution of Colombian identity through the cultural practice of music.

The essays collected in this volume are, on the whole, the result of dedicated fieldwork or detailed research. They seek to provide a window into the workings of a musical genre that has proven to be remarkably adaptive. As a practice of very humble origins, cumbia has managed to squeeze by and get away with things that are potentially out of reach for many other cultural practices. The object and hope of this volume is that we do it justice and manage to spark interest in students of Latin American culture so we can share cumbia's journey across the Americas and learn from its travails.

I.
Cumbia Music in Colombia
Origins, Transformations, and Evolution of a Coastal Music Genre

Costeño Music and Its Sociocultural Context

The Caribbean coastal region of Colombia is called the *Costa*, and its inhabitants are referred to as *costeños*.[1] The *música costeña* (coastal music) is a product of tri-ethnic syncretic cultural traditions including Amerindian, Spanish, and African elements (List 1980b, 1983), a merging that begins with the colonial period and continues into the republican period on the Caribbean Coast.[2] Traditional music from the Colombian Caribbean coast expresses its tri-ethnic costeño identity in various vocal styles and musical forms and through its type of instruments and the way they are played.[3] In this chapter I describe the aspects and circumstances under which *cumbia*, a coastal musical genre and dance form of peasant origins characterized by an African-derived style, has spread from its local origins in the valley of the Magdalena River to acquire a Colombian national identity, becoming in a few years a transnational musical phenomenon.

Through its heterogeneity, coastal ethno-organology reflects the different ethnic and cultural contributions that shape costeño culture. Instrumental ensembles are the product of this process of hybridization. They usually combine instruments of indigenous origin, such as the *gaita* (vertical duct flute) and the *maraca* (rattle); African origin, such as the *tambor alegre* and the *llamador*, single-headed drums of different sizes, the *tambora* (double-headed drum), the *caña de millo* (a millet-cane transverse clarinet), the *marímbula* (a large wooden-box lamellaphone), and the *marimba de napa* (musical bow); and European origin, such as the accordion and the wind instruments of the brass bands.

Most of the *ritmos* (as the musical genres for dancing are called) of Colombia's Atlantic coastal region—such as *tambora, bullerengue, chandé, mapalé, cumbia, porro, puya, fandango*—show some "Africanisms" present in their musical structure:

> The basic concept operative in most cases is the underlying reiterated cycle of pulses or time-span. . . . African influence is therefore to be found in the complex framework built above this foundation, involving pervasive offbeat phrasing, overlapping of call and response patterns, specific uses of the hemiola, and the employment of both disjunct and irregular cycles in the realization of the underlying time-span. These traits plus the density of rhythmic structure displayed in the performances of percussion ensembles relate costeño music to that of sub-Saharan Africa. (List 1980a: 16–17)

There are various occasions during the year when music is traditionally performed: during Catholic festivities,[4] such as Christmas and Easter, on patron saints days, and at carnivals and folk festivals (e.g., Festival Nacional de la Cumbia at El Banco, Festival de Gaita in San Jacinto, Festival de la Tambora in Tamalameque, Festival del Porro in San Pelayo, and Festival de la Leyenda Vallenata in Valledupar).

On the Caribbean coast, musical groups, or *conjuntos* (small instrumental sets with four to five elements), represent a further metamorphosis or evolution of the earlier tambora,[5] which, spread among the black communities along the Magdalena River, stands as an archetype. The tambora ensemble consists of percussion and vocals only, including a conical drum with a single head (*currulao*),[6] a cylindrical drum with a double head (*tambora*), and chant in the form of a call-and-response pattern performed by a male or female solo singer alternating with a chorus of women (*cantadoras*) and accompanied by the *palmoteo* (hand-clapping) or beating of the *tablitas* or *palmetas* (wooden paddles) of a chorus of women singing the refrain (Carbó Ronderos 2003). Its repertoire includes the *bailes cantados* (sung dances)—such as bullerengue, tambora, chandé, *berroche, guacherna*—and songs in call-and-response form (with a solo singer and chorus), accompanied by drums and handclap.[7]

As an expression of Afro-Colombian music culture, tamboras are quite common in the region considered the birthplace of cumbia, the Mompox area. Between the sixteenth and eighteenth centuries, many *palenques*, villages formed by fugitive slaves (*cimarrones*) during the colonial period, sprang up in this area.[8] In fact, from the organological point of view, the line-up of coastal conjuntos consists of drums that make up the tambora, to which the transverse clarinet, the caña de millo (cane of millet), or two vertical flutes (gaitas) were added, giving birth, respectively, to the conjuntos of *cañamilleros* and *gaiteros*. Throughout this instrumental development, there was a loss of the chorus of female singers (cantadoras) and, obviously, of the refrain sung by them (in some cases, sung by the same musicians). When the tune is sung, the vocal element appears in a call-and-response form and, consequently, the musicians in the group carry out the choral answer.

Origins, Dissemination, Instruments, and Forms of Cumbia

As a music and dance genre, cumbia is most representative of coastal oral traditional culture. It is the artistic and cultural product of the rural and artisan classes, who reveal a tricultural Afro-Indo-Hispanic heritage, although the African component is dominant. In traditional costeño music culture, the term *cumbia* has a variety of connotations: it refers at the same time to a rhythm, a musical genre, and a dance.

As music and dance, cumbia originates in the upper part of the Magdalena River, in the zone called the Mompox Depression, which is located at the confluence of the Magdalena and Cauca Rivers, between the cities of Mompox and Plato (Fals Borda 1986b: 132), and its epicenter is located at the nearby city of El Banco, where the Festival de la Cumbia has taken place since 1970. Later, the port city of Barranquilla, located at the mouth of the Magdalena River, became the center of dissemination of cumbia. Since the mid-nineteenth century, Barranquilla has hosted the yearly Carnaval, to which traditional music and dance ensembles come from all over the Caribbean coast and the valley of the Magdalena River to perform at the *desfile* (parade) called Batalla de Flores (Battle of Flowers), along with *comparsas* (dance ensembles) (Friedemann 1985).

The etymology of the term *cumbia* is controversial. According to the Cuban anthropologist Fernando Ortiz, "*kumba* is a very popular toponymic and tribal denomination in Africa, from the north of Guinea to the Congo." He adds, "The same root is evident among the Kalabari, who use the term *ekombi* for 'a certain dance of women,' also called *tukhube*" (1985: 183). The historian Carlos Esteban Deive (1974: 19) contends that the term *cumbancha* comes from *nkumba*, the word for navel. Nicolás Del Castillo Mathieu (1982: 221) suggests instead that the terms *cumbia* and *cumbiamba* probably derive from Kikongo *ngoma, nkumbi*, which signifies "drum." T. K. Biaya (1993: 204) claims that the name *cyombela*, which refers to the percussionist Luba-Kasai from the Congo, comes from *komba* (*ngoma*), meaning "beat on the drum." On the island of Annobón (Equatorial Guinea), the term *cumbé* indicates a square drum with legs, used to complement a dance with the same name. The drum is proper of Jamaica, where maroons called it *gombay* or *goombah* (Roberts 1926), and it arrived in Annobón during the nineteenth century through Freetown immigrants in Sierra Leone, which is where Jamaican maroons were taken, forming the Krio group (Creole in Sierra Leone; Horton 1999; De Aranzadi 2009).

Cumbé was also the name given to the towns founded by fugitive slaves in Venezuela (called *palenques* in Colombia and *quilombos* in Brazil) during the eighteenth and nineteenth centuries (De Granda 1970: 452; Bermúdez 1992: 61–62). The same name also turns up in the catalogue for Mexican string instruments, the *tablatura de vihuela* from 1740, where, among many dances listed from the colonial period, there is an entry for *cumbees o cantos negros* with the subtitle *cantos en idioma guinea* (Stevenson 1971: 162).[9]

The hypothesis on the origin of cumbia as a ritual initiation dance from Central Africa, based on etymological similarities, is also quite appealing: (a) In the upper region of Zaire, an initiation ceremony called *kikumbi* takes place, which includes dances comparable to the Brazilian *batuque* of Kongo origin (Mukuna 1979);[10] (b) *Likumbi* is the name of the shelter that houses a male initiation rite (*jando*) of the Makonde of northeastern Mozambique (Ndege 2007); (c) *Nkumbi* is the initiation ritual of the Mbo of the Ituri Forest in the Democratic Republic of the Congo (Towles 1993); (d) In the female initiation rites of the Tsonga, fertility songs are sung and the *khomba* dance is performed with the purpose of encouraging women's fertility (Johnston 1974).

Nevertheless Colombian cumbia bears no ritual connotation at all and, according to existing written and oral sources, does not appear to have had any in the past either. At present, just as in the past, the traditional occasions when cumbia surfaces are mainly folk festivals, carnivals (the Carnaval de Barranquilla, for example), and holidays of the Catholic liturgical calendar (e.g., the celebration of the Virgin of Candelaria by the hill of La Popa in Cartagena de Indias during November).

According to historical sources, cumbia does not seem very old; its origin does not appear to go back to the colonial era, but rather to the republican period. The first documented written comments on cumbia date back to the end of the nineteenth century, in the newspaper *El Porvenir* from Cartagena de Indias. On March 2, 1879, there is reference to the *cumbiamba* performed during the festival for the Virgin of Candelaria:

> At night you hear the *cumbiamba*, a popular dance whose music consists of a *flauta de millo* and a drum that produced a monotonous, but rhythmic sound. It is danced in a circle, and the man makes bizarre and graceful movements to the sound of the drum, while the woman holds a bundle of burning candles on her head, covered by a pretty handkerchief, which catches fire at the end, when the candles go out; that is the splendor of the dance.[11]

From the choreographic perspective, cumbia is a Spanish-like court dance that is characterized by a lover's duel, in which movements simulate a game of repulsion and attraction between two dancers (the *cumbiamberos*). A couple dancing in a counterclockwise circle around a group of musicians performs it. As it is usually performed at night, the woman carries a bundle of lit candles that she uses to push away the man, who pursues her by circling her with open arms. With the other hand, the woman holds the tip of her long skirt (*pollera*), and in a standing position, swings her hips and takes small steps, all while trying to remain untouched by her partner. The man dances around the woman with a hat (the traditional *sombrero vueltiao*, a staple of the Colombian Caribbean) in his hand, which he tries to place on her head as a symbol of amorous conquest.

In terms of musical performance, in its most conventional variety, Colombian cumbia is exclusively instrumental (Escalante 1964; D. Zapata 1967; List 1980b). The traditional caña de millo ensemble (or cumbiamba) is made up of the caña de millo (the transverse idioglottic clarinet), the *tambor alegre* (a conical drum with only one drumhead), the *tambor llamador* (a conical drum with one drumhead), the tambora (a cylindrical drum with two drumheads) and the *guache* (tubular rattle).

The caña de millo (also known as *millo*, *pito*, or *pito atravesao*) is not really a flute (Abadía 1983, 1991) but a transverse idioglottic clarinet, originally made of millet, nowadays often made from a palm called *lata* (Bactris guineensis). It consists of a short cane with four finger holes and a tongue cut in one end to act as a reed, which is fitted with a small thread that catches between the teeth in order to adjust the sound and produce the vibrato. The technique involves the inhalation and exhalation of air through the reed. The resulting sound is sharp and nasal-like.

The origin of this instrument is contentious. According to the Africanist perspective of the foremost ethnomusicologist George List,

> There is no evidence that the clarinet existed in South America in the pre-Colombian period. There are no archaeological findings of clarinets, no reproductions of clarinets on artifacts, and no references to such an instrument in early historical literature. . . . To my knowledge, a transverse idioglottic clarinet, that is, a clarinet held horizontally with the reed cut from the same body, and remaining attached to the tube of cane, is found in the Western Hemisphere only in the Atlantic coastal region of Colombia. Apparently, not the Indians, but the Spanish-speaking people from the plains are the only ones who play it. (1983: 61)

In Africa, the transverse idioglottic clarinet with a simple reed is found in the Sahel belt area, where pastoral nomadic populations use it (since it is the same area where millet is grown). According to List (1983), the caña de millo is a modified version of the *bobiyel* played by the Fulbe (Fulani) of Burkina Faso, of the *bounkam* of the Bissa of Burkina Faso, and also of the *kamko* of the Kasera-Nakari in the north of Ghana. Thus "the source of the caña de millo is Africa and the clarinets like the *bobiyel*, the *bounkam*, and the *kamko* are its progenitors" (65). These African examples are transverse clarinets made from a stalk of millet cane, with the reed cut from the side of the cane. The performance is based on the emission of sound while inhaling and exhaling without interruption. It should be noted that there are also surprising similarities with the transverse *libo* clarinet of the Hausa of Chad. This latter instrument also comes from the same type of millet cane and is also equipped with a small string that, when played, adjusts the sounds that are produced.[12] According to the hypothesis regarding the indigenous origin of the caña de millo (Abadía 1973, 1983, 1991; Bermúdez 1985), the Wayúu Indians from the Guajira Peninsula in northernmost Colombia use a very similar instrument, the transverse idioglottic clarinet called *massi* and *wotorroyoi*. However, it is possible that the Wayúu (also known as Guajiros) adopted these instruments recently from Afro-Colombian musical culture.

The *tambor alegre* (or *tambor hembra*, "female drum") is a conical drum,[13] with a drumhead made of goat skin, and is made of the wood of the *banco blanco* (*Gyrocarpus americana*). Its tension system in the shape of a v is made of wooden wedges and pieces of string from the *fique* plant (*Furcraea andina*). The *llamador* (or *tambor macho*, "male drum") is the same as the tambor alegre in form, material, and system of tension, but its dimensions are smaller.[14] The tambor alegre has the role of "cheering up," "improvising," or varying around a predefined rhythmic base, while the llamador performs a constant, unvaried isochronous pulsation on the offbeat.

The tambor alegre and the tambor llamador are single-headed drums with a "wedge-hoop" tension system that displays notable structural similarities with some African drums, such as the *sangbei* from the Susu and Mende peoples in Sierra Leone (List 1983), and with certain Afro-Venezuelan drums (*chimbangueles*), Afro-Panamanian drums (*pujador, llamador,* and *repicador*), and Afro-Brazilian drums (*atabaques*). All of these types of drums are very similar to the sacred *enkomo* drums of the secret society of Abakuá or Ñáñigos (Cuba), which makes up part of the Carabalí.[15]

The tambora is a cylindrical bass drum with two heads joined together with a "zigzag" tension system.[16] It is placed horizontally on a wooden rack and played with two drumsticks that alternate between the drumhead and the shell of the drum. Drums with double heads of this type are found in the Gulf of Guinea, such as the *tempe* drum of Temne in Sierra Leone and the *gbùn gbùn* drum of Kpelle in Liberia (List 1983; Stone 1982).

Finally, the *guache* is a tubular rattle, originally made from *guadua* bamboo (*Bambusa americana*). Today it is generally made of metal and filled with seeds.

Another group related to the playing of cumbia is the *conjunto de gaitas*, quite common in the coastal savannah region, which, roughly speaking, includes the departments of Córdoba, Sucre, and Bolívar.[17] Two gaitas flutes (*macho*, "male," and *hembra*, "female") with the maraca, the tambor alegre, and the tambor llamador traditionally form this ensemble (List 1973, 1983, 1987). The function of the *gaita hembra* is to play the melody, while the role of the *gaita macho* is to emphasize just a few notes of the melodic line. The best known example of this kind of band is the group Gaiteros de San Jacinto.

The gaita is a flute of indigenous origin.[18] Coastal gaitas are identical to the *kuizi* (*kùisi sigì* and *kùisi bunzi*) flutes of the Kogi Indians from the Sierra Nevada de Santa Marta (Izikowitz 1935; Abadía 1983, 1991) and are similar to the flutes called *tolo, suarra,* or *supé*, used in pairs (male and female) by the Kuna Indians of the Darién region near the Colombia-Panama border and the San Blas Islands (Garay 1930; Taylor 1968; List 1973; Marulanda 1984; Abadía 1973, 1983, 1991).[19] The maraca (*tani* in the Kogi language, *na* or *nasi* in Kuna) is a rattle of the Arawak Indians (Tro Pérez 1978), made from a dry fruit filled with seeds, called *totumo* (*Crescentia cujete*). Among the *indios*, the maraca has a dual function: it's the musical instrument for parties and the ritual instrument for the healing rites of the shaman. *Gaita* is also the name given by gaiteros to the musical genre corresponding to cumbia when it is played with gaita flutes.

As mentioned, traditional cumbia is an exclusively instrumental music genre (List 1980b). Later, singing was added to cumbia in the form of *cuartetos* (stanzas of four octosyllabic lines) sung by one of the musicians of the group, which alternates with the refrain of the chorus through a responsorial song (with soloist and chorus).

Cumbia is in double simple tempo (2/2 or 2/4). The *millo* (clarinet) begins and then the tambora follows, which alternates with the *paloteo*, the beating on the wooden shell of the drum using two sticks. Afterward the llamador comes in, giving a regular pulse offbeat, and the guacho is shaken upward and downward, emphasizing the binary scansion and accentuating the offbeat. The bullerengue (a *baile cantado*) could be considered a precursor of cumbia because its rhythm is also characterized by the offbeat played by the llamador. The tambor alegre plays a rhythmic ostinato with short variations at the end of each phrase. The song is fragmented by *revuelos*, rhythmic variations or improvisations. Improvisation is allowed to all instruments, with the exception of the llamador (whose role is to maintain a regular, repeated pulse), and its function is to carry the song to a climax, thus developing the same provocative function as the *gritos* (cries).

Media Distribution and Circulation

Since the 1930s, radio broadcasting has played a significant role in the diffusion of Caribbean and Latin American music (above all, the Cuban *son*, the Mexican *ranchera*, the Argentine *tango*, and the Brazilian *maxixe*), as well as the North American fox-trot. The first radio station in Colombia, La Voz de Barranquilla, took place in Barranquilla in 1929. Just a few years later, in 1934, a new radio station from Barranquilla, called the Emisora Atlántico, followed up. Around the same time, another radio station emerged in Cartagena, called La Voz de Laboratorios Fuentes (later simply called Emisora Fuentes). Cuban music (*bolero, son, rumba, guaracha, danzón*) had an immense impact on the Colombian audience; its success favored the process of "Cubanization" as a stylistic transformation of Colombian music.[20] In brief, radio stations of Barranquilla (La Voz de Barranquilla), Bogotá (La Voz de la Víctor), and Cartagena (Emisora Fuentes) all broadcast the recordings of Trío

Matamoros, Sonora Matancera, Sexteto Habanero,[21] Septeto Nacional, and the great Cuban orchestras (Benny Moré, Machito, Xavier Cugat, and Pérez Prado). Cuban bands such as Trío Matamoros and the Casino de La Playa orchestra toured Colombia in the 1930s, the latter performing on La Voz de la Víctor, La Voz de Barranquilla, and Emisora Fuentes (Betancur Álvarez 1993).

During this period, broadcast music was partly recorded and performed live at the radio station's studio. Each station had a stable orchestra that accompanied the guest soloists (as in the case of the Emisora Atlántico Jazz Band, the Orquesta Emisora Fuentes, and the Orquesta La Voz de Barranquilla). Programming could not sustain itself solely on recordings, because almost all were imported and, as a result, were quite expensive. Consequently this process led to the orchestration of folk music tunes, which had significant implications for contemporary Colombian popular music. The Cubanization of the arrangements was used to incorporate Afro-Cuban musical instruments: congas, bongos, maracas, claves, güiro, and trumpets.

Thanks to orchestral arrangements of many radio station bands, the cultivated "urban" interpretation of traditional "rural" melodies (originally performed by conjuntos and brass bands) led to a transformation of the folk repertoires into new urban musical forms: "Radio, then, not only provided a workplace for musicians and a point of circulation for their efforts, but also collaborated in the development of an urban musical culture for the Atlantic Coast" (González 1989: 27).

In the 1940s and 1950s the process of adapting traditional rhythms and melodies to cosmopolitan dance orchestras brought about a transformation from *música costeña* to *música tropical*. The rhythmic and melodic structures of costeño musical genres (cumbia, gaita, porro, fandango) traditionally interpreted by groups of gaiteros and *milleros* were stylized and orchestrated by composers and conductors such as "Lucho" Bermúdez (Luis Eduardo Bermúdez, 1912–94) and "Pacho" Galán (Francisco Galán, 1904–88).[22] Both had come to the regional music tradition of the coast to give stylized orchestral arrangements and big band sound to the music. Their music was halfway between the big band jazz style of Benny Goodman and the mambo of the Pérez Prado, Xavier Cugat, and Benny Moré orchestras. (Xavier Cugat toured Colombia in 1951, Benny Moré in 1955, and Pérez Prado in 1966; Betancur Álvarez 1993). At the same time, they were inspired by the *bandas de viento* (brass bands) from the towns in the Sinú River Valley, above all in San Pelayo (Córdoba), which was considered the "cradle of porro," and where the brass band style was strong and rooted in local tradition. Peter Wade clarifies:

> People such as Bermúdez and Galán came from backgrounds that had strong elements of the provincial middle class but had some links with rural lower-class experience as well; they had formal musical training, not always in a conservatory, but they were also familiar with Costeño instruments and styles from traditional peasant repertoire and from the *bandas de viento*. They knew, played, and often composed a wide range of styles, including *bambucos* and *pasillos*, but they wanted to bring Costeño music, albeit in highly adapted form, into the same arena—this was their way of making a mark. (2000: 87)

Since they conveyed supplementary meaning and rendered melodies recognizable to wide audiences, orchestral arrangements habitually respected the rhythmic structure of traditional genres. It is also imperative to consider the significance of the musical training of these musicians and conductors: "Lucho" Bermúdez, "Pacho" Galán, and Antonio María Peñalosa were all conductors who, during their youth, had participated in folk bandas de viento.

In the nineteenth century, bandas de viento emerged next to traditional groups in some towns in the department of Córdoba (San Pelayo, in particular; Fals Borda 1986a; Fortich Díaz 1994). Since then, folk music of the Sinú River Valley (porro and fandango) has been performed by traditional conjuntos (gaiteros and cañamilleros), or by a banda de viento, better known as *papayera*, made up of clarinets, trumpets, sax, bass drum, snare drum, and cymbals (Lotero Botero 1989).[23] Usually, *banda* musicians do not know how to read written music but rather play by ear. In other words, their training is still mostly through oral tradition. Young apprentices of wind instruments practice by making small lemon leaves vibrate between their lips, to imitate the trumpets and clarinets, making true brass bands called *bandas de hojita* (little leaves ensembles).

One of the most popular bandas de viento from the 1950s and 1960s, Pedro Laza y sus Pelayeros, is a quintessential example of this kind of cultural practice. Founded by Laza (1904–80) in 1952, its collection of works was made up mostly of porros and fandangos, in accordance with local banda tradition, and some cumbias as well. Its interpretation of coastal music was a unique combination of orchestral style and the typical sounds of village banda flavor, called *sabanera* (from the savannah).

Costeño music, particularly cumbia and porro, has strong African elements. Thus, to make it more accessible (aesthetically) and acceptable (socially) among the middle classes of the interior of the country and to contribute to its international diffusion, great ballroom dance orchestras reinterpreted it in a stylized and orchestrated form, eliminating all the African-derived musical instruments:

> *Cumbia* and other styles that belong to coastal music are a classic instantiation of a black inspirational tradition that, with time, has been turning "white." Previously, it was attacked, when in the past it was practiced independently by blacks. Nevertheless, it converts into a form that is more and more acceptable to the extent that it extends through the non-black world, losing its "Africanism" and its principal association with black people, although it retains its attractive quality of "hot." It is not a coincidence then that tropical music is also known as "hot, sexy" music. (Wade 1997a: 334–35)

The white and mestizo population of the Andean interior, who listened mostly to Andean music (*bambuco* and *pasillo*), began to listen and dance to coastal music (cumbia and porro), as well as Cuban genres (bolero, guaracha, son, and rumba).

National and international diffusion of orchestrated cumbia acquired a primary role in the relationship between music and national identity and the process of homogenizing tendencies of nationalism. Urban orchestrated cumbia begins to replace the bambuco, an Andean music genre till then considered the most representative form of traditional music in Colombia, as the flag of national identity:

> Colombia was no longer represented either at home or abroad by a style associated with the Andean interior, center of power, wealth and "civilization"; it was now represented by tropical music from the Caribbean coastal region, seen as poor, backward, "hot" (climatically, sexually, and musically) and "black" (at least by association, even if many of the musicians in the dance bands, even the Costeño ones, were whites or light-coloured mestizos). (Wade 1997a: 9)

Orchestras played in the social clubs for the elite in the large Andean cities, such as Bogotá and Medellín, or broadcast live on radio stations. Stylized and orchestrated cumbia by the great ballroom dance orchestras was popularized as *música tropical* (tropical music) in other Latin American countries: "Lucho" Bermúdez played with his orchestra in Argentina, Cuba, Mexico, and the United States; "Pacho" Galán played in Central America and Venezuela (Wade 2000: 173).

National record production was also fundamental to the process of diffusion of música tropical, especially the role played by the first Colombian record label, Discos Fuentes, founded by Antonio Fuentes (1907–85) in Cartagena (later transferred to Medellín) in 1934. Fuentes was the same person who had been so important as a promoter of the first radio station in Cartagena, Emisora Fuentes, and, who had also, in the 1940s, regularly transmitted the music produced by the Orquesta Emisora Fuentes. In the following years, other record labels that made history with Colombian popular music eventually popped up: Discos Tropical, founded by Emilio Fortou in Barranquilla in 1945, and Discos Sonolux, founded in Medellín in 1949.[24]

Currently, for the older generations living in the interior of the country, the term *cumbia* still refers to the stylized cumbia from the great orchestra shows of the 1940s and 1950s. Such a process of identification began when a young clarinet player, "Lucho" Bermúdez, recorded the track "Danza negra" (Black Dance),[25] a cumbia sung by Matilde Díaz; the song was so successful that people began to identify it as *the* Colombian cumbia (as the text of the song suggests). Nowadays, some hits from the 1940s and 1950s, such as the cumbias "Danza negra" and "Colombia, tierra querida" (Colombia, Beloved Country), or the mapalé "Prende la vela" (Light the Candle) by "Lucho" Bermúdez, are considered classics and known throughout the country, even today, half a century after their inception. Indeed these songs have become musical icons of Colombian national identity.

On one hand, the commercialization of cumbia has assisted its national and international dissemination through the production of recordings and increased radio playtime; on the other, it has also generated significant stylistic changes that have brought into question issues of authenticity and the alleged degeneration of cumbia. The musician Luis Antonio Escobar points out that the passage of cumbia from the "folk" to the "popular" domain caused a loss of authenticity:

> In this sense we have to consider another transition from folk to popular domain. Such is the case of famous musicians who adopted some native rhythms such as *cumbia* and *porro*, making arrangements and changing their character.
>
> I refer particularly to Lucho Bermúdez, a musician of immense musical talent and the author of numerous *porros*, *cumbias* and other forms, trying to represent a new kind of mixture between Indian, black, and white components. This new musical trend, synthesis of a new people of Cartagena, is another important expression, but it belongs to the Colombian popular music in some cases covered with international orchestration, which needs a certain number

of harmonies, rhythms, and instruments that are going to represent another musical level, perhaps more striking but less authentic. (1985: 84)

The folklorist José Portaccio writes, "One cannot deny that cumbias that have had national and international impact are the ones that are sung and orchestrated, contrary to the true and authentic performance, which corresponds to *milleros* and drum ensembles. The taped recordings of these groups hardly enjoy regional distribution and are very scarce through the entire country" (1995: 69). In fact it is surprising to note the enormous stylistic differences separating the two musical phenomena under the same name of *cumbia*. It's simply a matter of comparing, for instance, the "rural, traditional" cumbia played with autochthonic instruments by the cañamilleros of river towns like Mahates, Botón de Leyva, and El Banco, with a "popular, urban" cumbia, stylized, and with vocals, like "La pollera colorá" (The Red Skirt) by Wilson Choperena, sang by its composer and performed by Pedro Salcedo's orchestra (and successfully released by Discos Tropical), which eventually became a sort of popular national anthem.

The 1960s mark the progressive decline of ballroom dance orchestras and the rise of the smaller combos. With an instrumental structure made up basically of a brass band and two accordions (including the virtuoso *acordeonero* Alfredo Gutiérrez), Los Corraleros de Majagual contributed to the circulation and popularization of cumbia and *vallenato* in the entire country and in other nations where they played, such as Mexico, Ecuador, and Peru. Another band with a brief national popularity but a strong impact outside the country was Sonora Dinamita (inspired by Cuba's Sonora Matancera), renowned for its adoption of an electric bass and the accordion. The Sonora Dinamita, started in Cartagena in 1960 by Lucho Argaín (Lucho Pérez Cedrón), played a crucial role in spreading a simplified form of cumbia. This kind of *cumbia de exportación* (export cumbia; Escobar 1985; Pacini Hernandez 1992) began to circulate all over Latin America, enjoying particular acceptance in Mexico, Peru, Argentina, and Chile. As Deborah Pacini Hernandez writes:

> Other Colombian musicians and bands—recognizing cumbia's economic potential outside the country, also have continued to record cumbia produced exclusively for export to Central America and the Andean nations. Nevertheless, these cumbias have increasingly been transformed to adapt to the tastes of populations with very different aesthetic traditions than those from the strongly African-derived coastal culture from which cumbia origi-

nally emerged. Most noticeably, these made-for-export cumbias have lost the rhythmic complexity of their predecessor, the cumbia *costeña*. . . . As a result, these cumbias are uncategorically rejected by *costeños*, who refer to them politely as *cumbias del interior* (cumbias from the highland interior), or more scornfully as *cumbias gallegas*, the closest (figurative) translation of which I can think of is "honky cumbias." (1992: 292)

The commercial and standardized variant of cumbia spreading in all Latin American countries was so successful that it went through a process of appropriation and transformation according to the local taste. In the 1980s Peruvian cumbia, or *chicha*, for example, adopted the pentatonic melodies from the Andean *huayno*, adding the rhythmic structure from Caribbean cumbia. (Such is the case of the hit "El Aguajal" by Los Shapis, a chicha version of the huayno "El Alisal.") Then, in the 1990s, the Peruvian *tecno-cumbia* left the folk huayno component and mixed Colombian cumbia with Tex-Mex sounds. (Such is the case of the singer Rossy War.)

Cumbia and Other Genres

In the 1970s and 1980s, cumbia had to confront, at the national level, the emergence and growing admiration for another music genre, the *vallenato*. Named after its main center of dissemination, the city of Valledupar, vallenato is a musical genre played in its traditional form by an accordion ensemble, formed by the *acordeón* (diatonic accordion), the *caja* (drum), and the *guacharaca* (scraper), whose repertoire consists of four basic music forms: son, *paseo*, merengue, and puya.

With the encouragement of the first governor of Cesar and former president of Colombia, Alfonso López Michelsen (1913–2007), vallenato changed from a regional folk expression of La Provincia (the department of Cesar) into a national popular music for the masses. López Michelsen was a steadfast supporter of vallenato and the principal promoter of the now renowned Festival de la Leyenda Vallenata (established in 1967), together with a local politician, Consuelo Araújo, and the composer Rafael Escalona. Having garnered official validation thanks to a process of increased acceptance by the Andean middle classes and enjoying steady support by selected members of Bogotá's ruling classes, vallenato was losing its plebeian connotations (being an expression of the lower social strata of northeastern coastal populations) and an image closely associated with drug trafficking and smuggling during the late 1970s, to become a type of music disseminated and appreciated by the entire country and all social classes.

Vallenato's most recent revival as a widespread middle-class phenomenon took place in the early 1990s with the singer and actor Carlos Vives, who, after playing the role of Rafael Escalona on a hit soap opera produced by Caracol TV in 1991, asserted himself as a *rock-vallenato star*.[26] Vives's music found inspiration in the classics of the vallenato repertoire composed by Rafael Escalona and accordionists like Francisco "Pacho" Rada, Alejandro "Alejo" Durán, and Emiliano Zuleta, among many others. In this way, through the novel arrangement of instruments (integrating the gaitas, drums, and accordion to the electric bass and drums) and musical styles (blending traditional Caribbean ritmos, including cumbia, with contemporary urban rock), the singer from Santa Marta managed to bestow a modern and innovative air to vallenato, creating a new tendency that connects to the tastes of a large portion of Colombia's audiences, comprising both old and new generations, as well as different social classes: "By the early 1990s, *vallenato* had come to replace *música tropical* as the new popular Colombian sound" (Waxer 2001: 148).

In the 1980s the panorama of Colombian music began to change due to the influence of *salsa*, a Cuban-based popular dance music developed by Latinos in New York during the 1960s and 1970s. The music became apparent in the city of Cali, the principal urban center near the Colombian Pacific Coast, with a large Afro-descendant population. It is precisely in Cali and the nearby port of Buenaventura that the first groups of Colombian salsa emerged: Guayacán and Grupo Niche. But the first successful Colombian group was Fruko y sus Tesos, founded by Ernesto "Fruko" Estrada (formerly of Los Corraleros) in 1971, whose singer, the late Joe Arroyo, would eventually have an extremely successful solo career. The song "El preso" (The Prisoner), composed by Alvaro Velásquez and performed by Fruko y sus Tesos, was a hit for a long time in Colombia, becoming a classic of Colombian salsa. Colombian salsa takes the form of a variety of "sauces" with many local "flavors," inspired by rhythms of the Pacific Coast (*currulao*) and the Atlantic Coast (cumbia). For quite some time, Colombian salsa remained a decidedly regional and marginal phenomenon, with little national resonance and distribution, thus distinguishing itself significantly, in both style and form, from *música costeña* and *música del interior*.

Despite salsa's growing popularity and the advent of new, imported genres like Dominican merengue, commercial cumbia enjoyed substantial acceptance abroad throughout the 1980s, thanks to the success of songs like "La colegiala" (The Schoolgirl) by Rodolfo y su Típica.[27] The song became a hit in Europe when it was used as jingle for a coffee commercial. Actually, this song is not even considered a cumbia by most coastal musicians, but rather is considered contemptuously as *chucu-chucu*,[28] the derogatory, onomatopoeic term describing the kind of simplified and repetitive version of cumbia embraced by Colombia's recording industry studios after the 1970s.

In the 1990s cumbia was summarily included in the marketing of world music, awakening interest from British recording labels of world music such as World Circuit, Mango Records (a division of Island Records), World Music Network, and Globe Style, which released compilations of "old-fashioned" cumbias from the Colombian labels Sonolux and Discos Fuentes. In 1982, in Stockholm, during the ceremony for the Nobel Prize for literature, the Colombian writer Gabriel García Márquez introduced to a worldwide audience the Colombian singer Sonia Bazanta, otherwise known as Totó La Momposina, from a family of singers and musicians from the village of Talaigua, a small riverside town in Magdalena (an old palenque of fugitive slaves). Since then, Totó La Momposina has become a staple of the global circuit of world music, participating in WOMAD (World of Music, Arts, and Dance), the traveling festival of ethnic music from all over the world. Peter Gabriel started the festival in 1991, after successfully recording albums like *La candela viva* (The Burning Fire), by Totó La Momposina, for the Real World label in 1992. As the new emblem of traditional cumbia, Totó La Momposina has never altered her style or her traditional costeño repertoire to please the global market. Additionally, she has seldom strayed far from her roots (with the exception of some phases in her artistic career when she composed and interpreted some pieces inspired by the Cuban son), replicating coastal and river musical traditions in the finest way available.

In 2007 an unexpected and surprising event took place. The Gaiteros of San Jacinto, one of the most representative groups of traditional cumbia, won a Latin Grammy. Their album *Un fuego de sangre pura* (A Pure-Blooded Fire), coproduced by the Colombian recording artist Iván Benavides for the Smithsonian Folkways label, was awarded the prize for best folklore recording, celebrating the spirit of more conventional, unadulterated costeño music, the potential of a return to grassroots or, as many Costeños would claim, "to our very tradition."

Conclusion

Cumbia is the most representative musical form of costeño traditional culture of the Colombian Atlantic Coast as the cultural product of the Afro-Indo-Hispanic *mestizaje*, although the African component is its most relevant. Cumbia has its origin in the rural villages in the Magdalena River Valley, within the zone called the Mompox Depression, originally as an instrumental form only, played by the conjunto de cañamilleros. From the postwar period on, cumbia was popular in its stylized and orchestrated form in conformity with cosmopolitan taste, through national and transnational channels of diffusion (e.g., radio and records).

Big band adaptations of orchestrated cumbias in the 1940s and 1950s contributed to the processes of popularizing the sound, which became familiar as the new national music of Colombia, but at the same time redefined its social and cultural connotations with the erasure of blackness or Africanness. The process of "modernization" and commercialization induced by the national record market brought about its diffusion at the national level as música tropical, an urban orchestrated form, with the elimination of Afro-Colombian traditional musical instruments. To gain the acceptance of the Andean white and *mestizo* middle class, cumbia left behind its own regional connotations and acquired unofficially the status of Colombian national music.[29]

Fundamental to this process of commercialization or "modernization" and affirmation in the national and transnational market is the role of Colombian record companies (Discos Fuentes, Discos Tropical, Sonolux). In the 1960s cumbia was disseminated as música tropical in other Latin American countries (Mexico, Peru, Argentina, and Chile) through small groups made up of a wind section, a rhythm section, and an accordion set. In the 1970s and 1980s cumbia had to confront the arrival of other music genres, vallenato and salsa, mixing with them in some cases. In the 1990s cumbia, in its different forms, experienced a revival thanks to the boom of world music spreading throughout the global musical market.

From being a regional music genre with strong ethnic-social connotations and a musical expression of a local costeño identity, cumbia acquired the status of national music, transcending local culture and becoming the marker of Colombian national identity. A few years later, through a process of appropriation, reinterpretation, and commercialization, cumbia became a Latin American transnational style.

Filmography

Triana, Gloria. Cumbria sobre el río; series: Yurupari, 16mm, audiovisuales, Focine, 25 min., 1984.

Notes

1. The Atlantic Coast of Colombia extends from the Guajira Peninsula in the northeastern portion of the country to the Gulf of Urabá in the northwest, near the Panama border, and is made up of the departments of Guajira, Magdalena, Cesar, Atlántico, Bolívar, Córdoba, and Sucre, as well as portions of northern Antioquia (Urabá) and the northern arm of Chocó. The lower coastal and river plains are inhabited by Afro-Hispanic (*mulatos*), Indo-Hispanic (*mestizos*), and Indo-African (*zambos*) populations. The indigenous Kogi and Ika are located in the Sierra Nevada de Santa Marta, in the department of Magdalena, and the Wayúu are settled in the Guajira Peninsula.

2. In the past decades, the process of cultural mixing in the Colombian Caribbean coast and islands has been enriched by contributions from Middle Eastern immigrants (Syrian and Lebanese), called *turcos*, or the Turkish.

3. Manuel and Delia Zapata Olivella carried out the first notable recordings and investigations of ethnofolkloric interest regarding Caribbean coastal music in the 1960s (M. Zapata 1967; D. Zapata 1962, 1967). Before that, in 1959, the ethnomusicologist Isabel Artez, together with the folklorist Delia Zapata, started a campaign of fieldwork in coastal towns such as Palenque de San Basilio, Soplaviento, María La Baja, and San Jacinto (Aretz 1991). They were followed in 1964 by the investigations of the American ethnomusicologist George List, who did fieldwork in the town of Evitar (Bolívar) with the collaboration of Delia Zapata. This work brought about the publication of *Music and Poetry in a Colombian Village: A Tricultural Heritage* (1983). The ethnographical studies of Aquiles Escalantes (1954, 1964) about Palenque de San Basilio mark the beginning of interest in Afro-descendants culture in Colombia. One of the most interesting audiovisual source materials for the anthropological research has been the series of documentaries *Yurupari*,—including "Cumbia sobre el río" (1986)—produced by COLCULTURA (Colombian Institute of Culture) in the 1980s and directed by the anthropologist Gloria Triana. Even though there is still a demological character that remains in the study of ethnic music (Abadía 1973; Marulanda 1984; Ocampo López 1976), an anthropological and sociological approach is now emerging (Bermúdez 1992, 1994; Wade 1997, 1998, 2000).

4. In Palenque de San Basilio the *lumbalú* is still performed; it is a funeral ritual of the descendants of the *cimarrones* (fugitive slaves) that make up ancient *palenques* (Escalante 1964, [1954] 1979, 1989).

5. The term *tambora* has different meanings, but they all relate to one another: (a) a low cylindrical drum with two heads; (b) the rhythm (*golpe*) played on this drum (characterized by a ternary rhythm on a double meter); (c) the ensemble of voices and per-

cussion (including the tambora); (d) the dance associated with this music; and (e) the festive occasion with dances and songs performed by the tambora (Carbó 2003: 63).

6. The term *currulao* also indicates a genre of music and dance from the Afro-Colombian people from Colombia's South Pacific Coast, performed by a *marimba* ensemble.

7. Colombian *bailes cantados* present some similarities at the formal and stylistic level (above all, in the type of call-and-response songs that are accompanied by the drums) with other dance-music expressions broadcast in Caribbean Afro-Hispanic areas, like the *rumba* in Cuba, the *baile de bomba* in Puerto Rico, and the *baile de los palos* in the Dominican Republic. Petrona Martínez, belonging to a family of cantadoras, is the most representative singer of bullerengue (and in general of the bailes cantados repertoire) and has performed in many festivals in Europe, Asia, and North Africa.

8. In Colombia the *palenques* were numerous and very spread out, above all in the outskirts of Cartagena and Mompox, on the banks of the Cauca and San Jorge Rivers, in the Cauca Valley, in the mountainous region of Antioquia and in the Chocó, on the Pacific Coast, in the middle Magdalena up to the east in the Llanos (grasslands). The most famous palenque, which for the longest time was able to fight off the Spaniards, was Palenque de San Basilio.

9. Gonzalo Aguirre Beltrán, in the book *La población negra de México* ([1946] 1989), attributes the name Cumbás to the ethnic group Cumba-manez from the former Mali Empire: "In the second half of the 16th century black tribes such as the *Cumbás* and the *Zapés* were brought to Nueva España, and in general to America. These groups never appear again in the slave lists in the centuries to come" (119).

10. In Brazil the *cucumbis*, singled out during the nineteenth century in Bahia and Rio, were dramatic dances performed at the Christmas festivals and Carnival, which represent the clash between the black and Indian cultures; according to Oneyda Alvarenga (1947), *cucumbi* was also the regional Brazilian name for the black populations from the Congo.

11. See Enrique Luis Muñoz Vélez's (2006) "La cumbia: Trazos y signos de una historia cultural," www.musicalafrolatino.com/pagina_nueva_22j.htm.

12. This confirms the thesis regarding the African origin of the instrument, the fact that millet is originally from an Asian gramineaceous plant that spread out to Africa, Europe, and successively to America, with the arrival of Europeans, which excludes the use of *millo* in the pre-Columbian era.

13. The term *tambor alegre* refers to its function: "to make happy" or "to improvise," "to vary."

14. The term *llamador* means "caller." The function of a "call" by the drums is also recurrent in other Afro-American music traditions, such as Afro-Uruguayan *candombe*, Honduran *punta*, and Cuban rumba.

15. The Carabalí are Afro-Cubans of Efik/Ibibio origin, an ethnic group that inhabits the Calabar region in the southeastern part of Nigeria and uses the same drums called *ekomo* (Akpabot 1975).

16. In his monograph *Music and Poetry in a Colombian Village* (1983), List calls the tambora *bombo*, a generic Spanish term that identifies the bass drum with two drumheads and is used today on the Pacific Coast to refer to drums of this type.

17. The traditional genre performed by this group is the *gaita*, but in groups of *gaiteros*, the cumbia, the *porro*, and the puya also appear in their repertoire.

18. The Colombian gaita has no relationship to the Iberian *gaita*, a term that in Spanish and Portuguese means "bagpipe."

19. In the town of San Pelayo (Córdoba), one finds the *gaita corta* (called *pito cabeza de cera* in slang) that is distinguished by its dimensions from the *gaitas largas*. In addition, the gaita corta is played alone, not in pairs, as are the gaitas largas (Cantero and Fortich 1991: 120).

20. There is also a process of "Cubanization" of the Colombian repertoire on behalf of Cuban orchestras, as is the case with the porro "La múcura" (The Vase) by Crescencio Salcedo and reinterpreted by Pérez Prado, and the bambuco "Bésame morenita" (Kiss Me, Little Dark One) by Pedro Fernández and popularized by the group Sonora Matancera (Betancur 1993).

21. In some coastal cities during the 1940s, some sextet groups appeared that were imitations of Cuban groups, in particular the Sexteto Habanero, which formed in Cuba during the 1920s with the repertoire of son. The typical formation of the Cuban *sexteto* was guitar, *tres*, *bongo*, *maracas*, *claves*, and *marímbula* (later replaced by the double bass), while the Colombian *sexteto*—the Sexteto Tabalá of Palenque de San Basilio, the only one remaining in Colombia—includes *tambor alegre*, *timbal* (the same bongo), *maracas*, *claves*, and *marímbula*, with a repertoire of *son palenqueros*.

22. Some landmark songs include Bermudez's "Carmen de Bolívar," "Salsipuedes," "Tolú," "San Fernando," and "Colombia, tierra querida" and Galán's "Ay cosita linda" and "El merecumbé."

23. The *porro* is the slow version of the cumbia, with the same rhythm of the backbeat of the cymbal—the stress of the simple 2/4—that will be taken up by orchestras, played on a cymbal with a drumstick, and muffled with a hand. The term *papayera* has its origin in the typical musical apprenticeship of a *banda de hojitas*, accomplished by players who use papaya leaves vibrating between the lips, and for this reason it gets the name *papayera* (Fals Borda 1986b: 127).

24. The most acclaimed composers and interpreters of coastal music, such as Lucho Bermúdez, Pacho Galán, and Escalona, have recorded for Sonolux. Today this Medellín label continues promoting new Colombian talents.

25. See the LP *San Fernando y otros éxitos inolvidables de Lucho Bermúdez y Matilde Díaz* (Sonolux LP 12-267).

26. Rafael Escalona (1907–2009) was the most celebrated composer of classic vallenatos of the 1940s and 1950s.

27. This group was established in the 1970s by the coastal singer Rodolfo Aicardi (1946–2007).

28. This is an onomatopoeic term referring to the simple and commercial imitation of coastal music, very common in the 1970s. Another slang term with the same meaning is *música gallega* (lit. "music from Galicia").

29. Even though officially bambuco, a musical expression from Andean mestizo culture, represented the musical emblem of Colombian national identity at that particular point in time (Wade 1998, 2000).

JORGE ARÉVALO MATEUS WITH
MARTÍN VEJARANO

2.
¿Pa' dónde vas Marioneta? ¿Pa' dónde va la gaita?
La Cumbiamba Eneyé Returns to San Jacinto

Before leaving for San Jacinto to compete in the 17th Festival Nacional Autóctono de Gaitas, Martín Vejarano and La Cumbiamba Eneyé (LCE) performed at The Rose, a small club in the hipster enclave of Williamsburg, Brooklyn, which for the past few years has regularly featured artists involved with the local Nueva Colombia music scene.[1] What marked this event as special, however, was the presence and participation of Los Gaiteros de San Jacinto, the most recognized and highly influential *conjunto de gaita* from Colombia. As acknowledged bearers of the *gaita* tradition, a music genre inextricably linked to *cumbia*, Los Gaiteros have for more than five generations been its foremost practitioners, traveling internationally and bringing traditional folk musics such as gaita, *porro*, *puya*, and cumbia—the *ritmos* (or styles) that constitute the gaita tradition—to audiences worldwide. Scheduled to perform at Queens Theater in the Park in Flushing-Meadows the following day, five members from Los Gaiteros were present: Juan Fernández "Chuchita" Polo, Manuel Antonio "Toño" García, Gabriel Torregrosa, Dionysio Yepes, and Freddys Arrieta. Juan Nicolás Hernández, the senior leader of the renowned conjunto de gaita, did not travel to New York this time, due to recent health issues. In fact, except for special occasions, he rarely performs with Los Gaiteros these days.

Vejarano, announcing that it was going to be a special night because the *maestros*—their musical mentors, from whom they learned everything—were present, opened LCE's set with a *gaita corrida*, an instrumental piece whose rhythmic base is closely aligned with cumbia. In her notes accompanying the 2007 Latin Grammy Award–winning recording *Un Fuego de Sangre Pura* (A Fire of Pure Blood), Ana María Ochoa writes of Los Gaiteros de San Jacinto, "Through their own new compositions and through teaching young musicians, they are a crucial link between traditional gaita music and its contemporary renewal."[2] In honor of their special guests, LCE played their own version of the opening song from the Los Gaiteros CD, "Fuego de Cumbia" (Cumbia Fire). After performing several songs from their own repertoire—for example, Sebastian Cruz's composition "Marioneta," the title track and name of LCE's first release—Vejarano invited members of Los Gaiteros to perform with them on the small, dimly lit stage. Prototypically, "Chuchita," the *cantador* (voice or lead vocalist) began by reciting a *décima* as members of Los Gaiteros gradually replaced LCE musicians on *gaita macho* and *hembra* (male and female flutes) and *tambor alegre* (lead drum), while core members remained on *tambora* (or *bombo*, bass drum), *llamador* (timeline drum), and *coro* (vocal chorus). Together, as they played mostly slower tempo Afro-Colombian *bullerengues* as well as cumbias and gaitas, the paired gaitas were heard perceptibly clearer and the distinctively close musical interplay between the tambor alegre and gaita hembra was markedly evident on classic gaitas, cumbias, and porros, such as the ubiquitous "Campo Alegre." Indeed the performance demonstrated a rare example of master musicians and students performing traditional Colombian music together, sharing a stage in front of a mixed audience of Colombians, other Latinos, and New Yorkers of all kinds.

After several songs from the combined ensemble—by which point dancers had overtaken the floor—LCE regulars returned to close out the set.[3] The presence of Los Gaiteros de San Jacinto had clearly inspired LCE, motivating them to continue the performance with a renewed dynamic vigor. Whereas previously they had played confidently and efficiently, after playing with the masters they exhibited increased intensity that figuratively borrowed from the Smithsonian Folkways title *un fuego de sangre pura*.

Significantly in an urban setting, LCE's material tends toward faster gaita corrida and puya uptempo songs, undoubtedly to appeal to young urbanites wanting to dance. Demonstrating careful selection of audience-appropriate music and its interpretation, LCE's repertoire clearly leans toward the more traditional or authentic side of contemporary gaita/cumbia praxis, or its close approximation. Whether this was solely due to the presence of the masters or to present gaita "authenticity" in practice, the audience responded appreciatively, dancing, clapping, and singing choruses throughout the set.

Like their San Jacinto musical mentors, LCE demonstrates what Gil Olivera regards as central qualities of Sanjacintero musicians; that is, they exhibit "natural musicians[hip] dispatched with a tremendous force, making themselves heard throughout the world," as they "carry a gaita in the deepest folds

Figure 2.1. *Marioneta*, La Cumbiamba Eneyé's first recording, was released in 2006 on Chonta Records.

of their soul" (Gil Olivera 2002: 40, my translation). What is most striking, however, is that LCE and Los Gaiteros are both in the midst of a remarkable intracultural exchange and transformation involving several factors and elements, such as the relevance of place, the flows of transnational movements of cultural material, cosmopolitanism, and a classic encounter between tradition and modernity, conservation and innovation, to name a few.

In New York City, Martín Vejarano and La Cumbiamba Eneyé specialize in *música de gaita*, a genre that forms a substantial part of its core repertoire. The group claims to "perform in a variety of styles from Afro-Colombian music traditions—from both the Atlantic and Pacific coasts of Colombia—while retaining the styles' original formats."[4] This is apparent on their first U.S. release, *Marioneta* (2006), which contains traditional as well as original music in diverse genres and hybrid substyles, including *chirimía, currulao, puyamerenge, garabato-chande,* bullerengue, *champeta,* porro, cumbia, and gaita (figure 2.1).

Since arriving in 2000, Vejarano has worked diligently with Colombian and non-Colombian musicians, singers, and dancers, assembling one of the more visible and successful musical projects of the so-called Nueva Colombia/New Colombian music community in the United States. Insofar as LCE's Atlantic Coast repertoire is concerned, cumbia and gaita are not only genres or ritmos closely associated with San Jacinto's folkloric musical traditions; they are musical sisters in that their geocultural place of origin is traceable to the Sinú Valley, specifically the Montes de María la Alta region, or Serranía de San Jacinto in the northern coastal regions of Colombia. It is in this rural environment that the production of social life and racial *mestizaje* of *costeño* peoples have conspired to create an abundantly rich and enduring musical culture.

The region's mountainous areas, lowland savannahs, and *ciénagas*, located in the Department of Bolívar, lie southeast of the port city of Cartagena de Indias, only fifty kilometers from the Caribbean coast, located to the west. Within this area, the people known as *costeños*, populating such storied musical centers as El Carmen de Bolívar, San Basilio de Palenque, Sincelejo, San Pelayo, Ovejas, and San Jacinto, have contributed much to costeño culture and the many discourses and debates surrounding costeño music and dance, their history and significance, and the role they perform for local communities. The literature about the importance of *festivales patronales*, for example, where expressive cultures are dynamically maintained, is particularly abundant, rife with local and regional claims to cultural authenticity, proprietorship, and patronage (see Friedemann, Horner, and Villegas Jiménez 1995). And yet, most researchers agree that the distinctiveness of highly localized, microcultural expressions, evident in contemporary performance practices, reflect sociocultural change as they highlight tensions emanating from processes of cultural innovation vis-à-vis preservation. Among these and other issues, I am interested in querying how the musical field of the cumbia/gaita complex, given these contemporary tensions, extends and is impacted by *lo de afuera* (from the outside)—that is, by the Colombian diaspora.[5]

To illustrate this point, on LCE's first release, *Marioneta* (2006), the New York City–based ensemble included a fifteen-second spoken-word recording in which Nicolás Hernández, the elder and still active leader of Los Gaiteros de San Jacinto, is heard briefly, stating, "Eso no lo pueden cambiar nunca por la gaita, la que suena suena desde que usted la empieza a hacer. Hay un cardón [cactus] muy bueno, un cardón que . . ." (recording trails off).[6] Programmed between original compositions by the founding members Sebastián Cruz and Martín Vejarano ("Marioneta," a puya, and "Pachanga," a cumbia, respectively), Hernández's comments are included as a tribute to música de gaita and the centrality of its indigenous flutes. The authority with which he speaks is unquestionable. By incorporating Hernández's voice, Martín Vejarano et al. demonstrate the profound respect they, as modern, urban cosmopolitan proponents of gaita, confer upon the acknowledged masters and carriers of the tradition. Vejarano, however, takes the honorifics a step further. As a modern musician, he is interested in maintaining direct links with practitioners of traditional Colombian music *and* the places from which they derive; thus cultural preservation results from both action and mimicry, a necessary strategy deployed to gain entry into an "authentic" space. For Vejarano and his musicians, returning regularly to participate and compete in local traditional music festivals (e.g., San Jacinto) is empowering and enabling, allowing them to insert themselves into processes of cultural preservation while simultaneously emulating and advancing musical innovations that are intended to galvanize and even reinvent traditional costeño music (i.e., cumbia and gaita). It is a bold act, and Vejarano's experimentation—as a Bogotá musician connected to global networks via the New York diaspora— with the very construction of the gaita, attenuating and altering the instrument's "tuning,"[7] using different materials (e.g., PVC tubing), and even applying new performance and arrangement techniques, for example, suggests that participating, placing, or winning at the San Jacinto festival represents for *Marioneta* at least a modicum of acceptance by the tradition's authenticators—the authorities, as it were.

Thus, in this chapter I discuss processes and tensions that arise when local and regional folklore encounters global or world music ambitions. Issues of authenticity, innovation, and preservation are raised for both the indigenous gaita practitioners and the *new* gaiteros from *afuera* (outside). The focus of my study is música de gaita as performed by Martín Vejarano and LCE, performing in Colombia as Marioneta. The fieldwork and data take into account audience reception to their performance and participation in the local context of San Jacinto's annual Gaita Festival. Part ethnographic report, part reception study, the narrative is driven by the intersubjectivities of Vejarano, local festival organizers, and the audience's response.

I am concerned with transnational flows of Colombian music and musicians in the performance of genres from the Atlantic Coast that make up the gaita complex: cumbia, gaita or gaita corrida, porro, and puya. Again, questions of authentic tradition and definitions of *folklore* serve as a subtext, particularly in settings where gaita is performed by musicians from both within and outside the "official" festival cultural context, as they discretely bring new forms of innovation. "Innovation or musical creativity," as Ochoa points out, "transforms not only the instrument and the genre but challenges the ideologies through which both elements have been constituted historically" (1996: 40). With respect to sociopolitical and cultural economies occurring during the festival event (i.e., on the ground), these questions are raised in order to underscore significant musical innovation and shifts in meaning(s) for local audiences and cosmopolitan Colombian musicians alike (i.e., Vejarano), even as the thornier issue of Colombian identity is raised. Thus, as an ethnomusicology of gaita performance and its cultural meaning, the chapter aims to illustrate how one of Colombia's most popular music cultural resources, gaita, and its contemporary praxis elucidate processes of transnational and global cultural transformation along the cumbia axis while serving local and transnational desires.

Gaita

To determine the precise origins of gaita would require a suspension of disbelief and a general acceptance of vastly differing accounts and oral histories. Gaita is a music genre that developed primarily in and around a number of small costeño towns such as Carmen de Bolívar, Ovejas, and particularly San Jacinto (presently with a population of less than thirty thousand). Gaita is diffused throughout the coastal departments of Bolívar, Sucre, and Córdoba, and few music historians venture to date its origin; scholars such as List (1983), Miñana-Blasco (2000), and Zapata Olivella (1962), among others, have instead focused on gaita's tri-ethnic racial and cultural makeup to explain its derivation.

More recently gaita has received increased musicological and pedagogical attention for its indigenous antecedents and contemporary revival (see Convers and Ochoa 2007; Fortich Díaz 1994; *Revista Cultural* 2008). While many have commented upon gaita's relationship to cumbia (particularly its rhythmic structural similarities), ethnomusicologists have placed greater emphasis on, for example, the organology of flutes and natural materials native to the region, that is, *caña* and *cardón*, from which flutes are constructed (see List 1983). It has also been noted that throughout *la costa* a variety of flutes are used, including the *gaita corta* (the short cane flute of San Pelayo) and the paired gaita hembra and gaita macho duct flutes (of San Jacinto and elsewhere in the Serranía), with five orifices and a single orifice, respectively, both of Zenú provenance. While I am concerned with the gaita hembra and gaita macho, to speak of gaita generally refers to the native flutes of the Kogi and Ika tribes that continue to be played on the southwestern slopes of the Sierra Nevada de Santa Marta and the short and long paired sets of flutes played by both mestizo people of the lowland coastal regions and the Afro-

Colombian gaiteros on the littoral coast. In a more general use of the term, *gaita* also refers to the traditional music ensembles of San Jacinto that perform closely related musical genres (i.e., porro, cumbia, gaita, and puya). Each gaita (an abbreviated term for conjunto de gaita) thus comprises an ensemble of membranophones and idiophones, including paired gaitas, a large gourd maraca, and tambores (drums): a llamador, a tambor macho or alegre, and a tambora or bombo (figures 2.2–2.5).

Further complicating the term, *gaita* also can be said to represent the raced, cultural dichotomy evident in local music practices: one mestizo yet primarily indigenous, and one predominantly African—that is, *gaita negra* (or black gaita)—the latter traceable to Cartagena and its environs, where it remains prominently associated with a distinct drumming tradition found throughout Afro-Colombian costeño towns and villages such as Soplaviento and Palenque de San Basilio.[8] Significantly, the music and dance ethnographer Delia Zapata Olivella noted that while the organology and names of Afro-Colombian instruments and styles have changed from region to region, the choreography was conserved (Convers and Ochoa 2007: 32). This suggests that as variegated as gaita-related genres such as porros and puyas, or even *fandangos* may appear, gaita and cumbia are regarded as linked musical genres that evolved in tandem, over time and place, and as a result of intercultural, -racial, and -ethnic interactions over a historical continuum that has endured from the colonial era to the present.

In San Jacinto, gaita is decidedly mestizo in form, function, and content, retaining indigenous melodic elements and instrumentation, while incorporating African-derived drums and drumming patterns and perpetuating European choreographic styles, poetics, and social hierarchies. In the mid-1950s, for example, when Toño Fernández of San Jacinto began to set lyrics to traditional gaita melodies, this innovation was eventually adopted as common practice, and *cancioneros* (singers) have since performed poetic texts (i.e., often in the form of work songs), incorporating them with the once instrumental conjunto de gaitas—an ensemble that typically would play at informal social and community events such as *fiestas* and *parrandas*. For today's gaiteros, as in the past, the ability to improvise prose is one of the required performance skills; it is acquired from learning and reciting décimas, a decidedly Spanish-derived poetic form that continues to be significantly valorized throughout the region (figure 2.6).

Although gaita is a musical tradition that developed within costeño family and community structures, with the establishment and proliferation of fes-

Figure 2.2. *Gaita macho* and *maraca* (l.), *gaita hembra* (r.).
Courtesy of Juan Pablo Assmus. ©2012 Xqualo.

Figure 2.3. *Llamador*.
Courtesy of Juan Pablo Assmus.
©2012 Xqualo.

Figure 2.4. Juan Carlos "El Chongo" Puello playing *tambor alegre*. Courtesy of Juan Pablo Assmus. ©2012 Xqualo.

Figure 2.5. *Tambora*. Courtesy of Juan Pablo Assmus. ©2012 Xqualo.

Figure 2.6. Camilo Rodríguez, Martín Vejarano, and Juan Ospina of Marioneta. Courtesy of Juan Pablo Assmus. ©2012 Xqualo.

tivals celebrating local folklore—that is, traditional music, dance, and artisanship—its social context was altered, impacting performance dynamics for local artists and audiences. For example, one of the intrinsic aspects of local performance by San Jacinto's conjuntos de gaitas was the intense, raw competitions that took place between gaiteros engaged in heated décimas and *piquerías* and other forms of endurance contests held during informal gatherings and fiestas. As the Gaita Festival in San Jacinto gradually developed, however, the passion of local and regional rivalries was contained while the artistry of musicianship was elevated to specialized levels of professionalism. As a result, when principal gaiteros like Toño Fernández and the Lara brothers, among others, migrated to urban centers of the interior to educate people about gaita, the communal function was diminished somewhat, causing concern among some of San Jacinto's gaita elders. The weight of maintaining and carrying the gaita tradition fell squarely upon and largely emerged because of professional conjuntos de gaita, in particular, Los Gaiteros de San Jacinto.[9]

The San Jacinto Gaita Festival: Development and Displacement

Colombia is a nation with a penchant for celebration, recognized for its many regional and folkloric festivals as well as its carnivals and beauty contests. Of these, the Festival Nacional Autóctono de Gaita in San Jacinto is unique, but not for its size or level of media coverage; in fact it is one of the smaller festivals of the Atlantic coastal region, with only about five thousand people attending annually, primarily from nearby towns in the departments of Bolívar, Sucre, and Córdoba. Although receiving minimal print and broadcast media reportage, the festival nevertheless commands an exceptional degree of regional, national, and international attention.

The first San Jacinto música de gaita festival took place on December 2, 1988, and was dedicated by local town leaders as a tribute to Toño Fernández and the brothers Juan and José Lara, then leaders of Los Gaiteros de San Jacinto. Fernández, who believed that the gaita tradition was threatened and going to disappear,[10] together with other *hombres de color de tierra* (men of the color of earth), including the notable gaiteros Mañe Mendoza, Nolasco Mejía, Eliécer Meléndez, Nicolás Hernández, and Toño García, had been integral to growing interest in música de gaita (*Revista Cultural* 2008). Touring with Los Gaiteros nationally and internationally, teaching and performing in Bogotá since the 1950s, Fernández introduced countless people to costeño expressive culture through gaita. Although Fernández passed away on the evening the first festival opened, Toño, as he is fondly remembered, continues to be a cultural icon for the people of San Jacinto.[11] Yet it was more than local recognition of Fernández or his colleagues' musical contributions that impelled the community to establish the San Jacinto Gaita Festival as a cultural project of CORFOARTE, the local NGO. Town leaders recognized the importance of creating and developing a locally based organization that would promote San Jacinto and the Montes de María region as a vital site for cultural maintenance and conservation of música de gaita, which they presented as significant not only for the town or the Serranía but for the nation itself. Located in a region where since the mid-twentieth century intense armed struggle, civil war, and violence has perpetually victimized large segments of the costeño population, San Jacinto sought to appeal to the regional and central government (in Bogotá) for recognition and acknowledgment of its vulnerability, soliciting protection through and for its *culturas patronales* (local cultures):

"Today, the folkloric and artisan corporation of San Jacinto, from our deepest heart, struggles for the rescue and conservation of gaita music, which has served as San Jacinto's identity before Colombia and the world for a land keeping alive the most profound folkloric traditions of the region and that, with our work, places a grain of sand to transform the Montes de María into symbols of peace and progress for the land."[12]

Through cultural policy and advocacy, festival organizers have continued to make a case for supporting local folklore as a way to encourage cultural survival and economic stimulus through the valorization and conservation of its arts and artisanship. In the festival's annual event publication, *Revista Cultural* (2008), a historical review is provided that includes the following statement: "During this journey's trajectory, the last eleven festivals were organized, which made possible a peacefully shared space for our town and the region."[13] In the context of the costeño region's history of sociopolitical struggle, the gaita festival thus functions to maintain local performance standards of traditional music even as outside participation in the preservation of its culture is welcomed. Moreover, in the face of and beyond the daily realities of the ongoing civil war, música de gaita is promoted as a symbol of peace and national importance, representing efforts of local costeño leaders to celebrate identity—that is, convert the image of the region—while fostering inclusion within the nation's definition of the national project. Although only rarely mentioned in Colombian music scholarship (if at all), the sociopolitical conditions that led to extensive social displacement drove some gaita musicians to migrate from rural to urban centers in the 1970s and 1980s, particularly to the capital city of Bogotá.

Nevertheless, through participation in the annual festival, gaiteros (and *tamboleros*, as well as dancers and poets) who travel to compete and partake of San Jacinto's social and cultural environment, together with festival organizers and sponsors, continue to uphold gaita musical culture as an autochthonous folklore of the national culture—significant for a nation claiming to be formally receptive to its essential *mestizaje*. Gaita can therefore be viewed as a folkloric tradition and a conciliatory sociocultural strategy, but not strictly in an essentialist manner, as with the mainstreaming and whitening of cumbia and *música tropical* (see Fernández L'Hoeste 2007; Wade 2000; Waxer 2002). The San Jacinto Festival instead purports to embrace the present national mandate for constitutional multiculturalism (established by the 1991 Constitution) in accordance with and adherence to notions of authenticity by virtue of its indigenous and mestizo folkloric qualities. In doing so, the very transformation of that folklore is encouraged, as new actors (e.g., people from the diaspora) are invited to participate. Thus the conservation of culture and the security and safety of San Jacinto and the Serranía region that festival organizers strive for (and hope to achieve) are intertwined through social and cultural associations and connections. Gaita's renewal and popularization thus signals inroads toward the attainment of economic, social, and political support—and hence political and cultural survival.

In Colombia, however, folklore as an institutional and national commodity is concerned with purity of tradition, rescue from cultural loss, and the desire and "preference for accumulating and carefully cataloging information, [rather than] attempting to interpret" (Miñana Blasco 2000: 2–3) cultural expressions that fit well with a defined national imaginary. Moreover it is neither about "fakelore" (i.e., invented traditions or cultural spectacle) nor solely placing or making claims for music as either redeemer or savior, as Ochoa has critiqued from one theoretical vista. Rather the festival works to position gaita within an appropriate national niche, where it—and its people and culture—will somehow be protected from sociopolitical and cultural violence. Let us now turn to the festival and my case study of Marioneta to explore a prototypical current in this new direction.

Regresando a Colombia: The Festival, Cultural Patrimony, and Competition

Agua Chica, August 14 (6:17 AM)

At sunrise, after traveling nearly eleven hours on an overly air-conditioned bus from Bogotá, we pull into the Agua Chica station. Mules and stray dogs mill about as people wait around to make bus connections to unknown destinations. Throughout the first leg of the journey, for more than five hours of winding wet roads heading north to *la costa*, Martín Vejarano continued to instruct his musicians, talking through musical arrangements, reviewing *cortes* (musical breaks) in the songs they would perform, and playing rehearsal audio and video clips. With Carmen de Bolívar still more than five hours away and one of the musicians feeling ill, anticipation was building.

By early afternoon, in a light rain, with high heat and humidity, we finally arrive in Carmen de Bolívar, hiring two cars and drivers to take us the last few miles to San Jacinto. Upon arriving, we proceed directly to the Museo Etnoarqueológico de Montes de María, where we meet the festival coordinator Jorge Arrieta Caro, who greets the musicians, then registers Marioneta for the next day's aficionado-level gaita competition.[14]

Combining three émigré musicians from the New York group (LCE) and three Bogotá-based musicians, Marioneta reflects the joining together of two contemporary urban youth musical movements, one from the U.S. diaspora, the other from Colombia's central Andean capital city. Along with Vejarano (on gaita hembra), the New York–based Colombian musicians are Camilo Rodríguez (gaita macho and maraca) and Juan Ospina (cantador); the Bogotá musicians are Edwin Castellano (llamador), Freddy Urrea (tambor alegre), and Pedro Garzón (tambora). The sole aim was to form a gaita capable of realizing Vejarano's goals for the competition.

My fieldwork plan was to shadow Vejarano from New York to Bogotá, then to San Jacinto for the festival, where I would document Marioneta's rehearsals and performances before and during the competition. I also intended to interview and record members of the audience, specifically their reactions to the conjunto's performances. Postfestival activities were left open-ended but included the possibility of further travel and immersion into the Serranía region to meet, play music with, and further observe Vejarano's interactions with local gaita musicians.[15] As I discuss below, a related goal was to conduct a reception study among audience members during the festival in order to gauge audience reaction to *los de afuera de la region* (those from outside the region), thereby noting emic and etic concerns on the ground.

For Vejarano, the trip in 2008 marked the third time in as many years that, together with LCE musicians, he has traveled to take part in the San Jacinto festival. Aside from the desire to compete (and hopefully win) at the festival, returning to Colombia fulfills an important cultural and pedagogical function for Vejarano. The competition not only enables him to test and measure his own musical development as a gaita musician against local gaiteros; it allows replenishment of cultural and educational resources he relies upon for continuing to experiment with and expand upon his understanding of the so-called boundaries of the gaita tradition. Moreover returning to San Jacinto validates his innovations and contributions to a resurging gaita movement as well as the cultural representation he brings to the festival as an "outsider" to costeño culture. Further, it qualifies his participation in that it enables him to make certain claims for working *within* tradition while remaining sufficiently flexible to perform gaita in ways that are different, modern, and cosmopolitan, pushing the traditional boundaries of the genre. In other words, it provides Vejarano license to bring his own creative vision of gaita to the forefront of local and world music audiences.

Gaiteros, dancers, and poets from all over Colombia gather annually in San Jacinto in mid-August to compete for awards and cash prizes in several performance categories. In the conjunto de gaita competition, for example, there are three levels: children, aficionado, and professional, each of which must meet specific criteria for eligibility.[16]

Expectations for the 2008 festival were high, and Vejarano hoped it would culminate with a win by his coterie of young Bogotá and New York City musicians. In 2006, the first time Marioneta took part in the festival, the conjunto reached the finals of the aficionado (or serious hobbyist) competition, impressing the judges with their close adherence to traditional gaita praxis. At the time, many members of the public, including several judges, believed Marioneta merited first place. However, the ensemble missed the opportunity to perform in the finals due to a postponement and a miscommunication, as they arrived late to their stage call and thereby lost their standing. In 2007 Vejarano, along with two of his students from New York, won second place; according to a few accounts, it was a token gesture to encourage the *cachacos* (a somewhat pejorative term for Bogotanos) to continue returning to the competition. For the 2008 festival Vejarano concentrated on refining the ensemble's repertoire, including performing original compositions, which are not a requirement at the aficionado level. Thus Marioneta would not only meet the exigencies of gaita performance in terms of musical technique, content, and presentation, but would exceed them. That is, with respect to the rules of the competition and traditional gaita praxis, Vejarano hoped to go above and beyond the judges' (and the audience's) expectations for an aficionado-level conjunto de gaita, especially one not indigenous to the region.

On the evening of August 14, the opening ceremony for the 17th Festival Nacional Autóctono de Gaitas took place on the larger of two stages, located just across from San Jacinto's town plaza; a smaller stage for local and visiting gaiteros sat in the center of the plaza itself (figure 2.7). After a blessing from a Catholic priest and introductions of local dignitaries and festival officials by San Jacinto's mayor, the town's municipal band played the Colombian national anthem, followed by the municipality's anthem. A high school marching band then played porro and gaita melodies as majorettes danced with the hip movements particular to Afro-Colombian costeño dance (see Simon 1994). Announcers amplified to ear-splitting levels on the public address sys-

Figure 2.7. The *tarima*, or main stage. Courtesy of Juan Pablo Assmus. ©2012 Xqualo.

tem repeatedly promoted the festival's main sponsor, Cerveza Águila. Vallenato and cumbia recordings were played from nearby vehicles and market stands, adding to the strident and unyielding soundscape. Next was a *pelayera* band playing *corralejas*, porros, and fandangos, which in this cattle-raising region remain very popular. Accompanying even younger dancers, children's music groups also performed gaita and vallenato. At one point, the festive feeling of the ceremony was dampened somewhat when a local poet presented a lengthy poem about alcohol consumption and the damage it can cause; ironically this was followed by more Cerveza Águila promotions and copious public drinking of Ron Medellín Añejo, a favorite among festivalgoers. Culminating the opening event, local favorites Gaitambú, the young, very traditional gaita ensemble from San Jacinto, performed a short but dynamic set, followed by an incredible display of dancing, fireworks, and unbridled celebration. Throughout the opening night's festivities, several of the event speakers referred to the Latin Grammy Award received by Los Gaiteros de San Jacinto; the stage backdrop prominently featured the image that appeared on the 2006 Smithsonian Folkways recording.

In fact as one enters San Jacinto's archeological museum, which also serves as the festival's center of operations, the Latin Grammy Award is conspicuously and prominently displayed, front and center, in the entry foyer, indicating its significance as a source of local pride. The event's program flyers, posters, official festival publication (*Revista Cultural* 2008), and all related promotional literature feature the same photographic image, demonstrating a well-coordinated publicity effort to highlight the Grammy-winning gaiteros and the regional and international recognition the award represents.

At the conclusion of the festival's opening event, we met up with members of Marioneta at the entrance to the town plaza. Despite Camilo's lingering stomach illness, they were clearly excited and looking forward to performing. Vejarano, however, was particularly concerned about Camilo's health, especially since the next day was the first real day of the festival competition. Despite everyone's exhaustion, a group of fifty to sixty young gaiteros and their supporters gathered for a postopening *cumbiamba*, a sort of festival party parade. Heading northeast to a more residential part of town, we arrived at the house of one of the festival patrons, where chairs were set up and contributions were collected to purchase more Ron Medellín. The cumbiamba started at about 11 PM as a core gaita of five musicians started playing classic tunes. Occasionally, in the midst of a song, one musician replaced another in a transition that was remarkably smooth, even as each musician took turns playing different instruments; among this group of young musicians, unlike most older gaiteros, each was capable of playing all of the ensemble instruments. Couples dance with the hip movements typical of cumbia, in the long-established display of coquettish male-female courtship and seduction. The sense of camaraderie among the musicians was strong and appeared to be less a competitive display of technique and skills than a demonstration of friendly rivalries and sharing of musical knowledge among colleagues. After all, with the participation of very talented individuals such as Ivan Salcedo, Juan Carlos "El Chongo" Puello, and Ulianoth Daza Pérez, these were some of the young gaiteros energizing the present gaita revival movement regionally and nationally. Demonstrating the seriousness with which they approached their study of gaita, Daza Pérez said, "Gaita is entered into gradually and slowly developed. These musicians know well the history of the repertoire as well as the changes being made" (personal communication, August 15, 2008, my translation). After much dancing, drinking, and playing music, the crowd finally dispersed in the early morning hours, hoping to get a few hours sleep before the next day's final rehearsals, last-minute preparations, and the start of the competition.[17]

Concurso: Competition and Reception

En el festival, todos los conjuntos que llegan aquí a nuestro pueblo son buenos, los admiramos. En especial ustedes que son [de] tan lejos, como hizo Toño Fernández que se trasladó a otras partes. Entonces considero que lo mismo debe ser para ellos. Admirarlos, en especial por la inquietud que tenemos. Cualquier otra dificultad que tengan, eso se le debe anular un poco. El por qué? Porque tienen la voluntad, el ánimo de venir siquiera a unos pueblos de éstos, donde ellos vienen a recoger algo que de pronto ellos no tienen—la experiencia.

In the festival, all groups coming to town are good; we admire them. In particular you who are from so far away, just like Toño Fernández, who traveled to far away places. So I consider that it must be the same for them. We must admire them, especially given our concern. Any other problem they have should not be considered. Why? Because they have the will, the determination to even come to this sort of town, where they come to gather something they lack: experience.
—Tomás Hernández interview

The rules of competition are clearly outlined in the festival's *Revista Cultural* (2008), including details about who can participate, the requisite instrumentation, required number of gaita musicians, performance uniform or dress code, the selection of *aires* (songs), juror selection and judging procedures (rules for elimination or disqualification), and prohibitions (e.g., the use of microphones by contestants to address the public directly). In the aficionado competition there are two elimination rounds followed by a *finalistas* round, from which first-, second-, and third-place winners are chosen to receive plaques and cash awards.

The first round requires the performance of all four genres, or aires (more accurately termed *ritmos*). A three-member panel of *jurados* (judges) selects their order. Conjuntos that advance to the second round competition must subsequently play two of the four subgenres associated with gaita; again, the judges choose these. While most young gaiteros are primarily concerned with proper *ejecución de gaita*, that is, performing aires or ritmos in a traditional manner while adhering to strict performance standards, there is a self-conscious awareness, as Daza Pérez noted, that a new form of gaita is developing organically and by necessity.[18] Not unlike Martín Vejarano, Daza Pérez believes in the evolutionary process that gaita is presently undergoing, but as a local costeño from Soplaviento (Bolívar), his view is perhaps more radical since his ethnic subjectivity as a black gaitero makes it somewhat more difficult for him to break with established conventions or tradition. Although both Vejarano and Daza Pérez recognize the importance of maintaining traditional resources as they create or expand upon extant musical praxis, Vejarano's Marioneta project and proposal, as Tomás Hernández's comments suggest, is welcomed and perhaps allowed greater flexibility in terms of both juror and audience expectations. Nonetheless, when asked how he feels going into the first round, Vejarano responds that he has done all he can to prepare and now needs to just relax and have a good time (personal communication). With more than twenty conjuntos de gaita and musicians from all over the nation as well as the diaspora participating, the aficionado-level competition is exhausting, punctuated with everything from drunken brawls to power outages running well into the early morning hours.[19] In any case, each gaita presents itself as formally and professionally as possible, exercising great caution so as to not incur any infractions that could hurt their possibility of advancing to the next round or result in their disqualification.

As young gaiteros mill about the town plaza throughout the second full day of the festival waiting to compete, powerful rainstorms descend with unexpected frequency. Vallenato, salsa, and the music of *bandas pelayeras* compete fiercely for sonic space. Earlier that evening, as I prepared to film the first round of all the aficionado contestants, my field methodology and the logistics of interviewing audience members following Marioneta's first-round performance posed certain clear challenges. First, I had to generally identify audience members (including locals), taking into account (as much as possible) details such as race, class, gender, and age, where they came from, and if they attend the festival with any frequency. With only a small window of time available between performances, I was limited in the number of interviews that could be prudently collected after Marioneta's set. The questionnaire presented three key questions: (1) Did you like Marioneta? (2) Why did you like (or not like) Marioneta? and (3) Do you think Marioneta's work is good for the festival?

This line of inquiry was designed to measure the popular appeal of Marioneta and to record specifically which musical or performance elements were most appreciated or not. Most critical to this study, however, were the responses to my third question, which targeted Marioneta's perceived cultural contribution and overall public reception within the context of the San Jacinto festival.[20]

When Marioneta was finally called to the stage, as the penultimate aficionado ensemble to compete, they were met with a welcoming round of applause, perhaps indicating recognition or acknowledgment of the Bogotá–New York conjunto's previous appearances in San Jacinto. Opening their set with Toño Fernandez's classic porro, "Porro mangangueleño," Vejarano early on indicated a problem hearing the music through the stage monitor mix. One of the judges came forward to listen for himself and, standing behind the gaiteros, also noted the volume issue. Marioneta nevertheless remained concentrated and continued to play the porro for nearly *nine minutes*—well beyond the four-minute time limit allowed for each aire. Immediately following the song, Vejarano went over to the audio engineers to point out the problem with the monitor mix, then to the judges to offer further explanation for the interruption, even while the emcee reminded Marioneta of the strict time-limit rule. After audio engineers checked and readjusted volume levels (with some rowdy comments voiced by a few people in the audience), Marioneta proceeded with their second ritmo, "Pachanga," an original cumbia written by Vejarano, containing the following refrain between cantador and coro:

> (singer) Hay Pachanga
> (chorus) La gaita está sabrosa.
> ¡Colombia! Allá la gente goza.
> ¡Colombianos! Cantemos por la paz.
> ¡Hermanos! Hagamos ya la paz.
> ¡Mujeres! Armen una rueda.
> ¡Mujeres! y prendan las velas.
> [The gaita is delightful
> Colombia! There the people enjoy.
> Colombians! Let's sing for peace.
> Brothers! Let's make peace.
> Women! Make the circle,
> Women! And light the candles.]

These were followed in turn by Juan Lara's gaita, "El pensador," and the set closer, Toño Fernandez and Juan Lara's uptempo puya, "Maridita." Although the momentary disruption seemed to have caused some concern among the audience, contestants, and jury alike, the remainder of Marioneta's performance was impressive and powerful, clearly winning over the audience, who by the end of the set were dancing and clapping along with the music. A few reactions:

> Estaba chévere, o sea, fue espectáculo de los bogotanos que llegaron aqui a San Jacinto ... para ser de Bogotá y tocar gaitas sanjacinteras estuvo elegante.
>
> [It was great, it was a sight [to see] the Bogotanos that came here to San Jacinto ... to be from Bogotá and play San Jacinto gaitas was elegant.] (Omar Belina)
>
> Tocan alegre. Los muchachos son buenos. Tienen una facultad muy especial que [es] el ánimo.
>
> [They play joyfully. The boys are good. They have that special ability to play with energy.] (Tomás Hernández)
>
> Saben cantarlas, [y] tocar los instrumentos de una buena forma.
>
> [They know how to sing them (gaitas), [and] play the instruments with good form.] (Oscar Anillo)
>
> Sí me gustó, y por lo que escuché de más personas también quedaron encantados con el grupo.
>
> [Yes I liked it, and from what I heard from others, they were also delighted with the group.] (Marjelis Castro)

Thus the first round ended, and while Marioneta appeared to emerge undaunted, questions lingered: Would the excessive duration of the porro, the technical disruption, or Marioneta's handling of it result in penalization or otherwise adversely impact their chances of advancing to the second round? That evening there was evident concern among the musicians, and I could not imagine how the judges would overlook or reconcile the events surrounding their performance. The next day official results were posted in the museum courtyard, with Bogotá's Marioneta listed among the half dozen conjuntos de gaita that would continue in the competition.[21]

The second round of aficionado competition began late on Saturday evening, August 16. Marioneta spent the morning resting before rehearsing the two-song set, a gaita followed by a puya. As the last performers scheduled to play that evening, they selected the gaita "Golpe de chácara," most often attributed to Mañe Mendoza, which features some of Marioneta's more experimental arrangements including stop-time rhythms (*cortes*) and carefully executed melodic entrances, stops, and unison lines, rarely heard in San Jacinto. Closing with Juan Lara's puya, "La palma," the conjunto's set displayed inspired intensity and musical ability, which virtually assured Marioneta a place among the top three finalists. Audience members agreed, responding favorably:

> ¡Me gustó la puya! [I liked the puya!] (María Guzmán)

> ¡Hombre! Sí clasificaron. Si están en el final, es porque lo merecen. [Man! If they qualified, if they are in the final, it is because they deserve it.] (Lila Leyva)

> Había una muy buena energía entre ellos y estaban muy concentrados y lo transmitían, fue un buen rollo. [There was a really good energy between them and they were focused and they got it across; it was a good ride.] (Víctor Peñaloza)

> ¡Los instrumentos, los instrumentos, los instrumentos! Y realmente ellos lo hacen como si fueran sanjacinteros. Los interpretan como si fueran sanjacinteros. [The instruments, the instruments, the instruments! And they really play like they are Sanjacinteros. The interpret as if they were Sanjacinteros.] (Alberto Gómez)

> Es una agrupación maravillosa que se merece el premio porque lo hizo muy bien. [It's a marvelous group that deserves the prize because they did it very well.] (Zekiel Peña)

While most of the respondents' reactions were positive, there were also some negative comments made, as when Juan Pablo Assmus (my research assistant) overheard one man criticize Marioneta, referring to Vejarano as "el blanquito de ojos verdes" (the little white man with green eyes). Paraphrasing the local costeño, his comment was that Vejarano had not composed anything and yet wanted to change the tradition and the rules of the festival. Nevertheless, when I saw Vejarano the following day, we both knew that Marioneta had reached the finals of the competition.

Earlier that morning (with very little sleep after the previous night's performance) Marioneta participated in the festival's annual tribute to gaita ancestors, during which all gaiteros and dancers gather to parade from one end

Figure 2.8. Eliécer Mejía, an elder gaitero, plays at Toño Fernández's burial site. Courtesy of Juan Pablo Assmus. ©2012 Xqualo.

of town to the other, stopping at both of San Jacinto's cemeteries to offer libations, play music, and dance in a celebratory display of reverence, remembrance, and respect (figure 2.8).

Las Finales

On the evening of August 17, the festival finals were held in each of the competition categories. Scheduled to perform between the Encuentro de Danzas folclóricas de la Costa Atlántica (Congress of Folkloric Dances from the Atlantic Coast) and Canción inédita (unpublished song) finals, gaita aficionado contestants were instructed to prepare a program of all four ritmos in a specific order or sequence: first a porro, followed by a cumbia (both vocal pieces), then a gaita, and a puya to close the set; the last two genres are primarily instrumental, with the puya a characteristically uptempo piece. After a final day of rehearsal, Marioneta was decidedly ready. In the porro ("Cinco notas" by Toño Fernández) and the cumbia ("Cumbia continental" by Juan Lara), one could clearly discern commonalities, particularly in the introduction of melodic material, the approach to percussion entrances, similar rhythmic patterns and tempos, and the use of vocals and coro response. The relationship between cumbia and gaita, however, though also apparent, goes beyond similarities in rhythms or tempos. Cumbias contain lyrics (with strophic verses and choruses), whereas gaita vocals are typically limited to declamatory variations on uttered phrases such as "¡Uepa!," "¡Uepajé!," or "¡Uy!" (local vernacular expressions of excitement and joy). That is, cumbia is more closely associated with its related dance tradition, while gaita is significantly more closely linked to the conjunto's display of shared musical skills.

Marioneta's program was cleverly arranged so that the porro and cumbia were performed in a rather conservative manner, observing traditional characteristics and stylistic features of these genres, such as a close interplay between male and female gaitas and the intricate rhythmic interplay between the gaiteros and tamboleros (flutists and percussionists). With the gaita ritmo ("Llegó Mendoza" by Mañe Mendoza), the ensemble further demonstrated their ability to play traditionally while also applying uncommon methods, such as incorporating skillful musical breaks, played in unison. This specific type of musical element, which was not found in any other of the aficionado or professional gaita performances during the festival, underscores Marioneta's experimental approach. Moreover, when performing "El Indio" (The Indian), an original puya written by Vejarano, there were some rather unconventional performance elements, such as when Vejarano provided gestural musical cues. During the introduction to "El Indio," Vejarano cued the tamboleros' entrance with a right leg backward kick, which may have been necessary because of its difficult placement within the arrangement. This cuing gesture nonetheless highlights a performance aspect generally absent among traditional conjuntos de gaitas: the role of the bandleader. Most gaitas instead emphasize ensemble cohesion through communal experiences that bring musicians together to play, and even in a festival context, where the notion of honoring the gaita tradition trumps individual or ensemble innovation per se, there is rarely a leader functioning as musical director. This is also evident in the role of the cantador (lead singer); he or she is not leading as such but participates as an equal member of the conjunto.

In any case, Marioneta's selection of "El Indio," a *puya rápida* (fast puya), is also significant, especially when compared to idiomatically more conventional approaches to the subgenres.[22] As the set closer, "El Indio" encapsulated Vejarano's (and Marioneta's) proposal through its application of creative musical strategies: disruption of standard melodic formulas and rhythmic patterns; the use of expanded melodic registers and improvisational techniques; and highly synchronized musical breaks. Even the fast tempo is accentuated (i.e., ♩ = 160 bpm). Although percussion instruments are played in a technically prototypical style, with archetypal rhythmic patterns and adornments, the musical breaks that accompany the singer and coros' *gritos* (during which they shout "¡Hey!" and the singer concludes with a cry of "¡El Indio!") are highly uncharacteristic. Moreover the usual functions of gaitas are reconfigured, as when the *macho* plays an underlining repeated contrapuntal figure to the *hembra*'s melodic and fluttering ornamentations (also known as *gritos* or trills). Breaking from the standard pattern of a whole tone per measure, the macho's triplet figure suggests a ternary division of the measure instead of maintaining the puya's usually binarized duple meter. This manifests in an audible and perceptibly closer relationship between the male and female gaitas, as female melodies share in a greater musical exchange with the now more active and dynamic male flutes. Thus the hembra can be let loose to sing, while the macho responds in a more engaged, yet still supportive role. Intertwined to a greater degree than usual, Marioneta's gaitas thus generate greater musical force as a result. Alex Marullo, one of the aficionado judges, described gaita's dialogic relationship as follows: "The macho and hembra are like listening to a couple making love" (interview).

Given the unconventional approach and experimental flavor that Marioneta brought to the festival, there was a sense among the audience and judges that these young gaiteros from Bogotá and New York brought something fresh and revitalizing to the festival competition:

> This year's aficionado groups appear to be better than last year's. . . . The gaita from Bogotá [Marioneta] is very good. . . . They innovated *paradas* [stops] in the puya in an entirely different rhythm than the puya of the other groups. (jokingly) This is the first time I see that gaita has been deeply infiltrated by *los rolos* [costeño term for Bogotanos]. (Andrés Castro)

> The public is the best judge, the principal judge. . . . Marioneta is different from the other groups; they brought something new. Like I said, you have to innovate gaita, for good or bad; yet they did innovative things that all the judges appreciated. . . . We were happy, the public was also happy with Marioneta's evolution. (Emiro Cantillo)

Figure 2.9. Martín Vejarano and Marioneta win second place in the *aficionado conjunto de gaita* competition, San Jacinto, August 18, 2008. Photograph courtesy of Martín Vejarano.

Their presentation drove the public. . . . For me, personally, Marioneta's work is excellent. . . . I'm convinced of their talent, of their desire, I admire their project to search and learn carefully. . . . A group from the interior [of Colombia] that comes to investigate and admire the gaiteros of San Jacinto. They show the capacity to do things that costeños cannot, or will not do. (Alex Marullo)

At the conclusion of Marioneta's set, the audience strongly cheered them, many wondering aloud if they would or actually could win the aficionado competition. Although the festival winners would not be announced until all finalists had performed in their respective competition categories (early the following morning), Vejarano's musicians seemed pleased with their efforts. When the results of the aficionado competition were finally announced, Marioneta had won second place for the second year in a row (figure 2.9). That they placed evenly between two San Jacinto conjunto finalists, Gaitambú and Son de Gaita, is interesting and, perhaps, even fitting.

After four days and nights of music and celebration, the gaita festival ended with very little fanfare. By midday the rains had subsided, and with the sun blazing again, San Jacinto returned to its state of normalcy, which is to say, the town remains most definitely in the Third World, operating as if

Figure 2.10. Young soldiers on patrol in San Jacinto soon after the festival's conclusion. Courtesy of Juan Pablo Assmus. ©2012 Xqualo.

it were still the late nineteenth century or early twentieth. The streets lack drainage, trash is strewn about, the electrical grid continues to fail regularly, even as the central plaza's market activity resumed, accompanied by an incessant blend of battery-driven vallenato and salsa blasting from boom-boxes. While a few festival stragglers remained, Sanjacintero gaiteros and tamboleros were less visible. For the moment, the gaitas and tambores had been put away. Visiting gaiteros had left, returning to their home cities and towns all over Colombia to prepare for next year's festival, while others prepared to compete at the larger Ovejas Gaita festival, held during the month of October in the department of Sucre. The military presence in the area once again became all too apparent (figure 2.10).

La vuelta a Nueva York / Back to New York City

Shortly after returning to New York, I had the opportunity to ask Vejarano to describe his reactions to the festival and Marioneta's win. He answered, "Well, the first thing I have to say is that coming in second place for the second time in a row, it's the highest level in terms of reward—personal reward. . . . When you come in first in a contest like that, it means a lot, and it's a lot of responsibility involved in that title." He added:

> It's a recognition. They recognize we are good musicians, but also it's a way of showing the entire country that they accept and appreciate our efforts and our musical proposal, which to me is the reward, the best reward I could ever have. Just giving you a second prize, it's a symbolic thing, but it's more of a thank you; it's more of a "Well done, nice music, you guys are part of the family." . . . It's a very moving experience for me, very touching experience. I'm very happy in the personal sense because I conceived these arrangements, I conceived the repertoire, I worked with my friends and we traveled a long way to get there, and they gave us this recognition. That's beautiful. (interview)

Though he regards a second-place win as "the highest personal reward," Vejarano hopes to return to San Jacinto, most likely in a professional capacity. Not only has he proven his musical abilities and dedication to gaita, but he has also demonstrated the talent and drive required to compose and record new gaitas—the mark of a true professional. Speaking further about what the professional-level competition demands, as well as why the local focus is on traditional elements of gaita, Vejarano maintains that the difference lies in the musical production of people from the cities (like himself) and people of the region. Unlike young cosmopolitans, professionals focus on the traditional repertoire rather than putting forward sophisticated arrangements: "It's also because it's not what they [gaita professionals] have to offer." Unlike himself, "They didn't grow up learning jazz or rock or classical music. They are not into that stuff. They are into vallenato, música tropical, and other things" (interview). Explaining what he hoped to achieve, Vejarano said:

> I think it's our mission to bring, to offer and to propose a new approach and way of doing musical arrangements within the context of gaita music. Because if we do it well, in a good way, eventually, the people from the rural areas in Colombia, the real gaiteros, the real inheritors of this culture will adopt our approach to arrangements [and] try to make sure the flutes are in tune all the time [and] break down every little part or aspect of the melody and the counterpoint with the other flute. That's what we do. [We] make sure [to] try to work on the intonation of the background vocals, make sure the phrasing is accurate, and that everything is in place, a more meticulous, sophisticated

Figure 2.11. Marioneta with Nicolás Hernández of Los Gaiteros de San Jacinto. Courtesy of Juan Pablo Assmus. ©2012 Xqualo.

way of working. That's what we offer, and eventually they will adopt this if we do it in a good way. (interview)

Vejarano views Marioneta's participation as a win-win situation for the San Jacinto festival organizers and audience, as well as for himself and his musicians. Since his proposal was well received in San Jacinto, it lends his La Cumbiamba Eneyé project in New York substantial authenticity, cultural capital that helps to advance his musical and professional goals. Establishing their place as actors on the San Jacinto gaita scene—a scene no longer bound to geographical or cultural boundaries—Vejarano and Marioneta also help to mobilize and spread a carefully conceived and modified form of gaita across transnational borders. Paradoxically, in altering gaita to reflect a respectful yet cosmopolitan, postethnic identity, Marioneta continues the work of traditionalists such as Los Gaiteros de San Jacinto, internationalizing gaita while drawing attention to the expressive beauty, cultural resilience, and social survival of local indigenous elements and people (figure 2.11).[23]

Having established themselves as vigorous representatives of the gaita tradition, sufficiently so as to transport gaita beyond regional or national borders, Marioneta achieves transcultural, cosmopolitan goals even as they mediate local and regional concerns of the people of Los Montes de María. Through Marioneta's performance of gaita, San Jacinto also benefits from gaita's broadening transnational appeal: the small yet significant music festival gains greater media exposure and therefore larger national attention that helps to maintain all-important institutional connections to regional and national cultural organizations providing support for local and regional presenters of autochthonous folklore. Consequently San Jacinto's gaiteros are revered and upheld as cultural beacons of the region, empowering them as teachers and ambassadors of gaita while they travel, migrate, or are displaced to Colombian cities and the diaspora. Thus as the region benefits from media coverage and heightened public awareness, the culture of costeño hinterlands is preserved, disseminated, and valorized, even as the security of the region is enhanced.

Conclusion

The cover image of La Cumbiamba Eneyé's recording *Marioneta* (see Figure 2.1) depicts a gaitero marionette dressed in full traditional garb. The face is obscured; three strings are attached to the motionless figure as it holds a tambor alegre slackly by its side. The image raises several questions: Who is the marionette? What or whom does it represent? Is it a musician in La Cumbiamba Eneyé or Los Gaiteros de San Jacinto? Is it gaita itself? And who is working the puppet? What are the strings attached *to*? Where do they lead *from*? As a metaphor for La Cumbiamba Eneyé's musical and hence cultural proposal, the image of a performing marionette raises profound issues regarding cultural identity, particularly how it is defined, and toward what end. Though Turino's definition is useful, it leaves unanswered what actually occurs when individual or group identity is a product of vastly differing socioeconomic, racial, and political circumstances: "[Identity] is a public articulation of the sociocultural, economic, ideological and political makeup of an individual or group's identity, made patent through musical performance. That is, people perform music in a certain way as a natural product or extension of their personal and sociocultural identity" (1984: 253). Nevertheless, to paraphrase Turino, the status of gaita as an identity symbol continually shifts, as does mestizo identity according to the context of the definition. While we can often see evidence of this in musical details (e.g., tempo and meter variances; see note 22), reflecting local versus translocal and transglobal environments, for example, Colombia's self-definition as a predominantly mestizo nation remains a problematic construct in relation to the presence and persistence of distinct indigenous, African, and *criollo* identities constituting the homeland and diasporic populations (see Wade 2000). As a result, the internal and out-migrations of Colombians to large cities and cosmopolitan centers like New York City provide an opportunity to observe, document, and gauge the movements of people and elements of Colombian culture as they are transmitted transnationally through musical performance. How these are received and then return to mediate and alter local homeland culture is a crucial process that sheds light on both identity formation and cultural conservation. After all, how is it possible that a conjunto de gaita made up of young musicians from Bogotá and New York (formed in eight hours) can arrive in San Jacinto to compete and rank so highly among the local practitioners and authorities of "official" gaita? By positioning themselves as transnational carriers of gaita culture, these young, primarily middle-class mestizo musicians from the capital city are clearly taking on responsibilities that appear perilously close to either appropriation or mimicry—a problematic position, to say the least. However, in a country like Colombia, where regional and provincial divisions persist along ethnic, class, and racial lines, the commitment and respect these musicians demonstrate for gaita and their willingness to use their privileged social standing to gain access and promote gaita should not be underestimated or diminished. Moreover while Marioneta's role should be given critical consideration, one must also recognize that the transnationalization of gaita occurs on several levels: by Afro-Colombian gaiteros of Cartagena, such as Juan Carlos "El Chongo" Puello (figure 2.4), who tours internationally; by Los Gaiteros de San Jacinto, the "official" arbiters of gaita authenticity; and by Marioneta, the young New York City–based musicians whose gaita praxis has enabled several Afro-Colombian gaiteros and tamboleros to take a prominent place within the diasporic cosmopolis.

By rhetorically asking *¿Pa' dónde vas Marioneta?* (Where are you going, Marioneta?), this case study has shown how one group of young, cosmopolitan Colombian musicians (traveling between cities of the interior and the diaspora to the hinterlands) learn, experience, and negotiate gaita musical tradition even as they work to transform that tradition.[24] Turino's notion of *modernist culturalist reformism* allows us to understand theoretically how such projects demonstrate "the imagined possibility of forging a new synthetic social group and identity" (1999: 245). Noting the resonating value of Anderson's (1983) "imagined communities" and building his thesis on a

Peircian semiotic model, Turino writes, "The creative juxtaposition of localist and modernist indices, typical of modernist reformism, was intended to serve as an icon for the new locally unique, yet 'modern' nation" (1999: 246). In this case, however, the indices and icons of gaita serve a broader semiotic purpose, aiding in the symbolic construction of a transnation—as much for individual social identities in Marioneta's Nueva Colombia community (e.g., in New York) as for the communities of San Jacinto and the Los Montes de María region, where the intracultural exchange of symbols operates in multiple directions, from the local to the diaspora and back.

The second question ¿Pa' dónde va la gaita? (Where is gaita headed?) reflects back on itself, suggesting the real possibility that gaita and its set of substyles (cumbia, porro, and puya) are on a world music trajectory from authentic localism to constructed global product. As world music has become increasingly accessible through technological advancements in global media delivery systems (e.g., Internet, digital media files, portable drives) and sonic "worlds" travel farther and faster than ever to more people with the means to download digitized, hybridized ethnic sounds, what remains to be seen, heard, and understood is whether or not corresponding histories or authenticities will be lost in the translocal-global translation. As important as identifying the underlying motivations that drive gaita praxis, that is, hearing what people who play, dance, and listen to gaita are actually communicating, scholars of popular and traditional music will need to acknowledge that "only in recent years have proportional projects come into being, as there is an equalization effect between emerging social and economic cultures, that are having a profound impact on how international cosmopolitan music is being conceived and created, disseminated and enjoyed."[25] As we consider multidisciplinary approaches to contemporary ethnographies of musical communities and genres (e.g., gaita, a genre that hitherto has remained generally unknown despite its music industry success and genealogical link to the worldwide cumbia phenomenon), we must note too the formation of new social identities by what they are telling us, discreetly or openly, about shared Colombian realities and concerns.

While it would be reasonable (and perhaps simpler) to read this chapter as a national narrative about young émigré Colombians in search of their homeland cultural roots and modern identity via indigenization, or as a regional model of cultural resilience and the preservation of musical iconicity, or as a local narrative about local indigenous artists achieving international recognition and attention for their regional affiliation, at its base there lies the development of social identities in the process of shaping what music scholars have identified as Nueva Colombia (Santamaría 2008; Ochoa 2003; Cragnolini and Ochoa Gautier 2001; Ochoa Gautier and Botero 2009). Thus the formation of the nation, or the transnation, is contingent upon the validation of internal and external discourses regarding social and political identity; that is, these processes rely as much on the global as on the local exchange of cultural resources and material. As this study demonstrates, this conversation takes place not solely within cosmopolitan fusionist experiments in Bogotá or the official gatherings of cultural authorities sponsored by the Ministry of Culture; it also occurs at the local level of traditional music festivals and Brooklyn hipster venues. Neither the modernization and popularization of gaita—witness Lucho Bermúdez and Pacho Galán in the 1950s—nor the efforts to internationalize the music of Los Gaiteros de San Jacinto through recording and touring efforts are a new phenomenon. Música de gaita, in fact, has long been cultivated on different levels for different audiences: locally in San Jacinto as autochthonous folklore, nationally as cultural patrimony, and internationally as world music. What is significant about Marioneta's proposal as a *grupo de proyección* (Ochoa 1996) and its affect on local and world audiences, however, is the cyclical transnationalism, the multigenerational shifting of cultural proprietorship, and the extraordinary degree of acceptance and transcendence of cultural, regional, and racial integration—all with a populist goal toward sociocultural development, unification, and the transformation of severe social realities.

Interviews

Oscar Anillo (respondent)
Emiro Cantillo (judge)
Marjelis Castro (respondent)
Andres Castro (judge)
Alberto Gomez (respondent)
María Guzman (respondent)
Lila Leyva (respondent)
Alex Marullo (judge)
Zekiel Peña (respondent)
Victor Peñaloza (respondent)
Martin Vejarano (musician)
Ulianoth Daza Perez (musician)

Tomás Hernández (respondent)
Omar Belina (respondent)

Discography

Hector Buitrago. 2007. *Conector.* Nacional.
La Cumbiamba Eneyé. 2006. *Marioneta.* Chonta Records 003, CD.
Los Gaiteros de San Jacinto. 2006. *Un fuego de sangre pura.* Smithsonian Folkways Recordings SFW CD 40531.
Sidestepper. 2003. *3 AM (In Beats We Trust).* Palm Records.
Carlos Vives. 1995. *La tierra del olvido.* Mercury/Polygram Discos.
Various artists. 2004. *Historia musical de Los Gaiteros.* Discos Fuentes E20271.

Notes

I want to thank all of the Colombian musicians, dancers, and lovers of *gaita*, wherever you are, especially the members of Marioneta and La Cumbiamba Eneyé, Los Gaiteros de San Jacinto, and all the San Jacinto festival participants and audience. Special thanks go to Juan Pablo Assmus for his extraordinary photography, collaboration, and friendship. I am grateful for the Wesleyan travel grant (2008) that supported this fieldwork and to the readers for their contribution to this essay.

1. The August 1, 2008, event was advertised as LCE's "last show in NYC before our trip to Colombia, so don't miss it" (email, July 28, 2008). Current members are Nilko Guarín, voice; Silvia Sierra, voice; Juan Ospina, voice; Juan P. Uribe, soprano sax (not present in NY); Pacho Dávila, alto sax (not present in NY); Sebastián Cruz, percussion; Daniel Correa, percussion; Camilo Rodríguez, gaita macho, percussion; and Martín Vejarano, gaita hembra, percussion.

2. Ana María Ochoa, liner notes to *Un Fuego de Sangre Pura.* In 2004 Los Gaiteros de San Jacinto recorded a full-length compact disc in New York. Coproduced by the ubiquitous Colombian producer Iván Benavides, the recording *Un Fuego de Sangre Pura* was released on the Smithsonian Folkways record label in 2006, winning the 2007 Latin Grammy for "Best Folkloric Album," thereby garnering wider international recognition and interest in música de gaita. The recording is decidedly in the traditional gaita style of San Jacinto, hence its nomination and win in the folkloric category.

While música de gaita has long held historical significance as authentic Colombian traditional folklore and as a progenitor of cumbia, many of the sounds associated with costeño gaita are increasingly evident in Colombian popular music—for example, Carlos Vives's "Zoila" (*La tierra del olvido*, 1995), Hector Buitrago's "Música Somos" (*Conector*, 2008), Benavides's own Sidestepper project (e.g., "In Beats We

Trust" from *3 AM: In Beats We Trust*, 2003) — and in the efflorescence of the contemporary "fusion" music movements in Bogotá and its diaspora over the past decade. Winning the Latin Grammy would prove to have cultural and polemical repercussions for Los Gaiteros de San Jacinto, the San Jacinto community, and música de gaita itself.

3. After the first set, two LCE members left with Chris Michael, a non-Colombian drummer and percussionist very active on the Colombian new music scene, to go to another gig elsewhere in the city. (I too left after the first set.) Although I wanted to document this auspicious performance further, after speaking briefly with Martín Vejarano about the upcoming fieldwork in San Jacinto, it became evident that despite attempts at careful planning and trying to determine a viable research methodology, a great deal would be left to circumstance, chance, and improvisation.

4. Liner notes to LCE's *Marioneta* (CD, 2006).

5. As Fernández L'Hoeste notes, "In Bogotá . . . costeños are traditionally viewed as outsiders" (2007: 342). This outsider status, whether referring to the diasporic exterior of the nation or marginalized regions within national borders, is relevant to the discussion because Vejarano and LCE are exemplars of precisely those "scions of the Colombian urbanized middle class" who eagerly awaited a pivotal figure like Carlos Vives to emerge and use popular genres such as cumbia and, especially, vallenato to "combine tradition and modernity" (342; see also Vives's *La tierra del olvido* [1995] in the discography). Vives thus established a musical model that would be emulated by Colombians of all stripes and from all sectors of society.

6. "That's something that can never be changed in the gaita, that sound sounds from when you first start making it. There is a really good cactus [the material used to create a gaita], a long cactus that . . ." (La Cumbiamba Eneyé, track 4: "Voz de Nicolás Hernández," my translation). The gist of Hernández's comment, according to Vejarano's understanding of the tradition, is that the sound of gaita cannot be modified or changed if the gaita is well made and constructed from cactus, that is, from local materials.

7. I use quotation marks around "tuning" (and "scales") to indicate that each gaita macho and hembra has (a) its own idiosyncratic tuning, (b) tunings that do not strictly correspond to Western scales or even temperament, and (c) major and minor intervals are neither uniform nor standardized. See Convers and Ochoa (2007) for a description of a traditional gaita "tunings" and "scales" (part 1: 55–56; part 2: 27–31).

8. Catalino Parra, an elderly gaitero from Soplaviento, his grandson, Ulianoth Daza Pérez, who also competes at the annual Gaita Festival of San Jacinto, and Carlos "El Chongo" Puello from the San Fernando barrio of Cartagena exemplify ongoing efforts by black gaiteros, young and old, to maintain the black gaita tradition. Encarnación "El Diablo" Tovar remains perhaps the most revered black gaitero, a cultural actor and legend among tamboleros.

9. For a recent method book, including audio and video examples of gaita performance techniques and musical analysis, see Convers and Ochoa (2007). The authors also correctly point out that when gaita moved from the traditional rural areas to the urban cities, it lost much of its ritual (read: communal) character; thus to play folkloric music today is indeed a "profession," even though the music as part of daily life

endures (37, my translation; my use of quotes around "profession" is for emphasis). Also see Gil Olivera (2002), who recognizes that "*la gaita es la misma cumbia* / the gaita is the same cumbia," yet primarily differentiates cumbia from gaita based on its black influence, which he describes as more *alegre* (joyful), in major keys, while the gaita of San Jacinto is in a minor key (106), more indigenous and mestizo.

10. Quoted in Convers and Ochoa 2007: 34, my translation. For a history of gaita and its relation to cumbia, see Garzón 1987; Gil Olivera 2002; also see Fortich Díaz 1994, for an account of gaita as a precursor to porro in the *bandas pelayeras* of San Pelayo, an argument that remains contested among costeño scholars.

11. During this period the brother-and-sister team of Manuel and Delia Zapata Olivella advocated for Afro-Colombian folkloric traditions of music and dance, primarily from the costeño regions. Specifically concerned about the cultural loss of *gaita sanjacintera*, Toño Fernández similarly instigated the revival of the traditional style of gaita performance, which was being threatened by commercial popularization of "gaita" as performed by costeño bandleaders such as Lucho Bermúdez and Pacho Galán. Prompted by Colombia's recording industry, based in Medellín and Bogotá, to record and perform cumbias and gaitas *bailables* (danceable) with big band instrumentation, modern arrangements, and contemporary lyrics, the synthesis of orchestrated cumbias and gaitas gained wide popular acceptance among urban ruling elites (cf. Wade 2000).

12. "Hoy día, la corporación folklórica y artesanal de San Jacinto, en lo mas íntimo de nuestras fibras sensitivas, luchamos por el rescate y la conservación de la música de gaita, que ha sido para San Jacinto la identidad ante Colombia y el mundo de una tierra que aún conserva vivas las más profundas tradiciones folclóricas de la región y que con nuestro trabajo ponemos un grano de arena para convertir a los Montes de María en símbolos de paz y progreso para el país" (*Revista Cultural* 2008, n.p., my translation). Idiomatically, "poner un grano de arena" signifies "to make an effort," no matter how small. Present organizers of the Festival Nacional Autóctono de Gaita include CORFOARTE, Fundación SER, and Mutual SER, receiving help from Colombia's Ministerio de Cultura (federal), Gobernación de Bolívar (state), the Alcaldía Municipal (municipal), and the Fondo Mixto de Cultura, a coalition of national, regional, local, and NGO sponsors. Cost estimates for the festival are unclear, but the Colombian beer producer Cerveza Águila is clearly the event's main sponsor.

13. "Durante este trayecto recorrido, se han organizado los once últimos Festivales, que han posibilitado el espacio de convivencia pacífica para nuestro Municipio y la Región" (*Revista Cultural* 2008: n.p., my translation).

14. Marioneta refers to the conjunto de gaita organized by Vejarano made up of musicians based in New York City and Bogotá, including members of La Cumbiamba Eneyé as well as young resident musicians from the capital city who study *música costeña* (costeño music).

15. Martín Vejarano's willingness and desire to participate in this fieldwork, allowing me full access to both him and his musicians, would not have been possible without our first having developed a personal and professional relationship over several years.

16. There are also separate competitions for composers and lyricists in the *cancion inédita* (unpublished song) contest, as well as for décimeros and dancers in *décima*, *concurso de parejas bailadoras* (paired dancers), and *grupos bailadores* (group dance). The general rules for the gaita festival are published in its annual program, *Revista Cultural*; these include twenty articles outlining the festival's organizational structure, the competition arenas, presentation requisites (dress code and instrumentation), the elimination system, causes for disqualification, and selection of judges and the judging process. Usually first-, second-, and third-place winners receive plaques and cash. Cash awards vary considerably between levels and can be a source of contention for winners, who often have to negotiate with festival directors to receive the entire amount at the festival's conclusion.

17. Rehearsals were held at the home of Carmelo Torres, Vejarano's friend and a vallenato accordionist, who was joined by José Gallegos and Adolfo Rodríguez on tambor alegre. At one point, Camilo and Adolfo played what he called a "Twin Towers vallenato," with lyrics about the Taliban set to the tune of "Josa Mavilades."

18. At the beginning of the competition, in order to provide a fair and equitable basis from which to judge the conjuntos, the audio engineers set microphone and audio levels so that each gaita performs with the same sound settings. In addition, the performance of each ritmo is limited to four minutes, which, if exceeded, can result in point demerits from the judges.

19. Among the aficionado gaita cojuntos in the competition were Gaitambú (San Jacinto), Son de Gaita (Cartagena), Grupo Etnia (Bogotá), Makuna (Baranquilla), Son Sabana (Montería), Grupo San Felipe, Grupo Son Batuca, and Son Baracu (Bogotá).

20. At any rate, I maintain that the methodology of conducting brief but highly focused interviews immediately after Marioneta's performance yielded sufficiently significant reception data about the audience's candid reactions. The value and usefulness of the audience's comments, admittedly drawn from a small sample of randomly selected audience members, lies in the immediate and spontaneous public reactions they record. In addition, the necessary collection of respondent information was achieved subsequently by asking respondents their name, the name of their hometown and region, and if this was the first festival they had attended.

21. Among the gaitas that advanced to the second round of competition were Grupo Costumbres del Folklor (Tumaco), Gaitambú (San Jacinto), Tabagá (Bogotá), Son de Gaita (Cartagena), Los Gaiteros de Soplaviento, and Grupo Maigame (Cartagena).

22. For instance, as can be observed in the tempo and rhythmic variances of Juan Lara's "La palma" and Freddy Arrieta's "La bajera" or, in contrast, to Toño Fernández's "Maridita," a *puya lenta* (or slow puya) with vocals. According to an interview with Francis Lara collected by Convers and Ochoa, "The puyas that the older gaiteros played were not very fast" (2007, part 1: 85, my translation). This is borne out in the different tempos between the recording in the 1960s of "Puya san jacintera" by Los Gaiteros de San Jacinto, played at a tempo of ♩ = 152 bpm, and the recording of Freddy Arrieta's contemporary group Los Bajeros, who perform "La bajera" at ♩ = 160 bpm (Convers and Ochoa 2007, CD 1, track 11). Significantly, during the first and second

round of the competition, Marioneta performed both "La palma" and "Maridita" (a fast and a slow puya), each with an appropriate tempo; that is, they presented both types of puyas in accordance with standard tempos. It is important to note, however, that while all subgenres in the gaita tradition have "preferred" tempi parameters, many will exhibit at least some metric fluctuations within a song, especially in the fast-paced *puya rápida*. It is also interesting that LCE's recording of "El Indio" is at the slower tempo, ♩ = 152 bpm (La Cumbiamba Eneyé, *Marioneta*), whereas the puya played in San Jacinto is in the same tempo as "Los bajeros" (♩ = 160 bpm). In New York they generally play at a faster tempo.

23. A *cosmopolitan, postethnic identity* refers to a combination of cosmopolitan ethnicity (fluid, multidimensional, thick identities) and the multiethnic and multiracial cultural backgrounds and experiences of young Colombian transmigrant musicians in the diaspora. See Kasinitz, Mollenkopf, Waters, and Holdaway 2008: 361–91.

24. The source of this title is a bullerengue recorded by Los Gaiteros de San Jacinto, "¿Pa' dónde vas morena?," wherein the lyrics express curiosity, as they wonder where a young black woman is headed: San Jacinto? Cartagena? Or to a convent in Venezuela? It can be heard on *Historia musical de Los Gaiteros* (2004).

25. Bob Belden, liner notes to *Miles from India* (2007), the 2008 Grammy-nominated recording for "Best Contemporary Jazz Album."

JOSÉ JUAN OLVERA GUDIÑO

3.
Cumbia in Mexico's Northeastern Region

What is it about *cumbia* music that makes it so popular in northeastern Mexico? Why do so many of its Mexican followers ignore its Colombian origin? What are the elements that maintain its popularity through the years, even in the wake of new and diverse styles of music? This essay describes the panorama of cumbia styles in northeastern Mexico, a region that encompasses the states of Coahuila, Nuevo León, and Tamaulipas, and Texas in the United States. Since cumbia in the region is characterized by a great diversity of styles (*norteña*, *grupera*, *colombiana* de Monterrey, and *villera*), I compare the different appropriations of each style in terms of its emergence and evolution. I pay special attention to the uses of cumbia music in the construction of identity by various social groups in the region and the role of the relationship between center and periphery in the controversy regarding the legitimate definition of popular music in general and, in particular, of tropical music. This relationship between center and periphery within this sociocultural region is considered from both an internal and external perspective, with respect to large centers of economic and symbolic capital; its particular dialogue with other music genres, such as the ballad, *norteño* music, rock, and pop; and its distinct interaction with the culture industry. In addition, I aim to show that the most enduring and successful cumbia styles in northeastern Mexico—norteño, *grupero*, and *colombiano*—are those resulting from a hybridization that takes into account elements particular to a specific group, be it rural, regional, or transnational. Furthermore, the accumulation of cumbia styles validates this genre as one of the most popular musical expressions in northeastern Mexico.

Beginning with historical, geographical, economic, and social background information will allow us a better understanding of the emergence and development of the genre and its variety of styles. Subsequently the description of each of these versions of cumbia allows us to reflect on the interplay between different styles, borders, and collective identities. This historic and sociological approach omits musicological considerations.[1]

Regional Context

The city of Monterrey is a key economic and financial center in Mexico and is considered the nation's industrial capital. It is also part of a sociocultural region comprising the states of Coahuila, Nuevo León, and Tamaulipas and the southern portion of Texas, which has engendered historically related and mutually influential musical expressions. This context transformed Monterrey into a cultural boundary, despite its location 125 miles south of the Rio Grande. At the same time, the city became a capital or center of culture industries that promote norteña and grupera music.[2] This was mostly due to its early economic development (Cerutti 1983) and the corresponding appearance of electronic communications media (Pedroza 2006: 131–50; Sandoval 2006; García 2008).[3]

Beginning in the 1970s, Monterrey consolidated its position as a center for the culture industry, especially in the area of popular music. Before this period, the different styles of popular music from the region were circulated either by small recording labels from Texas (Del Valle, Ideal Records, Corona, Falcón) or Mexican affiliates of North American labels (RCA Victor and others). A few available local recordings were made outside the city. From among the variety of genres emerging from the northeast, only a few would eventually stand out: *corrido* (Mexican ballad), polka, *redova*, *chotiz*, and *huapango*. The critic Adolfo Duarte Ayala points out that the legitimating process resulting from the new revolutionary power in Mexico—and local means of communication—influenced the amount of attention awarded to these styles. As a result, such expressions ended up constituting genres that nowadays enact identity for all of the state (and for the region as well). Additionally, from the Texas side of the border, the scholar Manuel Peña describes an evolution of successful musical formulas in the first few decades of the twentieth century, symbolizing an ideological defense against the economic and political domination of Anglo-Saxon sectors of Texas (Duarte Ayala 2000; Peña 1993).[4]

This regional music, with its strong rural accent, enjoyed early access to the technology and resources of popular music, which emphasize mass appeal, commercial value, an urban character, and a bond to technological development. For the most part, this was due to its close proximity to centers producing such technology (in the United States). Moreover connections between Monterrey, San Antonio, and Houston contributed to the appropriation of new musical instruments at a faster rate than in other corners of Mexico. As a result, the music of the region gained an early urban following without neglecting rural areas.

Since the 1930s Monterrey has enjoyed commercial broadcasting that not only circulates fashionable national and international cultural expressions but also, starting in the 1940s, has become a vehicle for expressions of regional culture.[5] From that time on, Monterrey was influenced by the flow of national and worldwide communication, while also influencing the rest of the world. An example is evident in a study conducted two decades ago, which showed high reception of the city's principal and most powerful broadcasters (XET, XEG, XEWA) among the inhabitants of a town in the state of Querétaro, close to 250 kilometers (155.34 miles) from Mexico City and 800 kilometers (497.10 miles) from Monterrey (Olvera 1991).

Monterrey's contemporary music industry was born from the interaction between radio stations, record labels, publishing houses, event organizers, and artistic representatives that, beginning in the 1970s, gained the strength and support necessary to transform the city into a mandatory musical reference point for the entire country. Its centripetal force attracts musicians, businessmen, and mass media from other places, at which point it diffuses musical cultures—not necessarily its own—that have been produced, recorded, and circulated in this city, as is the case with grupera music.

Overview of Cumbia Styles in the Mexican Northeast

Cumbia arrived in Mexico in the 1950s through cinema, with films like *La liga de las canciones* (1941). At the same time, the first Mexican recordings appeared: "La pollera colorá" and "La múcura" (both Colombian classics); a short time later a few local music groups emerged. Upon its arrival in Mexico, cumbia encountered, particularly in the capital, other traditional Afro-Caribbean cultures already established there, such as Cuban, Puerto Rican, and Dominican. In some cases, such as *bolero*, *danzón*, and *rumba*, some musical genres had settled in the region decades ago, and in certain places, such as Veracruz, they had been there since the end of the previous century. In Mexico the tradition of rumba and bolero has contributed to an entire cultural infrastructure: countless orchestras, renowned international soloists, films immortalizing these stars, transnational music circuits, broadcasts popularizing the music, record labels, dance centers (*salones de baile*), and more. Given the strength of this musical culture, cumbia is viewed as a slightly less complicated musical style, with slightly lower artistic quality (Pérez 1995). Even so, its reception and diffusion into large cities was immediate; however, its main audience was rural folks who had recently migrated to the cities.

In northeastern Mexico, the styles of cumbia include, in order of appearance, norteña, grupera, colombiana de Monterrey, and villera. Before I describe each of these, a quick review of regional music and its exchange with tropical music will prove helpful.

The northern part of Mexico is both the receiver and the generator of multiple musical cultures, all of which are in some sense considered norteñas (Olvera 2008). Regional music, frequently mentioned in this essay, is shared by Tamaulipas, Nuevo León, and Coahuila and is collectively called the *conjunto norteño* or, quite simply, norteña music. In Texas it is called the *conjunto tejano*. They share the same roots, and continuous interactions between the two are part of their development. The accordion and the *bajo sexto*, a musical instrument with twelve strings in six double courses, are the principal instruments. Different combinations of the following instruments may accompany them: drums, saxophone, clarinet, and the acoustic or electric bass. Its original geographic location is the northeastern area of the state of Nuevo León, adjacent to the northwestern part of Tamaulipas; however, its historic evolution cannot be explained without contemplating its constant interaction with the southern part of Texas (in part because of the Mexican population residing there before the war with Texas and also because of historic migration to the area).

Norteña Cumbia

The process of tropicalization of northeastern regional music began in the middle of the twentieth century. Before cumbia, conjunto norteño music was in contact with bolero and *porro*. During the 1950s and 1960s, the popular norteña artists Juan Salazar, Pedro Yerena, and Juan Montoya played versions for the accordion and sixth bass of hits by Agustín Lara, Pedro Vargas, and

Los Panchos on each side of the border. Texan artists like Chris Sandoval even added orchestral instrumentation.

Porros and cumbias were heard on the radio and played frequently by local orchestras, but they had not yet become a regional expression.[6] It wasn't until the mid-1960s that accordion and sixth-bass performers of regional music (polka, redova, chotiz, and corrido) begin to experiment with cumbia.

Thus far, research has shown that norteña cumbia was born in the peripheral regions of northeastern Mexico and southeastern Texas, that is, "peripheral" in relation to the powerful regional centers: Monterrey, San Antonio, and, later, Houston and Dallas. In small cities, the hybridization of music bore the added charm of developing creatively out of newly discovered musical styles. In this way, there was no associated risk that musicians would lose respect as a result of the status or capital linked to a particular genre. However, this was an obvious risk for well-known singers in large cities, who performed only "legitimate" genres: the growing rock and roll of the period, music from the great orchestras, boleros, and ballads. In sum, experimentation in the capitalist recording industry frequently brings about the risk of losing an important audience; it is more profitable to try new models when these have already proven their success outside urban areas. During the 1970s, a group of regional companies located in Monterrey (Roble, DLC, DISA, DEM'Y) focused on promoting successful formulas tried out first in the peripheral regions.

On the Mexican side, the first established promoters of norteña cumbia were Beto Villa and the Populares de Nueva Rosita, with musical arrangements that translated various tropical rhythms to norteña cumbia through the use of accordion and the sixth bass.[7] Nueva Rosita is a small town in the northern state of Coahuila, in the carbon-mining region located one hour from the Texas border. By 1969, when the group started recording norteña cumbia, they had already spent years playing at popular dances in the region, achieving great success for this new genre. Additionally, in the 1970s norteña cumbia became an astounding success within the Hispanic population on the North American side. However, it would take years before it was taken up by the elite and integrated into their entertainment circles.

The influence of the Colombian music group Corraleros del Majagual, formed in 1962, was crucial to the process of tropicalization of the conjunto norteño. By 1968 the group had already toured the United States, thanks to their success in Colombia and spectacular interpretation of cumbias, porros, and *vallenatos*. One of these tours eventually led the Corraleros del Majagual to a short stint as residents in Nuevo Laredo, Tamaulipas. This contributed to direct access between northeastern audiences and the Colombian musicians, as well as to contact with exponents of both musical cultures. The two main influences were the previously mentioned Beto Villa (Mexico) and Aniceto Molina (Colombia), who remained briefly in this region after the group returned to Colombia.

Once the success of norteña cumbia was ensured in peripheral areas—which included songs by Cornelio Reyna and Ramón Ayala in the city of Reynosa—it gained acceptance in Monterrey and was recorded and distributed extensively, though not by the main established companies. Rather, emerging labels like Roble and DISA recorded the music, using regional groups like Los Martínez de Allende and Los Atómicos de Monterrey.

In 1970 the new label DISA (Sabinas Records, named after a city in Coahuila) produced "Cabellos largos" ("Long Hair"), by Beto Villa. It became one of his most famous hits, with another forty records to follow, most of them with DISA, which was owned by Domingo Chávez. According to Villa, Chávez realized his music was the cornerstone of the company and that, with time, it would become one of the most important brands of regional and grupera music. Demand for "Cabellos largos" was so high that Chávez, lacking the capital to produce a sufficient quantity of records, sold the original tape and ceded the rights to *MexMelody* in Dallas for its U.S. distribution.

In the United States, the history of norteña cumbia may be even older. The famous Mexican American musician Valerio Longoria remarks that, at one point, boleros and cumbia were played in the norteño style without making any kind of distinction. What is quite clear is that the dialogue between the norteño-Texan conjunto and other musical genres is evident from a very early stage. A good example of this is Ramón Ayala, a musician from Nuevo León who forged his fame in Reynosa, Tamaulipas, by belonging to the duet Los Huracanes del Norte with Cornelio Reyna in 1964. He started his own group, Los Bravos del Norte, in 1971. Some of his cumbias, mostly recorded in the norteño style, maintain a dialogue with rock and roll, from the simple hint or flirtation with the genre in "Pero yo no la conozco" (But I Don't Know Her), to the straight interpretation of rock melodies in the norteña cumbia style of "Despeinada" ("Uncombed").[8] Following what their ancestors did with bolero in the 1950s and 1960s, Ayala and other northern singers transformed the ballad and other pop music into cumbia and norteña songs.

Cumbia and Grupera Music

The most popular and active music culture in northeastern Mexico is grupera. It is not a genre, but rather a category imposed by the culture industry to represent a diversity of popular genres and groups in which there are no soloists, ballads in Spanish, rock, or ranchera music from the Bajío region.

Its roots are in the fully developed conjunto norteño, which has integrated more instrumentation and urban styles. It also has roots in the orchestra tradition, which played a central role in the urban music scene in Monterrey between the 1930s and mid-1960s (Duarte Ayala 1998).

One version of the origin of grupera is that it comes from a small musical group, between three and six members, that, unlike the orchestra, which has ten musicians, took advantage of the development of electronic pianos and synthesizers to play with an orchestral sound. They also added guitars and electronic bass, along with drums. These music groups developed in Mexico City and other important cities of the country during the 1960s. In the late 1960s, the most popular artist of cumbia and other genres of Colombia's Atlantic Coast was Mike Laure, a musician from the western state of Jalisco. Laure and later artists tried to "personalize" this music, moderating Amerindian and African elements while emphasizing European ones. During the 1980s, these groups consolidated into an actual music movement. Moreover musicians and artistic directors interviewed in the late 1990s mentioned another important change: a slowing of the rhythm in some cumbias and vallenatos, which were usually too fast for the majority of Mexican dancers.

Another version of its origin locates grupera in musical groups in Monterrey at the beginning of the 1980s, resulting from synergies in the radio, television, recording, film, and entertainment sectors in the city. The expansion of the culture industry opened the way for singers like Rigo Tovar, Fito Olivares, Bronco, Los Mier, Impacto de Montemorelos, Los Barón de Apocada, and Alicia Villareal, who influenced music scenes beyond their national borders. Monterrey became "the Capital of Grupera Music." Groups of young musicians from the rural and central states of Mexico arrived in Monterrey and started popular and successful careers without having to go to Mexico City.

Tejano Music and Grupera Music Crisis

Tejano music is a movement, which, up to a certain point, parallels grupera, appearing in the south of Texas in the 1980s. Its roots place it alongside conjunto tejano music as well as the orchestra. Artists such as Selena, Intocable, La Firma, Joe Olivares, and Bobby Pulido, among others, took up cumbia as an appealing genre in which to construct their musical style, much like what happened with Mexican grupero musicians. However, unlike grupero musicians, a good number of tejano musicians have formal musical training, and the business atmosphere is more regimented in this area of the culture industry. In addition, the surrounding cultural reality leads tejano artists to interact with other genres besides ballads and pop music, namely jazz and the blues.

Since the late 1990s, some observers have noted a crisis in grupera music in Mexico, resulting from a variety of factors. Among them, there is a lack of new musical innovation, unlike in North American groups, which have enjoyed more possibilities for growth. Also, just as fifty years ago, variables like the growing instability in the country resulting from the war against drug cartels led some Mexican musicians to settle in Houston to record and develop promotional strategies for their products, instead of building up the domestic industry. To top it all, piracy has destroyed entire sections of this industry that, for many years, generated a positive impact on the local economy. In this respect, we should keep in mind the following: the 1982 economic crisis in Mexico served as the trigger to start the rebuilding of Nuevo León's economy. Regional industrial groups have aligned with international ones, joining the productive chains of external markets while maintaining a historical link to the North American market (Pozas 1993; Cerutti, Ortega, and Palacios 1993). Their resources have reinforced their presence in sectors like tourism, education, and banking, placing them on a level to internationalize their investments. In this way, they will try to adapt, as they did eighty years ago, to the new conditions of the global market. Nonetheless record producers, artists, representatives of the entertainment businesses, and those who organize both national and international tours for the new and successful groups lack specialized professional development. They also live with a certain amount of isolation and disdain from those other participants responsible for the institutionalization of the culture industry (the government, universities, musicians with professional development, etc.). The result is the absence of a specific public policy in the economic and cultural fields to assist the development of this sector. Lack of preparation will show its strategic importance in situations of crisis, as in the current moment, when technological changes, corruption, and poor legislation in the field allow seven out of ten discs to be sold through piracy, bringing about the collapse of entire businesses.[9] Unlike other sectors of the industry with more experience and cultural capital in the handling of business, a lack of elements necessary to face these circumstances, to rework the industry, will become evident. Hip-hop culture is quite able to establish the infrastructure necessary for its production and reproduction, even at the local level. But grupera is linked to a very conventional culture industry, and, while its musicians currently make a living by touring, many related entrepreneurs fail along the way, trying to adapt to changing times.

Colombian Music from Monterrey

This urban musical culture began more than four decades ago in the marginal neighborhoods of Cerro de la Loma Larga, an elongated rock formation at low altitude that runs across the south-central part of Monterrey. Its inhabitants were rural migrants who arrived from the states of San Luis Potosí, Zacatecas, and Coahuila and occupied close to twenty districts, primarily the upper part of the Colonia Independencia. The conjunto norteño music and the *tambora* (a group using wind instruments that was common to many Mexican towns), just like the tradition of corrido, formed part of the cultural capital that confronted a hostile reality that marginalized them politically, socially, and economically. From all of the different musical styles offered at the time on the radio and at the discotheques, many of the migrants opted for certain Colombian melodies played on the accordion, an instrument that is also very important in Mexico's northeastern region. This kind of music alluded to rural or semirural reality and was easily identifiable to the people, especially when the songs told stories of love and tragedy. In order of appearance in Mexico, the principal genres of this musical culture are porro, cumbia, and vallenato, exhibiting a wide variety of themes and styles; all of these genres originated on Colombia's Atlantic Coast. This music was used by marginalized youth from these places as a strategy to develop cultural capital and to create a collective identity through dance, clothing, the use of the body,[10] and special attention to lyrics. By highlighting its veracity and poetic form, particularly in vallenatos, users ignored any other proposal emerging from radio. This universe of cultural practices and significations was known as the *colombia* from Monterrey, a sociomusical identity assigned by the rest of society and eagerly embraced by its users. A *colombia* or *colombiano* is a native of Nuevo León who lives according to these practices. For many years, the idiosyncrasies of this musical culture offered a world of options for different moods and uses. Thus it was not necessary to turn to other genres that were not Colombian to satisfy different needs. Even though both cumbia and vallenato may be danced, cumbia has more of a tendency toward dance and interaction between people, which generates a sense of happiness and chaos; vallenato tends more toward listening and reflection. At the beginning, deejays showed the way in terms of preference. These expert consumers gave life to festivals through their speakers and turntables. They were at the forefront of knowledge and in possession of the latest music coming from Colombia, which really meant the latest commercial versions (actually recorded at the studios in Medellín) of music from the Colombian Atlantic Coast. But also, and with great success, certain grupero musicians (especially those using the cumbia style in their music), such as Perla del Mar and Tropical Caribe, performed Colombian melodies.

In 1982 a local musician, Celso Piña, began a new period in matters of preference, forming a group that interpreted melodies with a sound as faithful as possible to Colombian originals in terms of instruments and vocals. From the sociological point of view, the most important aspect of this period is that, by respecting the style of songs imported from Colombia, this musical preference restored Amerindian and African components in Mexico. In this way, cumbia and vallenato, diffused and homogenized in grupera expressions, recovered their melodic and rhythmic distinctions.

By this point, the preference for Colombian music was apparent in many other suburbs and popular neighborhoods of Monterrey. New generations of Colombians or colombias, as they call themselves, created more music groups and styles of dance, dress, and use of the body linked not only to their marginality but also to a constant bond with the cities of San Antonio, Houston, and Dallas.[11] In terms of recorded music products, Colombian music took advantage of the infrastructure of the regional record industry, which had grown with the success of regional and grupera music. However, that was not enough to ensure the circulation of records. With the exception of the Vallenatos de la Cumbia, who gained national and international prestige during the 1990s, it was very hard to be accepted into the culture industry with a music stigmatized for its connection with drug addicts, gangs, and delinquents. We could claim, additionally, that the expansion of a preference took place despite the indifference or simple disdain of mass media, which paid attention to this market only after 2000, when Piña was relaunched by the culture industry as embodying fusion with other genres and music groups. The social spaces won over by the genre, thanks to the strength of its practices; the social validation that the government awarded this music on various occasions; and participation by middle-class and working-class intellectuals who participated in the diffusion and study of the musical phenomenon empowered a third generation of followers to cross borders, not only to play in grupero spaces but also to compete in some of the most respected places for music connoisseurs, like the Festival de la Leyenda Vallenata in Valledupar, Colombia. Admission into the culture industry at the end of the 1990s promoted a different way of engaging cumbia and vallenato, both of which had usually marched together within this music culture. It encouraged those with the most purchasing power to embrace Colombian commercial vallenato because of its romantic twist, which, in the urban context, offers greater prospects for marketing. Interesting tensions arise from these circumstances, some of which are described by the Colombian researcher Darío Blanco (2007: 89–106).

In the case of cumbia colombiana de Monterrey, its growth among audiences resulted from its adoption by the upper classes, as well as by the upward social mobility of marginal classes. In contrast, the *chúntaro* (hillbilly) style, which has more interaction with rock, reggae, ska, and the fusion movement, could be considered a particular appropriation of colombia de Monterrey by urban youth from the lower middle classes. In any case, it's important to underline that the new expressions of cumbia emerging from the Colombian Atlantic Coast did not become popular and were not embraced by colombianos from Monterrey, unlike vallenato, which generated an interest that kept up with novelties from this South American region. It was as though the music genre had been frozen in the 1990s. It is striking that young people keep listening and dancing to old cumbias by Andrés Landero, Policarpo Calle, Los Corraleros de Majagual, Alfredo Gutiérrez, and Lizandro Mesa, a phenomenon of musical longevity that merits particular research.

Cumbia Villera

Born in the poorest zones of urban Argentina to express the contradictions and drama experienced in that context, cumbia villera arrived in Mexico in the twenty-first century. Guadalajara, in western Mexico, was the first city to extend a warm welcome to this style, which empowers or acts as a catalyst for the soccer scene. Its trajectory into Monterrey has three sources: Tapatian bars (groups of soccer fans from Guadalajara), such as Barra 51 and Barra Irreverente; mass communication outlets; and Argentine soccer players themselves, who play on the city's team. From this starting point, the local fan clubs Libres y Locos and La Adicción have disseminated the genre by embracing melodies and changing lyrics to reflect their own circumstances. Beyond this context, it seems that decoding Argentine-influenced lyrics poses a serious limitation within certain popular settings.

Villera's vast diffusion is the result of a variety of factors; like many types of music, it offers something different and holds the audience's attention at particular moments. Moreover Monterrey consumers follow distant shifts in musical styles with the help of new technologies. Infrastructure around this sort of music is small, but it is growing. Between 2006 and 2008 its popularity was ratified by a number of shows in various Mexican towns, including Monterrey, by some of its most important representatives, coming all the way from Argentina, namely, Damas Gratis, Pibes Chorros, and Yerba Mala. Together with the international distribution circuit, in a short time the city has also generated a regional circuit with events by local bands like La Barra Libre, Los del Rinkón, Cumbia y Fuera, La Mafia Villera, and other groups from Guadalajara. At the same time, there are special bars in the city's downtown devoted to villera. Even so, recently merchants in city markets, where working-class sectors tend to shop, speak of a decreased interest in the genre.

The use of keyboards and synthesizers in villera and the intense sound of rhythmic instruments that are scraped contribute greatly to its appropriation by diverse groups, as the genre is relatively equal in appeal to fans of ska and reggae, as well as to those who enjoy colombiana from Monterrey. Above all, this music is most strongly embraced by soccer fans at matches.

Our research groups demonstrated different appropriations of the music by the lower and middle classes, as well as at the heart of each class. Rhythms and arrangements, with a more universal appeal, enjoy the greatest penetration across all social segments. However, its lyrics, which tend to be blunt and harsh, also bear the problem of a villero vocabulary. Urban youth from the lower middle and lower classes tend to decode musical messages most easily. Many young, educated fans have followed ska and reggae for years; thus they embrace lyrics. Other segments of the middle and upper middle classes use the music for dance, apparently ignoring the lyrics.

Discussion and Conclusions

Migration and borders are crucial factors in the historic shaping of cultures, particularly for Mexico, which houses some fifty languages and shares a northern border with the most powerful country in the world. On one hand, migratory flows usually activate processes that give birth to cultural developments: Mixtec migrants who travel to the United States and build a community there can form a new border (not necessarily geographical) with respect to the new cultures they face: Anglo-Saxon, Asian, or African American. They then negotiate their old ways with new and alternative cultures. They create solutions for new cultural necessities—solutions that were once considered deviant or, quite frankly, unorthodox by those with the most cultural capital. However, they will eventually be validated as central components of culture (Lotman 1998). Simultaneously processes of hybridization at geographic borders—in our case, the border between northeastern Mexico and southern Texas—also entail intense practices of negotiation for meaning amid complex actions and messages, since, at certain historic moments, border hybridization and international migration take place concurrently and with great intensity. For instance, the conjunto norteño with the accordion and the sixth bass emerged from a border culture with musicians arriving in Monterrey and reached the rest of the country by way of radio. By the 1950s it had grown into a popular regional music. This process runs parallel to the *bracero* (labor) program (1942–64), in which workers from all over Mexico replaced the U.S. agricultural workforce. Many of these workers, who were not from the North, appropriated this musical culture as an essential part of their world, since this experience (migration to another country) became crucial to their lives and because there was a radio industry in Monterrey with broadcasts capable of reaching Arkansas to the north and Querétaro to the south. Norteña cumbia and grupera cumbia were born and disseminated by this solid foundation of interaction between migration, economic policies, and collective identity.

Migration to Houston from Monterrey during the oil boom of the 1970s was another, perhaps less intense case, but of equal importance to the northeast, and it occurred parallel to the birth of grupera music. The possible relationship between this migration and the birth of a new segment of the cultural industry in Houston remains an open question, but it is a fact that, by the late 1970s, performers from this new scene, like Rigo Tovar and Renacimiento 74, left Houston and found success in Mexico. A different case relates to the growing internal migration from San Luis Potosí, Zacatecas, and Coahuila to Monterrey, specifically to the Loma Larga zone in the 1950s and 1960s. These individuals made up the future colombias, the musical culture called colombiana de Monterrey. In the years following the crisis of Argentina's economy, studies on recent Argentine migrations into the area and their impact on the diffusion of villera in Monterrey have yet to be conducted.

If one looks at northeastern Mexico not as a frontier border but as a location where two civilizations, North America and Latin America, converge, then it is possible to understand why practices of decodification are so vast. In addition, it is easy to realize the immense possibilities for the generation of new meanings within everyday life.

With respect to collective identity, I assert that, under certain circumstances, popular music plays a significant role in its construction, along with other factors. Helena Simonett (2001), in her work on *banda sinaloense* music, emphasizes the role that discursive practices play in cultural construction. Pablo Vila (2000), in his study on northern identity, highlights that identity relies on the articulation of certain narratives in dialogue with particular classificatory systems based on reality, of a hegemonic or alternative nature, thanks to which social actors gain self-awareness. Then again, Simon Frith (1996) reminds us that, as with most processes, this construction takes place through direct experiences, which are constantly renewed through the body, time, and sociability, integrating both ethics and aesthetics. Through music, the social group will build, both at an individual and a collective level, an ideal imaginary "self."

In this way, in the mid-1960s the same cumbias from the Colombian Atlantic Coast were received simultaneously by the inhabitants of the Colonia Independencia in Loma Larga and Monterrey and by rural areas in Tamaulipas and Coahuila. The appropriation of cumbia was different in each area, the balance between ethics and aesthetics being a direct product of different environments. The Loma Larga neighborhoods are urban areas that produced the colombiana de Monterrey music. In cities like Nuevo Laredo and Nueva

Rosita, the context is more rural, and it created different types of norteña cumbia. In both, the violation of aesthetic norms generated reactions among other social groups, and the relative position of "new musicians" awarded them a different burden of identity. On one hand, the inhabitants of small northeastern towns, including those at the poverty level, possess more cultural capital: they continue living in their places of origin, they have extended families with whom they are in constant contact, and the only risk they take is to experiment with local musical instruments, in general, to have a good time in their own environment. Rural migrants and their children, located in an urban enclave of Monterrey, not only know they are poor and marginalized (a large part of their social capital means little in the cities), but also know that others perceive them in the same way. Their musical preference is lived and defended with more passion, through a confrontational attitude. Nonetheless there is a common denominator in both processes. In a context marked by inferior social capital with respect to other groups, it is quite obvious that music that generates more harmony and confidence via a minimal use of resources — that is, with fewer instruments, less formal musical education, and less complex rhythms and harmonies — will often be favored and developed by this social group. Therefore groups conform to the musical experience elaborating a language and narrative that identifies and distinguishes them from others, even as the groups evolve. Their discursive practices are evident in dance performances, the way the music is played, and even in how they describe themselves. Nevertheless it would not be practical to draw larger, more restrictive conclusions about social identity from the discussion of cumbia.

Colombiana de Monterrey music displays a narrative of identity not just through vallenato, its most explicit narrative genre, but also through a combination of genres offering alternatives for multiple situations and states of mind that, together, include the possibility of claiming, "I am, or I can be, all of these things, according to what I need." Its fans share a musical repertoire that is identified, above all, by a certain way of interpreting cumbia, bolero, or vallenato, all in Colombian style. The same process takes place with conjunto norteño music. It is not cumbia that awards identity, but rather the norteña way of playing music, be it bolero, corrido, polka, or huapango.

And what if something were missing a complement for individual needs of expression or self-recognition? In social groups of working-class origin (except in the case of colombiana), there is a tendency to coexist with other genres: corrido and cumbia, with an emphasis on narrative or dance. Coexistence and dialogue are more the rule than the exception. In the socialization of certain genres of music, the family nucleus competes in influence with the school, the street, and mass media, generating a universe of preferences, along with constant disagreement and negotiation of one's liking: being colombiano and villero, colombiano and roquero, colombiano and *gruperillo* (a fan of grupera), or *potranquillo* (a fan of norteña).

Certainly, from the start, those who possess the cultural capital at the heart of the rural music industry have put down norteña cumbia or tejana, colombiana from Monterrey, grupera, and villera (Bourdieu 1999). Originating from social groups marginalized in the economic, cultural, or geographic sense, these styles of cumbia and the social groups that consume them have fought for recognition. The problem becomes more complicated with the evolution of the style and the social groups among which the music first originates, in addition to the rest of the social groups coming into contact with it when they migrate and negotiate existing musical cultures with their own experiences. In this sense, colombiana music from Monterrey seems to be in a vital predicament. Rap from this city, which grows rapidly, ventures local contemporary biographical narratives, whereas semirural references evoked by colombia have disappeared with urbanization. Besides, they always pertained to Colombia, not Mexico. A local narrative never developed; when they tried to be 100 percent Colombian, members of this musical following ceased being Mexican, at least partially. For example, in the northeast there is a clear relationship of continuity in time between the music of norteño and grupera groups, and between their respective cumbia styles. In a certain way, they both represent the evolution from the rural to the urban setting in large social circles. Conversely, it is not as easy to explain the return of conjunto norteño music and its type of cumbia at the end of the 1990s. Finally, to use a cumbia style as a sign of distinction (to praise tejana cumbia, to denigrate colombiana cumbia) tells us that the intersubjective dynamics that generate its diversity of styles in northeastern Mexico make this genre not only the most popular one in the region, but also a space of dialogue and confrontation between social groups.

Discography

Ramón Ayala y sus Bravos del Norte. *Con sus mejores cumbias*. DLC-523 EMI, 72438228504. Mexico.

Bronco. 1991. *15 Super éxitos*. Sony U.S. Latin. Catalog Number: 09196. New York.

Cumbias. 1997. DLV-EMIMUSIC 605. Mexico.
Celso Piña. 2000. *Antología de un rebelde.* MCM. CRH-6104. Monterrey, Mexico.
Tayer. 2000. *Río Bravo-Río Grande.* Tayer Fonogramas 002. Monterrey, Mexico.
Treasury of Northeastern Mexican Music. 1991. Vol. 1. Nuevo León. INAH 29.
Mexico City.

Notes

1. This essay revises material from the past ten years. Some of the first studies are "Monterrey," in *Enciclopedia Continuum de Música Popular del Mundo; Colombians from Monterrey. Origins of Taste and Its Role in the Construction of Social Identity* (Nuevo León: CONARTE, 2005); "Al Norte del Corazón, Evoluciones e hibridaciones musicales en el noreste mexicano con sabor a cumbia," paper presented at IASPM IV in Bogotá in 2008. A work in progress analyzes the reception of cumbia by adolescents; some of its first findings are used here as well.

2. Both genres are categories developed by the cultural industry to group varieties of popular music from northern and central Mexico, usually played by bands.

3. Rubén Hernández-León (2002) has documented the existence of a "bi-national, inter-urban region in Monterrey and Houston."

4. Peña (1993) indicates that the development of the combined Texas style does not constitute a counterculture, not in the sense of an object that is dominated and trapped, but rather that it should be interpreted along the lines of a defensive strategy.

5. Constantino de Tárvana initiated regular broadcasts from his radio in 1921. Ten years later, the first commercial broadcasts began: XET (1930) and XEFB (1931).

6. I am alluding to expressions that follow in the footsteps of *sonora* music and that fit into the repertoire of Colombian and Venezuelan groups, such as La Sonora Dinamita, Guayacán, Maracaibo, Barulera, and Oscar D' León, to the extent that they bear a number of features denoting their musical production. Extending into the center of the country, these bands come together and merge rumba with Colombian traditions and evolve together or follow the patterns that give rise to salsa in the United States, Puerto Rico, Colombia, and Venezuela. Music by groups like La Sonora Veracruz, Los Flamers, and Los Aragón will become some of the most popular broadcast expressions of cumbia in Mexico. Also, these music styles are found in urban centers in the northeast, but not as regional expressions.

7. Musicians in Monterrey, such as Los Hermanos Prado and Juan Salazar, have recorded cumbias in a norteño style since the 1960s, but they do not constitute a style of this genre.

8. Listen to Ramón Ayala y sus Bravos del Norte, *Con sus mejores cumbias*. The case of Ayala as the initial follower of the rock style makes him famous playing cumbias; it connects him with other famous singers, like Rigo Tovar (Tamaulipas) and Mike Laure (Jalisco).

9. Interviewed in Texas, Coahuila, Nuevo León, and Tamaulipas, artists, disc dis-

tributors, and singers discuss the impact of piracy in the local industry in the past ten years. The case of Margarita Robledo, owner of one of the major music distribution companies in Monterrey, explains the situation: while she describes the deplorable state of sales (which exceedingly worries the big transnational labels), she acknowledges that she ignores the Internet.

10. "Use of the body" alludes mainly to the adoption of tattoos and other treatments for the face and hair, which colombianos embrace to look different from other urban youth cultures in Monterrey's metropolitan area.

11. During the first decade of this century, the creation of a community of Colombian migrants generated a backlash toward those who embraced their music and hybridized it with other dances and attire typical of *cholos*. These were the colombianos from Monterrey.

4.

Rigo Tovar, Cumbia, and the Transnational *Grupero* Boom

As the lights of the TV studio slowly fade, the music starts with a repetitive, syncopated electric guitar riff accompanied by a rather uncomplicated harmonic sequence played on the Sonic City electric piano. The supporting musical structure is provided by a driving bass line and an incisive *cumbia* rhythmic pattern played by the *güiro* in counterpoint with the cowbell and bongos. The two guitarists of the band move rhythmically from left to right, following the cadence of the music in synchronicity, while a man wearing sunglasses plays the *timbales* and begins singing in a high-pitched, nasal voice:

> Ya tengo tantos deseos
> de conocer la mujer
> que será dueña de mi alma
> y dueña de mi querer.

> I have the desire
> to meet the woman
> who will be the owner of my soul
> and the owner of my love.

A large star-shaped medal crowned with a diamond is visible through the open, white, puffy shirt under the turquoise polyester suit worn by the long-haired singer. As the song moves into an instrumental middle section the singer improvises a simple but loud solo on the timbales; the audience goes crazy, clapping, whistling, and screaming in ecstasy. The excitement only grows as the performance comes to an end when the repeat of the sung refrain is rounded off with the singer jumping high into the air, extending his legs and arms, in his classic, signature dance move.[1]

This is just one of Rigo Tovar's typically engaged performances, for which he and his band, the Costa Azul, became immensely popular throughout Latin America and the United States in the 1970s and 1980s.

Although the image quality is rather poor, the old video is a witness to Tovar's extraordinary success, as well as the birth of one of the most remarkable musical tendencies at the end of the twentieth century, the so-called *grupero*, a cumbia-based musical trend championed by working-class *grupos* (bands) like Tovar's that took the Mexican media by storm in the 1990s. Who was Rigo Tovar? What made possible the unlikely success of a charismatic but vocally limited singer? What circumstances allowed him to become an idol among the Latin American working classes and to have such great success in a music industry on the verge of neoliberal globalization? This essay offers answers to these questions by exploring Rigo Tovar's cumbia style as a site for the intersection of class, ethnicity, race, and citizenship in Mexico and Greater Mexico during the 1970s and 1980s. I pay particular attention to the role of Mexican immigration into the United States in the changing attitude of Mexican media toward marginal working-class traditions. In analyzing this phenomenon I coin the theoretical notion of "dialectical soundings" after Walter Benjamin's concept of "dialectical images," and I argue that the transnational success of bands like Rigo Tovar y su Costa Azul allowed for the recognition of the marginal working classes and the validation of their cultural capital.

This study of Rigo Tovar and his music is not simply an attempt to reevaluate or reinsert in the history of cumbia a figure that has been overlooked in scholarly research about Latino and Latin American music, nor do I attempt to homologize changes in aesthetic taste among Mexican audiences with changes in the Mexican social fabric due to migration. Instead I invoke Rigo's success and his ultimate presence in the Mexican media as an index of the challenges that migration brought to mainstream Mexican culture in the 1980s and 1990s. The presence of Rigo Tovar and his music in the mainstream Mexican media is not a metaphor of social change but an example of social change. As such, I argue that the Rigo phenomenon in Mexico should be studied from a transnational perspective that illuminates how seemingly national mainstream practices occur within networks that exceed the national. In doing this, I understand transnationalism as "the idea that individual and even communal experience takes place within imagined communities that transcend the nation-State as a unit of identification" (Madrid 2011: 8). I show that it is precisely the type of culture exposed by the consumption of Rigo and cumbia (among other genres) by Mexican communities in the United States that redefines media practices in their country of origin.

"A orillas del Río Bravo/hay una linda región"
(On the banks of the Rio Grande there is a pretty region)

Rigoberto Tovar García was born on March 29, 1946, in the northeastern Mexican border city of Matamoros, Tamaulipas. His father was a low-paid carpenter, and, like most children from poor working-class backgrounds in the Mexican countryside, Rigo began working in early childhood to help support the family. In the early 1970s, he moved to Houston, looking for a job; it was there, while working as a waiter at a bar, that he received his first opportunity to sing for an audience (Carrizosa 1997: 108). There he sang and played with several pop and rock bands as well as a trio before getting together with his recently emigrated brothers to form the cumbia-based combo Conjunto Costa Azul in 1971. A year later the band released its first album, *Mi Matamoros querido*, named after Rigo's homonymous song, which was to become his first big hit. The cover of the LP shows Conjunto Costa Azul in front of the Mecom Fountain at Hermann Park, an architectural landmark in Houston's Museum District. The image is a testimonial to a fact stated by José Juan Olvera Gudiño (2005a: 40): that Houston and Monterrey formed the axis of a cumbia-based transnational, regional music industry that dominated the Spanish-speaking market of southern Texas and northwestern Mexico in the late 1960s and 1970s. In Rigo's case, it was the success of his first record among Mexican and Mexican Americans in Houston and Brownsville that caught the attention of music labels south of the border; when the talent-seeker Gastón Ponce heard the album, he persuaded Ignacio Morales from Discos y Cartuchos de México (DCM) to offer the band a distribution deal (Pulido 1981: 77).

According to the music critic Toño Carrizosa (1997: 108), Morales's distribution deal was unprecedented for DCM and was the reason for the label to morph into Discos Melody.[2] In 1979 *Billboard* published an article by Marv Fisher (1979a: 71) about the success of Discos Melody in an issue dedicated to independent music labels. Fisher wrote, "Such an outstanding artist as Rigo Tovar was typical of how Melody began to climb into prominence.... He had a phenomenal rise in success which only few in the country can claim. Naturally, his sales had a great bearing in establishing Melody as a driving force in the market."³ In fact the signing of Tovar by DCM/Melody coincided with the label's attempt to reposition itself in the Mexican music market. As part of this strategy, the label was searching for a band of *música guapachosa* (party music) to market against RCA Victor's new star band, Acapulco Tropical (Pulido 1981: 77).⁴ The transformation of Conjunto Costa Azul into Rigo Tovar y su Costa Azul capitalized on the charisma and personality of Rigo and quickly conquered what would prove to be a highly profitable market for Melody.

The label's marketing strategy for the band was rather simple. It consisted of extensive radio play and tours throughout the Mexican countryside and among the Latino—mainly Mexican and Central American—communities in the United States. It was quite successful. In less than eight years, Rigo became Mexico's pop music idol. Each new record sold more copies than the previous, and by 1981 his first ten LPs had sold more than seven million copies, while his single albums had sold much more than that (Pulido 1981: 74). In 1982 Rigo broke an attendance record in the northern city of Monterrey, Nuevo León, when he played for a crowd of 400,000 in the basin of the Santa Catarina River; the previous record was held by Pope John Paul II, who had visited the city and said mass in the same place in 1979, the year of his first visit to Mexico. To paraphrase John Lennon's infamous statement, one could say that Rigo Tovar y su Costa Azul were "more popular than Christ." That same year, the Chilean moviemaker Víctor Vío filmed *Rigo: Una confesión total* (Rigo: An Absolute Confession), a documentary that, according to the journalist Jorge Pulido (1981: 77), beat American movies like *Jaws* and *Star Wars* in the box offices of many Mexican towns.

Rigo became a phenomenon not only in Mexico, where he achieved sales records, selling over twenty-six million copies until his death in 2005,⁵ but also among Latinos in the United States (particularly in southern Texas and urban areas like Chicago, Los Angeles, and Las Vegas), where he held concerts at the height of his career. When Arnaldo Ramirez Jr., vice president of the historical Mexican American label Falcon Records, tried to reinvent his music enterprise, he opted for the promotion of concerts that responded to the changing demographics in southern Texas in the late 1970s; one of his main attractions was Rigo Tovar (Fisher 1979b: 12). Vío's *Rigo: Una confesión total* documents the excitement among the large crowd that congregated for a concert in Chicago's Aragon Ballroom in 1978. As he kept producing hit after hit and selling recordings at consistent record numbers throughout the next decade, Rigo's popularity among the Mexican Americans in Chicago grew noticeably. His presence as one of the main attractions at the 1986 Chicago

Pan American Festival, where he shared the spotlight with such Latino stars as Celia Cruz, Tito Puente, and El Gran Combo de Puerto Rico, attests to this extraordinary phenomenon.

Although still very popular at the end of the 1980s, Rigo had to eventually limit his concerts until he retired in the 1990s due to a problem with retinitis pigmentosa that affected his eyesight and led to complete blindness by the end of his life. This condition only added an extra element of tragedy to his personal story, which gained him more sympathy from his fan base. By the time he retired, Rigo had shown the mainstream music industry the enormous economic potential of a market that had remained neglected and marginal: the working classes. Although the first bands of what came to be known as *grupero* appeared in Mexico toward the end of the 1960s, it was Rigo's enormous success among Mexicans and Mexican Americans in the 1970s and 1980s that prepared the industry for the truly gigantic events of bands like Bronco and Los Bukis in the 1990s. Just as the Rigo phenomenon helped shape Discos Melody as an influential player in the Mexican and Latin American music industry, in the long run his success allowed for the transformation of the grupero trend from a local phenomenon into a true transnational music movement, with the establishment of an economically powerful music industry on both sides of the U.S.-Mexico border (see Madrid 2008: 58–61). By the time Rigo passed away on March 27, 2005, the entertainment industry in Mexico had been completely transformed, with the so-called *onda grupera*, which he helped develop, a dominant player in it. This shift in aesthetic concerns coincided with NAFTA and the validation of migrant culture in Mexico as its contribution came to be vital for the Mexican economy. In a way, Rigo was a type of NAFTA worker avant la lettre. His success in a type of postnational, transnational market allowed many to realize the type of marketing strategies to be expected under the new NAFTA provisions.

Rigo es Amor (Rigo Is Love)

Rigo's popularity among the working classes was partly the result of how his uncomplicated music allowed fans to identify him with their own grassroots origins. Rigo became the people's idol because he spoke in a familiar accent, he used unsophisticated words, and the lyrics of his love songs reflected the sensibility of millions of working-class Mexicans whose taste had been systematically ignored by the music and entertainment industry of their country. Rigo's public persona—his humbleness framed by long wavy hair and *Saturday Night Fever* suits—articulated the aspirations for cosmopolitan belonging of his working-class fan base within the familiar persona of the boy next door. His fans saw in him someone like themselves who was able to fulfill his dream of success. A member of the Pastorcillos de Rigo Tovar fan club interviewed for *Rigo: Una confesión total* said, "What we like the best about Rigo is his modesty. Our favorite song by Rigo is 'Oh que gusto de volverte a ver.' [Oh I am so happy to see you again.] Rigo's illness is retinitis pigmentosa; in due time this illness leads to total blindness, but with the well wishes of us all, all of the Pastorcillo members, we expect Rigo won't go blind. Long live Rigo!" Whether or not this testimonial was staged for the documentary, it illustrates the affection, sense of identification, and empathy Rigo's followers felt for their idol.

By the end of Rigo's career there were more than five hundred fan clubs throughout Mexico and the United States that adored the singer and cheerfully shouted the motto that identified them as his fans: "Rigo es amor." Many of these clubs were formed by low-income women who made a living as domestic workers and who would spend their free Sundays dancing and singing to Rigo's music either live or at the many *bailes sonideros* that slowly became popular in the 1980s.[6] Many sequences from *Rigo: Una confesión total* show women at Rigo's concerts screaming frantically for their idol and fighting each other to get close to him, take a picture of him, or even touch him. For them, Rigo was more than an entertainer; he was a true sex symbol, the embodiment of working-class masculinity, sensibility, and desire. Carrizosa (1997: 110) argues that although Rigo wanted to be close to the people, the enthusiasm of his female fans eventually forced him to hire bodyguards in order to keep them at a safe distance.

Rigo was aware of his iconic role among the marginal working classes and cultivated it thoroughly:

> I would panic if the middle classes, intellectuals, and rich people liked my music. . . . I am a *naco* [an ill-mannered person] and I sing for the *nacos*: for the people, for my friends who have feelings and goodness. The upper classes are like poisoned: they cannot win, they just take things away; they cannot admire, they just feel envy; they devour instead of eating; they speculate instead of sharing, they eat instead of savoring their food, they feel desire instead of feeling love. (Quoted in Pulido 1981: 80)

Rigo thus identified himself as a member of the working classes he sang for. His use of the term *naco* signifies the issues of class and distinction that informed not only the reception of his music by his fans but also the reception of the Rigo phenomenon by the Mexican upper classes. *Naco* is a term used in Mexico to describe bad taste, lack of sophistication, and lowbrow aesthetics. It is also often used to mark racial difference as well. Rigo's use of the word shows that he was well aware of how he and his music were perceived by the Mexican upper classes and that he was willing to play along with the discourse of difference as it allowed him to reinforce the aura of authenticity that made him popular among his followers.

La Onda Grupera: New Cumbia in the 1970s

The birth of the onda grupera in the 1970s and 1980s was the result of the increasing success of cumbia among the Mexican working classes during the 1950s and 1960s. By the 1960s Mexican groups like Mike Laure y sus Cometas, Sonora Santanera, and Chelo y su Conjunto had largely replaced the big Afro-Caribbean music combos of mambo and cha-cha-chá that dominated the popular music scene in central Mexico until the 1950s (Madrid 2008: 59). However, as José Juan Olvera, Benito Torres, Gregorio Cruz, and César Jaime Rodríguez explain (1996: 22), the Mexican appropriation of cumbia came with a number of instrumental and stylistic modifications to the Colombian genre; noticeably, the polyrhythmic practices of traditional cumbia were replaced by the simpler güiro rhythmic pattern that characterizes today's *cumbia norteña* (figure 4.1), the substitution of the accordion by the electric organ or the synthesizer, and the introduction of the drum set and güiro as the instrumental basis of the percussion section.

Peter Wade (2000: 174) has written that Rigo Tovar was one of the most visible musicians to take the process of stylistic simplification a step further by fully "dispens[ing] with brass and reed instruments" and developing a new hybrid type of ensemble.

Although in many ways typical of the simplified cumbia style described by Wade and Olvera, Rigo Tovar y su Costa Azul developed a very particular and unique sound. With its trademark keyboard-driven cumbias and a hybrid music style that combined *cumbia tropical*, rock, bolero, *ranchera*, and *balada pop*, the group became the first superstar band of the grupero movement

Figure 4.1. Simplified cumbia rhythmic pattern.

(which features the use of lyrical romantic melodies and cumbia rhythms). The band consisted of electric piano, two electric guitars, bass, and a percussion section composed of drum set, güiro, cowbell, bongos, and timbales. The harmonic and melodic elements are shared between the electric piano and the two electric guitars (a rhythm guitar and a solo guitar that would sometimes be distorted by effect pedals like the Fuzz Tone or Flanger). Particularly important is the familiar sound of the electric piano, a trademark of popular music of the 1970s. The electric piano would often introduce the melodic material at the beginning of a song and then retreat to the background during the vocal sections to play harmonic progressions made of long, sustained chords. During instrumental sections the electric piano would often improvise simple, repeated licks. Sometimes these improvisatory sequences would be shared with the solo electric guitar, which on most occasions would simply restate the main melodic material of the song. The percussion section provides the rhythmic structure of the song, which, in a cumbia, would be entirely based on the simplified cumbia rhythmic pattern discussed earlier, although it would be played by the güiro in a continuous drive from the beginning to the end of the song. The bass would reinforce the guitar and piano harmonies by playing sequences using the pitches of the triad in rhythmic augmentation of the simplified cumbia pattern played by the güiro (a quarter note followed by two eighth notes in the bass line).

While the Costa Azul provided the instrumental and rhythmic accompaniment, it was Rigo's high-pitched nasal voice, slightly out of tune, that characterized the sound of the band. However, his role in the group wasn't restricted to providing the lead vocals and public image of the band. Rigo was also behind the familiar if straightforward improvised timbale soli featured during the instrumental sections of the songs. And he was usually the composer of the band's own singles and the arranger of the instrumental ensemble—conveyed orally, as he was not able to read or write music. During a rehearsal recorded for Vío's documentary, Rigo explains how he organized and arranged his music:

The music ... I project it the way it should be. I give it an introduction, which is the first musical [instrumental] theme; then the first vocal theme; then a small change of key ... or a small little arrangement and I move into the second vocal theme. Then a transition comes, which is *el gozo* [the pleasure], as we call it among ourselves from the groups. And the final theme comes at the end; the end could be repeated.... The main theme should never be lost, I mean the first vocal theme. So I have to end with the main theme and make an end for it so that it can go into the final coda.

An analysis of his music shows that with small variations, Rigo's description—which applies perfectly well to a song like "No que no" and its Intro-A-B-Bridge-B-Coda form—is a very accurate representation of his formal predilections.[7] In this type of format it is precisely the instrumental sections such as the bridge (which Rigo eloquently calls *el gozo*) and quite often the final coda that lend themselves to improvisation and expansion. These sections allowed fans not only to freely express themselves through dancing but also to interact with Rigo, who would frequently provide soft-spoken love lines, unexpected dedications, or even blatant jokes during these moments.

Migration, Cumbia, and Transnationalism

Just as the 1960s and 1970s witnessed the arrival and escalating success of cumbia among the Mexican working classes, these decades also brought the end of the so-called Mexican economic miracle.[8] Between the 1940s and the 1970s Mexico developed a mixed economy, with the state supporting industrialization and establishing the economic infrastructure for private investment. Although migration to urban areas had been a constant during the process of industrialization, it was the mistaken economic policies of the 1970s and the ensuing inflation that exacerbated the phenomenon. Likewise, as the Mexican economy collapsed in the 1980s, with the resulting extensive impoverishment of the countryside and the reduction of jobs in urban areas, working-class migration to the United States increased significantly. Adding to the flow of immigrants from the Mexican countryside, the civil wars that battered Honduras, El Salvador, Guatemala, and Nicaragua in the 1970s and 1980s produced an enormous rush of refugees into the United States. This migratory flow helped concentrate large Latino communities in the American Southwest and states like Florida, New York, and Illinois.

Most of these immigrants came from working-class backgrounds, and an important constituent of their cultural capital was the musical genre that was quickly coming to dominate marginal neighborhoods not only in Mexico but also in Central and South America: cumbia. For a musician from the margins of Mexico like Rigo, who had himself been an immigrant worker in the United States (and had started his musical career in that country) and who was a border citizen used to negotiating border culture on a daily basis, these were natural markets. He shared not only these immigrants' social background and cultural experience but also their cultural capital and sensibility. Apparently the love songs and cumbias that he offered these audiences had little to do with their experience as immigrants; however, as Helena Simonett (2007: 124) argues for contemporary *bailes sonideros* in the United States, "Due to the spatial separation of the Mexican *sonido* fans residing in the United States, bittersweet and romantic songs speak of and to the experiences of those who have left. Romantic songs touch intimate feelings and deal directly with the private, emotional sphere." This was also the case for fans of Rigo in the 1970s and 1980s. Furthermore I would argue that Rigo performances were sites for the recognition and validation of a shared transnational cultural capital that immigrants from Mexico and Central America brought with them from their countries. Thus Rigo's music and its performances were sites that offered symbolic links to the land and communities left behind, a sense of communal experience while in the diaspora, and models to build a sense of identification beyond the constraints of the discourses of marginality and difference established by the hegemonic networks in their countries of origin. Rigo's cumbia dance events offered his fans a site where the liberated dancing body could intersect with the desires of the political body in an attempt to define a new type of transnational cultural citizenship in a rather hostile social environment.

Rigo's Cumbia as Dialectical Sounding

According to Toby Miller (2001: 2), cultural citizenship "concerns the maintenance and development of cultural lineage through education, custom, language, and religion and the positive acknowledgment of difference in and by the mainstream." By adopting the idea of cultural citizenship we recognize collective rights and culture beyond understandings of citizenship based on traditional conceptions of space and time. Central to the notion of cultural citizenship is the idea of recognition and tolerance. Cultural citizenship accepts the ability of migrants and their communities to negotiate sites of identification that ultimately allow for the recognition of their difference while still acknowledging their rights to belong locally and transnationally. Migration plays a central role in the current scholarly use of the notion of cultural citizenship, as the identity of migrant workers is separated from the place where they live and their status as citizens is guaranteed not by a nation-state but by "everyday customs and beliefs" (Shafir 1998: 19).

In order to account for the social and discursive implications of the articulation of cultural citizenship by music and expressive culture, I coined the theoretical concept of "dialectical soundings." This concept is inspired by Jill Lane's (2008) interpretation of Walter Benjamin's idea of "dialectical images." Benjamin developed the notion of the dialectic image as a tool to challenge the idea that the past could be understood only in the precise moment in which it is recognized—but never seen again—and "frozen" in an eternal image in the present. Instead he proposed that dialectic images work as "critical constellations" of the past in the present (Wong 2001: 31). Lane's reading of Benjamin suggests that these dialectical images appear in the present to recognize a moment in the past that has been rendered invisible through discourse and to provide a possible avenue into the future. I have taken Lane's provocative reading of Benjamin a step further and propose that if an image is able to trigger such a process, then music and its performance as audiotopia, as a site "of effective utopian longing where several sites normally deemed incompatible are brought together" (Kun 2005: 23), also provide a powerful space for such a process to take place. Music as dialectical sounding could work as a medium that makes visible the invisible via a specific articulation in the present and provides a possible place for that past in a new narrative of the present toward the future. I argue that the Rigo Tovar phenomenon is one such case.

The extraordinary success of Rigo's music should be understood in terms of cultural citizenship and the acknowledgment of marginal cultures by the middle- and upper-class mainstream, especially through their recognition by the media. In the case of Rigo, the grupero scene, and the working classes who embraced him, this process of recognition took many years, and there were many factors involved in its development. I would argue that there were at least three phases in this process. The first one concerns the reception of Rigo's music and his elevation to the stature of an idol by Mexican and Latino working classes on both sides of the U.S.-Mexico border as a result of the need of these individuals to find sites of cultural identification and validation. The second phase refers to the changing economic dynamics in Mexico and many countries in Central America as remittances from migrants became one of the most important sources of capital and as migrant culture began to make its way back into the countries of origin of these migrants. The third phase is the consequence of the democratization of the Mexican media (historically one of the most powerful media conglomerates in Latin America), which was partly a consequence of globalization, NAFTA, and the neoliberal polices of the past two decades, but was also the result of recognizing these working classes and their migrant relatives as an economically powerful market. I shall discuss now the issues of class and discursive invisibility at stake in the recognition of Rigo by the mainstream entertainment industry.

Due to the working-class character of the audiences who embraced Rigo, the Mexican mainstream as well as the elites initially reacted to his music with scorn. Rigo's statement that he was a naco and sang for nacos was a response to how he had been depicted by the mainstream media. Jorge Pulido's article for the middle-class-oriented Mexican monthly magazine *Contenido* is a good example of how the media reflected but also helped reproduce the feelings of the upper classes toward the working classes in Mexico. Although Pulido's article recognizes Rigo's remarkable and unprecedented economic success, its general tone is rather one of mockery. Pulido explains that Rigo became a popular music idol "without the upper third of the Mexican population noticing" and emphasizes that being "monotonous, badly structured, and meager," his music was artistically worthless (1981: 74, 80). Even Toño Carrizosa's book on the grupero scene, a project that seeks to celebrate this subculture, ends up stating that Rigo "shocked the true plebs" (1997: 109). In the classist rhetoric of the Mexican middle and upper classes, Rigo was a working-class naco who had inconceivably become a success.

Clearly the Mexican upper classes and elites of the 1980s were not ready to recognize not only the success of a member of the working classes but also the very presence of those marginal sectors as valuable members of Mexican society. In the tradition of what Octavio Paz (1981: 49) calls *ninguneo* (none-ness), "an operation that consists of turning someone into nobody" by which the Other is nullified, the Mexican mainstream media had systematically ignored the working classes, especially the most marginal members of this sector. As part of this process, the media had mechanically reproduced a hegemonic system that, as part of the discourse of the "Mexican Miracle," rendered invisible the lower classes as it imagined the country entering the consort of rich industrialized nations. The sudden success of Rigo and his naco music as well as his popularity not only among the "lowest two-thirds" of the Mexican population but also among those forced to migrate because of the lack of basic opportunities and citizen rights in their country and for whom the Mexican Miracle was nothing but empty rhetoric, represented a clear and present challenge to the dominant ideology. Pulido's article reflected the fear of the Mexican bourgeoisie; the Rigo phenomenon made the unattractive *ninguneadas* working classes into a very visible presence.

In this way, the Rigo phenomenon in the 1980s became a type of dialectical sounding in the terms I described, as a constellation of the past in the present and into the future. It rendered visible a subculture that had been neglected by both the media and the hegemonic discourse of the Mexican Miracle as well as the racially polarized American entertainment industry. The Rigo phenomenon offered a site for the imagination of a new future that would challenge the Mexican state's hegemonic discourse of progress as it exposed its flipside while advancing cultural citizenship as a viable option for the recognition of the marginal. It articulated its meaning at a historical moment when the economic crisis made migration an everyday aspiration for many Mexicans and presented both working-class Latinos and the marginalized Mexican working classes with possible courses of action to develop sites for the performance of cultural citizenship within their specific societies. It is this unknown path toward the recognition of the marginal Other that triggered in the bourgeoisie a sense of disorientation expressed in their fear of those "classless" individuals who slowly but surely were gaining spaces and alternative access to the public sphere. Furthermore, as these contradictions coexist in a new discourse that incorporates the formerly ninguneados, the dialectical condition of the phenomenon is evident in the fact that such recognition does not necessarily translate into more radical social change that may benefit them in their everyday life.

Rigo Tovar's success paved the way for the development of a grupero trend that, with the support of the Mexican and Latino media, was able to transcend class barriers in the 1990s within the transnational economic framework established by NAFTA. Rigo was also an influential figure in introducing cumbia into the Latino music scene in the American Southwest. The hybrid cumbia sound of bands like Selena y los Dinos and later Kumbia Kings owes much to his sound and his marketing experience in the 1970s and 1980s. The transnational success of bands like Rigo Tovar y su Costa Azul forced the Mexican media as well as the Latino entertainment industry to recognize alternative forms of citizenship and identity and challenged mainstream Latin American discourses of class and taste. Understandably, for the ninguneados who came to full visibility with his break into the music industry and who still sing and dance to his music, *Rigo es amor*.

Videography

Rigo Tovar: Trayectoria. Univision Music Group 103-6577. 2005.
Víctor Vío. *Rigo: Una confesión total*. Veracruz 6341. 1979.

Notes

1. This description is loosely based on the performance of "Cómo será la mujer" available on *Rigo Tovar: Trayectoria*, Univision Music Group 103-6577, 2005.

2. Discos Melody would later become Fonovisa and then Univision Records.

3. It is worth mentioning that at the time Fisher published his article, the roster of Melody artists included such stars as Angélica María, Raúl Vale, Diego Verdaguer, and the up-and-coming band Los Bukis. Yet the name that is noted as the gem in Melody's crown is Rigo Tovar.

4. The term *guapachoso* could be loosely translated as "flavorful," "tasty," or "festive." In Mexico the term *música guapachosa* is often used interchangeably with *música tropical* (music from the tropics) to label music with a certain degree of Afro-Caribbean or Afro-Colombian influence (see Madrid 2008: 78–79).

5. "Murió Rigo Tovar," *El Extra*, April 7, 2005, http://www.elextranewspaper.com/noticia/4084/1/0/registro.php.

6. *Bailes sonideros* are dance events where the music is played by a deejay instead of a live music band. Much cheaper than hiring a large band, group, or conjunto, bailes sonideros were an affordable entertainment option in poor communities of the Mexican countryside, especially after the Mexican economy's significant slowdown in the 1970s and 1980s.

7. This formal structure is also a standard in the bolero, another genre that Rigo Tovar y su Costa Azul also cultivated.

8. The Mexican Miracle refers to the continuous growth of the Mexican economy between 1940 and 1970.

5.
Communicating the Collective Imagination
The Sociospatial World of the Mexican *Sonidero* in Puebla, New York, and New Jersey

The innovative and unique forms of performative expression fashioned by diasporic communities have come to be recognized as some of the most notable features of globalization. Research of scholars in the arts and social sciences has revealed that the transnational movement of peoples, ideas, technologies, ideologies, and capital has inspired many marginal communities, especially immigrant subcultures, to express their sense of community in distinctively innovative and radical ways. Animated by a seemingly shared sense of displacement and, often, by a blurring of real and imagined representations of home and history, diasporic groups have availed themselves of new technologies, ideas, and experiences to create not only hybrid musical styles but also distinctively new performance formats, circuits, and distribution practices. While scholars (e.g., Garcia Canclini 1995: 231–32; Rouse 1991: 20–23) have pointed out the dynamism of "border zones" as crucibles for new expressive art forms, it is increasingly apparent that such zones need not be actual geographical boundaries but can also include the experiential borders created and invoked by diasporic groups, wherever they may be, through structured performances and sociomusical events. It is these kinds of localized events that support the notion that migratory movements result in the most extensive and lasting new social linkages, forcing us to rethink our understanding of the relationship between geographic space, social space, and performance space.

Some of the most inventive contemporary performance idioms, such as *technobrega* in Brazil and Colombian *picó* (see Pacini Hernandez 1993), center around deejays who manipulate technology as a means to present various forms and combinations of recorded and original music, sounds, and speech.[1]

In this chapter I discuss a unique form of social dance event that has been popular among the Mexican migrant and immigrant communities in New York City and nearby northern New Jersey for nearly two decades. It has an even longer history in Mexico City barrios and in the towns and villages of Puebla, from where the majority of these immigrants hail. In these weekend dances, the deejay, or *sonidero*, as he is known, together with those in attendance, create a powerful transnational musical and social experience. By manipulating music and simultaneously reconfiguring time and place, they turn feelings of displacement and marginalization into a collective sense of identity and connectedness, generating what Arjun Appadurai (1996) has called a "diasporic public sphere." In the process they dramatize and mediate their own experiences of a modern life that oscillates between and encompasses both Mexico and the United States. They effectively portray and create a modernity animated by both "real" and "imagined" interpretations of history, culture, and shared experiences of travel, dislocation, and a reinvention of their lives as both Mexicans and Americans. In many such communities, the deejay has emerged as a seemingly subversive and powerful force in facilitating the participation of individuals in the production, presentation, promotion, and marketing of artists and recordings utilized in the sonidero *baile* context. The sonidero tradition in Mexico City, Puebla, New York, and New Jersey is representative of a powerful transnational musical and social phenomenon that perpetuates individual agency within new social spaces and blurred geographical boundaries. While there are similar circuits for sonidero music between other U.S. cities and specific regions in Mexico, the research that directed the writing of this chapter was conducted in New York (in particular, Queens and Brooklyn), Paterson, New Jersey, Santa Isabel de Cholula, Puebla, and, more recently, Mexico City.

The Mexican population in the New York–New Jersey area has grown exponentially in the past two decades. Although traditionally outnumbered by Caribbean Latin Americans, New York City's Mexicans, both documented and undocumented, now number between 275,000 and 300,000, constituting the region's fastest-growing immigrant group (Smith 2005: 19–20). However, due to the large number of undocumented Mexicans, estimated at 75 percent, some unofficial estimates are in the range of half a million. In New York and New Jersey, the presence of Mexican workers in area restaurants, delis, bars, hotels, factories, and construction sites and as day laborers on the streets is visible on a daily basis. It is in these service industry jobs that the majority remain undocumented and, as a result, are often made to work long hours every week (Smith 1996: 74–75). Recently the Pew Hispanic Center reported that 95 percent of Mexican men in New York illegally were in the workforce.[2] In contrast to the deep-rooted Chicano and Mexican American populations in the West Coast and Southwest, New York–area Mexicans are relatively marginalized, exerting little impact on local sociopolitical structures and leading a relatively precarious economic existence due to the undocumented status of a large majority of the population. Two-thirds of the community's immigrants are from the region inhabited primarily by Mixtec Indians of Mexico, which includes the states of Puebla, Oaxaca, and Guerrero.[3] Most come from rural villages and towns in Puebla, such as Santa Isabel de Cholula (a rural municipality of Cholula), Piaxtla, Chinantla, Tulcingo del Valle, Tehauacan, and Atlíxco (Smith 2005: 15–17).

Many Mexican immigrants are men between sixteen and twenty-five who, during their first trip to the United States, typically remain stateside several years before returning home to visit. Newcomers to the sonidero bailes in the past decade are women and second-generation Mexican youth. My own conversations with the young immigrants revealed that many were sent by their families to work in the United States. Despite the difficulty of traveling to their homeland, many of them, like those on the West Coast studied by Rouse (1991: 18–20), remain in close touch with their relatives in Mexico and are often involved in family and business decisions. Depending on the economic status of his family, the young Mexican male often sends more than half of his earnings home and takes responsibility for helping other members of his extended family who choose to come to the city.[4] For most of these immigrants, Mexico is not simply an ancestral homeland to be regarded with nostalgia but a site in which they continue to be emotionally and economically invested. Rouse suggests that the expansion of international capital (in both the United States and Mexico) has allowed for a widening of the international border and the eruption of miniature borders throughout the country. David Gutiérrez takes this idea further by observing that "the influx of immigrants in recent years has expanded the ethnic infrastructure of jobs, communication, entertainment, and local cultural practices in the United States to the extent that, in many ways, Mexicans can now live in the United States as if it were simply a more prosperous extension of Mexico" (1998: 322). Their lives and future possibilities involve simultaneous engagements in locations that are associated with different experiences, cultures, and political systems.

Sonidero Bailes: Creating a New Social Space

For the many young migrants who reside in the New York region, the Catholic Church traditionally has provided the primary social space for community gatherings and maintaining social practices and customs. However, as this community has grown, Gutiérrez (1998: 317) describes what he calls "alternative social networks" that have begun to appear within local communities as they become more adapted to life away from Mexico. Organized social dances are an important way to examine how marginalized immigrant communities can transform the cultural landscape in this country and how they also affect communities back in Mexico. In the case of New York and New Jersey, Mexican sonidero bailes (deejay dances) are held most weekends in clubs, restaurants, community centers, and bingo halls in Queens and Brooklyn and in New Jersey towns with large Mexican populations like Paterson and Passaic. What the sonidero bailes in the urban neighborhoods of Mexico City and the small villages and towns in Puebla have in common with Mexican communities in New York and New Jersey is that they reflect distinct examples of both local and transnational networks that are a means to examine how marginalized communities can transform the social and cultural landscape in both countries. Whether in the streets of marginalized Mexico City neighborhoods like Peñon de los Barrios and Tepito or the sprawling market of La Merced, in rural municipalities like Santa Isabel de Cholula in Puebla, or in clandestine clubs, restaurants, and bingo halls in New York and New Jersey, the creation, production, and dissemination of music is tied almost exclusively to local neighborhoods and social networks on both sides of the border. Yet it is the sonidero who connects them all in the baile space.

The focus at these dances is the *sonido*, or sound system, of which there may be five or more set up at any given dance, with each sonidero performing roughly thirty-minute sets in a round-robin style. Thus, for example, in the Bingo Hall in Paterson, a popular baile location in New Jersey, the sonidos are typically positioned in a circle around the dance floor. The hall is decorated as it would be for a birthday party or wedding reception, with red, white, and green balloons tied to the tables and backs of chairs, streamers hanging from light fixtures, and a glittering disco ball suspended above the dance floor. Many of the sonideros will have erected their own banners, creatively designed with their stage name, logo, and visual image. At this event, as at most Mexican bailes, police officers are stationed at the front door to pat down attendees and discourage loitering. However, in Mexico City bailes tend to occur in public venues such as parking garages, plazas, and markets and in Poblano villages they are held in church yards, neighborhood streets, and plazas. In Mexico City sonidero bailes took to the streets in the mid-1980s (though pioneering deejays such as Arco Iris and Sonoramico were at neighborhood parties in the 1990s), where deejays simultaneously mediated between rival gangs and represented their home turf in late-night sonic battles. In New York and New Jersey, sonidero bailes occur somewhat under the radar of the general public and are viewed by attendees as opportunities to express personal desires as well as to connect to a Mexican identity and culture, though with caution.

On both sides of the border sonideros are responsible not only for the music but also for many other aspects of the event. At times, they are the organizers and promoters of the dances themselves, and they also provide the elaborate and colorful lighting systems and obligatory smoke machines. The sonidero, who is typically male, is recognized for his voiced personality, which he manipulates with myriad processed tape loops, prerecorded samples, and sound effects (such as delays, reverb, echoes, and phase shifters). With his synthetically distorted voice and other effects, he achieves the desired sound: big, loud, and superhuman.

The sonidero takes great and, one might say, fetishistic pride in his technology and his ability to sonically transport his audience. In conversations with me, sonideros would often begin with detailed descriptions of their equipment and its cost and their ability to simultaneously jockey the various required elements in order to construct the desired sonic and sociomusical environment. Jacques Attali (1985: 103) has described the recording industry as one "of manipulation and promotion," where the recording is "only a minor part of the industry." However, in this case, the expressive power clearly resides with the individual who manipulates the recording (and the industry) in order to satisfy the demands of his own community or subculture for the reinterpretation and creation of new meanings and a new sense of place.

Having the proper music is, however, essential for a successful baile, and the favored genre is a uniquely Mexican substyle of the Colombian-derived cumbia. The sonidero must have on hand the latest cumbia hits by such groups as Los Angeles de Charley (Charley's Angels) or Los Socios del Ritmo (The Partners of Rhythm) along with other Mexican popular music genres heard on both sides of the border, such as *música duranguense* and *rock en español*.[5] However, in recent years they are more likely to play cumbias by bands that are not those typically heard on commercial Spanish-language radio in Mexico or the United States but instead are widely sold in open-air flea markets (*tianguis*) and by street vendors in Puebla and Mexico City, often alongside pirated CDs and DVDs, and in small record shops in New York and New Jersey. This brand of *cumbia sonidera* often features a rootsy, Colombian *vallenato*-style sound, based on accordion (or keyboards) and *guacharaca* scraper, often with distorted or electronically treated vocals and slowed down to produce a deep, bass voice that unintelligibly punctuates the repetitive four-beat cumbia rhythm (with its heavy emphasis on beat 1 and secondary accents on 3 and 4). This style of cumbia was initially dubbed by sonideros in the northeastern city of Monterrey as *cumbia rebajada* (slowed and pitched-down cumbia) and popularized across Latin America by the accordionist Celso Piña and the deejay Toy Selectah. Unlike mainstream commercial Mexican cumbias, these songs generally last much longer than the typical three-minute pop song. Although lyrics and CD covers often contain distinct references to the genre's Afro-Colombian origins, Mexican groups predominantly record the songs. Many of the sonideros I spoke with said that they look for cumbias that have an identifiable "tropical" or Afro-Colombian sound, but, they always insist, the songs are performed and recorded by Mexican groups.[6] However, since the mid-2000s, almost all of the songs chosen by sonideros are by groups located in the same towns and villages in Puebla that immigrants come from rather than Monterrey or Mexico City.

In 2005, on the morning after a baile in Santa Isabel de Cholula, I went to a flea market with the nineteen-year-old son of a popular Brooklyn-based sonidero named Fausto Salazar (aka Potencia Latina). We walked through stall after stall with stacks of CDs and DVDs of bailes that had occurred in the many nearby villages over the past few weeks. We located one vendor who had been instructed by Salazar to collect several new recordings (some made just a few days prior to our arrival) by local cumbia groups for his son to take back to Brooklyn for his father to review for his next show. Salazar's son insisted that the public in Puebla had not yet heard these songs and that Salazar might be the first to select and mix them in New York. Mexican immigrants at bailes in New York and New Jersey would anticipate these new recordings just as they would a long overdue call from home.

Sonideros and their listeners vehemently reject commercial Mexican cumbias, initially recorded in Monterrey, as being *naco*, a slang word describing something that is "tacky" and excessively commercial or a person who is uneducated and lacking style.[7] Though the naco cumbias are more likely to be played on Spanish-language radio, the sonidero-sponsored recordings are aggressively marketed in local shops and flea markets on both sides of the border. They can also be found on sonidero websites, and some have even made their way onto Amazon.com. However, these recordings and artists are popularized primarily by the sonideros, for it is the sonidero's own choice, as publicized in the baile, that validates certain cumbias as authentically tropical, uniquely local (from Puebla), danceable, and worthy of popular consumption. In fact these recordings feature the sonidero's logo and name on the CD cover rather than the name of the artist.

In addition to his collection of personalized and "authentic" songs, every sonidero has a stage name, logo, and boastful tagline that makes him recognizable as a personality. Nearly all of the logos — displayed on business cards, vans, jackets, and T-shirts — use some combination of the colors of the Mexican flag: green, red, and white (though other colors might account for the eagle and snake atop the *nopal*); several also include the stars and stripes of the American flag, the Statue of Liberty, or other iconic U.S. symbols. Also typical are "tropical" images such as palm trees, coconuts, the sun, the beach, and bikini-clad black and dark-skinned women. These images are, in part, an "exotic" representation of Mexico (and Latin America) celebrated in the U.S. media, but they are also a way of authenticating the Afro-Colombian roots of the cumbia rhythm, which is at the heart of the music collected by sonideros (initially from Colombia and now created almost exclusively by Mexican groups).[8] This is not unlike the way sonideros in Mexico City and Puebla represent themselves, many of whom also publicly identify with specific barrios in Mexico City like Tepito or specific towns in Puebla, just as sonideros in New York and New Jersey identify themselves by local enclaves such as Jackson Heights in Queens and Sunset Park in Brooklyn or small, largely Mexican-dominated towns like Paterson and Passaic.

Sonic Travel and "El Disco Mobile"

While the cumbias favored in sonidero bailes are in their own way specialized, what is most distinctive and unique about the bailes is their social structuring. At the baile, the sonidero creates what Rouse (1991) has characterized as a sociospatial environment, acting as the voice of a displaced community whose emotions and attentions are constantly shifting between a fragmented reality of *here* and *there*, in this case, the United States, Mexico, and the pan-

Latino community in New York. The sonidero acts as a virtual navigator of the sound experience at the baile as well as the authoritative voice of the baile's distinct cumbia genre. He also encourages and mediates the involvement of the individual dance participants, who share in the creation of this diasporic public sphere, as the following description of a dance at a bingo hall in Paterson, New Jersey, illustrates.

The sonidero begins his set with a five-minute (or longer) largely taped prologue to the dance. His introduction is a sound collage comprising samples from radio advertisements and announcements, in English and Spanish, and musical excerpts, many of which are English-language popular hip-hop, house, and techno-pop dance songs. After the prologue, the sonidero segues into *la presentación*, which begins with a countdown to "liftoff" given in English (i.e., "Five, four, three . . .") and accompanied by "space travel" sounds and pronouncements about being transmitted to another place. The sonidero, in this case Potencia Latina (Latin Power), reminds attendees at the baile that the "disco mobile" (the mobile disco of the sonidero) is always "ready for travel." Frequently reiterating his stage name, he boasts of his powerful system and unique music selection: "la señal más potente" (the most powerful signal) or "música electrónica inteligente" (intelligent electronic music); throughout he reiterates his boastful tagline, such as "la máxima autoridad del sonido" (the maximum authority of the sound system) or "el destructor de leyendas" (the destroyer of legends). The presentation continues with more commentary about the authenticity of his musical selection and the sheer volume and power of his sonido. Echoes, phase shifters, and other effects alter his voice synthetically, producing that low-bass, slurred effect that makes many of his words nearly unintelligible. This nevertheless constitutes the trademark of his own recognizable sound, and each sonidero who performs after him constructs his own variation of this vocal sound and technique. He often repeats his stage name while welcoming and thanking other sonideros who are also performing at the dance. Some of the more popular sonideros are Caluda, Kumbala, Magia (Magic), Fantasma (Ghost), and Master. Fantasma and Master are sonideros from Puebla who often travel to New York and New Jersey to perform. In fact most of the larger sonidero productions that occur on the weekend and include five or more deejays often feature a guest sonidero who is from Puebla or Mexico City. In recent years, sonidero dances have included cumbia sonidera groups who also travel from Puebla to perform. There are a handful of such groups in New York and New Jersey, but the overwhelming preference is for the groups from Puebla.

In Mexico City and Puebla, bailes are often held outdoors in village plazas or urban neighborhoods or, in at least one instance that I observed in Cholula, Puebla, a church yard. Such bailes in New York and New Jersey would never occur in open-air public settings, partly because of concerns among local law enforcement about gang violence and among immigrants themselves, many of whom are eager to conceal their undocumented status. In some of the bailes I attended in Puebla, however, the sonidero, the sound system, and the promotion of the event were often paid for by a social organization of Mexican immigrants from that particular village located in New York or New Jersey. At one such event, a boys' club made up of fans of Fantasma (aka Cesar Juarez) whose ages ranged from thirteen to eighteen were hired by him to promote the event and to act as crowd control and security guards during the baile. Individuals of all ages and families attended this baile. (Bailes in the United States are predominantly youth dances.) As in the United States, these bailes occur on weekends, with larger events featuring several sonideros on religious holidays such as Christmas and Semana Santa (Easter) and celebrations honoring the patron saint of a village. In my conversation with Juarez (Fantasma) that evening, he explained that many of the larger events not only offer immigrants a means for maintaining ties to their families and friends but they also provide economic opportunities for the local community as a whole: "The people in New York who pay for these dances are not necessarily making a lot of money themselves, but they know they are better off than many people in their hometown so they feel obligated to contribute to make this happen. Plus, lots of young people are hired to do the promotion, help with sound and move equipment. Then there is all of the food and drink that is sold here by the mothers and grandmothers. Many families benefit financially from these bailes."

Back at the Bingo Hall in Paterson, during the presentation portion of the baile, most of the attendees are standing in a circle around the dance floor, waiting for the dance to start. Most focus on the sonidero, who is positioned behind his stacked sound system, standing completely out of view of the audience while turning knobs, changing CDs, pumping smoke onto the dance floor, and manipulating and adjusting lights while greeting and guiding his listeners, thus bringing to mind the affected voice of a superhuman Wizard of Oz, secretly operated behind a curtain by a very ordinary and human deejay prototype. Always visible, however, is the sonidero's crew, generally consisting of four or five younger men who assist him during performances. The presentation continues while the smoke envelops the dance floor and the dancers in a giant cloud. The effects and sounds transport them to another place that is part fantasy and part irony, as is particularly evident when the presentation ends with the thunderous sound of a spaceship landing and the *swoosh* of electronic doors sliding open.

After the "landing," the sonidero's voice becomes more audible and less distorted by effects. In place of the English-language techno and hip-hop that dominated the presentation and liftoff portion, we now hear a selection of Latin music styles, such as *salsa*, *bachata*, and *merengue*, but still not the cumbias people have come to dance to. The sonidero then directly addresses the audience. He welcomes the dancers to New York, New Jersey, and the bingo hall, and seconds later he also welcomes them to Mexico ("Bienvenidos a Mexico, bienvenidos a New Jersey"). When the sonidero plays the first cumbia the dancing actually begins. At this point, there is a feeling is that the baile locale has shifted closer to Mexico, but as the evening progresses, and through the sonidero's dialogue, there is also an affective shift back to the New York and New Jersey as the imagination becomes further imbedded in the reality of the collective experience of the dancers and sonideros. To borrow terminology from the ethnomusicologist Thomas Turino (2008: 26–27), the sonidero performance shifts from a scripted presentation mode to "participatory performance," at which time the sonidero acts as a facilitator for both dancers and those hoping to send shout-outs, salutations, and dedications to loved ones in Mexico. It is the participatory performance that is the most important feature of the sonidero baile. As Turino notes, the "primary attention is on the activity, on *the doing* and on the other participants, rather than on an end product" of a single performance (28).

Communication, Mediation, and Performance: The Complex World of the Sonidero

While other Mexican, American, and Latino popular music genres are present, cumbias constitute the core of the participatory performance of the dance. Rather than simply playing songs, the sonidero continues to speak through the microphone over the music. He boasts about the power of his sonido, reiterating his stage name, welcoming the other sonidos on the evening's bill, and acknowledging the local promoters of the show and the audience members he knows personally. He also might comment on the song's title or lyrics or, if relevant, the special day or event that is being honored, such as the Battle of Puebla (Cinco de Mayo, May 5) or el Día de la Virgen (Day of the Virgin of Guadalupe, December 12).

As the baile progresses, the sonidero's most important and clearly more taxing job is to read into the microphone the personal dedications and salutations that members of the audience and dancers are now giving to him, through his crew members, in great numbers. Attendees write the dedications on napkins, scraps of notebook paper, on the back of miniature playbills for future dance events, or whatever is handy. As more of these come in, there is less improvised banter by the sonidero. While he changes CDs, sets up recorded tapes, and manipulates effects and lights, he must also read these messages with creative flair, personality, and conviction, serving as a mediator, a ventriloquist of sorts, who articulates the thoughts and emotions of this community. The sonidero never changes any of the words that are written down and does not comment on what he has read. At dances in Puebla, attendees also request shout-outs and dedications. Many also construct large posters and signs with messages to their favorite sonidero or to someone living in New York (also featuring similar logos and icons from both sides of the border). These will be seen in DVDs that will be sold the next morning in the flea market and uploaded on the Internet for loved ones living in the United States.

At the end of the set in New Jersey, the sonidero's crew members begin the high-speed duplicating of CDs for the individuals who just had their salutations and dedications read aloud. The CDs contain the entire set (roughly thirty minutes for each sonidero), which usually consists of the prologue and presentation portion (with its liftoff and landing) and three to four cumbias, with the sonidero's banter and dedication-reading. They are also sold the next day in local shops with the baile date and place clearly marked on the jacket (as they are in the flea markets in Puebla). Also available in the stores are DVDs of the baile, featuring the distinctive dancing style noted for its continuous turns and for being unique to the local Poblano community. Significantly these CDs are not purchased for private listening at home or work; instead the young dancers might send them to Mexico or to relatives and friends living in other parts of the United States and for whom the salutations and dedications are written, or they might post them on YouTube or send them via email. It is important to note that in recent years, baile attendees have increasingly included second-generation, U.S.-born Mexican youth who come to the dances to "be Mexican." The birthrate among Mexican immigrant women has been the highest in the United States, with a 232 percent increase in births to Mexican women during the 1990s, and these American-born youth are coming of age and affecting the social dynamic of the baile. More than a sonic trip home, the sonidero baile is a decidedly Mexican space in a world where it is much easier to move between identities, nationalities, and realities. For many of them, this *is* Mexico. The sonidero remains very much the mediator of these realities and of a larger, more inclusive Mexican diaspora. A once popular sonidero living in Passaic, New Jersey, Angel Lezama (aka Orgullosito), described his role to me: "As a sonidero, you must capture the sentiment of the dedication and who it is being sent to. You are helping that person create an imagination, an image, something very special that will be sent to a family member or friend who is living somewhere else, maybe in Mexico, or someone that you want to get to know that is at the dance. They are all possible."

Lezama's own definition clearly indicates that these dances are not about nostalgia, or even the idea of simply returning to Mexico. Rather they evoke a newly constructed landscape of social life in New York that is built on a shifting of location, sounds, and images in which the Mexican immigrant youth lives and creates his own cultural and personal reality. Many of the salutations and dedications that Lezama, Salazar, Juarez, and other sonideros deliver are written in a loosely poetic, though fragmented style with varying degrees of effort to rhyme and utilize creative imagery. Many dedicate songs to girlfriends, friends, gang members,[9] neighbors, parents, other relatives, and the sonidero himself. Others simply want to acknowledge their presence at the dance, often naming the sonidero and stating that the individual is there, "presente," with the sonidero, "cien por ciento" (100 percent). There is usually mention of the individual's current home borough (Queens, Bronx, Brooklyn) or town (Passaic, Paterson, Union City) as well as the state and town in Mexico the person is originally from, such as Atlixco or Chalchiupan in Puebla. Sometimes these locations are deliberately jumbled, for example, "Puebla, New York" or "Brooklyn, Mexico." Mention may also be made of other cities in the United States such as Los Angeles, Chicago, and Las Vegas where friends and relatives are living and working. In Mexico, salutations are also written, recorded, and sent to the United States by parents, cousins, girlfriends, neighbors, and high school friends, which allows for a constant dialogue between individuals through the context of the baile experience and facilitated by the sonidero.

The sonidero's ability to travel to and from Mexico for performances helps keep Mexico alive in the immigrants' collective imagination. This sensation is enhanced by the physical presence of the sonidero, who acts as a conduit for communication between individuals on both sides of the border. He recognizes the validation of this experience and the authentication of this reality as a crucial aspect of his role. The sonidero is thus more than a mere messenger of dedications and salutations; his presence at dances and his travel between countries also enable his audiences to imagine themselves "presente, cien por ciento." As Salazar told me,

> When I am performing in Mexico, people often end their salutations and dedications with "presente, cien por ciento." That is to say, that they are here, with me, completely. Since I have traveled from New York, it is important for many people who have family and friends in the U.S. to send their dedications and salutations through me and say that they are with me. Also, in the U.S. it is the same for a sonidero who travels from Mexico to perform. They will want to be "presente" with him too. It is like you are "there" in Mexico, or with me you are "here" in New York. It also refers to being 100 percent Mexican, the music, the people, the place. You know, this is the music of our people and our heritage.

"It's just a way of transmitting a message," said another deejay, Francisco Flores, aka Sonido Candela, who is based in New Jersey and celebrated his sixteenth anniversary as a sonidero at a baile in 2011 in a rented Korean banquet hall in Flushing, Queens. "It's a way of saying, 'I'm here, I'm having fun, I'm doing well, and I'm sending you a greeting from over here.'"

The dedications and salutations presented below were collected at one of the bingo hall dances. Notice the references to location, such as Los Angeles and Chalchiupan, and placing Puebla in New York. Also of note are the colloquial expressions and references to the Mexican cactus (maguey) and mesquite plant, both powerful symbols of rural Mexico and Mexican identity. The dance styles—cumbia, salsa, and *danzón*—each originated in other Latin American locations (Colombia, Cuba, Puerto Rico, New York), but have become Mexicanized over time and have been adopted as Mexican popular music styles, particularly in the case of danzón and cumbia. Finally, many shout-outs and dedications praise the sonidero who is delivering the message.

Cumbia, Salsa y Danzón,	Cumbia, salsa, and danzón,
Lizbet te quiero	Lisbeth I love you
con todo mi corazón	with all my heart
Hasta Los Angeles, California	All the way to Los Angeles, California
De parte de Victor	from Victor
Cien por ciento Fantasma	One hundred percent [with] Fantasma

Espinas de mezquite	Thorns of the mesquite [tree]
espinas de maguey	thorns of the maguey [Mexican cactus]
Potencia Latina	Latin Power [sonidero]
la pura ley	the absolute law
Att: El Flaco y el amor	Att: "The Skinny" and the love
de su vida, Marta	of his life, Martha
Entre calaveras y esqueletos	Between skulls and skeletons
cuando llegan los primos	when the cousins [friends] arrive
e inquitos [sic] todos	and everything is a mess
se quedan vien quitos [sic]	they make it all right again
diavólicos sienporsiento [sic]	diabolical one-hundred percent
Primos: El Cholo, El Malaber,	Cousins: The Halfbreed, The Juggler,
El Ardilla, El Catrín, El Gato	The Squirrel, The Dude, The Cat
Puebla, Nueva York	Puebla, New York
yo estoy con el mejor	I am here with the best
el más chingón	the most "badass"
chabelo toño sagrado	the "guy" with the sacred sound
Fausto nacho polo	Fausto "nacho polo"
Puebla, Chalchiupan	Puebla, Chalchiupan
Puebla de los ángeles	Town of the angels

La máxima autoridad: The Sonidero as Archetype

As mediators of the baile experience, the sonideros use technology to assert *la máxima autoridad*, the maximum authority. Their electronically manipulated voices are painfully loud, garbled, low-pitched, and distorted. They call attention to themselves and the power they can assert, much like the border-blaster deejays on the Mexican side of the border with Texas during the early days of radio, who would overpower American radio stations and penetrate the United States as far north as Chicago and Washington's Yakima Valley. The sonidero at once authenticates and disrupts the cumbias he plays, perpetually talking over and electronically manipulating them. Yet despite his self-constructed image of power and authority, he remains respectful of the audiences and their dedications. In reading the salutations, he never interjects his own words or merely paraphrases the messages; he faithfully reads them as they are written. His popularity, as well as the success of the cumbias he chooses to play, derives not from the dominant commercial vehicle of radio and record sales but from his role as messenger, as authority, within the community of Mexican youth and from the sheer power of his sound system.

His community, whether in Mexico or the United States, trusts and respects the sonidero because, like them, he has also traveled and experienced the displacement, marginality, and ambiguity of the migrant experience. I learned that many of the sonideros I interviewed are or at one time had been undocumented. Prior to the September 11 attacks in New York, many sonideros traveled to perform at bailes with fake passports; now only those who can legally travel do so. This has opened the door for younger, up-and-coming sonideros, many of whom were born in the United States. However, the inability to travel has not deterred immigrant sonideros, as the Internet and social networking have made it easier for them to remain connected through live streaming, YouTube, and websites with sources and groups in Puebla and other parts of Mexico. Still, it is the mystery that surrounds the sonidero and his own experience of travel to the United States (or *la aventura*, as it is called by many) that continues to intrigue and link the baile attendee and the sonidero. The search for work has brought both the itinerant worker and the sonidero to oscillate between New York, Los Angeles, Chicago, Texas, Tijuana, Mexico City, and Puebla. The sonic experience they create together becomes a dramatization of that life, with its personal and collective history of living and traveling between two countries with complex and always changing political and social relations. The baile and the sonidero's role allow these Mexican migrants to metaphorically travel to Mexico, as Salazar put it. Through imagination, improvisation, and the constant real and imagined shifting of locales — of either here (*aquí*) or there (*alla*) — these young people are also learning to exist and thrive in the constantly fluid world of global America.

Conclusion

The sonidero bailes invite a variety of interpretive perspectives. At one level, they present yet another idiosyncratic fusion of tradition and modernity, in which the roots-oriented sounds of a rural vallenato-style cumbia has been transformed into a genre distinctly Mexican and is combined with the sonidero's space-age sound effects. The creative appropriation and cultivation of the Colombian cumbia to suit a specifically Mexican sensibility is another phenomenon with many parallels worldwide, and is worthy of further study in itself. The baile can also be seen as a variant of deejay culture, in which the deejay, in place of a live band, becomes the focus of a music and dance scene. The sonidero, of course, is a unique sort of deejay, who serves simultaneously as entertainer, as a vehicle for communication between distant parties, and, ideally, as a quasi-heroic figure who travels the same international migrant paths as his audience, albeit as a figure who is at once empowered and empathic.

Ultimately, however, the most distinctive features of the sonidero baile are not the specific music genre but the unique performance format and audience participation. The notion that everyone at the dance can participate in the shaping of the sound and the motion, whether dancing or writing salutations, is uniquely connected to this social experience that can also be shared transnationally. In effect, the music itself need not be overtly syncretic in character, since the sense of transnationality so essential to the event is achieved and dramatized by other means—especially the role of the sonidero and the innovative use of technologies and media. It has become commonplace to observe that diasporic music events frequently invoke memories of the homeland, particularly through renderings of specific music genres. At the same time, technologies have come to be used in various ways by transnational communities, which combine tracks recorded on separate continents, distribute the recordings in several sites, and sonically invoke both ancestral and new homelands that are now linked in new ways. The sonidero phenomenon can be seen as a strikingly original example of these sorts of practices—in this case incorporating music recordings, microphones, synthesized sound effects, CDs, handwritten dedications, and ultimately the postal system and the Internet. Just as the salutations and dedications are delivered from the United States to Mexico and vice versa, DVDs of the Puebla bailes are sent to family members and organization members that are able to share in the more public baile space in Mexico, thus erasing the notion of self-expression behind closed doors. In a sense a virtual neighborhood is created and expanded across the border through the baile experience in both locales, allowing the community to remain connected and current.

Those attending sonidero bailes in the United States, having varying degrees of actual memories of Mexico, develop a new sense of personal and national history, both imagined and real, based upon Mexican and American myths, their own experiences, and those of relatives and friends. Caren Kaplan (1996) points out the distinctive notion of memory among displaced communities, referring to the fragmented mental images these individuals still maintain about their home, along with those absorbed from the host society, which allow them to create a new history and a new identity. This is particularly true among the second-generation youth, many of whom have never traveled to Mexico, perhaps because one or both parents are undocumented. Sonidero bailes accommodate, dramatize, and legitimize this sort of ambiguous existence, memories, and constructed notions of Mexican life and identity, with their sense of presence and absence and their simultaneous investments in both the United States and Mexico. Baile attendees are able to imagine the presence of those who are physically absent and to participate in that exchange. They can speak to their absent loved ones and bring them into the local public space, while also addressing those at the dance who overhear the dialogue. In the case of the bailes in Puebla, Mexicans living in the United States can also participate simply by making the event possible. Together, they disrupt not only cumbias but also borders, displacement, and marginality and enable a flow of expressive culture and capital while circumventing the mainstream political economy of music and global markets in order to allow for individual and community-based creativity in accordance with their own sensibilities, desires, and experiences.

This shifting could be seen to exemplify the concept of the movable or expandable borders and the new space of the migratory homeland described by Américo Paredes (1993: 46–47) in his writings about Texas-Mexican border culture and folklore. Even more applicable to the sonidero world is Fredric Jameson's (1988) notion of "postmodern hyperspace," where there are no boundaries between Mexican and American culture. In order to locate oneself in this new space, a new set of images, new coordinates, and a series of more effective maps must be developed. Those attending sonidero dances are not only redrawing these maps but are metaphorically traveling on them, retracing the migration route many of them actually took to get here.

Last, and perhaps most overtly, the sonidero dances represent one more example of how communities and subcultures on both sides of the border are able to exploit features of a commercial music industry to create their own expressive events in accordance with their own sensibilities and desires. The collaborative construction of a unique sonic environment by the sonidero and those writing dedications metaphorically addresses and ennobles the needs, desires, and creative fantasies about the community's future in their new homeland. It bypasses the mainstream political economy of music, with its dominant patterns of music industry ownership and dissemination. The sound environment created by the sonidero, along with the salutations and dedications provided by the young dancers, can be seen as an example of Jacques Attali's (1985: 87) "future order," where the "noise" created by individuals represents the subversion of the stockpiling, commercialization, and corporate control of music. It is the noise of a community that is determined to maintain family and community cohesion despite being geographically scattered, socially marginalized, and politically powerless. The sonidero offers an opportunity for these individuals to feel at home and be heard, a place to share their experience with those physically present in the minds of the dancers themselves. Finally, these dances are a place for Mexican youth to socialize, to express a shared identity as Mexicans and Americans, and with the benefit of cutting-edge technology.

Notes

This chapter is an updated version of an article that appeared in the journal *Ethnomusicology* 47.3 (2003): 338–54.

1. *Technobrega* (cheesy techno) is a popular music genre created by deejays and producers by sampling, remixing, and reworking mostly American pop music from the 1980s. Its unusual distribution methods—street vendors manufacture, sell, and advertise the music—is featured in the Danish documentary *Good Copy, Bad Copy*. The documentary can be viewed in its entirety at http://www.goodcopybadcopy.net/.

2. See Pew Hispanic Center, "Unauthorized Immigrant Population: National and State Trends, 2010," February 2011, http://pewhispanic.org/files/reports/133.pdf.

3. In recent years, New York and New Jersey have seen a greater increase of immigrants from Mexico City (particularly from an impoverished settlement on the road to Puebla called Ciudad Nezahualcóyotl, nicknamed "Neza York," which has grown due to funds sent by Mexican workers in New York).

4. As one young man who had been living in New York for over eight years told me, "Where I am from, when you turn sixteen you are ready to go to the U.S. You are considered to be an adult and you are obligated to work and send money back home. You must do what you can to help your family."

5. *Música duranguense* is a popular music genre that grew out of a blending of popular brass bands called *banda* and the accordion-based *norteña* style among Chicago's Mexican immigrant population during the mid-1990s. It is now a sensation on both sides of the border. *Rock en español* is Spanish-language rock music that emerged in Latin American countries, particularly Argentina and Mexico, in the late 1950s.

6. This situation recalls the case of the picó deejays in Cartagena, Colombia, researched by Deborah Pacini Hernandez, but with a twist. Afro-Colombian picó deejays play early Afro-pop recordings, which have been renamed and redefined according to local aesthetics and conventions. The picó deejay extols the music's African

roots, foregrounding a local view of the community's African heritage as mediated by his stockpile of recordings.

7. *Naco* is a term often used by youth from Mexico City to describe a "hillbilly" from the northern region of Mexico (primarily states bordering the United States). The phrase *naco norteño* refers to a popular but less sophisticated accordion-based dance music (featuring the cumbia rhythm), also associated with the relatively rural border region.

8. Early sonideros such as Sonorámico and Arcoiris, who performed in Mexican barrios like Tepito, told me that they actually traveled to Colombia to search for obscure and classic vinyl recordings of cumbia to introduce to their growing legions of fans. These dances happened almost spontaneously and were typically held in the street, often continuing until the early morning. Today the Mexican government has strictly limited the number of outdoor bailes that each barrio may sponsor. See the collaborative website of researchers, scholars, sonideros, and fans, http://elproyectosonidero.wordpress.com/about/, for more information on the history of sonideros in Mexico City.

9. Though most sonideros deny any connection to gangs, they admit to reading boastful messages and shout-outs between members and groups. Some sonidero dances, mainly in Brooklyn and the Bronx, have been disrupted in the past by fights between alleged gang members. However, the police are a visible presence at most sonidero dances (even at the bingo hall in Paterson, which gang members are not known to attend).

JOSHUA TUCKER

6.
From *The World of the Poor* to the Beaches of Eisha
Chicha, Cumbia, and the Search for a Popular Subject in Peru

In 2006 a Peruvian television network scored a ratings hit with a miniseries based on the life and music of the singer Lorenzo Palacios Quispe, better known by the stage name that he adopted in the 1970s: Chacalón (Big Jackal). A pioneer in the *cumbia*-based style known as *chicha*, Chacalón fronted the band La Nueva Crema (The New Cream) from the late 1970s until his death in 1994. During chicha's heyday in the 1980s, his ability to convoke massive audiences drawn from Lima's Andean migrant community was legendary, a quality reflected in the slogan used to promote his performances: "Cuando canta Chacalón, bajan los cerros" (When Chacalón sings, the mountains come down). The son of migrant proletarians, a grade school dropout who had survived by working odd jobs in Lima's massive informal marketplace, succeeding by dint of effort and faith, Chacalón incarnated the archetypal protagonist of chicha lyrics. Invariably a member of Peru's marginalized Andean majority, fighting to get ahead within an opportunity structure that favored Lima's white minority, this figure was drawn largely from life, a life familiar to both Chacalón and his audience. The singer's story differed from theirs mainly by virtue of its denouement into popular acclaim. Despite his celebrity he remained closely identified with El Agustín, the rough neighborhood that had witnessed his birth, his success, and his death. When he died of heart failure and subsequent medical inattention, over twenty thousand fans reportedly attended his burial, beginning the transformation of Peru's "faraón de la cumbia" (pharaoh of cumbia) into a near-mythic emblem of subaltern triumph.

The success of the series *Chacalón: El ángel del pueblo*, whose plot interleaved the artist's biography with tales of contemporary urban life, suggested the continuing resonance of his narrative. It also seemed to vindicate a musical style that had been shunned by Lima's polite society, retaining an aura of seedy disrepute despite its popular success. And as a sign of renewed interest in local cumbia music, it was only one part of a much broader trend toward a serious recognition of the genre's place in Peruvian society. A number of scholarly articles had already explored the relation between chicha and its descendant, *tecno-cumbia*, which flourished between roughly 1998 and 2002 (Bailón 2004; Quispe Lázaro 2000, 2002; Romero 2002; Salcedo 2000). By 2007 Peru's national library had hosted a cycle of conferences on hybrid popular culture entitled "Lo cholo en el Perú" (roughly, "Indigenous and Mestizo Popular Culture in Peru"), in which the tecno-cumbia stars Agua Bella were invited speakers. The same year saw a revival of early Peruvian cumbia led by younger performers such as the rock band Bareto, rebranded as "psychedelic cumbia." Joining stars of the late 1960s and early 1970s, such as Los Destellos and Juaneco y su Combo, they brought the music to such centers of hipster cool as Lima's Botero Bar. This revival even took on a transnational dimension, with New York's Barbès Records releasing two CDs devoted to early Amazonian cumbia, one a compilation entitled *Roots of Chicha: Psychedelic Cumbias from Peru* (2007) and the other featuring the American band Chicha Libre (*Sonido Amazónico!*, 2008).[1] Finally, 2007–8 also saw a boom in contemporary cumbia from Peru's north coast, driven by bands like Grupo 5 and Los Caribeños, whose sound is heavily inflected by the sounds of *salsa* music. This latest style, attended by a self-conscious assertion of collective ownership, saturated the airwaves alongside admonitions to valorize "nuestra cumbia" (our cumbia) and was widely perceived to consolidate cumbia as a music of national scope and significance.

Together these trends are testament to the variegated nature of Peruvian cumbia and to its deep-rooted place within Peruvian life. And yet, with some notable exceptions (see Romero 2002, 2007), the existing literature on Peruvian cumbia is overwhelmingly devoted to the variant most commonly denoted as chicha, and in particular to its maximum exponents, Los Shapis del Perú. This focus derives in part from the group's highly visible role during the chicha moment of the 1980s, when they became the style's most recognizable public face. It also derives from the way that the music of Los Shapis seemed to emblematize certain academic theories of the era, especially those relating to Andean migration and social change in Lima. However, it has hindered a complete understanding of Peruvian cumbia as a musical style, and it has limited an effective understanding of what, precisely, chicha represented, as one stylistic moment within its history.

This chapter outlines the development of both Peruvian cumbia and academic commentary about chicha. Throughout, I demonstrate how changing musical sounds and notions of social legitimacy evolved in public discussions that drew in academic analysts, artists, mediators, popular commentators, and listeners. This network helped to establish a charged space of sociomusical discourse within Peru's overall public sphere, one that has recently become occupied once more by a broad-based discussion about cumbia music and its relation to social change within and beyond Lima. Against the background of this emergent discussion and cognizant of the analytical pitfalls that may attend it, the chapter has three main goals. The first is to explain why chicha became such a pervasive topic for academic commentators and also to suggest how the theoretical conclusions in this literature might be augmented by other viewpoints. The second, related goal is to highlight the contribution of cumbia artists besides Los Shapis, such as Chacalón, and thereby open possibilities for rethinking their place in Peruvian popular culture. Third, I briefly consider how contemporary developments in cumbia relate to the conclusions and predictions of earlier commentary, drawing upon the lessons furnished by the literature on chicha music to suggest how recent events both reflect and reshape their ideas. Overall my main objective is to suggest new avenues of investigation for scholars of music and popular culture within Peru.

Chicha Defined: Music as Metaphor and Detritus

Usually described as a blend of Colombian cumbia, Andean *huayno*, and rock music, during its heyday between the early 1980s and the mid-1990s chicha became a public touchstone for understanding Peruvian society.[2] Commentators analyzed its synthesis of Andean traditional and global cosmopolitan musics and its chronicling of migrant experience, finding in its ludic blend of distinct cultural registers a figure for the processes reshaping Peruvian society, particularly migration and its effects (see, e.g., Bullen 1993; Degregori 1984; Matos Mar 1984; Turino 1990). Since the middle of the twentieth century, indigenous and *mestizo* citizens from the underdeveloped Andes had flooded coastal Lima, erstwhile bastion of Peru's white *criollo* elite, reshaping the character of the capital. By the 1980s criollo hegemony seemed poised to recede before a demographic onslaught of "new limeños," second- and third-generation migrants perceived as culturally distinct from their rural Andean or urban criollo peers. Academics rushed to explore the particularities of migrant Lima, trying to understand this social sector in terms of shared values, practices, and worldview. Such studies often bore the stated or unstated assumption that this group augured a new, more just Peruvian society, one that would transcend the historic divide between the Andes and the coast (see, e.g., Franco 1991; Matos Mar 1984; Quijano 1980). In this context chicha music, a practice born of and for the "new Lima," became a site in which to observe the coalescing of a new popular subject, and therefore a key to the desires, mind-sets, and morals that would drive the future of the nation.

Viewed in light of such analyses, *Chacalón: El ángel del pueblo* might be seen as a belated bestowal of legitimacy upon chicha music and those associated with it. Any such evaluation, however, belies the continuing relegation of migrants and their manifestations to a lower tier of social respect and a continuing widespread disdain for those cumbia variants most closely identified with an "Andean" sound.[3] Perhaps the clearest sign of the stigma attached to chicha and its public is the way the genre's name has entered Peru's popular vocabulary: as a derisive term for migrant popular culture.[4] If intellectuals found in chicha a hopeful metaphor for the future, the middle classes by and large found a symbol of everything distasteful about a migrant sector they held responsible for the progressive decay of Lima. With state and civil actors unprepared or unwilling to accommodate its needs, migrant society had become defined by an improvisatory genius, a talent for working outside sanctioned channels to attain the employment, services, and goods necessary for life. Longtime residents thus watched with horror as Lima's infrastructure collapsed under the weight of the Andean influx, its streets filling with ambulatory venders and battered microbuses, unlovely shantytowns blooming in its desert outskirts. For many, the informal strategies behind these activities were not seen as mechanisms for survival in a precarious socioeconomic order but as evidence of an intrinsic lack of discernment and civic responsibility. This evaluation was in turn overdetermined by an entrenched racism that held Andean peoples incapable of fully adopting a modern subjectivity.

For many, chicha appeared to be a blend of found elements similar to that characterizing migrant life. Conflating aesthetics with the concrete realities of migrant existence, elite observers could not but read it as an inept attempt to imitate a musical modernity associated with more prestigious genres, a sonic equivalent of the makeshift qualities they decried in migrant Lima more generally. As used in contemporary Peru, the term *chicha* extends to other realms the kind of pejorative evaluations the musical style garnered in its early years: a derivative product of dubious origin, cobbled together from the unwanted detritus of local and foreign musics, born of the lumpen unlettered and thus graceless in its lyrics, sloppily constructed using substandard equipment, willfully ignorant of bourgeois aesthetic categories. Applied to residences, places of work and the products sold there, styles of dress, comportment, and cuisine, among other elements, the term is used mainly to disparage modes of behavior and material culture held to typify working-class Lima.[5] This usage even gave rise to a debate about which of Peru's cumbia-related styles and artists should properly be designated by the term. Many musicians whose careers predated it, particularly those from the coastal or Amazonian regions, strove to distinguish their music from chicha's acquired taint, preferring terms like *cumbia andina* or *música tropical andina*. In a similar vein, scholars have pointed to tecno-cumbia's self-conscious "de-Andeanization" as a contributing factor to its success in the late 1990s (see Romero 2002). Finally, the groups involved with the recent rise of northern cumbia have also seen fit to avoid the label, conspicuously classing up their music with terms such as *cumbia elegante*.

All of these rhetorical evasions call into question the extent to which the cultural manifestations identified with migrant Lima can be said to have attained a level of acceptance widely predicted a generation ago. Neither chicha music nor those associated with it attained the social capital promised during the boom of migrant scholarship in the 1980s. Even amid gains in economic might, migrant Lima "never generated a new bourgeoisie in Max Weber's terms, that is, not only people with money but also 'spiritual goods.' . . . [They have not become] a new guiding elite" (Neira 2004: 170).[6] Instead the coastal bourgeoisie retained its hegemony even while ceding select spaces for the expansion of migrant society, and contemporary Lima remains fragmented in terms of class and race.

There is a striking parallel between the literature on chicha and the broader literature on migrant society. Just as many scholars hoped that chicha's musical bricolage foreshadowed a peaceful revolution from below, a disproportionate number found promise in the black market and related strategies of migrant informality, seeing in them a protocapitalist ingenuity (see especially de Soto 1989). Of late, however, commentators have called for a reconsideration of such ideas (see, e.g., Degregori 2000a; Sandoval 2000). In an essay provocatively titled "Mesa Redonda and the Incineration of the

Social Sciences," alluding to the fire in 2001 that cost nearly three hundred lives in Lima's center of informal employment, the scholar Víctor Vich has challenged the premises that typified such works. Stating that the tragedy, which was traced to the unregulated sale of black market fireworks, "has challenged all those theories about 'popular society' and 'emergent modernity' that many of us have been proposing," Vich proposes a more cautious reading of Lima's working-class social formation, one that recognizes how it is shaped in and by conditions of profound inequality, replacing "the disproportionate glorification [*apología*] of the informal sector with a better understanding of its contradictions, practices, and politics" (2002: 105). In the spirit of this challenge, the remainder of this chapter applies a similar approach to cumbia music in late twentieth-century Peru.

Migration and Social Change in the Twentieth Century

Chicha music is both symbol and product of a historic transformation in Peruvian society that took place over the latter half of the twentieth century. Until that time, the national imagination had been divided along parallel lines of race, geography, and power established during the colonial period. In the sixteenth century, conquistadores and colonial administrators seized control of the Andean region, reducing most residents either to vassalage on Spanish landholdings or to nominally free subjects who faced fearsome tributary burdens. Spanish numbers within the Andes paled by comparison with the indigenous majority, however, and the capital was established not in the highlands but in the thin strip of coastal desert that separates the mountains from the sea. The Iberian center of gravity thus remained physically removed from the Andean region, and a colonial opposition between the lettered capital, seat of power and European cultural prestige, and an indigenous Andean hinterland, filled with unruly Indians targeted for tutelage and domination, became entrenched in perception. Never an accurate account of the colony's social relations, the separatism implied by this vision was continually traduced in practice. It was belied by indigenous peoples' early naturalization of European institutions and technologies, the emergence of a distinct mestizo sector, and the constant circulation of cultural elements among all of these groups. Nevertheless, from the viewpoint of Lima such fluidity was most often treated as evidence of the unsavory influence indigenous consociation could have on the weak-willed, and the notion of radical Andean alterity was largely an unquestioned truth. Meanwhile the eastern jungle lowlands, the third geographic entity within the Peruvian imagination, were barely inhabited until the twentieth century because of formidable barriers to settlement and resource extraction.

Neither did these patterns change with independence from Spain in 1824. If anything, they intensified, as landowners expanded Andean *haciendas* by dispossessing indigenous communities, and elites sought to shore up a nascent national identity rooted in the practices of Lima's European-descended criollos.[7] The exclusivity of the national project was emphasized in the late nineteenth century, when progress through industrial modernization became a guiding policy but resulted in patterns of investment that concentrated on Lima. With development benefiting the coastal milieu to the detriment of Andean landowners, most of the tiny highland elite fled to the capital, and in the postwar period a second economic expansion set in motion processes that would definitively blur Peru's ingrained lines of social demarcation. Continuing underdevelopment in the mountains and a coastal boom driven initially by the Korean War led increasing numbers of petit bourgeois mestizos and indigenous peasants to leave the Andes and seek opportunities in the capital. The dizzying pace of migration was clearly visible in Lima's census data, which saw the city increase from 145,172 residents in 1940, to 4,492,260 in 1981, of which 41 percent were migrants (Matos Mar 1984). Their arrival ended the exceptionalism of the city space. Violating the tenets of criollo teleology, according to which a Westernized minority would inevitably overcome and absorb a lamentable Andean majority, migrants did not usually seek to blend seamlessly into the social order that they found in Lima. Instead, even as they adopted some criollo lifeways and learned to finesse local legal and political structures, they recreated Andean social patterns and cultural practices within the capital, inundating the city with huayno music, patron saint fiestas, radio programs, and Andean cuisine. Commentators soon noticed, however, that such markers of Andean heritage were realized differently, adapted to the exigencies of city life, and incorporated elements from criollo or international sources. By the 1970s, with the emergence of a second and then a third generation of "Andean limeños," neither accepted as criollo nor entirely familiar with highland lifeways, progenitors of practices identified with neither of Peru's reified social blocs, "the new Lima" became a serious object of analysis.

Peruvian Cumbia: The Roots of Chicha

Chicha developed alongside this emergent popular class.[8] Its roots lie in the distinctly Peruvian versions of cumbia music that coalesced in the late 1960s. In the early part of that decade Colombian cumbia became popular throughout Peru, following earlier pan–Latin American successes such as *tango*, *ranchera*, *mambo*, and *bolero*. Eagerly assimilated by local performers and audiences, it generated different fusions in different regions of the country. By 1963 Los Pacharacos, a Central Andean group that performed huayno music, had begun playing their tunes over cumbia rhythms, using a traditional ensemble of saxophones and clarinets with harp or accordion accompaniment. They were quickly followed by groups such as Los Demonios del Mantaro, whose most outstanding contribution to the genre was its eventual title; according to most commentators, the term *chicha*, originally denoting an Andean corn beer, was drawn from their 1966 hit single, "La chichera" (The Chicha Seller).

Close on the heels of this cumbia andina, a different and ultimately more influential *costeña* (coastal) style emerged in Lima, pioneered by Enrique Delgado. The son of a *charango* player from the highlands, Delgado had performed in several different ensembles and in a wide variety of genres. He had played mandolin for the great huayno artist Pastorita Huaracina, and he had also dabbled in the *valses* considered emblematic of Lima's criollo society. By 1968 he was playing electric guitar in groups that performed *música tropical*, a term encompassing the many Caribbean genres that had been popularized by Peru's mass media. In that year, during a break in a performance, he tentatively essayed some solo tunes that he had created in the cumbia style. When the audience responded avidly, he was invited to release them through IEMPSA, Peru's foremost record label. Thus in 1968 the first recordings by the pioneering band Los Destellos hit the market, to great success. Under Delgado's leadership, this group fashioned a novel sound, largely retaining the melodic style and rhythmic feel of Colombian cumbia while adapting these elements to the instrumental format of a rock band, locally familiar since the late 1950s.[9] Two electric guitars, using distortion, reverb, delay, tremolo, wahwah, and other innovative effects as they became available, replaced brass and winds as lead instruments, and they quickly became the key sonic signifiers of Peruvian cumbia. Underneath their intertwining melodic lines, electric bass and percussion, usually including some combination of bongos, congas, *timbales*, cowbell, *güiro*, claves, and maracas, provided a rhythmic foundation.

Figure 6.1. "A Patricia" by Los Destellos: introduction (0:05–0:25) and *montuno* section (1:34–1:39).

Figure 6.1. Continued from previous page

The group's songwriting drew freely from the various traditions familiar to Delgado and his bandmates, recombining elements from all of them and adapting them to their instrumental format. The result was an adventitious juxtaposition of found objects from Lima's soundscape, usually arranged over a cumbia base. The distinctly Cuban sound of "El Avispón" (the B side of the group's first 45), the rock progressions that organized "Chachita," the use of the Andean warhorse "Valicha" (a huayno from Cuzco), and the laid-back cumbia rhythms on innumerable other tracks were synthesized in a way that was original and uniquely Peruvian. This distinctiveness is readily apparent in "A Patricia" (To Patricia), an instrumental number and one of their early hits (see figure 6.1).

In most ways, "A Patricia" is comparable to Colombian tunes of the same era. Performed at a medium tempo, the entire song relies on a harmonic template that alternates two chords, G minor and F major, over an interlocking foundation provided by the rhythm section. While the bass continuously outlines chord tones, leaving out the second note in each four-note grouping, bongos, timbales, guiro, cymbals, and cowbell play simple ostinatos that avoid the syncopated polyrhythm associated with other Latin American styles. Over this base, two overdriven electric guitars, one employing a wah-wah pedal, perform undulating, interwoven melodies, interacting in a call-and-response manner comparable to cumbia's brass and winds. If the melodies recall Colombian cumbia, however, the guitarists' delicate ornamentation recalls the playing style of Peruvian performers, in both Andean and criollo traditions. Periodically these melodies are punctuated by percussion breaks on timbales and cowbell, like those on the era's Colombian recordings. Finally, at 1:36, after the song's two primary melodic sections, a contrasting passage appears to reference Afro-Cuban principles of composition. Here the guitars switch to highly syncopated arpeggios, performing for several measures patterns that recall the piano *montunos* appearing in contemporary recordings of both *son montuno* and salsa.

If some listeners found this music derivative and uninspired, others diagnosed Peruvian cumbia as a resolutely local hybrid. Younger listeners, largely uninterested in such debates, quickly made the style their own. Thrilling to Los Destellos' modernist marriage of tropical dance music and effects-driven psychedelia, youths from across Lima's social divides united in musical consumption, flocking to live shows and driving the style up the charts in the early 1970s.[10] By then other bands had appeared, and groups like Los Ecos and Los Diablos Rojos became disciples of *cumbia costeña*. At the same time, a very similar style emerged from the Amazon, associated with artists such as Juaneco y su Combo and Los Mirlos. This *cumbia selvática* (jungle cumbia) was differentiated mainly by references to Amazonian customs in song lyrics and band members' attire. Though sharing a basic template, each of these groups created a unique sound, favoring different combinations of foreign elements, and the era's recordings integrate clear references to son, son montuno, *bugalú*, and other successful Latin American styles over a cumbia base. Groups from Peru's northern coast, many of which were also founded in this era, were a striking exception to this trend, a factor that may account for their relative anonymity at the national level before the 1990s. Instead, from the beginning their style appears to have hewn closely to Colombia's brass band format, which remained influential thanks to their play on radio stations in nearby Ecuador.

Cumbia into Chicha: Celebrating Community and Chronicling Marginality

At first Peruvian cumbia was publicly marked not as a subaltern phenomenon but as a youth movement, with appeal across Lima's diverse social spectrum. However, an increasing number of those involved in its performance and consumption were members of Lima's lower classes, and local scenes quickly cropped up throughout the city's migrant neighborhoods. Independent entrepreneurs moved in, seeking profits, and production largely moved to the informal sector. For if artists like Los Destellos had drawn upon personal connections to record for prestigious labels such as IEMPSA, other groups on the burgeoning scene had no access to such spaces. Small record companies, most notably the label Horóscopo, emerged to cater to artists of lesser pedigree. Meanwhile in the urban periphery, where migrants tended to reside, open-air venues called *chichódromos*, descended from spaces for huayno performance and controlled by migrant *promotores*, became the preferred spaces for cumbia shows, setting up in parking lots, circus tents, and any other available area. In the early 1980s many radio stations devoted to traditional Andean music similarly shifted to chicha broadcasting, and the former huayno titan Radio Inca emerged as the leading channel of dissemination.

It is in this period that cumbia enters murky definitional terrain. While most commentators agree on an initial division into coastal, jungle, and Andean cumbia variants, the 1970s saw performers blend traits from all of them.[11] Some began to compose songs that adopted a specifically migrant subject position. Many of them were "social" in intent, describing the everyday effects of the dismal socioeconomic situation faced by Lima's majority. The term *chicha* became attached to those tropical sounds identified with migrant youth, and if these performers did not initially present themselves as creators of a distinct genre, the terminological shift nevertheless marked them as different.[12] Some deejays and artists began to apply the word indiscriminately to all Peruvian cumbia, leading to disaffection within the scene itself. Artists whose careers predated its existence often resisted the term, viewing it as a delegitimizing label. Some observers have interpreted such attitudes as a capitulation to prejudice at best and an expression of disdain for migrant-identified cumbia at worst. Whatever the case, as a result of such debates, for some the term *chicha* includes all Peruvian cumbia, for others it is limited to cumbia created by and for the popular sectors, and for still others it includes only the specific blend of huayno and cumbia that dominated the 1980s.

The reactions of such established artists were not unfounded. The term *chicha* was often intended to delegitimize the cumbia of the age, expressing alarm at the uses to which a popular style was put by migrant artists, its increasing imbrication with their marginal environment, and its raw sound, attributed to lack of talent and resources rather than aesthetic preference or artistic intent. Though they were slanted by prejudice, these interpretations were not entirely unfounded, for the period saw a strong trend by emerging cumbia artists toward describing marginal characters and milieus. Such performers saw themselves as urban chroniclers, providing an underrepresented sector with frank and sympathetic accounts of their lives and giving them a space of emotional release. According to this position, their music simply reflected a shared reality. Their detractors, by contrast, accused them of reveling in marginality for its own sake and of promoting antisocial behavior by modeling it onstage and in song. It was through such debates that chicha became identified with a new kind of popular subject, and tensions over how to publicly represent this subject defined the genre's subsequent development.

Chacalón's career illustrates both the musical trajectory of Peruvian cumbia over the 1970s and the style's increasing affiliation with Lima's popular classes. He was born in 1950, the oldest of more than a dozen siblings; his mother was a huayno performer from the highland city of Ayacucho. Leaving school at an early age, he sampled various professions, including cosmetologist and tailor—both foreshadowing his later career onstage, where he became known for his ostentatious fashion sense. He and his brother Alfredo, popularly known as Chacal, had sung throughout their youth, favoring the sentimental boleros that stormed Latin America after midcentury.[13] In the early 1970s Chacal was invited to be the vocalist for Grupo Celeste, a cumbia costeña band managed by the Andean impresario Víctor Casahuamán. After recording several hits within a few years, however, he was ejected from the group. Meanwhile Chacalón, though he had achieved some recognition in 1972 with the song "Noche de invierno," had had an on-again, off-again musical career with few successes. His style was similar to his brother's, and with Casahuamán in need of a replacement, Chacalón stepped in.

Grupo Celeste had become known for songs that were heavily indebted to Cuban music, often described with the adjective *guarachero*. Chacalón's early effort with the band, "Viento" (Wind, 1975), was solidly within this vein, its melodic and harmonic structures appearing to emulate certain varieties of Cuban *son*. However, he brought a powerfully emotional interpretation to this simple song of poverty and migrant nostalgia, touching a chord in his audience. In the opinion of one chicha musician and scholar, this vocal delivery, "wounding and without affectation," would make Chacalón one of the two most important persons in chicha history (Hurtado Suárez 1995b: 171). Full of vocal breaks and other expressive gestures, it derived from the plaintive style of their mother's huayno music, a genre legendary (and often derided) for its melancholy tone and content. In a particularly effective passage, another investigator summarized its effects: "Chacalón was no great singer but he was an extraordinary performer. . . . Whereas Chacal tried for a careful execution, Chacalón reached, tried to cause a sensation, opened wounds, even if it meant ignoring vocal technique" (Leyva Arroyo 2005: 36).

Abandoning the polished tone of artists like Los Destellos and Chacal, Chacalón's rough-edged singing resonated among peers who recognized the vocal style and identified with the structure of feeling that animated it. His music became closely linked to Lima's popular classes, and the sound of earlier groups came, by comparison, to be positioned as "elegant," articulated to imageries far removed from the marginal aura that accrued to the rising star. As he moved from Grupo Celeste, to El Super Grupo in 1976, to La Nueva Crema in 1978, Chacalón's songs increasingly detailed the vagaries of migrant life.[14] These themes were not unique to him, but they achieved a new urgency in his interpretations, and they often seemed to define a distinct, shared popular subjectivity by speaking in its name. Such songs included "Pueblo joven" (Shantytown, recorded with El Super Grupo in 1976), which characterized the migrant slum as an idyllic space where hardworking proletarians remained humble but united, free from the petty jealousies of the wealthy. Elsewhere he described the alternating opportunities and frustrations of life in Lima in songs that are imbued with a sense of foreboding before the constant threat of failure, even as they are filled with a sense of triumph at staying afloat despite malignant forces.

"Soy provinciano" (I'm a Migrant, 1978), a standout hit for La Nueva Crema, is a prime example of the direction in which this group had taken chicha music by the early 1980s. The protagonist's origin is recognized in the very title, but greater emphasis is laid upon his identity as a worker, a young man "looking for a new life," who rises early to labor alongside his fellows, confident that he will succeed "with the help of God," and upon his urban milieu, which appears as the antagonist with which he contends, a place "where money is all and things are evil." Like all chicha songs it mimics colloquial speech, a trait that set the genre apart from the metaphoric huayno or the lyrical vals, densely poetic genres considered representative of Andean and criollo tradition, respectively. It is written in a register often criticized as "vulgar," not because of any slang or invective but because of its sheer pedestrianism. Musically the song shows the naturalization of Peruvian cumbia (see figure 6.2).

The instrumental format established by earlier bands persists, with distorted lead guitars (and vocals) performing over a rhythm section playing cumbia-style ostinatos. Its melody, harmony, and overall verse-chorus struc-

Figure 6.2. "Soy provinciano" by Chacalón y La Nueva Crema (lead guitar, bass, and vocals only): introduction and verse 1 (0:07–0:51).

ture, however, no longer resemble Caribbean or Colombian models. With a melody as simple and direct as its lyrics, the song's musical structure shows an effective marriage between form and content.

Songs like these have attracted much commentary in the reportage on chicha music, but they represent only one aspect of the genre's engagement with migrant existence. In a far greater proportion Chacalón, like most of his peers, sang tragedies of love and loss or else chronicled personal failings,

Figure 6.2. Continued from previous page

such as alcohol abuse and amorous jealousy. Tracks like "Por ella, la botella" (roughly, "Because of Her, the Bottle," 1982) describe the indulgence of these faults as part of a downward spiral leading the speaker to a pitiable state. Widely interpreted as glorifying machismo or substance abuse and as licensing listeners to indulge their weaknesses, this aspect of Chacalón's music attracted strident criticism and contributed greatly to the perception of chicha as a marginal genre. Condemnation was also widely accompanied by lurid statements about the growing association between chicha music, violence, and criminal activity, links thought to be specifically encouraged by Chacalón's "aggressive" personal imagery. Such commentaries came from within the Andean community, where these aspects of chicha music were seen as playing to the worst popular assumptions about migrant society, and without, where they were often seen as confirmation of migrant backwardness.

These concerns were not groundless, given the violence that sometimes attended chicha concerts. Furthermore Chacalón's songs of vice often eschewed moral condemnation, and he certainly cultivated a persona that seemed to glorify his marginal origins, modeling its emblems in a highly public setting. Clothing his imposing physique in flamboyant clothing, sporting long hair and gold chains, singing frankly about both the daily problems and the combative resilience of migrant life, his "migrante achorado" (uppity migrant) stance was intended to demonstrate pride in his background and its associated aesthetic sensibilities. For Chacalón's fans, however, his songs did not justify the behaviors they described as much as they recognized the temptation to indulge them and demonstrated an empathy for those who contended with such temptation. Indeed songs like "Por maldad" (Not Because I'm Bad) treat criminal activity as arising from situations of exclusion and want, even as they stress that such conditions can be overcome through personal dedication, a point sustained by Chacalón himself in public statements. Finally, if his public image was seen to challenge Lima's established hierarchies of taste, these evaluations betrayed apprehensiveness about the emergence of an unapologetically subaltern hero, one who did not readily submit to structures of aesthetic subordination, proud in his commitment to a distinct value system, and unafraid to seek and then flaunt success on his own terms.

Chacalón's music provided something of a bridge between the earlier, "elegant" cumbia and the full-blown emergence of chicha music. His defiant assertion of a marginal identity, his unabashed chronicling of its space of action, and the provision of spaces in which to gather those who followed him were all instrumental in rallying a new sort of public for cumbia. They were also instrumental in making cumbia, and chicha more specifically, into a uniquely migrant-identified endeavor. For if his songs were clearly associated with an Andean subject position, they were also thoroughly identified with Lima's cityspace. Far from a sense of helplessness, Chacalón's protagonists both demonstrate mastery of a limeño milieu distinct from that portrayed in criollo sources and recognize the precarious nature of their insertion into that milieu.

The World of the Poor in the Public Sphere: Los Shapis del Perú

The next shift in Peru's cumbia scene was marked by a sudden reversal, as chicha spread beyond the marginal confines into which it had retreated with Chacalón. It can be traced to the emergence of Los Shapis del Perú, chicha's first nationwide phenomenon and the first group to garner serious attention throughout the national media. Made up of experienced performers, the group coalesced over the late 1970s in the Andean city of Huancayo. Well connected to Lima, Huancayo had at an early date developed a cumbia scene linked to the capital, and the cumbia andina artists of the 1960s had mostly hailed from the area. Los Shapis partially inherited the style of these earlier groups, shaping their songs around the melodies and structures of Andean huayno music. In other ways they followed Lima-based bands, such as adopting the guitar-based format of cumbia costeña. Most important, they further developed the thematic interests of Chacalón and his associates, even as they sought to avoid his hard-line imagery. At the group's core were the songwriter and guitarist Jaime Moreyra and the singer Chapulín, "El dulce" (The Sweetie), university students whom one writer dubbed the "ideologues of chicha." In public statements, lyrics, and onstage imagery these organic intellectuals proudly acknowledged their migrant origins, essayed a more specific critique of Andean marginalization, and argued that chicha was the legitimate folklore of migrant society. In all of these endeavors, however, they cultivated a conciliatory tone. Creating a happy-go-lucky, media-friendly image, pairing it with a style of interpretation notably less ragged than Chacalón's, and instituting security checkpoints at the entrance to their concerts, they presented their message in ways that were palatable to a general public. And very quickly they managed to distance themselves, and chicha music, from the sordid aura that it had acquired, even as they further solidified its specific connection to migrant experience.

All of these characteristics made Los Shapis' music highly attractive for chicha consumers seeking social distance from Lima's marginal communities and for academic commentators seeking keys to an emergent Peruvian society. Scholars combed their lyrics for migrant-centered accounts of everyday life and hints of an associated worldview. However, Los Shapis were equally interesting for the markedly Andean direction in which they took chicha musically. Their huayno-based style has been described elsewhere (Romero 2002; Turino 1990), but it is worth reiterating the group's reliance upon this most Andean of genres. Their first hit, "El aguajal" (The Aguaje Grove, 1982), was simply a well-known huayno in a chicha setting, and similar cuts would appear on later records. In other songs they utilized huayno music's binary strophes, set to syncopated, pentatonic melodies, shifting between relative major and minor modes, alternately cadencing in each, principles that together define the genre throughout the Andean region. As a result, even originals like "Porque eres mujer" (Because You're a Woman, 1981; see figure 6.3), a lament of amorous betrayal, seem like huaynos in disguise.

Los Shapis were by far Peru's most popular chicha group over the 1980s, spawning numerous followers and leading established artists to imitate their

Figure 6.3. "Porque eres mujer" by Los Shapis (vocals only): verse 1 and chorus (0:39–1:09).

sound. The benchmarks of their success are legion, and it is little wonder that they are remembered today as chicha's most emblematic figures. At their peak, they drew crowds of over ten thousand on a regular basis, and after a 1986 performance in the soccer stadium of Lima's beloved Alianza team, they were invited to represent Peru at a World Youth Festival in France. They were recruited for political and advertising campaigns, in order to draw votes and capital from Peru's working classes. They even appeared as the stars and protagonists of a movie, *Los Shapis en el mundo de los pobres* (Los Shapis in the World of the Poor), which, though not a critical success, showed a newfound confidence in chicha music's drawing power.

Over the same period, however, independent labels glutted the market with stultifyingly imitative chicha records, even as multinational companies began to push *salsa romántica*, *balada*, and other pan–Latin American genres within Peru.[15] Chicha had declined significantly in popularity by the early 1990s, and while many groups continued to perform, others moved into other genres and some left the country. Argentina, with its comparatively strong economy and a large, nostalgic population of Peruvian migrants, became a magnet for chicha performers and impresarios. Some of these artists later returned as the stars of tecno-cumbia, a style that called into question the extent to which chicha ideologues had accomplished the goals they set out to achieve. Before arriving at this epilogue, however, it is necessary to place the literature on chicha in its context and describe its role in building a certain understanding of the style as metaphor and practice.

Chicha as Social Trope: "The Hopeful Narrative"

Chicha became such a compelling object for scholars, especially within the fields of anthropology and sociology, because it spoke to both the historic mission of these disciplines and contemporaneous shifts in social theory.[16] Charged from the start with investigating Peru's ethnic distinctiveness, and Andean life in particular, early scholars in these fields had begun by cataloguing the sheer variety of highland folkways and material culture, defending their value against a predatory modernity held to typify criollo society. Upon their disciplines' academic formalization around midcentury and infused with a holistic understanding of the culture concept, such scholars turned from the mere enumeration of traits to the elucidation of a unique and unitary "Andean" cultural system purported to underlie highland practices in general. While the essentialist conceits and preservationist bent of such work often seem quaint in light of later constructivist accounts, the drive to explain Andean culture as a complex system, with its own internal logic, was in fact a radical challenge to dominant understandings of Peruvian society.

Predicated upon defining an authentic Andean cultural formation against a domineering "modernity" outside its borders, this vision was severely challenged by the phenomenon of urban migration. As two supposedly discrete systems came into contact, many scholars turned to understanding and, often, ameliorating the changes wrought upon Andean culture in transition. Observing the changing lifeways of Andean citizens in the capital, a first generation largely diagnosed migrant society as anomic, typified by severe culture loss, in which individuals became alienated and depressive in the absence of familiar referents. A second wave quickly challenged these studies, focusing instead on urban adaptations as evidence of resilience. Attending to the re-creation of Andean practices, they argued that a deep-rooted cultural sense survived the transition to the capital's modern milieu and that such modified expressions served as a crucial aid for migrants adjusting to the city.

Despite their differences, all of these studies were marked by the dualistic assumption of Andean and criollo cultures as integral and antagonistic wholes, contending for subjects' personal affiliation and space in Peruvian society at large. By the 1980s, however, theories of social identity as multiple and malleable had begun to coalesce under such theoretical rubrics as *mestizaje* and *cholificación*.[17] Scholars paid new attention to cultural hybrids that had once been dismissed as aberrant and inauthentic. Urban practices were examined as strategies for success in a new milieu rather than evidence of inadaptability. Such studies were legion, but the book *Desborde popular y crisis del estado: El nuevo rostro del Perú en la década de 1980* by the anthropologist José Matos Mar (1984), can be taken as exemplary. Bringing together several strands of contemporary thinking, Matos Mar proposed a dynamic vision of migrant society, in which its hybridizing impulse accompanied a demand for socioeconomic inclusion. He interpreted disparate migrant activities, including land invasions, ambulatory commerce in defiance of municipal regulation, and cultural expressions that defied old dualisms, as a sort of generalized popular insurrection against the age-old limitations of a weakening nation-state. He argued that Lima's marginal majority had attained sufficient numbers, purchasing power, and control over public space, to be in a de facto position of social leadership, requiring a response from the waning structures of elite power. Matos Mar ended by predicting the imminent triumph of a new national paradigm, rooted in the mestizaje of migrant Lima.

Essayistic rather than technical in tone, *Desborde popular* was influential within and outside of the academy. Throughout the 1980s and 1990s academic and popular accounts of migrant Lima were similarly underwritten by the assumption, dubbed "the optimistic vision" by Sandoval (2000), that migrant ethics, structures, and practices augured an inclusive nationalism in abeyance. Given the continuing exclusion of Andean citizens and disdain for migrant-identified popular culture, however, these ideas have borne some recent reconsideration. In a twentieth-anniversary edition of the volume (Matos Mar et al. 2004), commentators noted that Matos Mar had overstated the self-consciousness of the challenge he described. Several suggested that migrant strategies such as informal commerce, in avoiding a direct engagement with the powers of exclusion, actually reinforced their authority to define boundaries of legitimacy (Pásara 2004). And Matos Mar himself acknowledged that despite very real pressures, Peru's ruling classes had effectively maintained the power to shape Peruvian politics and public culture, avoiding a serious integration of the kind that he forecast.

Academic treatments of chicha, and their relation to the genre's subsequent place in Peruvian society, follow a similar pattern. Matos Mar named chicha as a foremost example of his thesis, citing it as evidence that a broader change was nascent in the mestizo practices of migrant Lima. Others joined him in evaluating the style as a forerunner of the spaces where Andean and criollo worlds would dissolve to produce a unified national culture. This purported link between aesthetic and social realities, however, overlooked many of the characteristics that made chicha persuasive for its audience and unlikely to interpellate new national subjects. As a discursive practice, its effects were similar to the performances of Lima's *cómicos ambulantes* described by Vich (2001). Chicha songs did not directly challenge structural exclusion but rather "underlined an acceptance of the [state's] modern project ... reinterpreting it through daily life and the country's specific historical tensions" (14), even as their performers "emphasized the relations of power in which they were inscribed, connecting their intellectual lives to the group of which they felt a part" (51). Capturing listeners by appealing to their shared marginal condition, celebrating survival on the harsh terms posed by the city, and emphasizing the need to attain success by working in its interstices rather than challenging its premises, chicha adopted a resolutely subalternizing stance. Musicians revealed fractures in the state's historic interpretive structures but posited no effective demands for resolution. Precisely because it made marginality so central to its public while failing to challenge the terms upon which that marginality rested, chicha retained its status as a subaltern manifestation. If the style's mestizaje could indeed be read as a challenge to the dichotomous system that relegated Andean citizens to a place outside modernity, its popular appeal lay precisely in its empathy for migrant difference.

It is likely that different listeners partook of both readings, and this raises a second issue in relation to chicha literature. If scholars rejected the transhistorical fixity of cultural identities, they largely retained the notion of a causative link between expressive culture and personal identity, with the assumption that a change in one represented a change in the other. This "homology thesis," which dominated scholarship on music more generally, has been critiqued by scholars such as Peter Wade, who, following Richard Middleton, argues that such accounts "overstate the tightness of fit between the two levels, may understate the conflict over musical meaning within the social group whose identity is supposedly being reflected, and ... may overstate the element of subversion" (Wade 2000: 23). Just so, chicha was widely interpreted as the external reflection of a new internal reality, a shift in the collective subjectivity of its listenership, rather than as a practice likely to be meaningful in various ways for its various listeners, and one with many competing subvariants.[18] The ethnomusicologist Thomas Turino (1990) took a slightly different and more processual tack, evaluating chicha as a potential vehicle for a new identity, which might emerge through the process of collective consumption and mutual recognition. Most accounts, however, took the style as a rather mechanical response to social change, as evidence of an already completed change in consciousness, and were thus bound for disappointment when this identarian renovation failed to achieve its predicted sociopolitical vindication.

Such assumptions appear particularly weak if an understanding of the style is decentered from Los Shapis. Their widely imitated blend of huayno and cumbia lent itself particularly well to homological interpretation, supporting the idea that chicha was fundamentally an attempt to bridge Peru's binary divide via musical fusion. With few exceptions (see, e.g., Leyva 2005; Romero 2002), academic accounts have not described other cumbia styles nor their different social radii of action, instead inserting them into a teleological account where they become steps on the path to the synthesis of Los Shapis. A more inclusive history might have shown that the various musics designated as cumbia and chicha together constituted a phenomenon as varied as their audience. In this heteroglot space of encounter, musics were not synthesized as much as they were brought into contact, making evident the competing loci of identification that traversed Peru's public sphere without dissolving them. Such a history might note that, as a site where modernity, tradition, local, and foreign met and became confused, chicha was not as novel as often claimed. After all, huayno had itself been influenced by Mexican boleros and rancheras since the 1960s; tangos, *polcas*, and valses had been performed at highland parties since the 1930s; and of course, Spanish poetic forms such as the romance had prevailed as songwriting models throughout the region for centuries. Finally, a complete account would acknowledge that the category of chicha listener overlapped with more than one social identification, and conversely, that most *chicheros*, like most people everywhere, found many genres of music personally persuasive. Given all of these qualifications, taking chicha or cumbia to represent a single, fundamental moment of transformation in Peruvian society seems to reflect the demands of theory more than the facts of the matter.

Of course, it is easy to diagnose the missteps of chicha scholarship in hindsight, and scholars' conclusions were not entirely off the mark, particularly given how closely they hewed to the discourse of Los Shapis themselves. However, the disjuncture between the optimistic predictions that attended chicha music in its prime and its latter-day conversion into a term of insult might lead us to exercise caution when theorizing the efficacy of popular culture. As Deborah Poole (1988) has noted in a different context, the projection of neat, idealized social models on the subjects of scholarly research more often reflects the hopes of researchers than the conditions in which such subjects work. In approaching popular culture and its social effects, we would be well served by understanding that its manifestations "are formed under conditions of exclusion and subordination and that . . . the signs produced there are agonistically compromised with the reproduction of hegemonic ideologies even as they protest conditions of inequality" (Vich 2001: 184). If subaltern cultural practices often become effective symbols of resistance or collective identity, their creators also maneuver at a disadvantage within the public sphere, and a challenge to hegemony that fails to establish broader spaces of enunciation is unlikely to prosper as a national symbol. With this in mind, it is especially interesting to examine how later movements have resembled and departed from the case of chicha.

Epilogue: Dancing Cumbia on the Beaches of Eisha

Cumbia returned to prominence between 1998 and 2010 in three distinct waves that seized the imagination of the intelligentsia and the popular press, much as chicha had a generation before. With them returned the conversations about social justice that had attended the earlier style, but both the context and the music were different. Each of the new styles that emerged in this period were tied to different regions, the first being closely associated with the Amazon and the second with the northern coast around Piura, and together they shook off the Andean aura that chicha had given to Peruvian cumbia. More important, their protagonists achieved a social acceptance never dreamed of by chicha artists, reaching select spaces that had remained closed to performers even at that style's peak. Rossy War, the central figure of the first, Amazonian trend, garnered a listenership of 37 percent of the population, according to Peru's foremost statistics agency, making her by far the most popular artist in the country (Salcedo 2000). During the next wave, artists from the north coast were invited to perform their salsa-inflected cumbia in exclusive, criollo-identified spaces like the Gótica nightclub and Lima's beach resort of Asia. Such events generated an outpouring of commentary, most of it structured around the proposal that they heralded the arrival of Peru's long-denied moment of integration. If these working-class sounds could reach elite ears, it was widely felt, the barriers that chicha had not broken were soon to fall as well. For many, however, the success of these styles and their shifts in sound and image were rather too intimately related, leading to questions about whether or not they mark "integration or disguised prejudice" (Quispe Lázaro 2002).

The first wave, dubbed tecno-cumbia, was dominated by artists from the Amazon, an area long underrepresented in Peru's public sphere, and it marked something of a coming-out party for the region. It arrived in 1998, when Rossy War's song "Nunca pensé en llorar" became a hit, and soon dozens of imitators emerged. Many of these performers, such as Ruth Karina, had been working in the Amazon, absorbing elements of local popular styles like Brazilian *toada*. Others, including Grupo Néctar, were composed of former chicha artists who had left for Argentina upon the style's decline, picking up production techniques that were markedly "professional"-sounding compared with earlier efforts. A third group consisted of northern cumbia bands who took advantage of the boom to reach new audiences. All adopted a similar sound and image, however, and they dominated the airwaves until roughly 2002. In evaluating the genre's success among Peruvian elites, the ethnomusicologist Raúl Romero (2002) has argued that artists' stylistic and performative shifts were key to making cumbia palatable for consumers leery of chicha's national-popular taint. Though it retained the cumbia rhythmic template utilized by chicha artists, tecno-cumbia replaced guitars with synthesizers and avoided all hints of huayno-style vocalizing or pentatonic melody. Its lyrics became "happy and hedonistic, without any traces of melancholy or conflict with its social environment, as possessed by its ancestor, *chicha*" (Quispe Lázaro 2002: 109). Its "de-Andeanization" was accompanied by an emphasis on jungle-related imagery and sensual dance, both standing for a "tropical" identity perceived to characterize the performers. This tropicalism was widely perceived to situate tecno-cumbia, its listenership, and Peruvians at large under the aegis of a desirable pan–Latin American subjectivity, glamorous and globalized when set beside the parochial concerns of chicha music.

Amazonian tecno-cumbia, like chicha before it, declined in national profile almost as quickly as it had risen, and the next wave was associated with a different region and a different sound. Its rise was set off, however, by events within the world of tecno-cumbia. In 2007 several members of Grupo Néctar were killed in a bus crash, and the tragedy returned cumbia to the attention of the press. In a media environment newly curious about the status of this popular style, groups from the north coast, particularly Grupo 5 and Los Caribeños de Guadalupe, seized an opportunity they had missed during the tecno-cumbia boom, aggressively pushing their music on Lima radio and TV. The environment was propitious, and these groups also arrived with a sound radically different from both chicha and tecno-cumbia, one that was often described with the self-consciously elitist label *cumbia elegante*. This style brought slick, salsa- and *merengue*-inflected arrangements to the big band format that had long dominated northern cumbia and placed them beneath smooth, professional-sounding vocal interpretations inspired by popular Caribbean artists. Together these drew Peruvian cumbia even closer to the "international standards" taken to be defined by such Caribbean artists, and the effect was to intensify tecno-cumbia's nascent pan–Latin Americanism. It generated a much greater fervor than tecno-cumbia had, as radio and advertising became saturated with the sounds and images of Los Caribeños, Grupo 5, Grupo Mallanep, Hermanos Yaipén, Tongo, and their artistic compatriots. Perhaps no incident generated as much commentary as the appearance of cumbia groups at Asia, a resort south of Lima long accused of barring nonwhites from its premises. So synonymous with snobbery and exclusion that it is often used as a synecdoche for Peru's racist structures in general, its name is commonly spelled "Eisha" in such writings, with the Spanish-orthography rendering of its English-language pronunciation meant to lampoon the pretension of those who claim an elitist cosmopolitanism.

Finally, a third manifestation of cumbia chic emerged that was largely centered among Lima's bohemian, elitist intelligentsia, unlike the previous two waves, which were more general in scope. It involved a renewed interest in the classic, pre-chicha artists who were featured on the album *Roots of Chicha*, a compilation produced in the United States in 2007 consisting of what, until that moment, had been regarded as historical oddities, but that were given new cachet due to their uptake by American arbiters of hipster cool (see Clayton 2010). Taken together, such events led to the creation of a public narrative for these musics that placed their success within a sort of sociocultural rags-to-riches framework encompassing their creators and listeners as well. Like chicha, these cumbia-derived styles were initially identified with Peru's popular sectors, and as late as early 2008 Raúl Romero was able to state in an interview that "*cumbia* is still not valued by 'official' Peru" (Pajares Cruzado 2008). As such, their sudden uptake by Peruvian elites marked a real change in possibilities for cross-class identification and has been taken as marking the end of prejudice.

However, it should be noted that consumption, particularly of the musical kind, does not require a sincere identification with cultural producers. And it cannot be overlooked that the music produced has depended for its success upon marking a distance from lower-class origins and aesthetics, and from chicha in particular. One sector of Peru's commentariat holds this, in itself, to be a positive sign, a signal that noncriollos have achieved such numbers, such a level of integration, self-confidence, and power, that stressing migrant roots has become tiresome. For others, this position is belied by the continuing and specific exclusion of Andean-identified objects from the public sphere. In a cutting commentary, the scholar José María Salcedo, who maintains that all cumbia styles are in fact chicha in a greater or lesser degree of disguise, proposes that tecno-cumbia's demise came about precisely when it became clear that many of its artists were in fact former chicheros. He asks whether tecno-cumbia's success among criollo elites "could be because Argentina has been chichified, as demonstrated by their imitators of *chicha* . . . who come to Peru to show us that chicha can also be tall, blond, and blue-eyed?" (2000: 97).

The most pessimistic of these interpretations seemed to be confirmed in May 2008, when an incident involving Grupo 5 made headlines for weeks. In a radical and overdue gesture of inclusion, the group had been invited to pose in *Cosas*, Peru's glossiest of celebrity rags, and the magazine had photographed them in high-end tailoring from Lima's exclusive Designer's boutique. Upon the publication of the story, however, a local news program revealed the objections of the store manager to the use of her wares in this way. Stating repeatedly in an interview that clothes of the Giorgio Armani and Ermenegildo Zegna lines were not for use by "those people" but instead by "serious people," this unlucky individual became for some time the public face of continuing prejudice against both cumbia music and those who, by and large, create it.

This was not the only event to check the narrative of national harmony in cumbia consumption that has accompanied the rise of the northern style. Such occurrences would seem to argue that the barriers that chicha failed to rupture remain intact. While cross-class consumption has been achieved, mutual identification between consumers probably remains far more limited than the discourses surrounding contemporary cumbia seem to imply. However, these events have been accompanied by hopeful signs, perhaps indicating that something has shifted in the overall social context since chicha's prime. For if these incidents showed the persistence of prejudice, they were also reviled across Peru's media spectrum. They generated serious public discussion about the extent to which cumbia represents a site of encounter between elite and working-class peoples and sensibilities, showing a potential for a broad-based and participatory debate of the kind that chicha never fostered. *Cosas* even revisited the issue in an article titled "Fusión y discusión: La cumbia peruana está originando un nuevo debate sobre un viejo tema" (Kisner 2008), largely consisting of an interview with the sociologist Santiago Alfaro. As a foremost scholar of the contemporary moment in Peruvian cumbia, Alfaro conceded that cumbia "has become the musical background to Peru, in which the art is accepted but not the artist" (24). However, he also noted, "Music can create common sensations, and that is important. But we shouldn't ask it for more than it can give. Right now, cumbia is offering us a platform for discussing our interrelations, more so than resolving them" (25). In other words, it is possible that the current cumbia boom, arriving in a context of greater openness and popular will, is furnishing an opportunity for the kind of broad-based discussion that chicha was never able to generate. The resolution, and even the initiation, of such a debate will depend largely on the extent to which the inchoate sentiments of identification described by Alfaro can be backed up by projects of dialogue geared toward generating a sincere intersubjectivity. Given the wild-eyed predictions that accompanied an earlier generation of chicha, caution is in order; however, there is reason to be optimistic.

Discography

Chacalón y la Nueva Crema. 2004. *Lo Mejór del Faraón de la Chicha*. Nuevos Medios NM 15 832. N.p.

Chicha Libre. 2008. *Sonido Amazónico!* Barbés Records BR0017. USA.

Los Destellos. N.d. *Los Destellos, Vol. 2: Para Todo el Mundo*. IEMPSA IEM-0137. Peru.

Los Destellos. N.d. *Selección de Los Destellos*. IEMPSA IEM-0021. Peru.

Los Mirlos. 2000. *Antología de los Mirlos*. Orfeón CDL-16087. Peru.

Roots of Chicha: Psychedelic Cumbias from Peru. 2007. Barbés Records BR0016. USA.

Los Shapis. N.d. *Historia Musical de los Shapis*. IEMPSA COL-1362. Peru.

Filmography

Ciudad chicha. 2007. Directed by Rául R. Romero and Omar Ráez Jiménez. Peru. 47 mins. Documentary.

Notes

1. It might be further noted that Chicha Libre is an "American" band in at best a complicated sense, since several members hail from other countries, including France and Mexico.

2. Note that the Colombian cumbia referred to here is the commercial-popular format popularized internationally in the 1950s and 1960s, and not the rural-folkloric version.

3. Replete with product placement for local wares like Triple Kola, the series was a clear attempt to harness the purchasing power of migrant Lima and thus an implicit recognition of this sector's economic dynamism. Interpellation as a market, however, constitutes neither social acceptance nor integration.

4. Predictably, like similar slurs throughout the world, organic intellectuals and sympathetic academic commentators have adopted the term as a symbol of pride and identification. This usage, however, remains limited in scope and is premised upon the term's predominantly negative connotations.

5. The term is often applied to areas that may seem distant from migrant culture, particularly politics, where it indicates figures and situations characterized by dishonesty or graft, and popular entertainment, where it connotes such things as sleazy talk shows and yellow journalism. Its meaning in these cases, however, follows from the derisive application to migrant society, indicating an approach to the field in question that is "informal," backward, or distasteful, elements thought to be typical of migrant tastes.

6. Unless otherwise noted, all translations are mine.

7. Naturally there were challenges to these structures, with demands for Andean revindication becoming most prominently solidified in the *indigenista* movement of the early twentieth century. However, in general such challenges to criollo hegemony were sporadic and ineffective at changing broader patterns.

8. Establishing a precise account of the genre is difficult. Details on release dates, lines of influence, and the agents of innovation are often absent or the stuff of debate. Further, differing opinions about what constitutes cumbia, chicha, and tecno-cumbia make it difficult to reconcile existing accounts. Mindful of these problems, and also that succinct histories are available elsewhere, this review highlights those details most salient for the stylistic emergence of Peruvian cumbia, and later chicha, between the 1960s and the mid-1990s. It is largely synthesized from Bailón 2004; Hurtado Suárez 1995a, 199b; Quispe Lázaro 1994, 2000; Romero 2002; Salcedo 2000; and independent interviews conducted in Lima in 2008.

9. Though nearly forgotten outside the country itself, Peru developed a strong local rock scene at a comparatively early date, with Spanish-language covers of Bill Haley songs appearing in 1957 and local bands releasing albums of original material by 1963; see Cornejo Guinassi 1998.

10. This reception may have been aided by the dim view that the leftist military

government of the time took toward "imperialist" rock music, an attitude that led to official repression of its broadcast and performance.

11. In existing sources little mention is made of the northern coastal style.

12. It is not clear when the term entered popular usage in this way. Bailón (2004) affirms that the leader of Los Ecos used it as early as 1970 to describe the band's music. Others maintain that this usage dates from the later 1970s.

13. Their stage names derived from the world of masked wrestling (*kachaskán*, or catch-as-can), which had fascinated them as children and which their mother had practiced professionally. One figure, called Chacal (Jackal), stood out by virtue of his baldness, and one day when the young Alfredo's head was shaved as punishment for a misdeed, he acquired the wrestler's ring name as a nickname. It was later on that the older brother Lorenzo acquired, appropriately, the superlative version Chacalón, or Big Jackal.

14. Chacalón rarely composed his own songs. Víctor Casahuamán wrote "Viento," "Pueblo Jóven" is by Lerner Muñoz, and both "Soy provinciano" and "Por ella, la botella" are by Juan Rebaza.

15. Both factors can be traced to accelerating government policies of market deregulation over the 1980s. These led to the easing of restrictions on the importation of electronics and on the consolidation of radio stations under consortiums beholden to multinational music corporations.

16. For fuller details, see especially the excellent essays by Degregori, Mendizábal, and Sandoval in the collected volume *No hay país más diverso: Compendio de antropología peruana* (Degregori 2000a).

17. Derived from a colonial term for Westernized indigenous peoples, *cholificación* is the sociologist Aníbal Quijano's term for the hybrid popular culture of Peru's lower classes.

18. In a similar vein, Leyva notes, "Chicha studies ignore other kinds of popular consumption in Lima, so much so that sometimes one might think that the popular classes only consume that music" (2005: 29).

7.
Pandillar in the Jungle
Regionalism and *Tecno-cumbia* in Amazonian Peru

Tecno-cumbia thumped throughout the neighborhood, its pulsating beats growing louder and louder as we circled the Complejo, a popular tecno-cumbia amphitheater in Iquitos. The mood was festive, and young people doused in water and dusted with baby powder and cornstarch lurched out of *motokarros* (rickshaw motorcycles), tumbling to the ticket booth. We entered the sprawling compound, parked the motorcycle, and made our way to the throngs of people dancing to a Grupo 5 cover. The song faded out and the drummer began a quick-paced march beat that elicited screams of delight from the more than two thousand people crammed under the roof of the amphitheater, spilling out into a broad cement courtyard under the stars. The electric drum beat continued and a high-pitched, synthesized *quena* began to outline the familiar melody as the crowd began dancing in long, undulating lines, arms linked. Cornstarch was thrown in the air, falling on squealing dancers, leaving them dusty as it stuck to their sweaty faces. Out in the courtyard, a friend placed an empty beer bottle in the middle of our own group, and the line disintegrated as we formed pairs, skipping forward and backward around the bottle, taking turns "chopping" at the air above the beer bottle with our hands, imagining it was an *húmisha*, a decorated palm tree used at carnival. We danced, hopping back and forth, eventually coming together in a long line again, weaving around other revelers as they rattled off the rapid-fire lyrics to *pandilla* in unison with the performers on stage.

Pandilla is a folkloric genre of the Peruvian Amazon performed traditionally during carnival; during the celebration, community groups erect an *húmisha* (palm post), encircling it while dancing to pandilla. In recent years, however, electrified pandillas have become common year-round thanks to the Iquitos tecno-cumbia ensemble Explosión and the group's widespread popularity among Amazonians. Pandilla has incited regional pride and a desire by many *iquiteños* to attain a more prominent place in the national imagination. Although Peru boasts three distinct geographic regions (highlands, jungle, and coast), the coastal capital has often disregarded the jungle, relegating it to a "savage" culture good for little beyond interesting flora and fauna and (the equivalent of) "backwoods" villagers.

Along with its folkloric musical inheritance, contemporary popular pandilla owes a significant part of its sound to the influence of tecno-cumbia.[1] As Joshua Tucker discusses in this volume, tecno-cumbia is an offshoot of *chicha*, another popular Peruvian genre that dominated the country well into in the 1990s. Though often associated with Lima's Andean migrant population, its strong, Amazonian roots have earned tecno-cumbia significant local and national attention. Its current incarnation in and around Iquitos, in northeastern Amazonian Peru, has firmly represented and even propelled forward the area's difficult dialogue with cosmopolitanism as the city negotiates the forces of global modernity, attempting to maintain an Amazonian identity while also gaining more comprehensive entrée into the nation's imagination. In this essay, I introduce pandilla, a current tecno-cumbiaized trend with deep folkloric roots, describing how this genre represents a quest for regional cultural autonomy within an integrated national vision. I frame the understanding of contemporary pandilla in conjunction with its development in the tecno-cumbia sphere with a consideration of Iquitos's complex history and cultural identities that have been shaped by transnational influences. I then discuss the basic character of pandilla, examining its history, its musical and poetic character, the context of its consumption, and the importance of indexing indigenous Amazonianness in performance. Pandilla serves as a key connection between the region's past—molded by colonial dominance—and the present, which is steeped in cosmopolitanism and regional pride as urban Amazonians seek acceptance into the national imagination.

Iquitos: From Myth to Metropolis

The Amazon has always been considered a formidable territory, hardly penetrated by the Incas during their short and powerful reign (ca. 1400–1532). An unforgiving environment, the jungle presents numerous challenges to the explorer, not the least of which include extreme weather (heat and torrential rains), treacherous topography, difficult mountainous borders, and rapid rivers. This hostility of nature has informed past and present views of the forest and, by extension, its inhabitants. In the mid-sixteenth century the Spanish Crown sent explorers into the jungle in a desperate search for gold and the famed city of El Dorado. Instead they discovered an inhospitable, "savage" environment populated by disparate indigenous communities (see Dickason 1984).

Still, it was not until 1636 that the Catholic Church and the Crown sent a convoy of Jesuit missionaries to the area, representing a confluence of secular and sacred ventures. The city of Iquitos grew from a prominent mission, Santa Barbara de los Iquitos, located where the rivers Nanay, Amazon, and Itaya meet, cordoning off a slightly raised parcel of land. This was a strategic site for the missionaries and subsequent governors because of easy access to neighboring missions and towns as well as river traders coming from Brazil and Colombia.

After Peru's declared independence from the Crown in 1821, the small city grew, and in 1828 leaders established its first constitution. The capital of the Loreto Department, Iquitos became a tactical port city with an increase in river traffic, especially by merchants from Brazil and Colombia who freely navigated rivers leading into Iquitos, trading and selling *víveres* (goods) in exchange for labor or other services. These transactions with neighboring Amazonian nations inspired growing political and economic strength in the region, demonstrating its defiance of physical isolation.

Iquitos maintained a diverse population that included indigenous people, migrants from other parts of Peru, and Anglo missionaries and would-be entrepreneurs. Whereas the Incas never fully conquered the hundreds of native communities in the Upper Amazon, outside interest in the area during the late nineteenth century systematically exterminated dozens of tribes, especially as indigenous slave labor proved vital to developing entrepreneurial efforts. Bora, Shipibo, Yagua, and Urarina tribespeople suffered under subjugation by outsiders from the Andes and Europe.

The most visible abuse of indigenous labor appeared during the rubber boom (the first large-scale industry to develop in Iquitos), which was a short-lived trade that quickly brought tremendous capital to Iquitos and other Amazonian cities in Brazil.[2] Prior to this period, which lasted from approximately 1885 to 1907, Iquitos had a population of only about 1,500. The boom transformed the relatively slow, agricultural-based city into a cosmopolitan, urban port with a population in the tens of thousands. Europeans (Germans, Dutch, French, and Italians, among others) and North Americans flooded the area, exporting enormous quantities of rubber—nearly 3,029 metric tons (Flores Marín 1987)—and succeeded in further decimating native communities. Thousands of native people relocated from the jungle to Iquitos in search of employment and were subsequently used for slave labor.

Despite its isolation (or perhaps because of it), Iquitos transformed into a global, cosmopolitan city with extraordinary wealth in comparison with other Peruvian cities, especially after Peru's loss to Chile during the brief War of the Pacific in 1883. The rubber boom temporarily alleviated the nation's woes as it brought in tremendous wealth in a short period of time and put Peru on the map. The nation, however, saw Iquitos—and more broadly the Amazon—as a site of untapped wealth, ripe for exploitation. Heavily relying on what until then had been considered savage wilderness for its economic stability, the state only reinforced the Amazon's place in the Peruvian imaginary. The effects of economic prosperity (mobilized by upper-class *mestizos* and foreigners) on the public consciousness spurred exoticist visions of the jungle and its prospects. The region unified somewhat in an attempt to demonstrate its cohesiveness as a viable contribution to the state, but its efforts were underwritten by colonial history that dictated the Amazon's semipermanent position as a savage "other" place due to its wilderness and the perceived barbarity of its indigenous people.

The rubber boom ended with the export of rubber seeds to Asia, and foreign investors pulled out, submerging the recently modern city into extreme poverty. The rest of the nation filed the region under "lost wilderness," and its role in the national imaginary fell to simply wild jungle populated with backwoods natives. Building relationships with neighboring Brazil and Colombia, however, resulted in a stronger sense of regionalism. Its link with both nations is one based on Amazonianness: communication and trade with both countries resulting from geographical connection via rivers. While rivers in the Amazon stretch westward into Peru, they narrow significantly, physically prohibiting water traffic that would connect the region to the rest of the nation. This in turn has contributed to a larger identification with Amazonianness as opposed to Peruvianness.

This account suggests an ambivalent history for Iquitos, from without and within. The competition between cosmopolitanism, regional tradition, modernization, and hybrid musical and cultural styles serves to underscore the transnational and postcolonial relationships that the Amazon has maintained in the era of modernity (Garcia Canclini 1995). Most important, however, is the outsider's (inaccurate) perception of the city as savage wilderness, despite its clear position as an urban center. Although it no longer boasts an industry as developed as that during the rubber boom, it has a viable economy based on regular commerce, and this has allowed for ventures, such as the tecno-cumbia group Explosión, to thrive. As Ignacio Corona and Alejandro Madrid remind us in their recent volume exploring postnational musical identities, "the urban actually disrupts the meaning of the national" (2008: 17). Similarly the production and consumption of tecno-cumbia in and beyond Iquitos demonstrate the changing meanings of regionalism and nationalism, questioning what constitutes representative culture. The city's complex relationship with interlopers illustrates reasons for its exclusion from the national imagination, although its current public marketing of regional cultural products marks both an increasing regional pride and a desire to integrate culturally more fully into Peru as a whole, flexing Peruvian concepts of nation and region.

Pandilla: Amazonian Trend with Folkloric Roots

Pandilla is a folkloric music and dance genre associated with carnival in the Loreto Department. The style developed in the lower Amazon basin, in the Madre de Dios Department, where participants initially performed pandilla as part of patron saint festivals and it eventually became a crucial part of carnival. While its specific origins are unknown, current pandilla is likely a hybrid of indigenous and mestizo forms, eventually syncretized with *criollo* styles and firmly linked to carnival festivities.[3] According to the local folklorist Javier Isuiza Trigoso, locals understand pandilla as "the queen of Amazonian folklore" (2006: 21),[4] epitomizing Amazonian tradition; pandilla has become the dominant Amazonian musical form because people believe it is rooted in indigenous practice, even if they also recognize that commercial variants demonstrate other influences. The folkloric musician Carlos Reátegui concurs, declaring, "It is music from ages ago. . . . There are indigenous rhythms and . . . they've become more and more mestizo" (personal communication, February 2, 2007).

Despite its widespread popularity throughout the region, pandilla has not been discussed at length in publications outside of local weeklies (*Kanatari*, IIAP *Seminal*) and in the works of a few regional scholars and folklorists (Luis Alberto Salazar Orsí, Gabel Sotil, Joaquín García). While other regions in Peru have been informally assigned a *música típica* (typical, often folkloric or traditional music), such as the Andean *huayno* and the coastal *marinera*, the Amazon has not been appointed a representative musical genre. In summarily disregarding the region allegedly devoid of cultural traditions suitable for national projection because of its perceived wildness, Peru actually provided the Amazon with a blank slate; Amazonians have been freed to mold their own vision of folklore and tradition.

Ironically the musical style tecno-cumbia, a genre that signifies modernity and *mestizaje*, put the Peruvian Amazon on the cultural map. A region so often discounted for its savage roots became consumed nationally by an electrified genre. Pandilla, in turn, leaped from a solely regional fan base to a national audience in its electrified form. This change indicates the degree to which modernity, industry, and cosmopolitanism infiltrated the Amazonian urbanscape and promoted Iquitos—despite its isolation and "wild" jungle nature—to the level of sophisticated metropolis, at least to an extent. This process mirrors Gage Averill's description of Haitian music as a hybrid of "globally circulating practices, values, and beliefs with those that are more properly 'local'" (1997: 210). Similarly local pandilla, already a mix of traditional forms, fused and blended with glocal styles of tecno-cumbia. The background and development of pandilla merit further discussion, however, in order to contextualize the genre in its most recent formation.

Pandillar at Carnival

A typical carnival celebration in Iquitos (and, by extension, the entire Loreto Department) is a communal activity. The weeks leading up to the festivities are filled with pranks, parades, and initial preparation for the actual date, which is generally celebrated on the Sunday before Fat Tuesday. Customarily, small groups of families, organizations, or groups of friends pay into a community fund to purchase various supplies, including palm trees, gifts, sound systems, and alcohol.

The day before carnival, participants tie and nail together two palm trees to yield one extremely tall post. They then erect the *húmisha* (palm post) in the communal area (normally in the middle of an unpaved street), strung tightly to surrounding buildings to avoid a precarious fall. Participants tie gifts to the top of the húmisha, including washbasins, sandals, clothes, household items, and toys (figures 7.1 and 7.2).

When carnival arrives, groups of friends and neighbors gather at their re-

Figures 7.1 and 7.2.
The top of the *húmisha*,
adorned with gifts.
Photograph by the author.

spective húmishas and, with the rented sound system booming pandillas and chicha, dance around them, linking arms and skipping, stomping, or marching to the beat.[5] They dance in forward and backward motions, reminiscent of Bora and Shipibo indigenous dances in the area. Participants throw water, mud, paint, *achiote*, and other substances on each other, becoming quite filthy by the day's end. At sunset, after hours of dancing around the húmisha, everyone passes around a machete and takes turns slashing at the post, making pockmarks in the wood, loosening it for an eventual crash. Upon its fall, people dash madly toward the gifts, ripping them free from the palm leaves, eagerly stuffing them away in their homes.

In the song "Mix Pandilla 2007," by Explosión early lyrics assert the popularity of pandilla above foreign dance genres such as *reggaetón* and *merengue*, arguing that its singular rhythm is far more enjoyable. The narrator says that on the coast, in the mountains, and in the jungle, everyone wants to dance pandilla due to its singular rhythm. In the lyrics, the protagonist teaches an urban girl from Lima how to *really* dance. Because people from tropical areas such as the Caribbean and the Amazon are generally assumed to have exceptional (and sensual) dance skills, the narrator is effectively reinforcing particular stereotypes, primarily for local audiences, boldly positing the preeminence of provincial practice. This attitude is only partly in jest: pandilla lyricists specifically seek to exalt Amazonian culture, counterposing pandilla to Peruvian genres such as huayno and marinera that have dominated the national imaginary and media for so long, as well as the international genres that have a wide national listenership.

Pandilla lyrics also colorfully describe Amazonian culture. The songs clearly reference local foods, vocabularies, and customs. Often called *charapeando*, which is the process of speaking like a *charapa* (a local),[6] pandilla lyrics employ vernacular and slang known mainly to residents and migrants from Loreto. Another strategy is to emphasize the region's vitality and the many ways it differs from other parts of Peru.

Later in the song "Mix Pandilla 2007," Amazonian colloquial phrases pepper nearly every line, and local knowledge is required to understand the song's content. The story is a typical tragedy of a man who has been unfaithful to his partner and has unwittingly impregnated another woman, noting that both will suffer for it. The narrator sarcastically encourages the adulterer to keep partying, mentioning that it will be difficult to *tahuampear*, or dance at this party. He revels in his own life: "Y yo sigo *mashaqueando* tomando mi clavo huasca, comiendo *avispa juane* con su sopita flefle / Ahora si que te has fregado *buchisapa*." (I keep *lazing around*, drinking my *clavo huasca*, eating *meat juane* with soup,⁷ slurp, slurp / Now you're screwed, *beer belly*.)

As mentioned, what grounds the narrative in local experience is the use of language familiar only to charapas. Just weeks after arriving in Iquitos, even I became accustomed to these expressions, which are used by all generations. *Buchisapa*, for example, is a playful term used among drinking friends to refer to a person with a potbelly, often the result of too much beer; the suffix *-sapa* is a Quechua participle indicating largeness or fatness. As local languages continue to die, it becomes difficult to identify the source of such words and participles, but it is clear that roots, prefixes, and suffixes from countless Amazonian languages are found in local colloquialisms.

A pandilla's success depends partly on the number of local references buried in its text in this way. Most people are familiar with at least some Amazonian slang, and revelers get very excited at hearing local phrases in a song, several of which represent "castilianized" versions of Quechua words. During a local performance of "Mix Pandilla 2007," celebrants laughed hysterically at the *buchisapa* line, mocking the rotund singer who lifted up his shirt to reveal a large belly while clutching a beer bottle. When the singer repeated *huasca* several times, many people pretended to dance drunkenly, stumbling around and pretending to pass out on the concrete floor until their friends threatened to pour beer on them.

In order to mark their Amazonianness, more and more pandillas feature obscure local references and effectively function as a popular teaching tool. The orality of *loretano* tradition is a point of pride, and this informs the appreciation of pandilla as well. In the foreword to a compendium of Amazonian vocabulary, the local folklorist Jaime Vázquez Valcárcel focused on this phenomenon:

> We should feel pride of our form of speaking. . . . Our way of speaking is our existence. We were born with that characteristic and sadly, we're losing it. This book is not meant to make us feel guilty or responsible for this loss. The object is much greater and more noteworthy: to preserve and spread our orality. . . . We should always feel proud of our authentic expressions. To speak like *loretanos* is a way of being authentic. With this compendium, we will get to know the words that we have to express ourselves. It now falls on you, readers, to use the necessary cadence and tone so that our speech remains expressive in its glory. (Rodriguez n.d.: 6)⁸

The links Vázquez makes between authenticity, cadence, and tone are noteworthy. Charapas have a very distinctive cadence to their daily speech, a sing-song style that features a unique contour with deep pitches and elongated vowels; loretanos identify Amazonian authenticity with language use and daily communication involving such inflection. By referencing not only the vocabulary used but also the tone, Vázquez references another aspect of identity politics.

Pandilla dancing recalls indigenous Amazon culture, reflecting an engagement with native, local values. The marches' *saltito* (jumpy) style still constitutes the prototypical carnival music today, perhaps due to the communal aspect of the actual dance: couples change partners regularly while maintaining large, ill-formed circles, hopping and stomping backward and forward in a generally circular motion.[9] Because the central activity during carnival—dancing around the húmisha—generally takes place within neighborhoods or among small clusters of friends, the community aspect of pandilla is emphasized, tying the performance more tightly to local indigenous heritage that tends to center on communal gatherings and dance styles.

Pandilla instrumentation also reflects indigenous roots. As established by local folkloric ensembles, it includes some indigenous antecedents, but its combination of European, indigenous, and mestizo elements is considered emblematic of the syncretism that defines the genre. Contemporary folkloric pandillas are performed using *bombo* (bass drum), violin, *redoblante* (snare drum) and *quena* (end-notched flute). While many consider the violin a criollo instrument, its performance style is uniquely Amazonian. The bombo originated among Quechua speakers in the Andes, and it provides a basic bass line just as it does in the highlands. Though the redoblante probably originated in Europe, it has been adopted by native communities, where it is widely used to accompany dances and marches and is locally considered Amazonian. It plays a key role in effective performance of the pandilla, outlining the syncopated, march-like eighth and sixteenth notes that characterize the carnival sound. The instrument is instantly recognizable; participants in carnival begin dancing the pandilla when they hear the redoblante, before the entry of other instruments (figure 7.3).

The quena is of particular interest because (like the bombo) it is closely associated with the Peruvian Andes. Amazonian quenas probably derived from their highland prototype. Performers gradually adapted the Andean style to accommodate Amazonian aesthetics, which include lighter, faster,

El Shipibo Enamorado

Figure 7.3. "El shipibo enamorado," written by Eliseo Reátegui circa 1970. The ornamented *quena* line is characteristic of a folkloric pandilla, and the accompanying percussion lines, while often varied in concert settings, provide a basic feel for the pandilla rhythm. This recording is on an old cassette tape and may have been commercially released in the mid-1960s, although the original recording is currently unavailable. Folkloric ensembles perform "El shipibo enamorado" regularly today.

and higher melodies. Approximately one inch in diameter, the Amazonian quena is made of PVC pipe instead of bamboo and is significantly narrower than the Andean instrument. Its sound is thinner and higher-pitched, and it does not allow for the overblown partials heard in highland practices. The plastic Amazonian quena is often piercing, audible far above the pattern of the bombo; it looks quite modern yet creates a markedly indigenous timbre.

Because tecno-cumbia is the dominant musical style in and around Iquitos, the transformation of pandilla by groups such as Explosión into synthesized commercial music at times other than carnival is hardly surprising. As often happens to folkloric forms, local musicians reinterpreted pandilla, creating an electric version, perfect for mass consumption. In the case of Explosión, this hybridization earned the popular tecno-cumbia group acclaim throughout the region and beyond the Amazon's borders with migrants in coastal Lima. Explosión also decontextualized pandilla, popularizing it throughout the year not only as a method of asserting control and diffusion of a distinctly Amazonian genre, but also providing an easily accessible point of pride and regional identity for local consumers.

Electrified pandilla has come about as Iquitos faces an increasingly neoliberal economy, wherein the city's Amazonianness is challenged both nationally and regionally. As much as the area is attempting to integrate into the state, tight ties with the larger jungle region point to a difficult path paved with uncertainty about its economic future as well as a desire to be recognized for cultural (and other) achievements. Understanding tecno-cumbia and the tecno-cumbiazation of pandilla may help illustrate this local and transnational discourse coupled with regional identity.

Tecno-cumbia: An Amazonian Genre

The *tecno* of tecno-cumbia does not refer to techno music as it developed in the United States in Detroit in the late 1970s. Rather it refers to the implementation of electronics in the musical recording and performance of popular dance music in South America (Romero 2002). At the time of tecno-cumbia's genesis, electrifying music symbolized modernity, and the use of synthesizers, effects, and drum machines cemented an official entrance into cosmopolitanism for the Amazon.

Tecno-cumbia rose to national fame in the late 1990s and, with it, a temporary tolerance and even approval of tropical culture. As Tucker explains in this volume, tecno-cumbia's de-Andeanization of chicha provisionally pushed it into the spotlight, garnering previously marginalized peoples social acceptance in the capital city. Tecno-cumbia stars' rise to fame coincidentally paralleled the political campaign of the president and eventual dictator Alberto Fujimori in his quest to hold his position for a second term. Because Fujimori's main platform was the alleged rights of the migrant—himself the son of Japanese immigrants—he adopted the nationally accepted music genre in a blatant political ploy. This move reaffirmed the music as having "everyman" meaning. This was Fujimori's attempt to latch on to a genre that arguably arose from lower-class creativity in the midst of a stifling regime (Romero 2002, 2007; Turino 1990).

Las Tres Fronteras

Key to the development of cultural expressions like tecno-cumbia in Iquitos is the city's proximity to *las tres fronteras* (the three borders or frontiers). Iquitos—and, by extension, the entire Loreto Department—associates itself more with the Amazon region (including that of Brazil and Colombia) than with the Peruvian state. Just eight hours east of the city lie las tres fronteras, where Tabatinga in Brazil, Leticia in Colombia, and Santa Rosa in Peru meet in a confluence of borderlands on the Amazon River. Because of their nearness to each other, cultural overlapping and interchange are inevitable, and Iquitos is hardly exempt from borderland influences.

This regional association with the greater Upper Amazon does not preclude nationalism; in fact, iquiteños, and more broadly loretanos, also have strong nationalist tendencies during particular seasonal, isolated events. Individual and collective identity as Peruvians effervesces during Independence Day (July 28), soccer matches in which Peru plays against another country's team, and at a handful of other events. Amazonian affiliation, however, is far more prevalent due to shared colonial histories and economic and cultural exchange (Villarejo 2005).

In Iquitos the main external musical influences come from the neighbors of these borders. In the late 1990s until relatively recently, a dance form called *toada* dominated performances in Iquitos. Toadas are fast, commercial sambas allegedly native to the Amazon region of Brazil (although this fact remains disputed) that are danced in parallel lines. According to Paco Latino, a choreographer and dance historian from Lima, the toada developed in the

Peruvian Amazon as a hybrid song form, and it wasn't until chicha musicians popularized it through an invented, accompanying dance—mistaking the genre for Brazilian—that it became known more broadly throughout Iquitos.[10] This assertion most likely stems from an inherent competitive nationalism on the part of Latinos, especially considering that toadas are sung in Portuguese and appear to be popular in the Brazilian Amazon as well. Most Brazilians outside of the Amazon are unfamiliar with toada but associate it most closely with *samba brega*, a style often considered to be schlock.[11]

As Tucker relates in this volume, one of the cornerstones of chicha and tecno-cumbia is Colombian cumbia. Because of its location so close to the Colombian border, both cumbia and *vallenato*, another popular Colombian genre, have strongly influenced musicians and listeners in Iquitos. Because Latin dance crazes spread throughout South America through mass media, several tropical styles, such as salsa, cumbia, and *son*, merged with local sounds (Wade 2000). In Iquitos and the surrounding region, cumbia was especially prominent. Tecno-cumbia is part of the general genre of *música tropical*. Furthermore, iquiteños and limeños consider Iquitos and the Amazon part of the *oriente peruano* (Peruvian Orient), and the tropical influence has become naturalized.

Some scholars and laypersons meld chicha and tecno-cumbia into one fluid category. I choose to separate them based on several distinguishing sociomusical factors founded in part on Raúl Romero's (2002) description and my personal experience and in part on the political milieu that set the stage for tecno-cumbia's early reputation. I understand that these categories are hardly static and may be assigned to one or the other of the two genres, depending on context and perspective.

The Amazon-centric style of tecno-cumbia is key to differentiating it from chicha. References to Andean musics or performance styles fade, and in their place tropical styles predominate, including far more musical references to salsa, merengue, samba, and *son*. Tempos increase significantly in tecno-cumbia, and gone is the meandering, wallowing, sad love song. Lyrics tend to be more straightforward, lamenting love but celebrating fiesta culture. Furthermore, volume is of utmost importance. In Iquitos volume defines a successful gathering, party, or concert, especially in the presentation of a tecno-cumbia ensemble. Extreme volume also partially references modernity; hefty speakers often signify a wealthy, lucrative band. For example, Explosión's fifty enormous speakers display the group's wealth and prestige.

Dancing is the raison d'être of tecno-cumbia. Not only do female singers wear sexy pop-star outfits, gyrating to the rhythms, but additional young female dancers also dominate the stage. Explosión's owner, Raúl Flores, attributes the success of the group to the implementation of sexy dancers, clothed in barely there bikinis, dancing to sensual chorography: "I had to include female dancers in the group to do choreographed dancing. And so we got going with a bang, breaking the mold with this new system because it was something different, something spectacular in this part of jungle Peru. There's a lot of attraction because of the girls, the ladies."[12] Flores admits that part of the explosive popularity of his group is this distinct presentation of the sensual female charapa. As Romero (2002: 235) notes—and Explosión's performance attests—dancers' costumes incorporate perceived Amazonian heritage, with stylized "traditional" dress, including stereotypical feathers, beads, and woven tops and headdresses. Stereotypical costume styles often define a performance, not just among tecno-cumbia dancers but among audience members who recognize Amazonian elements and cheer loudly for them.

Perhaps the most distinctive characteristic of tecno-cumbia is, as Romero notes, mass mediation. Piracy thrives in Peru; musicians depend heavily on the circulation of pirated recordings to draw audiences to live performances to promote their product.[13] Tecno-cumbia entrepreneurs quickly realized its potential and targeted young consumers eager for new pop stars. A modified payola system assists groups with guaranteed radio airplay. This advantage has proven to be crucial to the success of pandilla as a tecno-cumbiaized genre, not only for promoting the style throughout the Amazon and beyond but for lending it a modern, cosmopolitan air and giving iquiteños cultural capital.

Tecno-cumbiazation of Pandilla

Until recently the highly profitable Explosión has been the dominant tecno-cumbia group in Iquitos for a number of years. Composed of several musicians formerly employed by Ruth Karina (see Tucker's chapter, this volume) and other popular artists of the mid- to late 1990s, Explosión proved a financially successful, enviable business model, actively marketing its cultural product, which included "authentically Amazonian" pandilla.

Explosión began its career in 1998 performing a combination of Brazilian toadas and Amazonian tecno-cumbia. Toadas, as I mentioned before, were popular, samba-infused dance songs that provided the soundtrack for mass line-dancing. Their popularity waned only in recent years as pandilla and other Latin American genres have supplanted them.

Explosión's tagline was *Grupo Explosión! El Orgullo Amazónico* (Group Explosión! Amazonian Pride!) long before the ensemble began performing pandilla; however, it was truly with the adoption of pandilla as its Amazonian cultural anthem that the logo gained more than just marketing value for its fans.

Although a number of factors most likely contributed to the resurgence in popularity of pandilla among Explosión listeners, there is a particular origin myth that has towered over local imagination, in part due to Flores's entrepreneurial finesse. According to several members of Explosión, it was early January 2003 when, after a long night of performing, someone in the group mock-drummed the march rhythm of pandilla. The keyboardists fiddled around, improvising a harmonic framework supporting a synthesized quena line. Soon a full-fledged jam unfolded, to which the tired patrons geared up again, dancing animatedly as if circling the húmisha at carnival. Explosión's musicians note that a local radio station, Radio Loreto, coincidentally sponsored that evening's show, and the station taped the impromptu performance. Later in the week, Radio Loreto broadcast the recording, and improvised pandilla became an instant local success. It was the most requested song for months after carnival, and Flores soon marketed it as *the* representative Amazonian music genre, comparing it to the marinera of the coast and the huayno of the highlands in terms of value as a generic Peruvian música típica. Its popularity skyrocketed, and now much of Lima and a few other cities familiar with the group recognize Explosión as a typically Amazonian band famous for its pandillas. According to Flores,

> We were going to be a kind of ambassador of our regional music. So the idea of fusion [entered] because typical music from this part of the jungle—like from what we call the quena, the *tambor* [redoblante], and the bombo—well, we changed the sounds, we created fusion through electronic instruments without abandoning the genre that we had to uphold. It was just a more ... more sophisticated sound. And it happened because today it's not just us from the Amazon who like it, but it's going to the national level. And this is great for us because it identifies us and all the while people like it more and more. Our fellow Peruvians, loretanos, jungle people identify with it, whereas before they were afraid, they were embarrassed to say, "I'm from the jungle and this is my music." But now, now they feel proud.[14]

Flores references the fusion of pandilla with tecno-cumbia. He implies that the goal is national airplay and a national fan base, and he indicates an affiliation or identification with the genre on the part of iquiteños. Flores also notes the inherent contradiction that faces Amazonians today: pride versus embarrassment at a strong cultural practice versus its historical context within a struggling, isolated society. His desire to be an "ambassador of our regional music" points to larger issues of desire for "authentic" Amazonian themes, underscored by an ineloquent history of debilitating colonialism and yet a thirst for cosmopolitan and urban sophistication. Turino's idea of "modernist reformism" as discussed in his volume on popular music in Zimbabwe is applicable here in the sense that the electrified pandilla is a result of "projects based on the idea that a 'new culture,' or new genres, styles, and practices, should be forged as a synthesis of the 'best' or 'most valuable' aspects of a local 'traditional' culture and 'the best' of foreign 'modern' lifeways and technologies" (2000: 16). Essentially Flores recontextualized pandilla, a form with significant connections to various indigenous cultures, by tecno-cumbiaizing it, thereby rendering it emblematic of a cosmopolitan project rooted in financial gain and marketing strategies. Flores and his musicians fused pandilla (tradition) with tecno-cumbia (new culture) to create a modern, Amazonian style that became an effective promotional tool and niche product.

Conclusion: Amazonian "Savage Modern"

The combined forces of colonization, through missionization and economic development, have created a space that is vulnerable to outside influences and yet creatively resistant, existing within its own tight-knit circle, creating new localities amid global trends. These histories have intertwined and converged to engineer particular constructions of ethnicity, selfhood, and regional identity that are uniquely local and yet remarkably urban, setting the stage for tecno-cumbia's progression from local attraction to national phenomenon. Local culture has been and continues to be deeply entrenched in the foreign, creating cosmopolitan spaces that signify sophistication, urbanity, and modernity (Turino 2000).

Although Lima is an enormous city made up primarily of Andean immigrants, wealthy criollos established its status as a thriving coastal metropolis long beforehand and set the precedent for regional comparisons. Iquitos is very isolated, located in the heart of the jungle; accordingly the charapa is largely marginalized by coastal elites and often, by extension, *nuevos limeños* (new Lima residents). For iquiteños, understanding the regional significance of the music that informs Amazonianness could perhaps uncover local strategies of shedding "savage" appearances in favor of urban cosmopolitan culture and becoming competitive with other Peruvian urban centers. Tecno-cumbia and pandilla are jungle genres, and yet their popularity is growing nationally, due to calculated business practices resulting from a changing economy and stronger development of local pride. This in turn allows the area to maintain a certain regional cultural autonomy while becoming a more visible and viable part of the national fabric (Martin-Barbero and Janer 2000).

Pandilla reappeared popularly at a crucial moment in Iquitos's history, when the area shed its postcolonial shadows with more fervor and embraced cosmopolitanism more enthusiastically. Media and entrepreneurial skills coupled with a certain exploitation of Amazonian pride encouraged one particular tecno-cumbia ensemble, Explosión, to showcase a popular local genre in a new setting, promoting an electrified regional style nationally on a platform already developed in the form of tecno-cumbia. Transnational influences stimulated strong regionalism, although in tandem with increasingly nationalist sentiments in attempts to become a recognized part of the Peruvian whole, shedding an association with savagery. Understanding these processes could unveil ways in which many iquiteños and Peruvian Amazonians carefully negotiate reception into that imaginary, culturally completing the old adage that Peru is indeed *sierra, selva, costa*.

Discography

Explosión. 2007. *Mix Pandilla*. Independent release.

Interviews

Flores, Raúl. Personal interview. June 22, 2007.
Latino, Paco. Electronic communication. April 18, 2008.

Notes

I wish to extend my deepest gratitude to Robin Moore, Emily Pinkerton, Becky Astrop, and the reviewers for their feedback. Any errors are my own.

1. While *popular* in the Latin American use has often denoted "of the people" or "folkloric," in this essay, I use the word to mean "commercially successful," similar to the way *popular* is used to describe such music in the United States.

2. With the arrival of the Brazilian steamboat *Marajó* in Iquitos on October 7, 1853, the era of new and more efficient transportation in the Amazon began (Rumrrill 1983). The rubber tree (*Hevea brasiliensis*) is native to the Amazon rainforest (AECI 2006).

3. Criollo styles include *vals* and *marinera*.

4. "Es la reina del folklor amazónico."

5. I joined my friend Mario Meder Seretti and his 2007 graduating class of the College of International Business at the Universidad Nacional de la Amazonía Peruana. We celebrated at the home of one of his peers.

6. The charapa (*Chelonia mydas*) is a freshwater turtle found in the Amazon Basin. Colloquially it is a derogative term used by people outside of Loreto (primarily in the coastal city of Lima) to refer to those who live in the Amazon. Within the Loreto Department, however, individuals often affectionately refer to each other as charapas.

7. *Huasca* is a local word meaning "drunk," and *clavo huasca* is a particular kind of tree that a strong liquor is made from. Associated with the San Juan festival, *juanes* are small bundles of rice, chicken, a hard-boiled egg, and olives wrapped in banana leaves. Juane is considered the most traditional loretano food and is even featured on billboards advertising locally brewed beer by the airport in Iquitos.

8. "Debemos sentirnos orgullosos de nuestra forma de hablar.... Nuestro hablar es nuestra propia existencia. Nacemos con esa característica y lastimosamente la estamos perdiendo. No es el motivo de este trabajo encontrar culpables o responsables de esta paulatina pérdida. El objetivo es mucho mayor y destacable: preservar y difundir nuestra oralidad.... Siempre hay que sentirnos orgullosos de nuestra autenticidad. Hablar como loretanos es una forma de ser auténticos. Con este trabajo podremos conocer las palabras que tenemos para expresarnos. Queda en ustedes, lectores, darle el tonito cadencioso necesario para que nuestro hablar quede expresado en toda su plenitud."

9. Few scholars have described the pandilla, and that which has been written is primarily by local folklorists such as Javier Isuiza Trigoso, whose thin volumes are some of the only resources on urban culture in and around Iquitos. "[La pandilla es un] masivo baile público. Tomados de los brazos en pareja, forman columnas y se desplazan realizando una especie de saltos sutiles. Algunas veces retroceden un paso atrás y vuelven a emprender con regocijo la danza [(The pandilla is) a massive public dance. Arms linked, couples form columns and they move in a kind of subtle jumps. Sometimes they go back and forth, and return to the beginning, enjoying the dance]" (Isuiza Trigoso 2006: 21).

10. Paco Latino, personal communication, April 18, 2008.

11. The *lambada* was also popular in Iquitos until relatively recently, and its imprint can arguably be found in toadas and even in some of the dance styles of tecno-cumbia.

12. "Había que incluir dentro del grupo musical, ballet de chicas que bailen para hacer la coreografía y entramos de arranque y rompimos esquemas con ese sistema porque era algo diferente, algo espectacular en esta parte del Perú de la selva, hay mucho atractivo por las chicas, por las señoritas" (Raúl Flores, personal interview, June 22, 2007).

13. Henry Stobart (2010) and Barry Kernfield (2011) address the impetus for piracy in detail in Bolivia and the United States, respectively, in their recent publications.

14. "Nosotros íbamos a ser una especie de embajadores de nuestra música regional y bueno, de ahí la idea de fusionar, porque la música típica de acá, de esta parte de la selva, a través de lo que nosotros llamamos la quena, el tambor y el bombo, que es típico de acá entonces . . . entonces nosotros ya cambiamos de sonidos, fusionamos a través de instrumentos electrónicos sin salirnos del género que teníamos que mantener, solamente que ya con un sonido más, más sofisticado y . . . y se hizo esto. Hoy por hoy no solamente [nos] gusta a nosotros que somos de acá de la Amazonía sino ya esto . . . esto se está expandiendo a nivel nacional, y ahí bien por nosotros, porque nos identifica y cada vez va gustando más a la gente y adonde vamos esté. Nuestros paisanos loretanos, selváticos, se identifican; les gusta mucho. Antes ellos como que tenían un poco de temor, de vergüenza de decir 'yo soy de la selva y ésta es mi música'. Ahora no; ahora se sienten orgullosos" (Raúl Flores, personal interview, June 22, 2007).

8.
Gender Tensions in *Cumbia Villera*'s Lyrics

Due to the novel character of the studies of music and identity in Argentina, quite often there are no studies available on a particular musical genre. That is why, in many cases, musical research in Argentina cannot follow the canonical writing format used by the social sciences, in which a thorough review of the literature and a positioning of the research in relation to that literature are mandatory. In most cases, there is only a small amount of research to take ideas from or to compare one's research with and show how one is proceeding.

Therefore in most cases, one has to rely (very unwillingly) on what has been written on similar musical genres elsewhere to position one's research in the academic field. This creates a problem and an opportunity at the same time: analyzing a particular musical phenomenon without taking into account the historical processes that make it unique can produce perverse effects of interpretive projection. However, if one is fully aware of those possible effects, it is still possible to illuminate the phenomenon under investigation and, at the same time, to reveal the situated character of the interpretive proposals. This productive tension has been a constant in our research, and its outcome has been a radicalization of the anthropological dimension that serves as its guiding muse.

Thus, while the popular musical genre we were studying approximately resembled something "out there" (there are cumbias in several Latin American countries, as evidenced by the essays in this collection), in the process of our research, our perspectives on the topic gradually changed, and we were able to understand the idiosyncrasies of *cumbia villera* in a novel manner. In that way, and based on an interpretation that recognizes the feminist perspective but, at the same time, radicalizes and singularizes its effects (we fully understand gender power dynamics and the necessity of dismantling male domination in both society and the social sciences), we make visible the nuances and complexities that we believe are very important, stressing the singular historical circumstances in which cumbia villera occurs. Additionally, the current conditions of performance of our research subject are so idiosyncratic that any comparison with musical genres elsewhere makes little sense.

While looking for ideas on how to analyze gender relationships in cumbia villera, we did not find much previous academic research done in Argentina, but we did find a couple of pathbreaking studies done in Latin America on *salsa* and *bachata* (Aparicio 1998; Pacini Hernandez 1995). Therefore our analysis of cumbia villera's lyrics is influenced by what Pacini Hernandez and—especially—Aparicio found in their research (which was highly influenced by feminism's second wave). However, our analysis departs from theirs in most cases because the complex web of linguistic and nonlinguistic practices (what we call "discourses") in which these lyrics are performed and interpreted (their different layers) is completely different.

We are fully aware that gender power relationships are constitutive of social interactions and, as such, should always be considered in any analysis of the social. But at the same time, we agree with Wetherell and Edley, who write, "Most men benefit from patriarchal practices and most women do not. There is certainly a considerable 'patriarchal dividend' most men accrue which produces masculine characters. But it is also possible to identify 'subordinate masculinities' and 'complicit masculinities' where the alignment with hegemonic forms of masculinity is more complex" (1998: 159–60). We also believe that gender power relationships are only one component (one of the most important, to be sure) of any social relationship, and such a universal presence is always actualized in a singular way because it is shaped by all the other components of the particular whole to which it belongs.

At first glance, the lyrics of cumbia villera seem to fully comply with male "symbolic terrorism," a discourse analysis influenced by second wave feminism found in many musical genres around the world in general and Latin America in particular. Frances Aparicio has been a pioneer in this type of analysis regarding Latin American music, particularly in the cases of *bolero* and salsa. Deborah Pacini Hernandez was a pioneer as well regarding Dominican bachata, and Peter Manuel regarding Caribbean dance music. All of these outstanding authors, as should be the case, relate their interpretations of the lyrics to how their interviewees interpreted those same lyrics, clearly showing that many times, what the analyst found in the lyrics is not the same interpretation that people who follow the genres stress about the songs. In this chapter we follow a similar strategy, but we add a dimension that is not always explicit in the work of these authors: the complex web of discourses that surround the emission and reception of cumbia villera lyrics. (We understand discourse as explicated by Laclau and Mouffe [1987], that is, as those linguistic and nonlinguistic practices that carry and confer meaning in a field of forces characterized by the play of power relationships.)

By *emission*, we mean all the social performances (here understood as linguistic and nonlinguistic discourses) that accompany, in different ways, the artistic presentation of a particular song. As Middleton aptly reminds us, musical "meanings result from the social context of performance and reception; but the performance itself has metamusical aspects . . . [such as] bodily movement and social interaction" (1990: 242). Thus some of the dimensions of emission of the songs are pretty close to the musical performances themselves, such as the way of singing, the corporeal movements of the singers, their facial expressions, the movements of the dancers who almost always accompany the performance of cumbia villera songs, their facial expressions, their comments before and after their dancing, the comments of the announcers before and after the song, and the expressions of the public who go to the shows in which those songs are performed.

Some other dimensions of this larger contextual emission are a little more distant from the actual performance of the song, acting as a general cultural background against which those songs are performed. In the case of the highly sexualized songs that characterize cumbia villera as a genre, we consider the way that sex is publicly discussed in the media outlets (television, radio, and magazines) that cumbia villera fans usually consume and the way sex is talked about in the everyday conversations of these youths.

We believe it is impossible to understand how cumbia villera's lyrics connote sexuality in the way they do without taking into account all these other linguistic and nonlinguistic (performative) discourses that are always linked to the emission of those songs. When one does so, the lyrics acquire a very different meaning and, in many cases, clearly contradict a literal textual analysis. Thus when one reads the lyrics without watching the performances, they appear to be a clear manifestation of the masculine symbolic violence well researched by second wave feminism. That is the reason one of the most important Argentine sociologists, Maristella Svampa, is correct, but only partially so, when she writes:

> Women are constantly ridiculed and denigrated [in cumbia villera lyrics], especially on the sexual plane. Far from accidental, the virulence of these at-

tacks arises out of complex social processes: on the one hand, we are referring to the marked warping of the masculine universe in which a man's identity is anchored in work and his role as breadwinner; and on the other, to the emergence and affirmation of female protagonism as witnessed in present day social movements not only in Argentina, but in the globalized periphery in general. (2005: 180)

However, only after exploring the thorough meaning of those lyrics, in their enunciation and reception, is it possible to get a much more complex and revealing image of the culture of the social group wherein cumbia villera circulates. This image does not negate gender conflict, but it perceives that conflict with a greater complexity and allows the appearance of tensions, hues, and subversion points in relation to an initial masculine domination image perceived as complete and absolute.

This is so because only one of the possible readings of the lyrics of cumbia villera comes into view when those lyrics are analyzed using what has nowadays become the hegemonic academic view (both in descriptive and normative terms) regarding gender. The field of cultural studies has adopted the critical perspective and set of values of the literature influenced by second wave feminism (in its different incarnations), which has placed a well-deserved emphasis on the way social practices are continuously crossed by a dimension that is always present in any kind of social interaction. We are referring here to gender power relations that historically, in the vast majority of cases, have meant the domination of one gender (feminine) by the other (masculine). This literature has been instrumental in revealing that, behind the apparent neutrality of any system of categories (including those used by popular music), there is always a set of power relations that, if not questioned by the social scientist, contributes to its reproduction.

Therefore it is necessary to put forward such a reading of the lyrics but, at the same time, to challenge it, to problematize it in the way we do in this essay. Our position is that the analysis of gender power relations does not have to assume the existence of gender positions that precede the social configurations that frame them; man and woman are neither essential nor universal subject positions. At the same time, we believe that power relations are never relationships of absolute and eternal domination, even though, by definition, they always reveal social asymmetries.

In this vein, to the textual analysis proposed by the literature influenced by second wave feminism à la Aparicio we want to add all the considerations that make such scrutiny much more complex. Influenced by some developments of so-called third wave feminism, but especially by current research done on popular cultures, we use those types of analysis that illuminate the relative power of all subordinate people, not just women, and the kind of social analysis that denounces the fact that, behind the good intentions of analysts, they often identify with the type of power they are questioning. In the case of popular culture studies, that kind of research tends to equate, using sophisms, the culture of poor people with a poor culture. (We are referring here to the approach advanced by Grignon and Passeron [1989] about the kind of analysis that, attempting to bring back the social and historical character, that is, the political nature of aesthetic categories, relies on the dominant categories that they reveal.)[1]

Thus what we have learned from recent third wave feminism (Baumgardner and Richards 2000; Henry 2004; Karp and Stoller 1999) is the importance of trying to "recast femininity as a transgressive opportunity for women to claim sexual power and to create feminine subject positions through their sexuality.... Debbie Stoller and Michelle Karp, the founders of BUST magazine, have most vocally supported the idea of 'girlie,' defining it as 'Girl Culture—that shared set of female experiences that includes Barbies and blowjobs, sexism and shoplifting, Vogue and vaginas' (Karp and Stoller 1999: xv)" (Keenan 2008: 379–80). As Melanie Waters reminds us, "The girlie brand of feminism that BUST promotes is seen to constitute an important rebellion against the false impression that since women don't want to be sexually exploited, they don't want to be sexual; against the necessity of brass-buttoned, red-suited seriousness to infiltrate a man's world; against the anachronistic belief that because women could be dehumanized by porn . . . they must be; and the idea that girls and power don't mix" (2007: 258).

In a similar vein, for authors like Baumgardner and Richards, this kind of pro-sexuality feminism also implies "staking out space in areas identified with men, such as . . . porn, and judgment-free pleasure and sex" (2000: 80). This theoretical approach, on the one hand, proposes a celebration of sexuality in itself and, on the other hand, claims that women deserve rights *as women*, including regarding those things that specifically make them women. Thus Baumgardner and Richards claim that those "women things" can actually give women power. That is, if women are stuck living in a "man's world," then they might as well take advantage of those things that allow them power in that world, even if those things are signifiers of traditional femininity, a claim that implies a complete redefining of what domination and empowerment may mean in the context of sex: "'These days putting out one's pretty power, one's pussy power, one's sexual energy for popular consumption no longer makes you a bimbo,' wrote Elizabeth Wurtzel in her 1999 glory rant *Bitch*. 'It makes you smarter'" (Baumgardner and Richards 2000: 306).

For third-wavers, feminism is an empowering drive to affirm women's sexuality and to claim their own sexual appetite; it is a movement that claims a particular female sexuality based on a belief that desire is not exclusively a male prerogative (Kimmel 2005). In other words, they believe that there is power to be found in embracing not only femininity but sex itself (Baumgardner and Richards 2000). In brief, third wave feminism embraces femininity in the guise of some traditional feminine signifiers, yet it is linked with empowerment and a desire for independence and sexuality *for themselves* rather than only engaging in sex for the pleasure of men. Accordingly many third wave feminists are quite sensitive to the fluid notion of gender, the performative character of sex, and the potential oppressions (and, of course, empowerment) inherent in all sexual and gender relations.

When we analyze the lyrics and their multiple interpretations, we apply many of the insights we got from reading Aparicio's, Pacini Hernandez's, and Manuel's pioneering work on gender relations in Latin American popular music, but we try to add complexity by entertaining some of the ideas brought forth by third wave feminists, complexity that accounts for the contradictions this pioneering work cannot account for due to the idiosyncrasy of our own subject of study. At the same time, for the kind of analysis of lyrics we are doing it is crucial to consider the complex web of discourses that surround the enunciation of those lyrics, a consideration that opens up new analytical venues that a less thorough analysis of lyrics cannot traverse to. But before entering the complicated field of cumbia villera's conditions of emission, a brief account of the history of cumbia as a musical genre is necessary.

Cumbia and Cumbia Villera in the Argentine Music Scene

There is no agreement about when cumbia first appeared in Argentina. According to some connoisseurs, it arrived in the 1940s with Efraín Orozco, who came to Argentina with his jazz orchestra and played cumbia with the stylistic variations in fashion at the time. According to Héctor Fernández L'Hoeste (2007: 347), it was only after the 1960s, with the arrival of the Colombian band El Cuarteto Imperial, that cumbia gained a firm presence in Argentina.

Considering that cumbia records and radio play have greatly contributed to the spread of the genre in all of the Latin American regions in which cumbia has taken root, we cannot ignore these avenues either.

However, the bulk of scholarship regards the late 1950s and early 1960s as the point at which tropical music became popular in Argentina, and the names of two pioneer cumbia combos occupy center stage in such a development, Los Wawancó and Los Cinco del Ritmo. It is important to point out that cumbia's rise to popularity was framed by the decline of *tango* as the most important dance genre in Buenos Aires. Starting in the early 1950s and linked in complex ways to the arrival of internal migrants to Buenos Aires, tango initially shared its popularity with the folk rhythms those migrants brought with them (above all, *chamamé*) and with American and Caribbean rhythms. Later it was almost totally replaced by them. By the early 1960s chamamé and cumbia had become the favored dance genres among the popular sectors of Buenos Aires, partly because the accordion served as their most important melodic instrument and embracing couples could dance to both.

Although the dominant sectors of Argentina's society viewed cumbia as reflecting popular bad taste, the genre was first heard in Buenos Aires in middle-class *confiterías*, showing that cumbia was accepted by Buenos Aires high society. In the mid-1960s Los Cartageneros, La Charanga del Caribe, and Fuego Cubano joined Los Wawancó as the main exponents of the genre.

Through the late 1960s and the 1970s, cumbia remained popular and blended with native Argentine rhythms, most prominently with chamamé, the most danceable among them. From this blending, *chamamé tropical* was born, a rhythm that reigned in the 1970s and early 1980s. One of the most important combos of this genre was Los Caú (The Drunk Ones), who, mimicking the American rock band Kiss, painted their faces black and white. Humor was their distinctive characteristic, and they made fun of everything, including rock *nacional*, the most important musical genre of the period. For instance, Los Caú facetiously titled one of their albums *Los Caú en Obras*. The height of success for Argentine rock bands at the time was to be invited to perform at Obras Stadium. Los Caú never performed there, let alone recorded a live album there. The photos on the album cover poked fun at the rockers' aspirations while showing the class differences that separate cumbia's musicians and audience from those of rock nacional. The photos show the members of Los Caú attired and equipped as working-class masons literally *in obras*—that is, building a house.

According to Eloísa Martín (2011), the opening of the Tropitango dance hall in 1981 inaugurated a new period in tropical music. In addition, the first program dedicated to tropical music, *Fantástico* (later renamed *Ritmo Fantástico*) aired on the Splendid radio station in 1986. The program would lend its name to the first middle-class discotheque-type dance club devoted exclusively to tropical music when the Kirovski brothers, owners of the Magenta record label, opened the Fantástico Bailable, with a capacity of thirty-five hundred, in the Buenos Aires neighborhood of Once. The club, which still operates, is on Rivadavia Avenue, with its many bus lines, and close to the Once train station, making it easily accessible not only from all parts of the city but also from all over Greater Buenos Aires. Martín also maintains that the two most important record labels of the genre, Leader and Magenta (and their related undertakings) were especially important in what is considered the boom of tropical music in the late 1980s and 1990s. This is so because the recording companies owned a number of radio stations and dance clubs in Buenos Aires and Greater Buenos Aires; they also produced TV programs and published magazines dedicated to tropical music.

For Esteban De Gori (2005), the *bailanta* boom of the 1990s appears to be linked to the fantasy of infinite consumption and well-being that was called *la fiesta menemista* (the Menemist party), referring to the neoliberal policies of President Carlos Menem. De Gori and other scholars emphasize the new class alliance proposed by Menemism in which both dominant and popular sectors would benefit from pegging the Argentine peso to the U.S. dollar, selling state-owned enterprises at bargain-basement prices, and establishing a strong strategic alliance (baptized *relaciones carnales* [carnal relationships]) with the United States. Supposedly such neoliberal policies would benefit Argentine society as a whole and would finally transform Argentina into a first world country.

The model worked for a few years. It was effective in modernizing services such as energy, water, telecommunications, and transportation, which previously had been provided by the state, and in increasing the consumption of consumer goods. The fiesta menemista was celebrated by the popular sectors and ensured President Menem's reelection in 1994. According to De Gori (2005: 356), "Such festivity, deprived of social and political belligerence, was expressed and spread by cumbia." Menem's sociopolitical experiment ended in the worst economic disaster in Argentine history and the first default of a country in the modern era. That is the story that the next incarnation of cumbia, cumbia villera, narrates.

But in the late 1980s, before artists like Pablo Lescano and groups like

Damas Gratis and Los Pibes Chorros became popular in the first decade of the twenty-first century, the most important representatives of *la movida tropical* (which had cumbia at its most important representative) were singers such as Alcides, Antonio Ríos, Miguel "Conejito" Alejandro, Pocho la Pantera, and Ricki Maravilla, along with groups such as Adrián and the Black Dice, Malagata, Karicias, Chévere, and Green.

The artists of this period came from the popular sectors and reproduced their aesthetics. Before they became famous, they had earned little, working as waiters, photographers, small shop owners in outlying neighborhoods, and clerks. Some even made a living doing odd jobs. In many cases, even successful artists had to keep those part-time jobs because it was the owner of the group who made the money; the musicians were little more than his employees.

According to Martín (2011), the increased visibility of cumbia in the media in the 1990s coincided with an aesthetic novelty that broadened its spectrum of patrons. After the group Sombras appeared on the tropical music scene in 1993, bands made up of good-looking and stylish young men became increasingly common. They replaced the grown men with indigenous features and provincial tastes (i.e., *mestizos*, in this particular case) who had initiated the boom.

In the world of tropical music, power was in men's hands from the start. The owners of record companies and musical groups, entrepreneurs, and song and lyrics writers were usually men. Women were seldom seen except on stage as dancers or singers, and they almost never achieved the fame of the men in the group. During this period, however, three women—Lía Crucet (nicknamed "La Tetamanti" for her bustline), Gladys "la Bomba Tucumana," and Gilda—became exceptions to the rule in cumbia. Despite her short career, Gilda became the object of much media attention after her death. Numerous articles appeared in mass-circulation newspapers and magazines; her life story and the miracles she performed were told and retold on radio and TV.

According to Martín, the cumbia business really flourished in the 1990s:

In 1997, half of the best-selling CDs in Argentina fell into the cumbia category; sales of the top ten totaled almost 3 million copies. . . . Total income from record sales and dance club tickets was estimated at $130 million for 1998. The forty tropical music groups recording on the Leader label sold 3.5 million CDs, including more than two hundred thousand by the group Red. Magenta

> accounted for 2.5 million in record sales. In 1999, Leader was third in sales among all recording companies in Argentina, including multinationals such as EMI.... Contracts signed with recording studios are extremely unfavorable to the artists. Record companies do not pay royalties, and they "deduct" from earnings what musicians receive for live performances on TV shows owned by the companies themselves. (2011: 36–37)

The 1990s also witnessed increased exposure of cumbia in the media, with many radio and TV programs dedicated to the genre:

> The genre's first network TV program, "A Pleno Sábado," debuted on Channel 2 in 1996. It was three hours long and presented a variety of artists. The trend spread quickly, and by the end of 1997, seven network and cable TV programs — twenty-seven hours of airtime per week — were dedicated to tropical music. "Tropicalísima," which had the highest rating on the state-owned channel, and "Tropihit" were both owned by Magenta; "Fantástico TV" and "Fantástico TV de la Tarde" were broadcast on TVA; and "La Máquina," "Todo Ritmo," and "Hoy Sábado" were broadcast on the América channel. "Pasión Tropicalísima," with the same length and format, aired on Saturday and Sunday afternoons on Channel 9 the following year. (Martín 2011: 37)

All these developments can be considered the antecedents of the popularity of cumbia villera in the late 1990s and early twenty-first century. According to Martín, cumbia villera became popular in Argentina in a historical context in which remnants of a country once considered the most developed in Latin America persisted amid unprecedented structural and social changes. The genre opens a window onto the world of young people growing up poor in Buenos Aires and in the Greater Buenos Aires neighborhoods. As De Gori (2005: 355) points out, cumbia villera "intends to be a reading and a language of the profound devastation and de-collectivization of the social bonds." He continues:

> The neoliberal project was able to dissolve the institutional net that the state re-created with its public intervention, producing not only an economic change but also a profound cultural change, expressed in diverse dimensions of subjectivity. In Argentina, this project meant the destruction of the industrial infrastructure, widespread unemployment [about 20 percent], political disciplining of the trade unions, and the beginning of unheard-of impoverishment. But it also started to produce a subjectivity marked by both instability and insecurity. This was so because the social bonds based on not only labor

relationships but also all of the state, religious, and trade-union social networks (which historically provided social references and the place to solve social problems) were dissolved. (362–63, our translation)

Martín writes:

> [In the songs of cumbia villera] as constructed musically, being poor implies neither impoverishment nor suffering. Instead, characteristics that the mainstream stigmatizes are viewed in a positive light. In an operation similar to Helena Wendel Abramo's analysis of punk behavior, cumbieros "crudely take up the negative perception of poor young people crystallized in the society at large and use it to describe themselves, seeking to make explicit their condition and the character of the prejudice at one and the same time: 'Yes, we're poor, ugly, have no future and are dangerous'" (Abramo 1994: 100). In that way, in cumbia villera, the adjective "villero," used judgmentally to refer to those living in shantytowns, is elevated and invested with pride. This, in fact, is the distinguishing feature of the genre. In the eyes of others, being a villero is worse than being poor: it means liking and deserving poverty. In practice, using the term stigmatizes something or someone as, by definition, ontologically inferior. Cumbia villera does not hide the characteristics associated with poverty; rather, it transforms them into lyrics that constitute an aesthetic ideal. If performers of so-called romantic cumbia were chosen by professional producers because they were thin and good-looking and had European features, cumbia villera producers by the same token prefer "*negros*." (2011: 38)

The man who is generally considered the creator of cumbia villera is Pablo Lescano, whose first group, called Flor de Piedra (in a clear allusion to marihuana), appeared in 1999. Other groups, such as Yerba Brava and Guachín, appeared around the same time. A short time later, Lescano himself created and led a new group, Damas Gratis, even today one of the most important representatives of the genre. In 2000, Los Pibes Chorros, Meta Guacha, El Indio, and Mala Fama appeared, and the following year Bajo Palabra, Dany y la Roka, and Sipaganboy were born, as was La Piba, one of the very few female performers of the genre.

> In a matter of months, cumbia villera had become an unexpected commercial success, selling about three hundred thousand CDs . . . and representing 25 percent of all records sold in Argentina, according to recording companies' figures. This percentage does not take into account pirated editions, which make up 50 percent of total record sales. Cumbia villera groups also

Gender Tensions in *Cumbia Villera*'s Lyrics 199

performed dozens of shows each week at popular bailantas and on TV. . . . Beyond its traditional market sector, cumbia villera appears in a variety of mass-media products, including prime-time variety shows, investigative reports, and video clips. In addition, 2002 marked the opening of two Argentine movies—*El Bonaerense*, directed by Pablo Trapero, and *Un Oso Rojo* [A Red Bear], directed by Adrián Caetano—in which both Colombian and villera versions of cumbia were played. Cumbia also served as background music in *Tumberos*, a TV series portraying life in prison; the genre and its artists now provide background music to illustrate many popular-sector "customs" and aesthetic in TV soap operas and drama series as well. Thus, although airtime for programs dedicated to tropical music dropped from twenty-seven hours in 1996–1997 to twelve in 2000, the genre has gained greater exposure than ever before in diverse mainstream formats. (Martín 2011: 39–40)

Having set the stage to understand the place of cumbia villera in the history of Argentine popular music in general and la movida tropical in particular, we are now better prepared to comprehend the complex role cumbia villera songs play in the construction of gender relations in contemporary Buenos Aires.

Cumbia Villera's Conditions of Emission

As an analyst, what do you do when you encounter lyrics such as the following?

Que peteás, que peteás, qué pete que te mandas, que peteás, que peteás, qué bien que la cogoteás. [How you suck, how you suck, what good head you give; how you suck, how you suck, what good head you give.]

Dejate de joder y no te hagás la loca. Andá a enjuagarte bien la boca. Me diste un beso y casi me matás. De la baranda a leche que largás. [Stop messing around, and don't act crazy. Go and wash quite well your mouth. You gave me a kiss and you almost killed me. From the bad odor of milk that you have.]

Hay que locura que tengo, el vino me pegó. Y te veo con mi amigo, entregándole el marrón. [Ay, how crazy I am, the wine hit me hard. And I see you with my friend, handing over your ass.]

No me vas a dejar así, yo sé que sos alta gata. De amor no te cabe nada, por guita [dinero] abrís las patas. [You are not going to leave like this (without having sex), I know that you are a high-priced prostitute. You don't understand anything about love, but for money you open your legs.]

Ella es una chica así de fácil. Es de bombachita [panty] floja. Si al hotel no la llevás, no sabés cómo se enoja. [She is a very easy girl. Her panties are very loose. If you don't bring her to your bed, she gets very angry.]

Laura, siempre cuando bailas a ti se te ve la tanga, y de lo rápida que sos, vos te sacás tu tanga . . . y le das para abajo, para abajo y pa'bajo. [Laura, when you dance we can always see your thong. And because you are so fast, you take off your thong . . . and you go down, down, down, down.]

A mover ese culito mamita, que a los pibes vos se las dejas bien durita. A mover el culito mamita, que los pibes mueren por darte una apoyadita. [Shake that little ass, mommy, that the kids' dicks get very hard seeing you. Shake that little ass, mommy, that the kids die to touch it with their dicks.]

One's first impulse is to download everything one has learned from the feminist critique of patriarchal society and analyze these lyrics in terms of their symbolic terrorism and their phallocentric, objectifying, and fragmenting undertones, treating women as if their only role in society is to please men. We follow such an impulse in the pages that follow, but before doing so we show that the use of overtly sexual language is a characteristic not only of cumbia villera in particular, but of contemporary Argentine culture in general. The fact that cumbia villera is the first musical genre to conspicuously display this language in songs does not mean that such a discourse is absent from Argentine popular culture. We also show that what first sounds like a very aggressive language changes its character when contextualized in relation to the discourses and performances that conform to the media culture that the fans of cumbia villera consume on a daily basis.

The meaning of these lyrics that sound so misogynistic cannot be fully understood if we do not relate them to a certain change in the cultural platform of the popular life world where sex has become autonomous from love and reproduction and where the interest in different forms of pleasure and in pleasure for its own sake have contributed to a preoccupation with anal and oral sex not only among men and not necessarily in the terms that a decontextualized reading of the lyrics would presuppose. What is perhaps new in the social scenario that frames the advent of cumbia villera is the sexualization of women in public forums rather than their sexualization in mainly male, restricted environments, which was the way women were mostly sexualized in the past.

In other words, explicit sexual discourse constitutes a common and extended cultural platform in the language of men and women in contemporary Argentina. This kind of sexually overt public discourse constitutes the external layer of cumbia villera's emission. It is not directly related to the singers' performance, but it is the background against which those performances acquire a particular meaning. It is beyond the scope of this essay to fully analyze this phenomenon; therefore we will mention only some of its major manifestations and how they are connected to cumbia villera's own discourse.

Argentine radio and television broadcast a number of shows featuring female counselors who share with young and mature women alike the advice of *ser perras* (being like bitches) in bed, of *sacar la perra de adentro* (bringing out the bitch inside), of being a "real whore" to give and get pleasure. At the same time many programs offer multiple humorous references to the possibilities women have to attend male erotic shows, which are part and parcel of an array of calls that promote feminine sexual initiative at the mass-media level. In those programs, sexuality and genitalia appear within the logic of a generalized autonomization. It is legitimate to talk about sex, different ways to perform it, its relationship to pleasure, its central role in a love relationship, but also its autonomy as a fantasy dimension in which, for instance, the subjection that often is attributed to the woman who offers oral sex is instead described as being a partner, being able to play a game, *ser gauchita* (being a little gaucha). Thus it was described by Nazarena Vélez, an actress closely related to cumbia's life world, when a radio interviewer asked her if she practices oral sex with her casual male partners. Magazines that target female youths are full of advice about how to please men but also highlight a range of sexual activities in which female readers themselves can find pleasure. In articles in which sex appears separated from love, marriage, and engagement, the authors vindicate an autonomous space of sexual enjoyment. One example among many is that of the sexologist Alexandra Rampolla, who, in a very popular program on daytime TV, recommended to her female audience the kinds of massage they should perform on their jaws to overcome the fatigue produced by a long session of oral sex.

The kind of television programs that cumbia villera fans watch are full of explicit, direct sexualized and genitalized images. And sex appears in all its varieties: group sex with a majority of men or women, anal sex, oral sex with receptive or provocative women, and more. Not in a direct way—at least not always—but very often sex appears in choreographies, verbal references, and jokes in which women assume their own voice and claim for themselves sexual liberties that were historically restricted to men. To ignore all the hedonistic dimensions that these images project and to dilute all the complexity of this sexual imaginary, claiming that we are dealing with the old and always present machismo, not only is epistemologically erroneous but also, and more important, takes away power from the subalterns whose defense this stance supposedly assumes.

We think that it is a mistake to claim that in these collective and public scenes women are only sexual objects, because the depictions of oral sex in the media show women as active agents, able to give others and themselves pleasure. Whereas only a few decades ago the sexual liberalism of some actresses and singers was criticized as immoral, that same liberality is nowadays accepted as compatible with the traditional roles of mother, partner, and fiancée.

If this generalized sexual discourse is the outer layer of the emission of cumbia villera's lyrics, what occurs in the performances themselves constitutes the inner layer. Cumbia villera is performed with the active participation of women, who are highly influential through their dancing and facial expressions or their commentary on what is occurring in those performances. Thus it is necessary to point out that in all the television programs in which cumbia villera is performed, the dancers play with the (usually sexually charged) expectations of the men in the scene. At the same time, they disavow those same expectations in scenarios that follow their dancing or in interviews they grant on the same television programs. On the one hand, the dancers' movements are executed as the lyrics dictate. (The dancers usually laugh at the insults they receive or ironically act surprised, as though saying "See the horrible things they say about us!") On the other hand, in the scenes that follow their dancing in the same television programs, they portray themselves as being "normal" or exhibiting "proper" behavior. These portrayals and irony clearly send a message; instead of signifying "We are the sluts the lyrics talk about," they imply "We choose when and where we want to play being sluts."

At the same time, in the usual venues of the genre (bailantas, concerts, and TV shows), the performance of the lyrics adds a twist that subverts what the lyrics say explicitly. For instance, when cumbia villera is performed on

TV, with choreography and a live audience, the singers (almost always male) combine aggression with admiration. This is accompanied by the complicity of the dancers, who interpret the meaning of the lyrics with their bodies. Singing with smiles on their faces, the singers joke about the capacity of the dancers to play the part of the "sluts" the lyrics talk about. The way singers use their facial expressions and joke around in response to the dancers acting out their lyrics is a characteristic not only of cumbia villera performances, because facial expressions are commonly used to convey jokes in many cultural settings. As Peter Lyman explains in his case study on sexist jokes, "The ordinary consequences of forbidden words are suspended by meta-linguistic gestures (tones of voice, facial expressions, catch phrases) that send the message 'this is a joke,' and emotions that would ordinarily endanger a social relationship can be spoken safely within the micro-world created by the 'joke form'" (1998: 173). The singers use their facial expressions to convey their lyrics in a light manner, so that dancers and audience members interpret as acceptable language normally considered to be insulting. This obviously has its correlation with what occurs in the most popular television programs that we described earlier, where women who are recognized by their professional or family roles do not lose respect because they publicly perform audacious erotic scenes. In those programs, it is implicitly understood that there are areas of conduct that are evaluated differently, that a woman (or a man, for that matter) has to be "good" or "proper" in her family roles and also in her sexual roles, and that those good performances can refer to a conflicting set of values.

Thus the parodist intention and the (self-consciously) overacted astonishment that the singers exhibit (and whose function is to comment on the song and get a reaction from the dancers) is a good example of the contextualization of the lyrics that modifies, in large part, an initial reading in terms of female objectification and disrespect.

After the songs are over, the dancers usually demonstrate that they can perform other roles (more prudish and familiar), or they comment on their sensual performances with some critical distance. These performative discursive actions give other meanings to the lyrics besides the literal. That is, the irony moderates the objectifying character of the songs, and the feminine agency transforms into a dialogue what initially appeared to be only a male monologue.

Women as "Easy"

A very popular topic in cumbia villera's lyrics is the portrayal of women as "easy," that is, willing to have sex. In Argentina such female behavior is usually labeled *puta*, a term that is also used to refer to a prostitute. It is only the context of the expression of the label that determines its meaning. The song "Maria Rosa" by Yerba Brava is a good example of *puta* denoting "easy."[2] The singer is absolutely sure that Maria Rosa, with her sexy dance movements, "provokes" her male audience. And she does so because she wants somebody to buy her a drink. Buying her a drink is a cheap price to pay for the sexual services she will provide. Such behavior supposedly transforms her into an "easy girl."

In the lyrics, "her panties are very loose / if you don't bring her to your bed / she gets very angry." The use of the metaphor "loose panties" reveals a certain reconstruction of the standards of metaphorization in current Argentine music: while historically Argentine musical genres had almost no direct genital references, cumbia villera employs very popular, sexually explicit expressions of contemporary Argentine males.[3] The lyrics clearly state Maria Rosa's preference for casual sex and the fact that her dancing is related neither to the pleasure of dancing per se nor to the search for a lasting romantic relationship.

At the end of the song the negative value ascribed to Maria Rosa is insinuated and finally asserted. She "doesn't care" about the consequences when she "gives herself" to a man who is not her partner (she will be an easy target for "what people may say," her "value" in the marriage market will be lowered, and she will lose the respect of other women who know her, her *comadres*).[4] She does not even care what the action of "giving" (*entregar*) suggests in Argentina, that is, anal sex, which can be considered an autonomous key to pure sexual pleasure because it is not related to reproduction or, perhaps, a simple consent to men's (usually insistent) will.

The object desired by men as a trophy, and generally given bit by bit by women in different forms of negotiation, gets another value in this particular case. In this signifying context, being first in "getting it" clearly makes the male protagonist of the story a "good lover." This is so because males are looking for a situation in which they can be "the first" or "the exclusive owners." In a cultural context in which virginity has lost its traditional value, men fantasize that "all the girls surrender [their virginity]," "all of them are sluts," and actively search for that trophy that will make them the only one, the first one. However, the claim of exclusivity over a sexual practice less frequent than the "legitimate" one is not working alone in this signifying context; it intersects with two other elements that complete the connotation of what the song wants to convey. On the one hand, in the popular imaginary anal sex implies a greater female granting, a greater recognition of the male partner, both in terms of domination of his female partner and of his performance as a lover. (Good lovers obtain that "prize" because they get their partner sexually excited; great men get that prize as a response to their magnitude.) On the other hand, "surrendering her ass" directly implicates the female protagonist as a subject compromised by pleasure in itself. If it is true that, in the case of the song we are analyzing here, the protagonist liking anal sex is signaled offensively in terms of her "licentious" character, it is also true that in many instances of popular discourse, many women are praised precisely for such a "vice," for instance, in the celebration of their feminine movements, or their being "hot," or their skills performing oral sex. We want to address the constant tension that exists between what is being criticized and what is being recognized and praised in a language that, even though it is still critical, describes women as real agents in the sexual encounter, something that often is highly admired by men.

But in the song we are analyzing, it is clear that Maria Rosa is willing to "give it" even if doing so reduces her "value" and adds greatly to her negative characterization. She, who is not interested in love, is revealed as a voracious and "licentious" female, and so she is characterized as being "easy."[5]

Typical of this musical genre is the use of a piece of clothing related to female sexuality to represent a woman. This kind of operation can be considered in terms of what Aparicio (1998) refers to as compartmentalization and objectification.[6] According to Aparicio, the heart functions as the totalizing metaphor that connotes the possession of the affective and emotional life of women; thus we could say that in songs like "Maria Rosa," the thong or panty works as a totalizing metaphor that implies men's possession of women's sexuality. In this sense, the only thing of any value for cumbia villera's men is the sexual possession of women, without any further interest in the affective or emotional dimensions of such a possession. In this (de)gradation of objectification, we go from the heart to the panty, passing through the ass, and end up equating women with a piece of clothing with clear sexual connotations. Therefore, if in the synecdoches using body parts (the heart in bolero, for instance), those parts are "reduced to a status of instruments of the masculine desire and fantasies" (Aparicio 1998: 135), in the specific case of "Maria Rosa," the parts reduced to mere instruments of men's desires and satisfaction are the entrance orifices (the permitted one in vaginal coitus and the forbidden one in anal coitus—forbidden because it goes against the normative ideal of reproduction), represented metaphorically by a female garment.

Additionally, considering the point of view of the narrator (implicitly a heterosexual man, as are the majority of cumbia villera singers), it is clear that the targets of María Rosa's sensual movements are heterosexual men, and the goal of those movements is to promote their sexual excitement. Here the way sexuality is treated clearly shows a man's point of view, without any consideration of a woman's perspective. As Aparicio (1998: 209) points out, it is a sexuality imposed from the outside, "from the man's sense of power over her body, identity, and life. While female desire is alluded to . . . it is never self-defined but rather marked precisely by the absence of any female voice. Masculine desire, in contrast, is overdetermined."[7] There is no other possibility in the story, such as that Maria Rosa dances to enjoy herself, to express herself, or even to arouse other women. In most cumbia villera lyrics, female desire and sexuality are invisible, repressed, and, above all, built by this specific masculine perspective.

However, this particular song also offers another possible reading of its content. For example, in the line "Loose panty, how that pleases," who is being pleased? What if Maria Rosa is the one feeling pleasure? When the lyrics state that she doesn't care, perhaps it is because she is not concerned by what people say about her attitude; maybe she actually wants and prefers what she is doing.

Our theoretical point is that a critical reading of the lyrics à la Aparicio is correct, but also partial, because the idea of objectification applied by the previous analysis presupposes that the "others" are always the ones who objectify, and that objectification by "others" is always a bad practice. This idea can be criticized from different perspectives. From the point of view of psychoanalysis, for example, there are no natural sexual objects for human beings. This assertion implies that totalizing is impossible, and love and sexual discourse, by definition (by the mere fact of referring to the other), are always fragments; therefore the very culture of the psychoanalyst fragments as well, although she is often unaware of doing so. This claim is related to what many nonwhite, non-Western, nonheterosexual feminists criticize about feminists of the second wave, that is, to confuse the experience of white, Western, heterosexual women with the experience of women in general makes invisible the differences of women of color, third world women, and lesbians in relation to the "norm," that is, themselves. It is here, we think, where the topic of the fragmentation of the other and its criticism becomes ethnocentric and loses a great deal of its analytical capacity. That is the reason we believe that, in fact, any discourse objectifies and fragments, where the difference can be found in the logic behind the fragmentation but not in the fragmentation itself.

If this is so, an analysis of cumbia villera lyrics influenced by the feminist second wave is really proposing that one kind of objectification and fragmentation of women is wrong but another is acceptable. If this is so, it would seem that the only admissible objectification and fragmentation (and obviously one that is not recognized as such) is the one proposed by a discourse on sexuality that stresses the discussion of sex within the limits of the heterosexual couple, a discussion about sex as a problematic and recurrent dimension of the marital life of those middle-class social actors who are usually the ones who analyze cumbia villera's lyrics. Egalitarian ideals are the norm among those social sectors, which implies the construction and design of the relationship as an integral dialogue, and where the sexual chilling or lack of correspondence in that regard is frequently the cause of legitimate separation.

Thus fragmentation is not only a cumbia villera practice. However, from the standpoint of those who observe only how "others" objectify, those are neither fragmenting nor objectifying practices. The contrast that we have just made does not tell us a lot about what is going on in the realm of cumbia villera, but it does tell us something about the extreme care we have to take with the presumptive neutral and universal patterns of interpretation we apply to cultural artifacts and behaviors, something that, in relation to gender and sexuality, we have learned from those feminist approaches that reacted against the second wave's gynocentrism.

In relation to the objectification that some analyses read in cumbia villera's lyrics, we believe that it can be revealing something more than a man's complete reduction of a woman to a simple anus. On the one hand, we believe that what is performed in the song and the dance hall in a comedic key, as a humorous representation, speaks of an acceptance and an ironic distancing in relation to the sexist discourse deployed by the lyrics. This is so, above all, if we take into account (as we pointed out earlier) the context of the emission of the songs, where women appear with their distancing comments on what the lyrics seem to denote. At the same time, the assumption that the feminine self-definition is not taken into account comes from the presupposition that such self-definition always has to come from the singer's voice. In this sense, a straightforward textual analysis demands that the male singer give women the role of autonomous subjects through his allocation and not portray them as simply passive objects of his own sexual activity. Of course, we are in complete agreement with this requirement, knowing that representational practices have real effects upon the people who are thus addressed. However, this kind of interpretation of the lyrics many times concludes that women are passive subjects. It is not the case of the author we are quoting here, because in her timely book Aparicio also analyzes how her interviewees interpret and make their own (through a very interesting process of re-appropriation) those lyrics that objectify them. However, we want to go a step further regarding Aparicio's analysis and point out that the voice is not the only mechanism that confers identity; self-definition is produced by the body as well. Therefore passivity is neither pure nor total. If we take into account that women accompany with their bodies, their presence, and their interpretations their sexualized presentation in the lyrics, it is possible to speculate that the interpretation of passivity is not a property of the phenomenon being analyzed. This is so because the phenomenon of cumbia villera is much more than the lyrics; it also comprises the web of discourses in which the songs are expressed, including the social choreography in which these songs flourish.

An interpretation of the lyrics that does not take into account the complex web of discourses that surround their emission deprives the scene of its ambiguity, its tension, the productive activity of usually subordinated actors (women) who do not have many opportunities for linguistically articulating their own vision, considering the very few *cumbieras* who are active participants in cumbia villera's scene. This is so because the lack of a prominent voice of their own does not mean that women are totally dominated in cumbia villera, since many of them exercise their agency in other instances that are opened in the complex relationship between the emission and reception of the lyrics of the genre.

Another example of the "easy woman" character in cumbia villera, in which a thong replaces the panty, is "Se te ve la tanga" (Your Thong Is Visible), by Damas Gratis. "Se te ve la tanga" mixes astonishment and insult to describe the sexual activity of women. The singer cannot but laugh when he sees the girl of the story (Laura) dancing in a miniskirt. Why? Because while dancing in such a small piece of cloth she is constantly showing her thong, which he equates with her ardent desire to be taken as soon as possible to a motel to have sex. At the same time, the singer is absolutely sure that Laura is doing all this for pleasure, not for money. According to him, Laura is a "fast girl" who quickly takes off her thong and "go[es] down, down, down, down . . . back and forward, back and forward" that is, has sex with passionate enjoyment.

Here again is the image of the "easy woman" represented by the metaphor of being "fast." It is quite clear that the one who cannot wait here is the woman, who is impatient in her search for a pleasure that is happy-go-lucky. She dances just to arouse men because, according to the narrator, she is the one who "desires it." The act of making love is graphically described in the song: "Le das para abajo, para abajo y pa'bajo. Y le das para atrás, pa'adelante y pa'tras." [And you go down, down, down, down, and you go back and forward, back and forward.] Women's sexual activity is deployed and privileged in this image in the same way that some years later it was deployed and privileged (but this time in the context of mainstream television) in the image of women pole dancing, many times performing a social imaginary with polyandric and Amazonic connotations.

However, and in addition to all the contextualizing dimensions that we discussed in our analysis of "Maria Rosa," we firmly believe that any analysis done from a gender perspective has a great deal to gain by moving from only criticizing men who supposedly reify women to a perspective that tries to decipher the infantile attitude with which these men, dominant but besieged, contemplate the lively sexual activity of some women and fantasize that most of them are like that. Naked kings, but unaware, they only vaguely intuit the fragility of their kingdom. Maybe because of that, before crying out of fear, they laugh with a qualified laughter that signals their tenuous grip on reality. We think the fact that the narrator of "Se te ve la tanga" laughs at Laura's acts is very symptomatic ("You dance in a miniskirt, it makes me laugh"), because the masculine voice no longer describes a passive object; instead it describes a power, a force. Such a laugh shows either a difficult complacency or, perhaps, a masculine attempt to assimilate the blow or to try to maintain a control (or at least the appearance of having control) that has been lost. The woman addressed by the laugh no longer is what she was in the previous interpretation of the song. The latter is a "possession," subordinated and diligent, or a complementary companion; the former doesn't fit in the place men design for her and isn't motivated, not even in men's stories, by a simple masculine solicitation.[8] In this regard, the fantasized "voracious chicks" of many cumbia villera songs perform the role of the imaginary scenario that tries to address the anxious question these young men do not know how to answer: "What really do these young women want from us?" (Žižek 1989: 114). As such, cumbia villera also provides the coordinates of these young men's desires, constructing the frame enabling them to desire something.

Conclusions

The general picture we get after an analysis of the lyrics, their internal tensions, and the context of emission of the songs is that in their attempt to put their everyday experience into words, men talk about a femininity that they can no longer understand. They insult, humiliate, and joke about what they see as both new and threatening. In this way, the jokes in cumbia villera lyrics function to "indirectly express the emotions and tensions that may disrupt everyday life by 'negotiating' them, reconstructing group solidarity by shared aggression and cathartic laughter" (Lyman 1998: 172). Given that men fear sexually active women, they cope with their insecurities by making women the butt of their jokes in their lyrics.[9] Here is where the fantasized construction of these sexually active women, whose only purpose seems to be to please men, occupies a prominent role in the lyrics of this genre, because it is only through fantasy that these young men can relate to these women, that is, insofar as they enter the frame of their fantasy (Žižek 1989: 119).

If some of the women of Argentina's popular sectors, as portrayed by cumbia villera, do not advance their new identities in a well-defined and complete voice, if they do it subverting the symbolism that used to be masculine-centered, that doesn't mean that they don't advance a new identity, at least in some way. Perhaps the men who joke about these sexually active women are revealing concerns that are difficult for them to recognize. We won't accompany them in their deception with our analysis.

Notes

1. While Bourdieu denounces domination using its own language and makes visible its exit points, some of the feminist literature denounces masculine domination without taking into account a certain margin of feminine agency that, although it does not comply with what most of the feminist writers understand as "plain agency," nevertheless is opposed to masculine dominant practices.

2. Considering the amount of money that was requested by the authors of the songs to publish the lyrics we analyze in this chapter, it was impossible to quote

them at length. Academic works like this one are treated the same way commercial products are treated, as if thousands of dollars on copyright royalties were going to end up in the pockets of the authors, which of course is not the case. The absurdity of this treatment makes even less sense given that the lyrics are readily available in the Internet. The lyrics of "Maria Rosa" can be accessed at http://www.musica.com/letras.asp?letra=1516740 and of "Se te ve la tanga" at http://www.mp3lyrics.org/d/damas-gratis/laura-se-te-ve.

3. It is important to clarify that this type of symbolic construction is not exclusive to cumbia villera. In the 1990s a very popular combo (with a lot of television exposure), Macaferri y Asociados, popularized the hit "Bombacha Veloz" (Fast Panty). Thus this type of expression already had an important media presence before cumbia villera was born, but only in comic venues, many times targeting males, although in this particular example there were no age distinctions.

4. This point is not a folk anachronism. In popular sectors' everyday life, *compadrazgo* (a nonegalitarian fictive kinship relationship very common among women) mediates women's relationships with men. It implies support networks, collaboration, and also the articulation of those hierarchies that have their center in a particular valued male. Women in that context are not only women, but also sisters-in-law, daughters-in-law, and so on. All these relationships, not always horizontal and in many cases highly vertical, are shaken if any agent in the network behaves in such a way that challenges the network's expectations. The "she doesn't care" of the song can have severe consequences for some of these women. On a related matter, this can also help to explain something that has to be taken into account as contextual data: among many members of the popular sectors, women's status is one of subordinated inclusion in hierarchical family units that center on a masculine vertex. Women are *de* (that is, they "belong to") fathers, husbands, or brothers, and from a symbolic point of view that is still hegemonic (but less hegemonic in actual practice), female work outside the household is a situation that menaces the value of the household.

5. *Licentious* is one of the several adjectives used to describe the woman who, from men's point of view, desires sex without any amorous or reproductive interest. Interestingly, in Peter Lyman's study of sexist jokes in U.S. fraternities, women are often thought of similarly to how Maria Rosa is described, as sexual objects. Lyman found that when his male participants defend sexist jokes, "intimacy is split from sexuality in order to erotize the male bond, thereby creating an instrumental sexuality directed at women. The separation of intimacy from sexuality transforms women into 'sexual objects,' which both justifies aggression at women by suspending their relationship to men and devalues sexuality itself, creating a disgust at women as the sexual 'object' unworthy of intimate attention" (1998: 178). The male protagonist in the lyrics distances himself from any type of intimate or serious relationship with Maria Rosa because he views her as a purely sexual object that does not deserve any respect from him; he sees her as simply a source of sexual gratification.

6. Aparicio writes, "[In the bolero] the object of desire is systematically alluded to mostly through her parts, yet very infrequently, if at all, as a whole subject who thinks

and feels. . . . Indeed, the most central metaphor for love, *corazón* (heart), suggests the compartmentalization of the woman or the beloved into one of her bodily organs or parts as a prerequisite for its possession" (1998: 134–35).

7. Even though, musically speaking, salsa doesn't have anything to do with cumbia villera, we found Aparicio's book very helpful, as her analysis of the lyrics basically coincides with ours and some of the comments she got from her interviewees are very similar to the ones we got from ours.

8. As Manuel points out in his discussion of misogynist lyrics in Caribbean music, "Some expressions of misogyny in popular music may be indicative less of the actual social subjugation of women than of angry male backlash and resentment against genuine female emancipation. . . . The prodigious amount of overt misogyny in dancehall might indicate a *greater*, rather than lesser, degree of female autonomy in Jamaican society" (1998: 18).

9. In Lyman's case study on the role of sexist jokes in male bonding, he found that men with the least interaction with women told the most hostile, misogynistic jokes (1998: 176). Men defended these jokes by differentiating intimacy and sexuality, which ultimately turned women into sexual objects (178).

9.
Feliz, feliz

Pablo Lescano exemplifies tradition and modernity at the same time. Pablito, the master of rhythm, the creator of *cumbia villera*, acknowledges the paternity of his child as an inevitable fate: marked by a *chamamecero* (a performer of *chamamé*, a regional folk genre) grandfather from Corrientes province, and his precocious adventures at Tropitango de Pacheco, Buenos Aires (the grand cathedral of Colombian and Peruvian cumbia), it could be no other way. "La cultura se va haciendo" (Culture is made along the way), explains the musician who loathes the stiff discourses of those who think they know, yet at the same time, he demonstrates a profound knowledge of his art and of his tropical passion. Capable of historicizing the genre from the middle of the twentieth century and knowledgeable about cumbia in all of its versions, Lescano is a researcher of what he actually does. To the point that it was he, born and raised in the shantytown of La Esperanza in San Fernando (in northern Greater Buenos Aires), who first began playing with a deejay friend until he mixed cumbia, the most popular rhythm in the continent, with electronic and psychedelic paraphernalia created with synthesizers. Pablo Lescano played at Luna Park (the most important concert stadium in Buenos Aires) with his all-time band. Pablo Lescano played with Miranda (a well-known pop band) at the Roxy (a theater), becoming a hit with the keyboard on his shoulder. Pablo Lescano was at the Žižek parties (an avant-garde Buenos Aires night club, named after the Slovenian philosopher Slavoj Žižek), where a handful of "mods" seem to him "a mountain of lemons" because of the "*lime* they have in their heads," he says.[1] Pablo Lescano, without calculation or marketing ornaments, reigns in the rhythm he created, and now it crosses all borders. Mexico. Spain. New York. Paraguay. Bolivia. Ecuador. Pablo Lescano is the king wherever he goes.

This is an interview with Pablo and a nosy peek into the work of Alberto Sánchez Campuzano, an artist and filmmaker who followed Lescano through the streets of his neighborhood and through infinite performances on Saturday night when Damas Gratis (Lescano's cumbia group) played fifteen shows for fans in the Argentine capital and Greater Buenos Aires. Alberto, the thirty-five-year-old from Cali, Colombia, was in Buenos Aires (on a scholarship from the National Fund for Culture and the Arts of Mexico) on a search that brought him from haughty Palermo to the Cildañez shantytown, where he ended up helping a group of "pibes chorros" (thieving kids) start a cumbia group. Alberto has an expert ear that allows him to identify, on Buenos Aires soil, subtle aspects of his countries—Mexico and Colombia—in local songs. From repeatedly going to the Tropi de Pacheco (along Panamericana, close to Route 202 in northern Greater Buenos Aires), he met "Yanque," a guy with a nerdy face who happened to be the son of two Argentines who migrated to the United States and gave birth to him in Los Angeles. "He arrived in the 1990s in San Fernando with an arsenal of two thousand CDs that accounted for all the cumbia he had listened to with his friends over there," Alberto told me in a travel diary that he sent from Monterrey, where he tracks down cumbia to finish his movie. "Cumbia is music of migrants: Colombians arrived in Mexico and generated a new cumbia in the 1970s and 1980s. Yanque arrived in the 1990s, and appears to be the *sonidero* of villera cumbia."

Lemons

When I saw him in May, after a long waiting time at the door of *Pasión de Sábados* (Saturday Passion), the TV program on which he usually plays, Pablo Lescano had spent the previous night with a "reporter from New York," whom he had brought to the dance halls so that he could "alucinarse."[2] "Of course, keep in mind he was going to Niceto [an upscale nightclub], where they mix cumbia with *electrónica* [synthesizers], or *reguetón*. Then followed a little rap, next a little bit of cumbia, and reguetón one last time. It is a marvelous invention. I told him 'Come with me,' and I took him to Fantástico Bailable, to Jessy James, and to a few more places [alluding to dance halls whose customers are working-class folks]. The fellow couldn't believe it," says Pablo, from his apartment with a wonderful river view, on an avenue in San Isidro (an upscale Buenos Aires suburb).

The North American friend is Jace Clayton. That same night, Pablo put us in contact with each other over the phone. Jace was returning to New York in a week and I was traveling to a seminar in Manhattan. We met at an Oriental restaurant, where he invited me to eat dinner with him and his wife, a Catalan artist. Jace, a black fellow from Boston who lives in Brooklyn, young and smart, happened to be DJ Rapture, a guy at the vanguard of the global electronic music scene, who for many years has been dedicated to exploring alternative rhythms. Having had enough of Africans and Orientals, he investigates Latinos with enthusiasm. He had been sent to Buenos Aires by a New York magazine, *The Fader*, an ultrachic publication, dedicated to fashion, global tendencies, and music. In it, he published his journey with Pablo through the Buenos Aires scene and described the nights at Žižek and his international and modern audience, and the mass of *cumbieros*, "one hundred percent black," as Pablito's back claims in tattooed letters.

How do you feel about the fact that cumbia is mixed, more and more, with electronic sounds?

As a matter of fact I started that trend, with Taz, a deejay friend. He, like myself, after taking so many drugs, became crazy. He ended up in Borda [the most important neuropsychiatric hospital in Buenos Aires]: he became psychotic. I and many others ended up like that. He came to my house all bearded. My mom grabbed him, "Get yourself a bath, remove that beard," she demanded. He had a complete studio and, when he returned, only his keyboard was left. They stole everything. I bought him two changes of clothes and Snickers, so he could more or less get around. I bought him a new computer. And I said to him, "Do something, come off drugs." Everything that now happens in Žižek began with him throwing me [track] bases and me playing the keyboard.

How does this new, transformed cumbia catch on with people?

What we did was used afterward in the film *El Bonaerense*. We didn't do it in such a flashy or crazy way. It was cumbia. What happens in Žižek is that it is made for *limados* [wasted people]. I like using new words, and now I laugh with one they taught me: freaky [in English]. Since they're so strange, they made everything even crazier. For those clubs [Niceto and Žižek], it works. But, if these same deejays went to *bailanta* [the working-class dance hall], on the third track, get them offstage, because they will throw bottles at them. People say this isn't cumbia, hip-hop, or anything.

Colombian Passport

Alberto Campuzano began as a painter and sculptor. He has a Master of Arts degree from the National Autonomous University of Mexico (UNAM) and won a national award in his home country, Colombia. Afterward he moved to Mexico City and became a curator and collaborator for art magazines from the United States, like Clayton. The only thing he doesn't do is play an instrument. While roaming around with his camera through Buenos Aires shantytowns, recording scenes for *Llena mi alma de cumbia* (Fill My Soul with Cumbia), the documentary that will include cumbia scenes from Buenos Aires, Lima, Santiago, Guatemala, Monterrey, and Los Angeles, he considers, "My lazy wandering allows me to notice how my body moves along, discovering the origin of body movements (anaesthetized by Gancia [a cheap liquor] and other cheap alcohol beverages that young people drink from big jars) that cumbieros flaunt in the bars of Greater Buenos Aires. In the cumbia world in Buenos Aires, I discovered my body playing *chúntaro style* in the cold *porteño* winter. It was like a muscular epiphany." In Mexican slang, *chúntaro* is synonymous with something raucous, unsociable, and uncouth. Alberto cannot refrain from comparing, from recognizing the rest of the continent in this southern corner, and asking himself: Why in the hell do they dance cumbia like this over here? He is surprised by the fact that it is a mix of body movements coming from *murga* (Argentine street carnival music), chamamé, Mexican *sonidera cumbia* (the cumbia from Colombia, recycled in Monterrey), and Andean rhythms, "those that have arrived by bus from Peru, Bolivia, and the provinces in the north of Argentina." "Cumbia is a producer of territorial ties," he concludes.

Colombia is always a presence in the musical ear of Pablo Lescano. The initiation of the cumbiero arrived early; he was ten years old when, for the first time, a female friend of his mother, Norma, took him to Tropitango with her child, who was a little bit older. For more than twenty years, Tropitango has been building a music tradition that mixes groups like Los Mirlos, from Perú, with Los Diablitos, friends and mates of Pablo who used to accompany him during tours, creators of *Los caminos de la vida* (The Paths of Life). For the show, Pablo's mother ironed a shirt that used to belong to his father, always the same one, and with this "adult" appearance he ventured into cumbia dance halls. "The Tropi was the only dance hall that played Colombian music imported directly from Colombia. For this reason, it continues to be 'La Catedral,' it goes against the grain, and it's doing well. They do not bring in commercial groups," says Lescano, driving an immaculate all-wheel-drive truck. Los del Bohío, Los Palmera. On one side, there's Colombian cumbia, and on the other, Santafesina cumbia.

What is the difference between those who listen to Santafesina cumbia and those who listen to Colombian cumbia?

The southern zone is Santafesina. The northern zone is Colombian. However, some supporters of Santafesina sometimes go to the north zone and the opposite also happens. Los del Bohío, Los Leales, who are from Quilmes [a southern Buenos Aires suburb], Los de Marañao, Los de Fuego, come and go from the south. The north zone is accordion. It is a Hohner Corona III, specially made for *vallenatos*. It is like a *bandoneón* (the quintessential Argentine tango instrument), but it has three little whistles. The south zone is more guitars and a gentler accordion, like the one from Los Palmeras, or Los del Palmar.

What kind of influences does cumbia villera get from those styles?

I went dancing at the Tropi. I listened to foreign music. I began playing in the group Amar Azul, and this group gave me the opportunity to know Argentina, from Ushuaia to La Quiaca [the two opposite geographical regions of the country, La Quiaca to the north, and Ushuaia to the south]. And I began listening to other things. But when I was sixteen, I also started going to Constitución [the transportation hub that serves southern Greater Buenos Aires] to dance at the Super Tropi, where I came across Santafesina. Because many people that go to Super Tropi come from Lanús, from Quilmes [two southern Buenos Aires suburbs]. Santafesino groups that play accordion, like the cumbiamba, went there. At that time, from outside of Argentina, the Sonora Dinamita was very popular; it was the best. Afterward Mexicans began to come who played Colombian sounds, the *sonideros*. Not long ago, the Sonora Escándalo came and, three weeks later, another sonidero group came that does all the songs of Aniceto Molina, Jorge Meza, Lisandro Meza.

Do the Mexicans listen to your songs?

If Mexicans are anything at all, it is professional copycats. They do my songs in Guadalajara and Monterrey. Like everything else, when something becomes a hit, we're all on the lookout. It truly doesn't bother me that they play my songs. Here, did you see any punks at the bailanta? In Mexico you can see them! With a mohawk, tight pants, "punkie," and you cannot believe it.

Sun without Drugs

Pablo already knows Mexico. He played in Mexico City, Monterrey, and was in Guadalajara, where they suspended the show because the police could not guarantee the place's safety. But it was not easy for him to be successful in Mexico. The first time, he was there for only two days. He had a manager who realized that supervising six cumbia groups at the same time (he was managing their careers at the peak of their popularity) meant it was necessary for Pablo to feed himself with music from other places. Thus, off the cuff, he sent him to Mexico City. The guy who was going to show him around was a big man with little affection for nightlife or the streets. Pablo was overcome by the fear of not being able to move around in an unknown place. He wanted to visit Tepito, a traditional working-class Mexican neighborhood famous for its counterfeit merchandise. They wouldn't let him. He went anyway. So, fed up, he returned to Argentina in two days.

When did you return?

We went back in 2002, after De la Rúa had left by helicopter.[3] It was the first time [sic] I went to play in Mexico, but I couldn't enjoy it. I was holed up at the Hilton in Monterrey. [It was] a really shitty time. I had a very hard time over there. Even today, I regret that I didn't manage to leave the hotel. I went to the show and right back to the hotel, and I only went out into the nearby neighborhoods in search of action of some sort and nothing else. Finally, the third time was a gem. There are little dives where groups play cumbia. For me, that was a country of marvels.

The bars of Monterrey, packed with live music, are landmarks in the sonidero world. Alberto Sánchez Campuzano had a second epiphany after finding Argentine cumbia swinging in his body. It was at Tropitango, when, behind the figure of Yanque, he glimpsed the origin and evolution of sonidera cumbia in full swing at Talar de Pacheco (the Buenos Aires suburb where Tropitango is located). There it was: stereo murmur in the background, the deejay speaking over the songs, riding on the music, like an announcer giving off his messages on the radio. Mexican sonidera cumbia has Colombian roots and is distinguished by community messages that alternate sentimental content with comments on what is happening on the dance floor, as though it were a soccer game. Alberto experienced an epiphany and surrendered himself to the mouths of Tropi for many, many days. There he understood *parlanteras*, those girls who wiggle their butts by the speakers or on top of them, making the dance floor heat up a little bit more, and still a bit more, while they defend their space, threatened by other girls, newer girls, newcomers who pretend to remain at a spot that seems to belong to no one but hides strict hierarchies. Alberto watches them, seduces them, and talks to them about his view of the sonidero, like a heartthrob of cumbia.

> What is a sonidero?
>
> The sonideros are migrants who return from the United States to their Mexican homes. Los Angeles is a city in which the cumbia experience is intense. They return and transform it with background messages and new melodies. Since the 1980s, they have been in charge of cheering Monterrey parties, originating the "Colombias de Monterrey" [Colombians from Monterrey], a music and aesthetic culture that takes cumbia and *vallenato* as its identitarian source. This identity alludes to the 1940s in Colombia. Amid violence, migrations from the countryside to the city took place, and cumbia transformed itself into the rhythm that identified a whole nation, which associated cumbia with happiness and peace. That's why, for me, Yanque is so important. It is one of the links with the mobility of cumbia and migrations.

Drugs without Sun

Pablo Lescano enjoys great prestige among his fellow musicians. If you hear any criticism by chance, it comes, at the very least, from his main competitors in the cumbia villera world, Los Pibes Chorros, the most important of many bands that emerged from the commercial apparatus of the Kirovski brothers, owners of the tropical scene and its historic record label, Magenta.[4] If at one time they invented the band Commanche—blond, lanky guys who moved around in basically choreographed pelvic moves—later, after the success of the bands produced by Pablo (Flor de Piedra, Los Jedientos del Rock, and Meta Guacha) the Kirovski brothers staged many copycat bands that emulated testimonial lyrics that were packed with images of strong drugs, misogynist messages, and prison stories. Pablo is a great musician. No one can question his ear, or his musical formation. He studied. He feels proud of that, and this has been, at the same time, his lifesaver in his worst moments. The phoenix that emerged from a long recovery, and several escapes from farms and communities for drug addicts, found his strength in the cumbiera tradition from the northern zone, the tradition on which he was raised since he was a young boy who slipped into the Tropi.

In Pablo's household, the Guarani voice of his Correntino (from Corrientes province) grandfather was paramount, as well as the sharp ear of his uncle. Grandfather left him a respect for the culture of the Argentine Northeast (the provinces of Corrientes, Entre Rios, and Misiones). He still feels the same each time he goes to Corrientes with Damas Gratis. "They know that my elders were from over there, so the vibe is still better," he says. The cumbiero uncle was the one who performed the role of music censor. "Do you remember break dancing? My mom made me an outfit with quilted fabric and I break-danced. I looked like African Americans and did those turns with a little step back and my arms electrified. When my uncle saw me, he got mad. He didn't talk to me for a couple of months!" he remembers and laughs. He returned to cumbia like a convert who repents and is fortified in the faith of an initial dogma. He began to study guitar and keyboards. Eventually they hired him to play keyboards for Amar Azul, a group with which he learned how to play fifteen shows a night and toured the interior of the country. They didn't do badly. They sold up to 250,000 CDS. "Cumbia business is a lot bigger than any other genre. No one beats it, not even rock," he says.

Amar Azul's bonanza resulted in several investments. On one hand, he put together the band Flor de Piedra, with which he enjoyed his first hit, "Sos un botón" (You Are a Cop). Afterward he bought a motorcycle, first a Honda XR 80; later on, a Honda CBR 450. Once he loved speed and wind more than nightlife, and he bought a Honda CBR 900. "That was in 1998. It was summer; I went looking for a Portastudio [a portable four-track recorder] in Tigre [a northern Buenos Aires neighborhood] and, when I returned, an idiot at a light did a U-turn and hit me. I was clueless. I fractured both legs, and was left lying there. I was in bed for six months, with an exposed fracture and another one in my femur. At that time, I needed an operation, to pay for the clinic, a physical therapist, and a lot else. The managers didn't pay for health insurance. With Flor de Piedra, I managed to pay for the clinic."

This is the story that founded the myth of Lescano: the accident. His official website tells it, as well as the websites of fans and many newspaper articles. It is one of those lucky misfortunes that change the life of an artist. With much humility, without a tinge of pretense, he retells it. "I wrote those songs because I was lying down all day long in a bed watching TV and playing the keyboard. After that, I paid a studio, I made the second album for

Flor de Piedra, and went on to record the debut for Damas Gratis in a wheelchair. They were in a hurry to release the album and I told them, 'No, wait a bit, I can't walk.'" They released the album anyway. So, ten years ago, Pablo debuted in Damas Gratis with broken legs. That's how it happened. The first night, they did three shows: the Patria Club in Fuerte Apache (a very poor Buenos Aires neighborhood), the Tropitango in Pacheco, and another dance hall he doesn't even remember. Yes, the image haunts him, being helped by two people to get on stage with crutches; later, clutching the keyboard in front of the audience, without any chance of moving, afraid of falling. "With 'Se te ve la tanga' people went crazy, totally wild, we couldn't control anything. After that, there was a boom, because everything that is new becomes a hit."

Most people think that the cumbia villera boom has already passed. However, you again filled Luna Park.

When I started playing, there were not many groups and music was in short supply. I began doing shows without playing on TV, just with a demo. Here, there are many groups that release a new record and last only a year. This is not like rock-n-roll, where bands release a bad record and fans buy it anyway; they support the band no matter what. With cumbia, if your second record is bad, you're done.

What remains of cumbia villera?

The groups are there, the point is which ones work. When there is the opportunity to play in Mexico, for instance, Meta Guacha, Los Jedes, or Flor de Piedra don't make a fuss and they only send the singer; there, they play a record as backup, he does playback, and they're done. Damas Gratis isn't like that. We are much more; we all go, or no one goes. I don't do playback, nor am I going to go alone with a CD as backup. I worked a lot with Fidel Nadal [an Argentine reggae musician], and he goes to Mexico, and there he has a band. I think that you have to feed everyone behind you. You must support people. Our band is like a live deejay, but with the backup band playing all the time. On TV, we are the only ones, with Leo Matiolli [a very well-known cumbiero], who don't use playback. Also, we do not use playlists. We do what comes to us at that very moment. My musicians follow me to the death. They already know where I am going. We know each other.

Tropicalísima (Very Tropical)

Cumbia has its rules. Tropical music, which goes beyond cumbia, does not. One can go from cumbia to tropical like a dry frontier up north (in Argentina), through a path where nobody asks for papers. Like those deejays in the Rupture style (Jace Clayton) who have come to cumbia to stock up on new melodies and rhythms to sample, some artists cross the line of what's popular and embrace *non sancta* aesthetics related to cumbia. In 2008, the highest point of this tendency was an art show at the Ricardo Rojas Cultural Center, a cultural center linked to the Universidad de Buenos Aires, curated by young Máximo Jacoby. It was called *Tropicalísima*, and, in a well-understood excess, the author of this chronicle was part of the exhibit, with some printed texts of his book *Cuando me muera quiero que me toquen cumbia* (When I Die, I Want Them to Play Cumbia) hanging on the walls of the exhibition room. The exhibition lasted a few weeks. On the walls, the already well-known work of Javier Barilaro stood out: scenes of the cumbiero world that privilege written texts in the playful manner of cumbia. Jacoby and Barilaro are outsiders in the art world, but this doesn't keep them from being refined in their proposal. The inclusion of tropical music in the world in which they belong, loaded with excluding codes, is a tribute to the consecration of a genre that encapsulates a lot more than rhythm or dance in its execution and enjoyment.

In the exhibit, Pablo Lescano accepted a date for a public interview during which he would talk about cumbia. But he went on tour to Paraguay with Damas Gratis, and there, it was Mother's Day. The tour went on without a return date. Pablo didn't show up at the Rojas Center. But the Rojas was packed with fans. There was a little bit of everything in the audience that wanted to hear him speak about cumbia, from transvestites to academics and mods. When the exhibit closed in the room that leads out to Corrientes Street (the Buenos Aires entertainment venue par excellence), the doors were wide open. The band Fantasma played quasi-improvised cumbia sponsored by Lescano, who promised to produce an album for them. The band performed some cumbias that the public danced to until the end. Among the dancers, one could see Kiwi Sainz (a well-known marketing analyst and journalist); the dean of the Social Studies Department at the University of Buenos Aires, Lucas Rubinich; and various families of *cartoneros* (very poor people who pick up trash in the street, mostly cardboard, to sell it) that were passing by and stuck around. The central piece of the exhibit was a model that emulated a city of whimsical buildings made from cardboard bought from a cartonero. The children of cartoneros who were present understood it as a game and stomped on the boxes until they turned them, again, into a mountain of waste. So the work of Barilaro and Ramona Leiva became what it had been before.

Later Pablo Lescano, king of cumbia, shared the stage with other groups, invited by many rock and pop artists who are his fans. Boundaries were constantly transgressed, from left to right, and vice versa. Lescano played as guest for Miranda at the Roxy and later starred with Dante Spinetta (son of the Argentine rock legend Luis Alberto Spinetta). In the show he gave at Luna Park, he played with Juliana, from Miranda, and later on with Dante. The days when cumbia did not dare to go beyond the trail that goes from Tropi in Constitución to Tropi in Pacheco are long gone. Loyalty to his neighborhood does not prevent him from flirting with pop. Within him, modernity and tradition are not contradictory.

What has changed since you began?

When I started, there was all this commotion, the Buenos Aires night scene at its fullest. Back then, on Monday, the Tropi of Constitución was open; on Tuesdays, there was another dance hall in Morón [a western Buenos Aires suburb] called Aéro, for old people; on Wednesdays, Popularísimo in Once; Thursdays, the Metrópolis; Fridays, it was time to go to work [i.e., touring many dance halls on the same night]. There was something to do everyday. But now, the thing is there are families to support, you know?

So things aren't the same now?

I'm not kidding, the Tropi of Constitución, that used to be open on Mondays, closed down. I almost died! It was a great pain for me. Now you can ask, "Where are we going?," and I don't know. With drugs, everything went to hell. I had five bands; I couldn't produce them anymore. I stayed with my own. I had to say I couldn't be in the studio all day locked up because this involves more strength than I've got.

So, just like rock, there is a relationship between drugs and the tropical scene.

The relationship is there, but you can't blame the scene. It is the individual. Look at me. I had all the wisdom from the streets. I would see guys who took drugs by the corner, and I knew that anyone who went out to rob was not drugged out. Anyone who makes money can't take drugs, because if he does, *se agila*.[5] If you go out to rob drugged out, they kill you, because you aren't well. When I started taking drugs, it wasn't because of dances and cumbia. I was always able to say no, no, no, until the day it all went to shit. Everything became blurry. The sound tech left, and returned the next day. And I went, "Hey, you just arrived?" For me, only three hours had gone by. Everything was on high speed. And at first, drugs encouraged me to record, but afterward I couldn't manage. You think that you make something great one day, and the next day you listen to it and say, "That's shit! I couldn't have done that! I'm a bastard! Look at what I did." You have to be with your guns loaded, because if you are all muddled up, everything goes to shit. You lose clarity.

What were the consequences of this experience?

I didn't work for a year. I was burned out. Burned out, okay? I had to pay for treatment. And to continue managing things outside, the kids, there goes the money. My mom separated from my dad and stayed with me. I have a house with a studio. But it is in *Esperanza* [the shantytown]. I was born there, nobody can tell me anything, because they all know how I am. If you gave me the chance to choose a neighborhood, I would live there, but I can't.

Pablo gets around in his all-wheel drive, comfortable with his fame. Wherever he goes, there is someone who shouts at him, greets him, throws him kisses, hollers. He will star in Alberto Sánchez Campuzano's documentary, now being finished and edited in Monterrey. He is continental, transnational, just like the cumbia that gave birth to him. Driving his truck, he crosses a street in San Isidro, and on the corner, in front of a light, a young kid stops him.

"Pablito Lescano! Give me some change?"

He hands some change through the window and tells him, "In any case, you are going to see me every day."

Honest, upright, the king moves around in his territory.

"These are new guys on this corner. I know everyone."

He says it, proud of knowing his steps, where he walks.

Notes

1. This is a play on words that makes little sense in English. *Lime*, in this context, means having their brains *limados* (filed down), that is, going crazy.
2. This is a term favored by young people in Argentina to describe seeing something extraordinary. A literal translation would be "to hallucinate."
3. This is in allusion to the sudden resignation from office of President Fernando

de la Rúa, forced to leave the Casa Rosada (the Argentine equivalent of the White House) by helicopter to avoid an angry rally against him and his economic policies.

4. They own many bailantas in the Greater Buenos Aires, where their cumbia groups constantly play.

5. This is a *lunfardo* expression to address a person who loses his sharpness for some reason. In other words, he becomes stupid.

10.
El "Tú" Tropical, el "Vos" Villero, and Places in Between
Language, Ideology, and the Spatialization of Difference in Uruguayan Tropical Music

Ay, como la voy a gozar, pronto se les va a acabar,
Ay, como van a llorar.
La Plebe! ... Cumbia Plancha.

Ah, how I'm going to enjoy it, soon it'll be all over for you,
Ah, how you're going to cry.
La Plebe! ... Cumbia Plancha.
—La Plebe, "Como la voy a gozar," 2004

At first blush, the lyrical passage from the Uruguayan *cumbia* group La Plebe seems most interesting for the us/them duality that it invokes. Emerging from the depths of the economic crisis into which the River Plate region sank at the turn of the twenty-first century, La Plebe's brand of cumbia—known as *cumbia plancha*, the Uruguayan take on Argentina's *cumbia villera*—left little to the imagination as it articulated a new poetics of urban poverty. In the song "Como la voy a gozar," La Plebe warns its addressees, the "crooks in suits" (i.e. a corrupt Uruguayan political and economic elite), that it will soon be time to settle scores on behalf of the "kids who beg in the streets." The song's lyrics are punctuated on two occasions with the spoken phrase *cumbia plancha*, which underscores the emergence of this new musical subgenre in intimate connection with the figure of the *plancha*, a hoodlum hailing from the shantytowns that grew with alarming speed in Argentina and Uruguay in the late 1990s and early twenty-first century. Perhaps in part because of their explicitness, musical expressions of this sort in the River Plate have generated significant academic attention and debate in recent years (see, e.g.,

Larroca 2009; Cragnolini 2006; Pardo and Massone 2006; Vila and Semán 2006; Vila and Semán 2011; De Gori 2005).

When viewed in greater historical depth, however, La Plebe's proclamation of the cumbia plancha subgenre acquires additional dimensions of interest and polysemy. For one, while cumbia has been the rhythmic base of choice, virtually without exception, for plancha groups like La Plebe since their emergence around 2003–4, the term *cumbia* has been applied to a variety of music and dance forms in Uruguay since the early 1960s. Earlier performers of this music rightly insist, however, that their musical influences derived partially from cumbia, but perhaps more centrally from Puerto Rican *plena*, subjected to various local inflections. Those who make this correction tend to prefer the generic descriptor *música tropical* (tropical music) as a more accurate term than *cumbia*. And yet *cumbia* is the overarching generic designation that has stuck in popular parlance for decades, uttered oftentimes with an air of condescension that is not lost on the genre's adherents.

This chapter is thus about an Uruguayan cumbia that has not always been cumbia in the strictly musical sense. While the rhythms involved have varied, however, the generic designation *cumbia* has been a flashpoint of social contestation at numerous moments that predate significantly the emergence of cumbia plancha. It is those earlier and comparatively understudied moments that I focus on here. In doing so, I aim to elucidate how this transnational genre has mediated understandings not only of inward-looking us/them dyads of the kind invoked by La Plebe, but also, simultaneously, of regional cartographies that situate Uruguay at varying degrees of proximity to the social realities of "the rest of Latin America." The history of Uruguayan cumbia, that is, has been largely about questions of here/there, as the genre has entered into different vectors of tension with venerable notions about Uruguayan socioeconomic, political, and racial exceptionalism within the regional context. In what follows, I trace some of these tensions in a semiotic analysis that proposes to locate musical semiosis amid a constellation of signs that are not only musical and bodily but also linguistic. Thus my focus falls largely upon Uruguayan cumbia lyrics.

Popular music lyrics have been mined productively, of course, at the levels of propositional content and poetic structure by scholars in a range of disciplines, but comparatively little attention has been paid to the semiotic implications of the linguistic forms per se in which popular music is enunciated.[1] As scholarship continues to pose questions about what transnational itineraries imply for musical significance and signification—about how musical practices point backward toward purported points of origin or forward toward new social lives—valuable insights are to be found in the linguistic stuff with which genres like cumbia are so thickly imbued. Indeed few genres seem to suggest this sort of linguistic analysis as strongly as cumbia, which traversed virtually the entire, richly heterogeneous Hispanophone world in the span of a half century.

To illustrate the utility of closer attention to language in transnational musics, I consider here, from among the multiple linguistic phenomena that help to shape cumbia's sociospatial indexicalities in Uruguay, the case of second-person address forms. This sort of analysis calls first for an understanding of the linguistic, musical, and more broadly social histories that have intertwined in the course of cumbia's social life in Uruguay from the 1960s to the present. I then consider four separate moments in this history in which the genre's indexicalities—the national and regional cartographies toward which it points—shift. Each of these shifts depends fundamentally upon choices between second-person address forms (the *voseo* and the *tuteo*) in ways that illustrate the dense entanglements that can emerge between musical and linguistic modes of semiosis. In what follows, a comparable relationality becomes apparent between both of these expressive modalities and the social histories that they not only reflect but also work to shape and concretize.

Linguistic Background: From Pronouns to Ideology

Histories of second-person address forms in Spanish (Carricaburo 1997; Fontanella de Weinberg 1999; Lapesa 1980) often note a peculiar movement of the pronoun *vos* along Brown and Gilman's (1966) semantic axes of "power" and "solidarity." Originally a deferential alternative to the second-person singular *tú*,[2] *vos* was supplanted during the colonial period by *vuestra merced* but endured in more peripheral areas of the Spanish colonies, where it came to signal ever greater levels of reciprocal intimacy or nonreciprocal condescension. The story of *vos*, in other words, is the story of a "v" that became a "t."

Argentina and Uruguay figure prominently among those areas of Spanish America where the career of *vos* continued its "downward" spiral. Currently *vos* is considered the least formal and most intimate of the region's second-person singular pronouns, with *usted* (which supplanted *vuestra merced*) signaling the highest levels of mutual distance or nonreciprocal deference. In Argentina academic and nonacademic observers alike note that *vos* has grown so robust as to virtually eliminate any real choice between *vos* and *tú*. Thus as early as 1971, David William Foster could applaud a recent new edition of Ernesto Sábato's *El Túnel* for its exclusive use of *vos*—a choice that, in Foster's estimation, "evokes the entire structure of [Argentine] society, a structure that is broken when one uses the international *tú*" (1971: 354). Concurrently with this displacement of *tú*, *vos* has also gained significant ground in exchanges that would have called for *usted* earlier in the twentieth century, for example, a young clothing store employee's greeting to middle-aged customers (see Weinerman 1976). The same basic process has transpired in Uruguay, although *tú* does persist there as a viable—but nearly always marked—alternative to *vos* in certain social contexts that I will explain further (Bertolotti and Coll 2003).

At first blush, the case of the River Plate would seem to affirm Brown and Gilman's (1966: 264–69) general thesis regarding the triumph of the solidarity semantic due to a growing "distaste" for the grammaticalization of differential power. While such a reading would not be without validity,[3] it would also obscure much of what continues to make second-person pronouns socially and semiotically interesting in the River Plate region. For if indeed the history of *vos* and *tú* can be tracked along the axes of power and solidarity, it is also a history *of movement and differential distribution in geographical and social space*. Accordingly linguists have devoted significant energy to specifying the relative frequencies of *vos* and *tú* in distinct regions of Spanish America (see Carricaburo 1997). This variation in space is reckoned and codified, in turn, by a set of situated River Plate language ideologies.

When Foster invokes a binary opposition between the "international *tú*" and (we can infer) the autochthonous Argentine *vos*, he performs a "literalization" analogous to the operations that Silverstein (1985: 244) attributes to both seventeenth-century English Quakers and non-Quakers and twentieth-century U.S. feminists. Foster's binary, that is, projects a variation in the pragmatic domain back onto the semantico-referential system, thereby laying open the latter to all manner of socially and politically driven contestation and change (Silverstein 1985: 240–44, 252). And it merits mention that the pragmatic phenomenon seized upon by Foster's binary—namely, regional variation in pronominal usage—is no more neutral or innocent than the status and gender discriminations treated by Silverstein or the articulated valuations of gender, rationality, Christianity, and modernity that Kulick

(1998) sees driving choices between Taiap and Tok Pisin in the Papua New Guinean village of Gapun. If language ideologies are indeed never only about language (Woolard and Schieffelin 1994: 55–56), Argentine and Uruguayan ideologies about pronominal variation imbricate *tú* and *vos* in a long discursive history of exceptionalism, within which this region has tended to accentuate its own geographical, social, and cultural distance from the rest of Latin America. In this sense, pronominal variation and cumbia music and dancing take on meaning within the same ideological matrix—a matrix concerned with understanding social difference at the national level in the context of broader regional imaginaries.

On Being Tropical in Uruguay

We are better. When in Switzerland I had the honor of attending a banquet, the President of the Commune said to me, "We are honored to know that you are ex-President of Uruguay, the Switzerland of America." When it was my turn to speak, I said, "I am honored to be in Switzerland, the Uruguay of Europe."
—Luis Batlle Berres, president of Uruguay, 1947–51, ca. 1957, quoted in Caetano and Alfaro 1995

If claims to uniqueness and even superiority have formed part of the repertoire through which many modern nations have been imagined (Anderson 1991), historians correctly note a particularly vehement and perdurable insistence on two mutually reinforcing tropes in the imagining of the Uruguayan nation: "the Switzerland of America" and "the whitest country of Latin America."[4] Such constructions are informed by a number of factors that arguably did distinguish Uruguay from much of the region in the first half of the twentieth century, among them the massive influx of European immigrants into the River Plate region in the late nineteenth century and early twentieth, the consolidation of a robust liberal welfare state, and the burgeoning, by the first decades of the twentieth century, of one of the region's largest middle classes (see, e.g., Caetano 1992; Andacht 2000). These factors enabled not only an imagining of Uruguay in close proximity to Europe, but also a concomitant renunciation of the Latin American continent, as exemplified by the reflections of Foreign Minister Enrique Larreta of Uruguay upon returning from a trip to the United States in 1949:

In our country there are no insoluble problems because destiny has favored us with an exceptional situation. Even the United States has an insoluble problem, that of black people, and if, descending a bit, we pass over the continent we find an oppressive climate, with a tragic mix of races and with all the problems that derive from that mix. . . . Any one of us, upon returning to our Uruguay, has "rediscovered" this race of ours with its manifest unity, white, clean, healthy, apt, intelligent, although this yes, not very inclined toward work, and it is this race of ours that occupies with a scarce number of inhabitants a territory relatively large and rich, in which one finds millions of animals. . . . I think that from this equation there cannot result any problem for which, with a bit of firm dedication, we cannot find a happy solution. (Quoted in Caetano and Alfaro 1995: 185–86)

If social geographies have been reckoned thus from Uruguay since the early twentieth century, then a pressing question emerges: What is cumbia *doing here*? This question speaks not only to the pathways through which cumbia and other "tropical" rhythms reached Uruguay, but also to the sort of social work they have performed over time.

As mentioned earlier, a number of musics from the Spanish-speaking Caribbean, cumbia prominently but not exclusively among them, had begun to find their way into Uruguay by the late 1950s,[5] and as was the case throughout Latin America, these "arrivals" were made possible by the emergence of new technologies of musical recording and distribution (see Wade 2000). Musicians from some of the first Uruguayan tropical orchestras speak of scrambling to get hold of records by Caribbean bands, many of them from Cuba in the early years and then from places like Colombia and Puerto Rico after the imposition of the U.S. embargo on Cuba in 1962.[6] Driven by these musicians' zeal for reproducing what they "imported" from the Caribbean, the 1960s in Uruguay became a period of dances in huge halls, featuring multiple tropical orchestras and as many as several thousand attendees. Musically, as mentioned earlier, a variant of Puerto Rican plena, inflected with certain influences from Afro-Uruguayan *candombe*, came to hold particular importance in the repertoire of these orchestras, and many agree that the ascendancy of this *plena-danza* rhythm owed largely to the relative ease with which dancers could follow it. Cumbia, however, was a consistently strong presence in these orchestras' repertoires as well, with particular dominance in the *charangas* of the rural interior, which were further distinguishable from the *sonoras* of Montevideo by their preference for accordion over wind instruments.

From this period of consolidation in the 1960s the Uruguayan tropical music scene continued to thrive through the 1970s and 1980s, with some amount of original musical composition entering into the repertoires of certain groups. While other musical genres (e.g., rock, *murga*, and *canto popular*) suffered significant censorship and repression during the military dictatorship of 1973–85, the tropical scene was largely left alone by the authorities. The dance went on for tropical music, in spite of political conditions, a fact whose importance would be difficult to overestimate for the purposes of locating tropical music's social significance in Uruguay from the 1970s to at least the 1990s. In the more immediate sense, the fact that tropical orchestras did not become a channel of explicit political protest during the dictatorship has led to the genre's dismissal as frivolous by critics from many points on the political spectrum.[7] In a broader sense, however, it is the link to a dancing lower class—to massive halls where the bar sells sausages in addition to beer and, purportedly, legendarily, deodorant is two pesos per stroke in the men's bathroom—that forges such potent linkages between this nonautochthonous suite of musical expressions and manifestations of social alterity within Uruguay. Tropical musicians themselves reinforced this linkage frequently in band names, album covers, and song lyrics that emphasize fun, flavor, fiesta, passion, love, and, of course, exploits on the actual dance floor.[8] This is the dense indexical field that surrounds the term *cumbia* in Uruguay for much of the second half of the twentieth century and gives it such a charge of otherness in relation to some of the dominant discourses of Uruguayan nationhood. This cumbia, in other words, is not so much a discrete musical rhythm as an "other" cultural poetics (Stewart 1996; Limón 1994): cumbia tropicalizes social difference in a place long imagined as the antithesis of the racially mixed and socioeconomically troubled tropics. And for much of its history, when Uruguayan cumbia spoke in lyrical form, it employed the second-person *tú*.

El Tú Tropical

As mentioned earlier, the "triumph" of *vos* has not been as complete in Uruguay as it has been in Argentina. In many Montevideo offices, for example, the pronoun *vos* still sounds too informal for exchanges involving one's superiors or clients, or even coworkers of equal rank with whom one has little or no relationship outside of work. Since *usted*, for its part, sounds increasingly hyperformal, speakers often choose *tú* as an acceptable middle ground. This choice, however, operates at the pronominal, not the verbal, level. Unless they are from one of the two rural areas that make exclusive use of *tú* (Rona 1967: 59, cited Carricaburo 1997: 30), speakers virtually never complement a switch to the pronoun *tú* with a switch to the corresponding verbal conjugations. Instead they continue to employ the conjugations corresponding to *vos*, while perhaps avoiding altogether inflections in which the *voseo* and the *tuteo* differ. So, for example, certain stock greeting routines prove more advantageous than others in a scenario in which speakers aim to avoid both the pronominal and the verbal *vos*:[9]

Example 1
A: ¿Cómo *estás* (N)?
B: Bien, ¿y *tú* (T)?

Example 2
A: ¿Cómo *te* (N) va?
B: Bien, ¿y a *ti* (T)?

Note that in both examples, Speaker A has made no commitments: the *tuteo* and the *voseo* do not differ in their present indicative conjugation of the verb *estar* or in their construction of the object pronoun. Indeed the only way Speaker A can commit in these situations—grammatically speaking, at least—is by adding one or the other subject pronoun in sentence-final position: ¿Cómo estás tú? // ¿Cómo estás vos? Otherwise the choice devolves to Speaker B, who in both of the examples opts for the *tuteo*, using the subject pronoun in Example 1 and the prepositional object in Example 2. (The *voseo* constructs the prepositional object as *vos*.) Contrast these examples with the following:

Example 3
A: ¿Cómo *andás* (V)?
B: Bien, ¿y *tú* (T)?

Such an exchange could certainly be heard in contemporary Uruguay. If Speaker A were extremely concerned about committing to the *tuteo*, she might avoid the verb *andar* altogether, since the *tuteo* and the *voseo* conjugate it differently in the present indicative tense. That said, Speaker A has not crossed the proverbial Rubicon in Example 3—and this is precisely because she does not have the option of substituting *andas* (T) for *andás* (V).

The same point emerges if we return to Examples 1 and 2 and imagine that Speaker A has walked in on Speaker B just as the latter is about to complete an important report. If Speaker B, having just committed to the *tuteo*, must ask Speaker A to return in five minutes, the exchange has a high probability of ending in the following fashion:

A: ¿Cómo *estás* (N)?
B: Bien, ¿y *tú* (T)? ¿*Decime* (V), *podés* (V) volver en cinco minutos?

Clearly, Speaker B could avoid entirely imperative forms like *decime* (which the *tuteo* constructs as *dime*), and she could replace *podés* (V) with the conditional *podrías* (N). Unless she is from the Department of Rocha or certain towns on the extreme northern border with Brazil, however, she would *not* opt for *puedes* (T). The point of these rudimentary examples is that while the pronominal *tuteo* may be marked for formality or distance but be common in contemporary Uruguayan usage, the verbal *tuteo* is marked for something entirely different: nonautochthony. Meanwhile the valorization of this nonautochthony—and therefore the full indexical plenitude of the *tuteo*—emerges not so much from workaday routines like the ones described earlier as from the richer and more elevated plane of semiosis that is cumbia.

The Uruguayan group Karibe con K recorded the song "Karmencita" in the mid-1990s, when certain important changes were already under way in the look, sound, and consumption of Uruguayan cumbia. (I discuss those changes in greater detail below.) Nonetheless a song like "Karmencita" reproduces many of the important characteristics of the tropical music that took hold in Uruguayan dance halls as early as the 1960s. For one, it is a cover of a song originally written and performed by Puerto Rico's Gran Combo; Karibe con K, as was its wont, simply changes the "c" in the song's original title, "Carmencita," to a "k."[10] It also adapts the song's original rhythmic structure to the variants of plena and cumbia that had come to characterize Uruguay's brand of tropicality. At the linguistic level, Karibe con K follows what was, by the time of this recording, a well-established practice of leaving in place the instances of clearly nonautochthonous *tuteo* contained in the original lyrics—with one brief but highly revealing exception.

Chorus	Soloist
Qué será, qué será, qué será, *dime* (T) qué será?	
	Ay qué será lo que *tienes* (T) *tú* (T)?
Qué será, qué será, qué será, *dime* (T) qué será?	
	Tiene una cosita que me gusta a mí
Qué será, qué será, [qué será, *dime* (T) qué será?]	[Esa cosita que] *tú* (T) *tienes* (T)
	A mí me entretiene
	Bueno, y ahora
	un corito bie::n afinadito, a ver?
Mi Karmenci:::ta:::	
	No:: loco no!
	Esta es de la con K, *bo'* (V)!
De qué?	
De la con K:::!	De la con K:::!
(laughter) . . .	(laughter) . . .
Qué será, qué será, qué será, *dime* (T) qué será? . . .	

Uruguayan address forms, it will be recalled, do establish a place for the subject pronoun *tú* in certain speech registers. That place corresponds, however, to situations of distance and formality, and neither of those two conditions seems to apply to the reflections on "I don't know what" in "Karmencita." Moreover the pronominal *tú* is framed in this example within multiple repetitions of two uses of the verbal *tuteo*: *tienes*, the present indicative of *tener*, and *dime*, the imperative of *decir*.

By far the most noteworthy moment of "Karmencita," however, comes at the bottom of the right-hand column in the excerpt, when a percussion and trumpet break coincide with a rending open of the song's poetic texture. To this point in the song, chorus and soloist alike have addressed themselves directly to Karmencita, using the *tuteo* to implore some clarification on just what it is about her that proves so captivating. During the break, however, this narrated event (obsession with the mysterious Karmen) gives way abruptly to the narrative event (Bauman 1986), and we are inserted into a joking metamusical exchange between the soloist and the chorus. The soloist requests an especially pretty rendering of Karmencita's name, and the chorus responds with a mocking, ironic intonation in a nasal register bordering on falsetto. This rendition meets with the scorn of the soloist, who reminds his singers, just before an outburst of generalized laughter, that this is not just any Carmencita under discussion, but rather the one whose name begins with a "k." Seconds later, the narrated event returns, with Karmen once again as the addressee. This fleeting shift of address and of frames (from the narrated to the narrative) takes place principally in the soloist's speech, which adopts irregular prosodies and tempos characteristic of, in a word, speech instead of singing. Almost as central to this frame shift, however, is what Paul Friedrich ([1966] 1979) has referred to as pronominal "breakthrough," that is, a moment in which a shift in pronominal usage signals a fundamental renegotiation of the terms of an unfolding social interaction:

No, loco, no!
Esta es de la con K, bo (V)!

Here *vos* makes its fleeting appearance in the guise of an abbreviated sentence-final vocative used with extreme frequency in both Argentina and Uruguay. And within the logic of this specific text, the pronominal breakthrough into *vos* coincides with what could be construed as a breakthrough *out* of full performance (Hymes [1975] 2004). *Vos* "breaks through" here, that is, in a jesting, contemporaneous aside that recognizes its own disruption of the text's optimal realization. This is also precisely the moment at which Karibe con K widens the intertextual gap (Briggs and Bauman 1992) between its rendition of the song and the original version by El Gran Combo; no percussion break of this sort takes place in the original version, and Karibe con K uses the musical occasion to underscore its orthographic revision of the song's title while simultaneously departing from the original's *tuteo*, which it reproduces faithfully at all other moments in the recording. In these ways, the structure of "Karmencita" embeds a reflexive awareness of the mutual dependence between the *tuteo* and the Uruguayan tropical.

Musicians who were active in the tropical scene between the 1960s and the 1990s expressed this same awareness to me on multiple occasions, and those musicians extend their commentary beyond questions of the *tuteo* and the *voseo* to touch upon issues of prosody and phonology as well. A fair degree of consensus exists, for example, around the status of Santiago Salas of the long-running Combo Camagüey as one of the best lead vocalists on the tropical scene in the 1970s and 1980s. Nicknamed "El Chileno" on account of his country of birth, Salas's roots in a linguistic context other than the River Plate purportedly made it easier for him to pronounce "ll" and "y" as j instead of ʃ. In other words, El Chileno made for a more convincing Puerto Rican or Cuban, in ways that musicians themselves describe in dialectological terms.

El Vos Nuestro

Yo no escucho salsa, a mí no se me pega el "*tú* (T) . . . ya *sabes* (T) . . . *tú* (T)." . . . Vamos a tratar de decirlo como es, el lenguaje nuestro.

I don't listen to salsa, it wouldn't occur to me to say "*tú* (T) . . . ya *sabes* (T) . . . *tú* (T)." . . . Let's try to say it like it is, in our own language.
—Fabián "Fata" Delgado

In 1996 Fabián "Fata" Delgado left the group Karibe con K to found his own group, Los Fatales, which led an unprecedented surge in tropical music's popular reception in Uruguay. Beginning in the second half of the 1990s, groups like Los Fatales and Chocolate achieved deep insertion into a space that none of their predecessors had ever been able to access fully: the Uruguayan middle class. Delgado himself deserves significant credit for this development. His agenda was at once artistic and commercial. Commercially, groups like Los Fatales grew more selective about the types of dances that they would play, opting instead to accept a higher (sometimes stunningly high) volume of private gigs at weddings and birthday parties. Delgado himself was also tropical music's pioneer of the "children's theater" circuit that emerges during every period of school vacations, launching Fatales para Niños in 2001, an experiment also without precedent in the history of the tropical music scene.

Artistically, these groups drew upon certain innovations that Karibe con K had begun to explore, most especially more elaborate staging and costuming that followed the conventions of Uruguayan Carnaval rather than the fashions of Caribbean recording stars. Groups like Los Fatales and Chocolate, however, were also explicit in ways that their predecessors had not been in incorporating more local musical influences. Choruses adopted the harmonies of Carnaval *murga*, sometimes accompanied by the rhythms and instrumentation of that genre's *batería* (snare, bass drum, and crash cymbals), and while candombe had long been present at some level in the rhythms of Uruguayan tropical music, groups like Delgado's incorporated candombe *tambores* themselves as both a musical and a visual element, something that antecedent groups had rarely done, if ever.

Finally, the groups of this period placed heavier emphasis on writing their own music and, as the quote from Delgado makes clear, speaking their own language, which meant eschewing the mimetic *tuteos* of their predecessors. Witness one of the megahits produced by Los Fatales in 1999, "Comadre Compadre," which began with several spoken lines over a percussion break:

¿*Querías* (N) Fatales?
¡*Tomá*! (V)
Andá (V) llevando.

Before it even reaches its first verse, this new style of Uruguayan cumbia— which Delgado and others attempted to rebrand not as cumbia or as música tropical but as *pop latino*—announces forthrightly that it will speak a more local sort of language, with two consecutive second-person imperatives conjugated for the *voseo*, as well as a "ll" that is clearly, almost exaggeratedly, a River Plate ʃ (English "sh") rather than a Caribbean j (English "y").

While all of these devices drove a period of unprecedented localization of Uruguayan cumbia, the turn of the twenty-first century did not see anything akin to tropical music's universal embrace as shared musical patrimony in Uruguay. Delgado himself, in a complaint echoed by many of his counterparts, explains that while individuals from all sectors of Uruguayan society now eagerly try to book him for private engagements, many of those same individuals will, in more public scenarios, dismiss his version of pop latino as inconsequential lower-class cumbia, while the mainstream media pays little heed at all to what is by far the largest audience- and revenue-generating sector of the popular music scene. Nevertheless developments of the late 1990s did open new commercial, social, and semiotic spaces for Uruguayan cumbia around the turn of the century, making possible at least one notable return to the *tú tropical*—this time in a format that staked its claim to the tropics in more explicitly racial terms.

El Tú Re-Tropicalizado

Ay, mamá mamá,
como te mueve(s) (T) me va a mata(1)
—La Bola 8, "Como Te Mueve," 2002

The group La Bola 8 emerged in 2002 onto an Uruguayan cumbia, música tropical, pop latino scene that had grown large enough to permit exploration of some niches, and the group's producer and composer, Carlos "Bocha" Pintos, conceived of the project explicitly as a *grupo de morenos*, the next phase in the development of black music in Uruguay, which would fit somewhere within the tropical scene.[11] While the majority of the group's first CD consisted of original compositions, the first hit that brought wide public attention to La Bola 8 was a cover of a 1997 song by the Latin hip-hop artist DJ Sancocho. If the song was not original, however, the arrangement certainly was, with Afro-Uruguayan candombe drums—arguably the most important element of La Bola 8's musical and visual brand—supplanting the original recording's dance beat, assisted by *tumbadoras* in the execution of a *plena-danza* reinterpretation. Keyboards outline the original recording's montuno patterns, but, as if to complete its collection of sonic tokens from various black musics of the world, La Bola 8 also adds scratching turntables and a female gospel choir that emerges over the song's final coda and fadeout. The cumbia of La Bola 8, in other words, points toward blackness at the musical level, in accordance with Carlos Pintos's vision for the group, through indexical linkages to the tropics *and* far beyond.

Lyrically, meanwhile, La Bola 8 revises certain moments of the song's original lyrics in the interest of creating a lyrical text with greater interest for an Uruguayan listenership and greater articulation with Pintos's goal of branding a grupo de morenos. For example, where Sancocho speaks of walking through Upper Manhattan around 190th Street, La Bola 8, unsurprisingly, chooses to speak of walking down the main avenue of Montevideo's downtown, 18 (i.e., Avenida 18 de Julio). Similarly, when the protagonist of Sancocho's lyrics refers to himself as a *tíguere con clase*—a Caribbean lexical item referring to a man astute in the ways of seduction and romance—*La Bola 8* chooses simply to substitute the phrase *negrito con clase*. When it comes to the linguistic forms under consideration here, however, no such translation or localization occurs, and almost all of the forms nonautochtonous to

Uruguay (with the exception of *tíguere*, which would be largely incomprehensible to the Uruguayan public) are left in place or even accentuated. The pronominal and verbal *tuteo* co-occur throughout the song text in phrases like *cómo tú te mueves* and *qué tú tienes*. Specifying the spatial indexicalities of this *tuteo* further are lexical items foreign to the River Plate but prominent in the Caribbean, especially the adjective *chulita*. Note also the lateralization in the foregoing epigraph of word-final "r" to yield *matal* instead of *matar*—one of the more distinctive phonological characteristics of the Spanish-speaking Greater Antilles. Finally, the song's very title, "Como Te Mueve," not only performs a verbal *tuteo* but also makes graphic the aspirated or deleted word-final "s" considered nearly universal in the Hispanophone Caribbean. In other words, while La Bola 8's music can range globally in its invocations of blackness, and while its revisions to the referential plane of Sancocho's lyrics can perform certain adaptations to the local context, decisions at the level of linguistic form return resolutely to the tropics as the indexical grounding for a new Uruguayan cumbia whose otherness is racialized in unprecedentedly explicit ways.

Each of these examples foregrounds, in its own way, the dense relationality between musical expression and language use and their attendant ideological matrices. In the Karibe con K and Bola 8 examples, cumbia taps the verbal *tuteo*'s preexisting indexicalities of geographical otherness. In this sense, the *tuteo* helps to tropicalize cumbia. Simultaneously, however, cumbia draws the *tuteo* into a dense semiotic field all its own, thereby associating this set of linguistic practices with a richer and more specific repertoire of images, sounds, discursive tropes, bodies, smells, and so on. In this sense, cumbia tropicalizes the *tuteo*. Throughout this process, the spatial imaginaries that work through the *tuteo* may well serve the Uruguayan lower classes as a resource for fashioning a subcultural style in the sense that Hebdige ([1979] 1991) envisions. Alternatively, the case of cumbia may add spatial deixis to the list of expressive devices that Warner (2002) identifies as critical for the constitution of counterpublics. Even if one were to adopt one of these two views, however, it would remain the case that difference cannot be difference without the dominant gaze.[12] And in this respect, cumbia's poetics of social difference has given the dominant gaze an easy route to displacement and ironic dismissal. Within an already well-rehearsed discourse, detectable on both sides of the political spectrum, the difference invoked by the *tuteo* is quaint and cumbia at large is at best tacky or at worst debased. Both are annoying but ultimately innocuous and easily dismissed. Drawing on semiotic resources cultivated within cumbia itself, these discourses conclude that the tropical was never from here, or *about* here, in the first place.

It should come as little surprise, then, that deployment of the *voseo* was a part of efforts in the late 1990s to popularize cumbia with the middle and upper classes—efforts that met with partial but by no means total success. At first blush, the linguistic strategies of Los Fatales may seem to suggest a simple, "one-way" sort of instrumentality, in which the *voseo* localizes cumbia without receiving much by way of semiotic feedback. Quotes like the one from Fabián "Fata" Delgado, however, must also be recognized as explicit interventions into understandings of what constitutes "el lenguaje nuestro [our own language]." In this sense, Delgado's brand of cumbia *does* also contribute to a kind of localization of the *voseo*. As the most recent chapter in cumbia's history demonstrates, however, the localizing thrust of the *voseo* can work to accentuate cumbia's otherness just as easily as it can suppress it.

El Vos Villero and the Other "Other Uruguay"

A *vos* (V), *te* (N) la vamo' a dar
Si te llegan a largar
Como *te* (N) la vamo' a dar
Hijo de puta
La Plebe, "A Vos," 2004

No *te* (N) *hagás* (V) el divino, que *vos* (V) *tomás* (V) vino
Sabés (V) que no miento, le *das* (N) al cemento
La Monada, "El Divino," 2004

As mentioned earlier, the economic crisis of 2001–2 brought unprecedented levels of economic woe, political instability, and social disarticulation to the River Plate region. By most measures, the situation in Uruguay was one of significantly greater calm than in Argentina at the end of 2001 and through much of 2002. In August 2002, however, even as indications emerged that the Uruguayan banking system would remain solvent, images of malnourished children and of looting for foodstuffs issued forth from a band of neighborhoods skirting the periphery of Montevideo. A few days later, the entire downtown was shuttered up and abandoned shortly after lunchtime; rumors had circulated that truckloads of looters, many of them armed, were headed for the downtown area from the *cantegriles* or *cantes*, the poor shantytowns that grew vertiginously around the city's periphery during the first years of the century.

The fear and dismay that hung in the air during this period were palpable.

Clearly middle-class Uruguayans feared for their own livelihood. But as the deserted downtown of August 2002 also demonstrated, many Uruguayans were also reeling over the emergence of a previously unthinkable social and political subjectivity: a desperate and angry urban poor, here in the "Switzerland of South America." As the epigraphs to this section demonstrate, this subjectivity found room for its own voice within cumbia. Clearly, though, this cumbia, *cumbia plancha*, differs in important ways from all of the variants described earlier. If pop latino renounced some aspects of the tropical in the interest of localization, cumbia plancha's renunciation of the tropical was more complete and more aggressive. Musically speaking, almost all acoustic instruments, including tumbadoras and other "tropical" percussion, were supplanted by synthesizers. More important, lyrical themes shifted from lighthearted tales of fun and seduction to bitter denouncements of political graft and economic inequality or varied descriptions, often celebratory, of the multiple forms of violence and substance abuse that run rampant in the cantes. However one chooses to locate the resistive potential of such an "other" cultural poetics, the spatialities at work here are clearly opposed to those described for earlier phases of cumbia. Cumbia plancha gains nothing from the elaboration of an otherness that passes through some remote geography. This is a brand of alterity that seeks instead to present itself as autochthonous and endemic to a particular moment in Uruguayan history that calls not for rapprochement with venerable ideas about middle-class Uruguay, à la pop latino, but for confrontation. If this is the case, the foregoing discussion helps to explain the near total avoidance of the *tuteo* in cumbia plancha. The problem is not that these musicians and fans do not use the *tuteo* in their daily speech. Neither did the majority of musicians and fans from the era of Karibe con K or La Bola 8. The *tuteo*, in other words, is not inadequate as a sign of identity; it is, on the contrary, *overdetermined* as the index of an alterity that is too remote from the cantes to be of any use.

Conclusions: The Music-Language Nexus in Uruguayan Cumbia

Cumbia traveled great distances indeed to reach Uruguay. Those distances are best measured not in miles or kilometers but in terms of the sociospatial remove that dominant discourses of nationhood sought to establish between Uruguay and the rest of the continent throughout the twentieth century.

While this essay does not pretend to be a comprehensive account of cumbia's history in Uruguay, it should make clear that the genre has never fully closed that distance. It is still quite difficult, that is, to imagine claims about Uruguayan cumbia as national heritage or patrimony in any proximal future, and it is precisely that quality of being "out of place" that has given the genre such powerful semiotic and political potential. Language—understood here as the linguistic forms in which cumbia lyrics say what they say—is one of the principal modalities through which this semiotic and political potential is actualized. How, though, are we to theorize these histories of mutual signification and resignification between music and language?

In an essay exploring the "language-culture nexus," Silverstein suggests that even as individual discursive events concretize sociocultural conceptions into an interactional "here-and-now," all such events are simultaneously situated within more macrological "ritual centers of semiosis," which "exert a structuring, value-conferring influence on any particular event of discursive interaction with respect to the meanings and significance of the verbal and other semiotic forms used in it" (2004: 623). Understood in strictly linguistic terms, and in relation to the second-person address forms discussed here, Silverstein's formulation points toward an understanding of cumbia as one of the most important "ritual centers of semiosis" valorizing the *tuteo* and the *voseo* in Uruguay. It is largely within and through cumbia, that is, that the *tuteo*'s nonautochthony becomes a certain kind of Otherness and the *voseo*'s autochthony becomes a badge of the Local. As I have been at pains to point out, however, the valorization in cumbia is far from unidirectional. For the cases discussed, that is, the more apposite move is to think of the *cumbia scene*—a sprawling, technologically and commercially mediated network of singing, playing, recording, and distributing, and of listening, watching, dancing, and consumption—as itself a ritual center of semiosis that comes to bear upon music and language alike. When the *tuteo* appears in "Karmencita," the linguistic construction and the music *tropicalize one another in equal measures*. Within the cumbia scene, in other words, we find what might be termed a music-language nexus: a mutually constitutive relationship between, on the one hand, ideologies regarding where this music comes from and for whom it stands and, on the other hand, ideologies regarding where particular linguistic practices come from and for whom they stand.

At the same time, cumbia music, singing, and dancing per se can be understood productively through linguistically grounded conceptions of genre as "the historically specific conventions and ideals according to which authors compose discourse and audiences receive it" (Hanks 1987: 670). Within this framework, genre becomes an emergent feature of ongoing communicative practice, subject to re-elaboration according to the agendas and the social constraints governing any given performative act (Briggs and Bauman 1992; Bauman 1986; Kapchan 1996). This iterated, emergent, and contestable understanding of genre is clearly congenial with the case of Uruguayan cumbia, given the multiple indexical recalibrations discussed here and the ongoing social contention over the genre's status and meaning within Uruguay. To cite just one example: a fairly elaborate phonological and prosodic register has developed in recent years around the cumbia plancha subgenre, in imitation of the figure of the *plancha* himself. I recall listening transfixed in 2009 at a karaoke set in which a male performer sang, in this plancha register, multiple songs belonging to earlier (i.e., non-plancha) moments in the Uruguayan tropical music repertoire. While I was unable to locate this singer after he left the stage to ask him what he had intended, it seems legitimate to presume that at least some members of his audience were left with questions similar to mine. Was the performance a parody of the new plancha aesthetic (which is, indeed, vehemently rejected by adherents of some earlier subgenres), or was it a celebration of cumbia plancha's rising primacy? Or might the singer's "miscalibrated" speech have been intended as a mockery of the entire cumbia scene, insofar as it failed to acknowledge or respect subgeneric distinctions? A definitive reading is less important than the recognition that this transgression of generic expectation pointed in multiple directions of social significance—and that it was accomplished more or less exclusively through language.

For the case of Uruguayan cumbia, then, as for many other popular music genres, attention is due to both discrete performative negotiations with generic precedent and broader reconfigurations of "ritual centers of semiosis." Within both analytical modes, however, closer attention to linguistic form—of which second-person pronouns are just one example—offers clear dividends to understandings of musical significance and signification.[13] When an analysis of the Uruguayan case widens to discern choices between *tú* and *vos* (or ʒ and ʃ, or "c" and "k"), it becomes far clearer that the semiotic horizons of cumbia are none other than the horizons of a "Latin America" that has been a foil, a threat, and an occasional object of desire from different Uruguayan vantage points, and that is likely to remain a constitutive "outside" during an ongoing period of deep social change.

Discography

La Bola 8. 2002. "Como Te Mueve." *Corré La Bola*. Obligado Records, Montevideo. Original music and lyrics by Norberto Cotto and Luis Tineo. Original recording by Sancocho, 1997, *Rumba te Tumba*. Cutting Records, New York.

Los Fatales. 1999. "Comadre Compadre." *Revolución Fatal*. Sondor, Montevideo.

Karibe con K. 1996. "Karmencita." *De Vuelta en Kasa*. Sondor, Montevideo. Original music and lyrics by Rogelio (Kito) Vélez. Original recording by El Gran Combo de Puerto Rico, 1983, *La Universidad de la Salsa*, Combo Record Productions, New York.

La Monada. 2004. "El Divino." Montevideo. Original music and lyrics by Néstor Criscio, Pablo Fraga, and Diego Machado.

La Plebe. 2004. "Como la voy a gozar." *Cumbia Plancha*. Star Music, Buenos Aires. Original music and lyrics by Eduardo Britos, Juan Carlos Cáceres, and Alejandro Jasa.

La Plebe. 2004. "A Vos." *Cumbia Plancha*. Star Music, Buenos Aires. Original music and lyrics by Eduardo Britos, Juan Carlos Cáceres, and Alejandro Jasa.

Filmography

Historia de la Música Popular Uruguaya. 2009. Directed by Juan Pellicer. Documentary in 15 parts. Original broadcast release June 2009, Canal 5– Televisión Nacional de Uruguay.

Notes

1. Exceptions include Fox 2004 and Samuels 2004.

2. Brown and Gilman (1996: 255) trace this form of honorific pluralization to the Latin *vos* that was used to address the Roman emperor.

3. The case for Argentina is particularly strong here. Scholars from a range of disciplines have noted that Peronism linguistically enacted the leveling of social differences through an insistence on *vos*. In the regime's de facto anthem, recorded by Hugo del Carril in 1949, the famed singer addresses Perón himself with the verbal *voseo*: "Perón, Perón, qué grande *sos* / Mi general, cuanto *valés* / Perón Perón, gran conductor / *Sos* el primer trabajador." See Carricaburo (1997: 25–26) and, for a more general treatment of Peronist popular culture, Ciria (1983). James (1988: 25–30), in

turn, suggests that much of what made Perón's speech "popular" to begin with was an intertextual linkage with tango's lyrical tropes and linguistic style. It is worth noting that if this history of *vos* in Argentina affirms Brown and Gilman's (1996) thesis, it does so at a level of historical detail and specificity that the authors themselves do not achieve.

4. While this chapter cannot, for reasons of space, undertake a full analysis of the singular history of race in Uruguay, it should be noted that even according to official census figures, around 5 percent of the Uruguayan population claims primarily African descent. Moreover varied organizations within what could be termed the Afro-Uruguayan civil rights movement have been reinvigorated since the 1990s by linkages with the internationalization of certain Afro-American agendas. See Ferreira (2003), and for a historical overview, Andrews (2010). The manner in which race becomes visible and audible in the history of Uruguayan cumbia is discussed in passing here but deserves fuller consideration, especially insofar as race seems to be one of the primary axes of differentiation between the social histories of cumbia on either side of the River Plate.

5. When viewed in the light of the dense cultural traffic that has long traversed the River Plate, the case of tropical music would seem to be one point on which Argentine and Uruguayan cultural history differ substantially—at least in Uruguayan tellings of the story. Many prominent Uruguayan figures from the 1960s and 1970s emphasize that Argentina was not a principal referent for them—that their first goal was to reproduce what they heard on imported recordings, and that, secondarily, they tended to incorporate musical influences unique to Uruguay, especially Afro-Uruguayan candombe. The director of one of the most prominent groups of this period synopsized the matter succinctly for me: "¡Me importaba un pepino lo que hacían en Argentina!" (I didn't give a damn what they were doing in Argentina!) Later in the history of tropical music, in the 1990s, Peruvian influence on Argentine cumbia became quite pronounced in ways that did not occur in Uruguay, for reasons that seem to relate to the proportionally small impact of Peruvian migration to Uruguay as compared to Argentina (see Massone and De Filippis 2006). The one point at which Argentine influence on the Uruguayan tropical scene is recognized seemingly universally—including from the Uruguayan side of the River Plate—is in relation to the most recent period of cumbia villera and cumbia plancha. All of these observations are of a preliminary nature, and they suggest the need for a more in-depth regional study of tropical music that accounts for convergences and divergences across the River Plate.

6. This brief history is informed largely by oral accounts given to me between 2004 and 2010. I am particularly indebted to Benjamin Arrascaeta, Daniel Astrada, Fabián Delgado, Carlos Goberna, and Rodolfo Martinez for their generous insights. While much of the history of tropical music in Uruguay remains untold, one invaluable new source on the topic is Juan Pellicer's consummate fifteen-part documentary, *Historia de la Música Popular Uruguaya*, the first account in any format, to my knowledge, that affords a space for tropical music within the rubric *música popular*.

7. It is important to acknowledge that political protests *did* emerge occasionally from tropical music during the dictatorship, that dances *were* periodically raided by

the police and the military, and that the protagonists of the tropical scene during this period have expressed nuanced positions regarding the practical and moral challenges that they confronted in continuing to play. See Goberna 2008; Pellicer 2009.

8. Examples abound, but see the discography of Karibe con K for album titles like *Passion of the Multitudes, Agents of Flavor*, and *What Temptation*. Los Fatales, another Uruguayan group, dominated the cumbia scene of the 1990s with albums like *The Captains of Joy, Exporting Joy*, and *Mozzarella Pizza*.

9. For all of the following examples, I use (V) to note a pronominal or verbal choice corresponding to the *voseo*, (T) to note a pronominal or verbal choice corresponding to the *tuteo*, and (N) to note a "neutral" choice, for instance, the simple perfect preterit in which the *voseo* does not differ grammatically from the *tuteo*. (The example of the simple perfect preterit does not apply universally. In other parts of Spanish America, the *voseo* and the *tuteo* do perform this conjugation differently.)

10. The rich indexicalities of the letter "k" in the history of tropical music constitute a topic worthy of consideration in its own right.

11. See "Con Bola 8: La Renovación de la Movida Tropical," *Diario La República*, October 12, 2002. More recently, Pintos has distanced the music that he produces more resolutely from the monikers *cumbia* and *música tropical*.

12. The choice is a significant one, not least because Hebdige ([1979] 1991) presupposes the social formation "working class," whereas for Warner the public as a kind of social formation is called into being by virtue of being addressed. For some helpful caveats regarding the analytical declaration of counterpublics, see Briggs (2004).

13. As should be clear, I also want to suggest that the inverse is true: scholars of language will often find in popular music a highly fertile terrain for the cultivation of language ideologies.

II.
On Music and Colombianness
Toward a Critique of the History of Cumbia

To speak about cumbia is to speak about Colombianness. At the same time, to reflect on cumbia entails a focus on a narrative of idiosyncratic resistance and collective obstinacy. Just as in other latitudes, as an expression of identity, musical genre, and cultural practice, cumbia speaks to us, from the beginning, about how the presence of diverse social and ethnic groups was articulated in the context of a national reality. For the most part, in Colombia the history of cumbia, polysemic and polyvalent, packed with fissures and displeasures, is the chronicle of an alternate history of the nation. This is why, through a tracing of this genre from its uncertain origins to its controversial present, it is possible to uncover a more reliable — and critical — approach to more irrefutable forms of Colombian identity. From my perspective, problematizing cumbia is a way to undermine or subvert official or governmental discourse, particularly if we contemplate the extent to which music of this variety has become an object of concern for government interests (i.e., for efforts supported by the Colombian Ministry of Culture seeking co-optation). On the whole, a keen approach to the circumstances of a musical practice renders possible a more profound analysis of the validity of certain ideas of nation, since, upon identifying the limitations and disagreements of musical production, given its proximity to national influence, the contradictions that drive state-sponsored processes of identity come to light. As an elusive cultural product, making little distinction between officially sanctioned and popularly supported spaces, cumbia offers a vehicle of study unlike any other, providing an enormous opportunity to explore the arbitrariness of our ways of conceiving of the idea of nation, above all, in terms of rhythm and difference.

It is precisely from the analysis of an exercise of identity of this nature that one can argue the following: Colombian cumbia, sponsor of successful cultural forms through the entire hemisphere (call it *cumbia sonidera*, *tecnocumbia*, or *villera*), achieves its greatest effectiveness and cultural penetration through methods that, at a national level and proper to each period, have generated considerable rejection and awakened distrust, up to the point of disavowal, by its traditional followers. At each step of its evolution, cumbia has signified an expansion of the idea of nation, transgressing racial and social barriers and experiencing a strong domestic and international struggle. The greatest test of this argument is simple: in other corners of the Americas and the world, music that is more closely identified as Colombian cumbia represents, quite evidently, cultural forms with little prestige within the Colombian national context. In other words, within this musical genre's conventional environment, by and large its most successful version has habitually been the object of staunch rejection by purists and reactionary sectors, who have been consistently opposed to cultural change and more in agreement with the celebration of more rigorous versions of this music.

The history of this rejection is an account of the predicaments of the Colombian idea of nation (and, in some instances, those of other nationalities). It happened at the end of the nineteenth century, when black and mulatto populations were repudiated at the outskirts of the walled city of Cartagena de Indias, at the heart of Colombia's Caribbean coast. It happened again at the beginning of the twentieth century, with the decline of *bambuco*, the folk music genre from mountain regions, as Colombia's national genre. In the 1950s it took place through the ascent of orchestrated cumbia, dressed up for the enjoyment of the bourgeoisie of the interior of the country. It also came about in the 1970s, with the taking off of the *chucu-chucu*, *raspa*, or *paisa* sound, all namesakes for the same musical phenomenon. And it is happening today, thanks to the success of musical varieties of sudden acceptance, like *tropipop*.

Broadly speaking, it is possible to divide the history of cumbia into three phases. The first phase covers the period from its remote origin, for which there exists a range of theories; a nineteenth-century flourishing; and its growing popularity at the beginning of the twentieth century. In plain terms, it narrates the infancy of the genre. The second phase narrates a process of social mobility, thanks to the music's whitening and marketing, largely attributable to two important Colombian orchestras during the middle of the twentieth century, with a corresponding peak as a national popular form. This stage corresponds closely to a period of strong, rebellious adolescence. The third phase, akin to its years of maturity, takes place during the late 1960s and early

1970s. It narrates the subsequent evolution of the genre toward a variety with regular, monotonous finishes but with very effective cultural penetration in international markets. From this period on, more recent developments, in which new generations look for a balance between traditional forms favored by their parents and their own preferences, influenced by dreams of modernity, are not as striking. To a certain extent, despite embodying a potential foray into unchartered territory—after all, previous phases have already been the subject of detailed documentation—this last stage reveals, in a very clear fashion, the genre's determined transnational penchant.

To speak about the historical origin of cumbia is to allude immediately to the center of a controversy. While there is agreement and some shared positions, there is no unanimity when it comes to the birth of cumbia. Thus, more than positing an actual affirmation of the birth of the genre, I wish to discuss its possible origin. In general terms, there are three overarching theories, and all are centered on the ethnic character of the practice, a feature that seems potentially underhanded, particularly when one considers the lack of mainstream problematization conferred on ethnicity in Colombia. To some, the most important aspect is indigenous nature. This position has been criticized as an intractable negation of African heritage or as an example of interpretive naïveté. Yet to others, cumbia is music of *zambo* origin, that is, a sound that combines indigenous and African lineage. In this case, criticism has centered on the exclusion of a European contribution. For others still, the genre signals the musical meeting point of the three main cultures arriving in the Americas, contributing almost instantly to an impression of duplicity with politically correct versions backed by the social and cultural establishment. While a fellow contributor to this volume embraces this approach, I think it fails to problematize ethnicity in a more subtle manner. In any case, the most likely conclusion is that the origin of cumbia goes back to some corner of the greater Bolívar, the former province under the control of Cartagena de Indias, a geopolitical entity that, with the passing of the years, was divided into the current departments of Atlántico, Bolívar, Sucre, and Córdoba in the Colombian coastal Caribbean.

After all, when it comes to a birth date for the genre, these three principal theories allude to alternating points of this geographic background. For the master composer José Barros, author of the celebrated song "La piragua" (The Canoe), cumbia was born in the countryside called Pocabuy, in the lower Magdalena, comprising the towns of El Banco, Chiriguaná, Chimichagua, Mompox, Tamalameque, Chilloa, Guamal, Chimil, and Guataca, which form an indigenous nation extending along the banks of the Tucurina River (now called the Magdalena River). His interpretation emphasizes the indigenous ancestry of the music. Other famous cultural practitioners, such as Lisandro Meza, one of the most renowned interpreters of Colombian accordion music, also praises the indigenous theory but locates cumbia's origin in Monte Faroto, a place that contributes a name to the music as well as to the neighboring indigenous population.[1] According to Meza, these indigenous populations were the ones who created for the first time the flute-like instrument the *gaita*, which gives cumbia its melody. Other reliable sources, such as the researcher José Portaccio Fontalvo, also refer to the *faroto* character of the gaita in order to point out a possible origin for cumbia.

In general, Colombian music historiography goes back to the indigenous traditions of the Zenúes, Arhuacos, Caribs, and Farotos to highlight a point of departure for the cultural practice of cumbia. The object here is to underline the importance of the *chuana* or gaita, an instrument made from *cardón*, a type of giant cactus. However, the connection to gaita is sometimes a stretch. In the Montes de María, located in the coastal department of Sucre (toward the south of the former territory of Bolívar), the instrument is known by the name *chuana*. For the Kogi Indians, today situated in the Sierra Nevada of Santa Marta (on the other side of the Magdalena River, in a neighboring eastern province), it is called the *kuizis*; it is called *suaras*, *suanes*, or *supes* by the Cuna Indians, a group of people from the Colombian part of the Darién Gap, which is close to the border of Panama, toward the extreme western coast of the Colombian Caribbean (Camargo Franco 1994). Clearly, examining musical instruments in order to discover the genre's beginning is no joke. To make a gaita, you need only to pull from the ground a giant cactus (whose pulp serves as the backbone for the instrument), cut it about 80 centimeters long (32 inches), peel it, and pull out the pulp with a hot rod, making a hole in the lower part. This routine was almost the same throughout much of the Colombian Caribbean, with few variations. The "male" gaita has only one hole. The "female" gaita is perforated with five holes 6 centimeters (2.4 inches) apart. Without a doubt, gaita provides a great indication of the beginning of cumbia, but it is not enough to clarify the music's hybrid nature, the result of mixing indigenous wind instruments and the beat of drums of African origin.[2]

There are also those who support a series of old accounts, such as the memories of a general from Cartagena de Indias, Joaquín Posada Guttiérrez, in which, although he never explicitly mentions cumbia, circumstances related to the practice are described; particular examples from the Cartagena press from March 1879, where the gaiety of cumbia is mentioned; the travel journals of a Frenchman, Henry Candelié, dated 1880, where again cumbia is spoken about; the journals of Miguel Goenaga, a traveler from Barranquilla, in 1888, where the celebration of cumbia is already established in the center of the city; the announcements in the *Gaceta Municipal* of Cartagena in 1904, where the sum of one and a half pesos is charged for a cumbia dance; and a note by Generoso Gaspé in the *Boletín Historial* of February 1917, in which cumbia or *cumbiamba* (the name of the practicing group) is associated with the Virgin of Candelaria festivals in Cartagena de Indias. Most plainly, these accounts allow some to praise the role of this Colombian port in the emergence of a cultural form of mixed indigenous and African descent.[3]

According to these relationships, cumbia, as well as some of the less popular sister genres such as *mapalé*, was already a common practice during the earlier part of the second half of the nineteenth century (Posada Gutiérrez 1929). Despite the popularity of vocals in cumbia, it is suggested that its preliminary form was purely instrumental. Vocal elements would have come later, once Spanish had imposed its linguistic norm. The testimony of Posada Gutiérrez, for example, points out how, toward the beginning of February 1865, during the festivals to honor the Virgin of Candelaria (the patron saint of Cartagena de Indias), the crowd ventured from the corners of the walled city to the foot of La Popa hill. It bore witness to dances in circular patterns, with the participation of black, mulatto, and indigenous populations. Amid the merriment, the black and mulatto peoples danced in pairs, accompanied by drums, while the indigenous peoples limited themselves to large circles of men and women dancing to the sound of gaita. On this date, these groups had already mixed, bringing about dance practices related to cumbia and mapalé. Also mentioned as proof of intimacy between the black and indigenous populations is the valuable contribution of San Jacinto of Luango, a village located in the Montes de María and home to famous gaita players. The text makes clear that Luango was populated by a group of blacks from colonial Cartagena, so music, once it had attained a more structured, stable form, had migrated inland.

The third theory of cumbia's origin, and perhaps the most well-known one, given the support of Manuel and Delia Zapata Olivella, champions of things Afro-Colombian, and Guillermo Abadía Morales, another honored chronicler of national folklore, highlights the African ancestry of the music, going back to the origin of the name, which, according to the works of the Cuban author Fernando Ortiz, is related to the term *cumbé*, of wide usage in West Africa.

Other researchers, such as the North American scholar George List and the Colombian Rocío Cárdenas, also highlight the African character of cumbia, though they justify it through an analysis of the music's structure, which is polyrhythmic, with added cycles of rhythm (fundamental in the extensive use of the eighth note, a common trait in African composition, according to them), or in the structural elements of its practice as dance, identified with the traditions of San Basilio de Palenque, a safe haven for runaway slaves from Cartagena de Indias. In this context, despite a superficial recognition of the contributions of the indigenous community or the attributions of European character, African tradition takes priority, going back to the legacy of the slave period.

Independently of the theory, what remains clear is that, at the beginning of the twentieth century, cumbia already was a cultural form with a certain prominence in the context of Colombia's Caribbean. Inevitably it was to grow in popularity—through the Virgin of Candelaria festivals, Cartagena's independence celebrations during late November, and Barranquilla's carnival in late February—until it became the candidate par excellence to replace bambuco (of Andean origin) as the incarnation of a national musical form. In this way, cumbia was practiced in an expansive manner until the arrival of a ballroom dancing boom in the northern hemisphere, which, while endorsing the growing popularity of jazz bands in the style of Glenn Miller and Tommy Dorsey, impacted favorably on the viability of commercial cumbia. Thus cumbia ventured farther away from its provincial origins and traveled readily into the Colombian Andes, so detached from any recognition of African culture.

The path to the second phase of cumbia's development is the product of the coming together of a series of factors. With the arrival of new technologies, initial recordings of Colombian music were made. Between 1910 and 1917, Emilio Murillo had recorded some melodies (including the national anthem) in the Columbia and Victor studios in New York City. Additionally, Victor studios recorded the duet of Wills and Escobar in Bogotá in 1914. Years later, in 1929, this very duo would represent Colombia at the Ibero-American Exposition in Sevilla. By the 1920s a few bambucos had been recorded. Throughout these years, this genre was assumed to be the greatest expression of national character, discounting the fact that its appeal was circumscribed to a few inner provinces. Lack of national communication and a harsh topography substantiated this approach.

Toward the end of the decade, in 1928, songs like "La pringamoza" by

Cipriano Guerrero had been recorded, gesturing toward Caribbean music as a more representative agent of Colombianness. According to the British researcher Peter Wade (2000), in terms of recordings, the most important exponent of coastal music from this period was perhaps Ángel María Camacho y Cano, who, coming from a wealthy family in Cartagena, was put in charge of directing an orchestra at the Café Paris in Medellín.[4] Around 1929 and 1930 he recorded melodies of Caribbean origin for Brunswick and Columbia at their studios in New York. In this city, even musicians from a variety of nationalities, such as the Puerto Rican composer Rafael Hernández, recorded tracks throughout the decade, identifying them with coastal names like cumbia, *porro*, and mapalé. Along these lines, Colombians began to familiarize themselves with new kinds of music, not just the abundant selection of national production (broadening their understanding of nationality) but also a good portion of Latin American musical production from this period. In this sense, the awakening of a national musical tradition in Colombia appears within the context of wider sensibilities, though later than other Latin American nationalities (such as Mexico and Brazil), accompanied by a great variety of rhythms and musical elements from other traditions in the hemisphere.

Which brings me to another consideration. A good part of the success of cumbia during this second stage of transition is due to the companionship (in terms of commercial success) of genres like porro. Just as mapalé is related to cumbia in terms of its nineteenth-century lineage, with the emergence of a commercial market through rudimentary recordings and works by great orchestras, porro was the rhythm that contributed the most to interpretive importance. In musical terms, the principal characteristic of porro is the prominence of wind instruments, thanks to which low tones prevail. The genre has a simple time (4/4), with a strong repetitive melody, a trait that, according to fans from this period, assisted in the penetration of the Andean music market, given its meager demand for aptitude in dance or melody. The popularity of porro came from the maturity of a tradition of wind instruments of European lineage on the Colombian Atlantic Coast, additionally encouraged by the strong influence emanating from North American jazz. Despite the importance of an autochthonous tradition regarding wind instruments, as noted in the analysis of gaita, the musical peak of cumbia and porro comes from replacing gaitas with clarinets and saxophones, accompanied by a set of trumpets. Having arrived during the early nineteenth century, a good part of this European instrumentation was used by military bands that were generally led by foreigners or creoles from the middle classes with uneven music schooling, but made up, for the most part, of people of humble descent and incipient knowledge. In other words, these were performers from the villages, who, with time, took advantage of these instruments to give free rein to cultural expressions closer to their roots.

This musical juncture generated what became known decades later as the music of *papayeras*, a name given in the northern Caribbean area of Colombia to the large wind ensembles from the countryside, proper to rural settlements, and customary entertainers of village festivals in the region. In any case, this tradition promoted, strengthened, and nourished, among other things, the ascent of porro, with a rhythm and style of dance appealing to middle-class audiences in the interior of the country. Beginning in the 1930s, the popularity of porro facilitated a true takeover of dance halls at social centers in cities such as Medellín and Bogotá, despite protest from archconservative segments in these capitals. For these groups, beyond any process of musical stylization experienced by coastal music genres, these melodies continued being rather "black." Once again, at the moment of achieving new heights of popularity—as had happened in the past, when cumbia embodied the effervescence and vigor of populations of African and mixed origins in Cartagena de Indias—the music genre stood out for its flexibility in terms of identity constructs and its interpretive resistance. To validate itself as an alternative representation of nationality, it had to overcome, as in previous situations, barriers of class and ethnicity in the interior of the country.

To emphasize the significance of this particular moment, this was also the time of the appearance and consolidation of the first purely Colombian record labels, such as Discos Fuentes (1934), initially located in Cartagena and later in Medellín, and Discos Tropical (1945), with its headquarters in Barranquilla. Barranquilla, a port town located close to the mouth of the Magdalena River, fulfills a vital role in the diffusion of cumbia and porro, finally overshadowing Cartagena as the favorite location for musical convergence. Simultaneously with cumbia's maturing, this transformation came as the result of a series of lucky coincidences. In the matter of a decade, Barranquilla became the headquarters for the first commercial airlines of the Americas (1919), the first air postal service (1919), and the first commercial radio station (1929). During the same period, accompanied by airs of modernity and an entrepreneurial spirit, a number of European, Middle Eastern, and North American immigrants arrived in the city. Immediately following this demographic displacement, an economic surge began, which affected, among other things, the dynamics of the communications industry. In those days, hoping to please the taste of the recently arrived and reflect the styles of this period, the media sponsored great orchestras that played live for particular radio broadcasts. During the early 1930s, the practice of evening concerts and first-rate arrangements, emulating the aesthetics as well as the sound of the most renowned big bands from the United States, sparked the transition from folkloric genres to popular rhythms with commercial appeal. An Italian immigrant, Pedro Biava Ramponi, for example, played a key role in the process of disseminating the music, given his connections with the city's music scene, in particular through his work at the Escuela de Bellas Artes (School of Fine Arts) at the local state university, the Universidad del Atlántico, where groups like the Orquesta Sosa, the Emisora Atlántico Jazz Band, and the Orquesta de Conciertos Víctor practiced regularly. In fact Biava's work had a significant impact on two of the greatest masters from this period: the Soledeño Francisco "Pacho" Galán (from the town of Soledad, Atlántico) and the Bolivarian Luis Eduardo "Lucho" Bermúdez (from the town of El Carmen de Bolívar, in the now fragmented province of Bolívar).

Without a doubt, the 1930s and 1940s were a prelude to the golden age of coastal music in Colombia, with musicians like Guillermo Buitrago and José Barros as the major architects of this musical vanguard. Later, as strong demand for coastal music materialized, Bermúdez and Galán were the main promoters of cumbia and porro. In particular, Bermúdez, who moved to the center of the country and switched partners, beginning a new life with Matilde Díaz (a native of Tolima, a province in the interior of the country), the vocalist for his orchestra, contributed amply to the building up of coastal music in the record market in the interior of Colombia. In *Music, Race, and Nation: Música Tropical in Colombia*, his noteworthy chronicle of coastal music as an expression of the idea of nation, Peter Wade (2000) documents this process diligently. He alludes to the scant contact between the coastal population and the inhabitants in the interior cities, so reluctant to problematize difference beyond their customary framework. In contrast, at this point in time coastal people were, to a certain extent, used to contact with people from various walks of life, given their culture's peripheral nature. However, the interior populations, with their untainted, mountainous topography, still had not experienced continuous contact with people from other locations. In Wade's text, the clash between coastal idiosyncrasy, open and informal, nurtured by the Caribbeans' lack of social inhibition, and the ritualism of Andean societies, less worldly and less accustomed to declaring interests outright, was quite blatant. In the 1930s, when people from other provinces arrived to live in cities of the interior for the first time, Bogotá was a gray city with an eternally leaden sky (despite other changes brought about by global warming, this meteorological aspect still hasn't changed), buried in the stupor of the high plateau, which is why it is portrayed in this fashion in Gabriel García Márquez's work. Medellín, on the other hand, was hardly even a city; governed by deeply rooted conventions and with an entrepreneurial spirit worthy of admiration, life in its surroundings was almost absolutely void of motivations for recreation and entertainment. Bogotá's population followed the path of religion, with churches everywhere, and a somber and prudish image prevailed in its manner of dressing. In Medellín life revolved around commercial activity and work in a very serious and unyielding manner. Around the time the tango star Carlos Gardel died, in 1935, Medellín's milieu still incarnated a withdrawn and sorrowful culture, far from the influence of dance music orchestras. Generally speaking, while Barranquilla benefited from the business fervor of its groups of immigrants, becoming, in a matter of a few years, a cosmopolitan city with a remarkable penchant for fleeting styles of imported origin, Medellín and Bogotá still did not benefit from the premature development of Colombian air transportation or the solicitous character of its geographic centrality. Hence cumbia's rise as a national genre is framed by an opposition in the definition of national identity by these three cities.

The resulting racial tensions were predictable. Unlike the populations from the interior of the country, where mixed indigenous and Spanish descent is the main ethnic component, blacks and mulattoes are an unquestionable part of the Atlantic coastal population in Colombia. The arrival of young coastal people in both cities in search of educational opportunities at distinguished academic centers sped up the contact with a music tradition that, to the terrified eyes and ears of the Andean community, seemed boisterous and vulgar. In a country like Colombia, in which regionalism, even today, is the established rule of identity, the upbeat nature of coastal people, tinged by a lettered tradition bent on the ignorance of others and the overall superiority of the political and cultural center of the country, was interpreted as an indisputable symptom of lack of common sense and rudeness.[5] Their music, with a rhythm that, according to some, invited sensual joy, embodied, for the older generations from the interior of the country, an unambiguous sign of perdition. For their youth, it signified new material to explore and even displayed hints of modernity. In the context of the capital city's hermetic society, the lack of inhibition and informality fostered by the new music were a refreshing change of air, thanks to which the youth could take pleasure in new freedoms and a greater understanding of the body.

Additionally, the role of media, which broadcast Caribbean music in the interior of the country on radio programs dedicated to the youth, was noteworthy. After the dawn of Colombian radio in Barranquilla, numerous radio stations followed in the interior of the country, such as La Voz de la Víctor and Radio Santa Fe in Bogotá, both beginning in 1930, and La Voz de Antioquia and Ecos de la Montaña in Medellín, both created in 1931. The programming for many of these stations included shows dedicated to Caribbean music, including the contribution of coastal varieties, dressed up as nationalist display and playing to the sympathies of the local record industry, which began to recognize the great commercial potential of this type of cultural production. In the catalogues of record companies like Fuentes and Tropical, apart from releasing foreign recordings resulting from licensing agreements with international record houses, tropical music groups were listed favorably. In fact for the most part, recording was eclectic and improvised, combining members from different groups to maximize the number of possible sounds, genres, and musical arrangements. In this way, after barely organizing a group, a studio like Fuentes could try out new musical formulas that would render possible a tangible expansion of the record market. In the late 1940s, motivated by prevailing protectionism—during a certain period of time, the importation of music was banned in the hope of inciting the birth of a national recording industry—companies like Sonolux and Discos Vergara appeared in Medellín and Bogotá, respectively. Slowly but surely, an irrevocable process of concentration of the recording industry began to take place in both cities, distant from the music industry on the Atlantic Coast. In other words, at this point it became clear that the central economic apparatus would use the cultural production of the periphery to hegemonize the rest of the nation.

The 1950s and 1960s marked the climax in popularity of coastal orchestras, with a prestige substantiated in the placidity of porro, the favored genre for a growing musical exportation. Within the record industry, despite realizing the difference between genres, everyone discussed things in terms of cumbia. This way, given the success of orchestras playing coastal music, with arrangements and accompaniments strongly influenced by the great jazz orchestras, it became common to speak in terms of cumbia to allude to almost all of the music genres coming from the Colombian Caribbean. When it came to music, the sound production of Lucho Bermúdez, the great representative of the tradition of coastal music in the interior of the country, independent of orchestrating *fandangos*, *sones*, *pasodobles*, mapalés, or the well-known porro, was synonymous with only one thing: cumbia. In the case of Pacho Galán, his attachment to his homeland reinforced the connection even more, since Soledad, his native city, held a remarkable reputation as the vital center of a penchant for cumbia.

However, unlike Galán, who would later reap international fame thanks to the implementation of hybrid genres like the *merecumbé* and who was not inclined to abandon the comfort of his familiar environment (despite tours to Central America, Venezuela, and the United States), Lucho Bermúdez demonstrated an exceptional capacity for adaptation. By 1944, for example, he had already taken charge of the music at a nightclub in the capital. In time, Bogotá's cold chased away a good number of his musicians, who were promptly replaced by musicians from the interior, more light-skinned and of noteworthy musical scrupulousness. It is unknown whether this change was deliberate or circumstantial; what is certain is that it contributed to criticism that Bermúdez "whitened" the coastal music tradition with the purpose of dressing it up in "coattails."[6] On the other hand, a more flexible perspective could construe Bermudez's evolution as the result of a more pragmatic, open attitude to national culture, willing to engage other parts of the country and, along the way, popularize a musical norm centered on Caribbean expressions. Whatever the truth is, in 1946 Bermúdez was invited to Buenos Aires, where, together with his singer and partner, Matilde Díaz (no other Colombian musicians were present), he recorded more than forty tracks for RCA Víctor.[7] In 1948 Bermúdez traveled to Medellín, the city in which, thanks to his performances at the Voz de Antioquia and Hotel Nutibara, he was known as a good composer, conductor, and arranger of music. Later he would participate in tours to Cuba, Mexico, Central America, and the United States, turning into a figure of prominent international importance.

In the same way, aside from the success of Bermúdez's and Galán's orchestras, it's imperative to point out contributions by Venezuelan bands like Billo's Caracas Boys, headed by the Dominican Luis María "Billo" Frómeta, and Los Melódicos, led by Renato Capriles, during the late 1950s and throughout the 1960s and 1970s. In some cases, the arrangements of Colombian songs on the part of these Venezuelan orchestras enjoyed more popularity than the originals. It was as a result of the style of these bands, which used to incorporate more electronic instruments in their performances, that a transition began in musical taste and access to recordings. And so cumbia's transnational propensity began to surface. In particular, these new groups favored the use of the Solovox (the organ by Hammond), a bass, drums, clarinets, and two or three horns in place of the traditional sax and trumpets. At the end of the 1970s, the rhythmic structures of coastal music began to lose complexity and gradually acquired regularity, giving rise to a style that became known by the pejorative nickname *chucu-chucu* or *raspa* (scratch), alluding to the repetitive character of compositions and the devotion of groups to the *guacharaca*, an instrument that is scratched to mark the rhythm. For a certain number of musicians, toiling to defend a theoretical interpretive purity, the building up of this variety of cumbia outlined a reductive process since, to their ears, new compositions sounded more and more monotonous and predictable. (In a way, this transition evokes the stylization of cumbia when it migrated to the interior of Colombia.) As such, this new sound was readily endorsed by *paisas*, the inhabitants of Medellín, who, at this point, ran the Colombian record industry in a competent and iron-fisted manner. It shares signs of *música gallega* (Galician music), that is to say, indications of a new feel or groove that democratized dancing and greater uniformity in its rhythm section parts, fostering the impression of harmonic simplicity. In addition, while this evolution proved essential for the migration of the form, it substantiated links between paisas and those of Spanish ancestry. Thus, in the discussion of this kind of music, it became evident that, for many conventional critics, for a genre to be considered properly Colombian, it had to sustain certain essentialist constructs of nationality, according to which the preferred way of reflecting identity was to account for musical complexity and harmonic coherence. Musically speaking, though this idea of nation contemplated heterogeneity, it also endorsed firm adherence to unchanging principles of demographics, as if the actual circumstances of Colombia's population weren't shifting.

In short, in the effort to maximize earnings and secure the music market long term, Medellín's record labels became eminent promoters of tropical genres, and therefore of the unveiling of a particular style of music most often recognized as cumbia. Aside from Venezuelan orchestras, there was an entire segment of groups like the Sonora Dinamita, Los Hispanos, Los Black Stars, Los Teenagers, Los Tupamaros, El Combo de las Estrellas, and Los Graduados, whose trademark was their ability to reproduce coastal sounds in regularized versions using musicians from the interior of Colombia. In plain terms, when it came to performances and recordings, a good part of the production sanctioned as cumbia came from musicians from the interior of the country. On a practical basis, the coastal art of the great orchestras of tropical music had been dismantled and even "improved" to facilitate an agile and uncomplicated interpretation. This represented an authentic gold mine in commercial interests, since it enhanced interpretive viability (music could be played by less skilled performers from anywhere in the country) and assisted contractual negotiation (it relieved the necessity of contending with difference). At this point, despite the fact that there was already a tradition of contact with the record markets of other Latin American countries, the appearance of these groups, with very rhythmic but predictable melodies, was the decisive step for the dissemination of cumbia throughout the continent. In general terms, the music that many people in Mexico, Peru, and Argentina recognize as Colombian cumbia relates to production from this period, and not to the classic period of porro, with arrangements reminiscent of North American bands. Once cumbia was packaged for exportation, the very straightforwardness of its structure facilitated its adoption and reproduction by disenfranchised groups in other latitudes. Galán and Bermúdez required a full team of well-trained musicians; these new sounds demanded much less. This exemplifies a great irony since, for the purpose of the internationalization of the genre, the most successful variety of the music was the one with minimal artistic approval within the national context. As usual, cumbia thrived under a mantle of disdain. Once again, honoring obstacles proper of customary processes of identity in Colombia, a particular form of nationality prevailed despite heated criticisms and rants against it.

The end of the 1970s brought an overwhelming onslaught, forcing cumbia into a long period of inactivity: the peak of *salsa* music as an urban Caribbean expression (despite having come from the Nuyorican neighborhoods of Manhattan and the Bronx); the arrival of disco (openly hedonistic, with a trifling disposition); and the festive, deceptive hegemony of Dominican *merengue*, a genre that would dominate a good part of the 1980s, mimicking the advances of cumbia, relatively speaking. Throughout these years, slowly but surely, Colombian cumbia inspired the maturing of regional versions in remote corners of Mexico, Central America, the Andean countries, Argentina, and Uruguay, thanks to the advances of the paisa sound. In more practical terms, this phase stands as the transnationalization of the genre, when it was embraced by other nations and adapted locally, giving birth to national varieties more conducive to the reflection and problematization of more proximate circumstances. In Peru, for example, upon mixing with *huayno* (a local folk genre), cumbia fostered the birth of *chicha* and later evolved into the rage of tecno-cumbia. In Argentina, the atmosphere of *bailanta* (working-class dance celebrations) would do its part, though the staging of cumbia's more discordant descendant, *villera* (cumbia from the *villa*, or slums), would still take a while. (Eventually its rise would be triggered by the crumbling of the Argentine economy at the hands of brazen politicians and rampant corruption.) During this time, in Colombia, cumbia survived thanks to its Antioquia version, while other, related genres watched closely—chief among them, coastal accordion music, which, with the passing of time and thanks to revisionist political schemes, ended up being called *vallenato*. Still other manifestations perdured—choreographies from the Ballet Nacional de Sonia Osorio, the folkloric group of Delia Zapata Olivella, and the recordings of Totó La Momposina—but in terms of diffusion, their actual impact was minor. Throughout the 1980s, while the middle-class appeal of rock in Spanish evolved and merengue flirted with Jamaican dance hall and North American rap, in a lapse that would engender Puerto Rican *reggaetón*, there was a generational changing of the guard in Colombia's cultural industry. In the early 1990s, just as cumbia had displaced bambuco and *pasillo*, vallenato popped up as the new music genre of national stature. Its execution, in which the conventions of indigenous music were more visible than in paisa cumbia—thanks to the reappearance of gaita—giving way to further diminishing of African ancestry, facilitated the conquest of the Colombian music market, already in the hands of companies from the interior located in Medellín (the ones of national origin) and Bogotá (those belonging to multinational conglomerates).

This success, however, was marred by a problem that remained. Unlike their embrace of cumbia, musicians from the interior found it hard to identify with the new genre, and even more, to master the use of the accordion. Vallenato ensembles proliferated, but their type of tropical music, with key coastal exponents, was difficult to co-opt. This circumstance remained untouched until 1993, when a young fellow from Santa Marta, having aspired to be an actor and recorded a few ballad albums—even some rock in Spanish—pointed the way forward. In less than a year, thanks to the extraordinary success of the album *Clásicos de la Provincia*, a compilation of songs resulting from the biographical soap opera of the composer Rafael Escalona, the singer Carlos Vives became the knight in shining armor of the Colombian music industry. Initially the phenomenon was interpreted as the arrival of the internationalization of vallenato, though later, with the development of a recording career for Vives, who stubbornly pointed out the link between his music and cumbia, circumstances shifted. To evoke the demographic change of his generation (the sustained urbanization of the country), Vives integrated strings and electric instrumentation into his sound, proper to pop and rock, genres that enjoyed great acceptance among middle- and upper-class urban youth. Along the same lines, to emphasize cumbia's ancestry, he revived gaita, the flute, and even the *llamador* (a small drum), instruments from its first phase, when it was still bound to vernacular interests. This display of conscientious arrangements was supported by persistent claims, according to which his cultural production (in its new-fangled version of accordion music) not only recognized the importance of cumbia's musical legacy but also attempted to insert itself into its historical narrative. For this reason, Vives would repeat incessantly in interviews, "Mother cumbia is behind everything" and "Vallenato has taught me it comes from cumbia."[8]

Likewise, suggesting a personal mythology, Vives underscored the importance of the discovery of the rhythmic pattern of cumbia in the electric guitar as a key moment in the development of his music project, thanks in large part to his band's guitarist, Ernesto "Teto" Ocampo, who, like the singer, has coastal ancestry (Abello Vives 2002). In this way, in just a few years, Vives created an image evocative of the success of coastal orchestras from forty years earlier; in fact, by dexterously managing his image, he nurtured a link between his music and cumbia's earlier tradition, effectively establishing continuity for the history of the genre (and reframing the periodization suggested at the beginning of this text). At an international level, his maneuvering was even more skillful: conscious of the enormous potential of his production in the U.S. market and hoping to be well known in the rest of Latin America, Vives used the metaphor of the white child with a black soul, selling himself as a Colombian Elvis who took advantage of his country's musical tradition (think of accordion music as the Colombian blues) and translated it into a more cosmopolitan context.[9] Within this framework, Barranquilla was compared with New Orleans, another Caribbean port near the mouth of a large river, with avid followers of carnival and a flavor of ineffable and joyously decadent tropical partying. In more recent production, in which, pressured by record companies, Vives stopped recording old tunes and authored his own material, he emulates the music of innovators like the Dominican star Juan Luis Guerra, who, despite dabbling with a Taino legacy, moved away from a folkloric sound. (Like so much of Quisqueya's cultural establishment, Guerra deals, consciously or not, with the "whitening" of his national context.) There are those who interpret Vives's music as a recovery of folklore;

in fact it does embody a process of this nature, though with the mitigating factor of a rushed updating, in many instances in open contradiction to any sort of ethnomusicological project.

Once Vives's success became obvious, other sorts of random recordings began to appear with a similar finish. Within this context, the most immediate cases, Tulio Zuluaga and Moisés Angulo, indicate the small difference between an ill-fated copy and an attempt at greater substance. Groups like Café Moreno, Karamelo, and Luna Verde also contributed to the hasty exploitation of the model. Nevertheless, over time it became obvious that this production went beyond a passing fad. It began to build up its popularity and even came close to conceiving a style; by 2005, hardly a decade after the release of *Clásicos*, it was already common to hear the term *tropipop* describing these groups, the musical offspring of Carlos Vives. New groups and singers like Cabas, Bacilos, Bonka, Lucas Arnau, Mauricio y Palo de Agua, Sin Ánimo de Lucro, Fonseca, San Alejo, Fanny Lu, Pernett, Jerau, and Wamba, some of whom enjoyed recognition from awards like the Grammys, Billboard, Lo Nuestro, or the Principales in Spain, contributed greatly to the consolidation of this musical trend, in which the rhythm of cumbia or the hints of accordion frequently mixed with the riffs of an electric guitar or vocals evocative of melodies by Guerra or Vives. Amid so many new figures, little did anyone notice that, thanks to tropipop, cumbia had advanced to a new experimental stage. In other words, it had gone through a transformation like that of the late 1960s and early 1970s, when, at the expense of the Antioquia record labels, it had been possible to take the music out of the hands of coastal performers. From this viewpoint, tropipop represents, for the music of accordion and chucu-chucu, what chucu-chucu embodied for orchestrated cumbia: a musical opening to more flexible tastes and an expansion in terms of identity that is judiciously packaged in a Caribbean format.

The vectors for this change presuppose that, on social matters, the evolution of the genre has been vertical, from the lower class to the middle class or from the middle class to the upper class. With regard to ethnicity, though there is criticism of porro (predictably rooted in whitewashing), now it is feasible to talk about even greater suppression of the code of African ancestry. All in all, it is legitimate to talk about the co-optation of a musical practice. Going beyond purist or essentialist positions, given a narrow perspective on the question of musical legitimacy, tropipop validates the music produced by a certain cadre of small groups from the interior, who feel pressured to clarify that their music is inspired by a Caribbean tradition, far from intending to incarnate it. In tropipop, although coastal performers sometimes highlight the vocals and instrumentation (the accordion, for example, is still played mainly by coastal musicians), the music has given free rein to the sensibility and harmonic contribution of performers from the interior of the country. At an individual level, with the ascent of performers like Fonseca, a native of Bogotá; Lucas Arnau from Medellín; and Fanny Lu, a native of Cali, it was clear that the path to follow was that of a sensibility closely related to the music tastes of the middle class in the interior of the country rather than to the traditions of a coastal working class or a folkloric or rural basis. In terms of musical performance, groups like Mauricio y Palo de Agua, Bonka, and Wamba evince the significance of a common context, that of having attended middle-class, all-male schools in Bogotá, for example. These bands, with barely any female participation, are accustomed to bringing together youth from the privileged classes and do not endorse an introspective, critical disposition. They are used to wearing emblematic symbols of nationality from the northern Caribbean area, such as Arahuaco handbags, proper to the tribes of the Sierra Nevada de Santa Marta, and *sombreros vueltiaos*, alluding to day laborers from the Sinú River basin at the opposite end of the Atlantic Coast. But more problematic facets of this environment (i.e., the fact that, in terms of infrastructure, these settings have been traditionally forsaken by Colombia's central political establishment) are promptly ignored.

Consequently, as an evolutionary stage of cumbia, tropipop works in a contradictory fashion. To make itself worthy of public recognition, tropipop reiterates the traditional obstinacy of cumbia when it comes to matters of identity, overcoming class and ethnic barriers during the nineteenth century; displacing bambuco and pasillo at the beginning of the twentieth century; becoming a national expression by means of porro; and, despite complaints by purists, conquering foreign markets triumphantly during the rise of chucu-chucu. In this case, as in the past, attacks have been immediate.[10] Some radio stations have come up with campaigns against tropipop. In terms of music and arrangements, tropipop is accused of watering down cumbia (and vallenato) as an "authentic" expression of Colombian folklore. In terms of lyrics, there is criticism of frivolity and impetuosity, given the flippancy of their repertoire, rather detached from harsh Colombian realities. Vives himself, at the moment of alluding to differences of race or class, is used to making comments with an easy and conciliatory tone, taking little notice of implicit difficulties in discussing issues of this kind. Nonetheless, despite what may be immediately obvious and beyond consideration of any tangible flaws, the ascent of tropipop entails an achievement, since it involves an expansion of identity past the established confines marked by those who wish to control the evolution of cumbia. In Colombia, to succeed in a shared expansion of nationality, regardless of orientation, involves considerable effort.

On the other hand, perhaps the most problematic aspect resides in the alignment of change, more favorable to the interests and points of view of the affluent classes. With the rise of tropipop, cumbia has validated the course of its trajectory through the twentieth century, when there was still hope for cultural vindication, given the development of marginal identities in the construction of a national being. Its direction is very clear now, passing from being an affirmation of local musical and cultural values to an instrument of national hegemony. In the advantageous hands of a certain sector of the cultural and commercial establishment in the interior of the country, cumbia becomes a binding ingredient in a new sense of nation, very close to the upstart multicultural spirit of the 1991 Constitution. If this tendency came with an exchange of capital, a revaluation of differences in the country, and a shift in the social policies of the government—all of which could facilitate a more appropriate assessment of national inequalities—tropipop wouldn't be so questionable. The sad part is, close to two decades after constitutional reform and following a beneficial increase in musical tradition and trade, both of which have signified substantial gains, the degree of general inequity in Colombia remains intact, at one of the highest percentages in the hemisphere. (That is to say, with a few exceptions, it has seldom been music's responsibility to effect social change; however, one cannot help but feel that the rise of cumbia could have contributed to greater social consciousness among Colombians, an event that clearly hasn't taken place.) In the context of the 1990s, one of the most violent decades in recent history, music's relation to social mindfulness was attenuated, as political awareness no longer figured as motivation for any of the warring parties. In a country bleeding to death, its key association was with projects of *convivencia* (coexistence), championing a feel-good mentality.

Following Vives, cumbia has regained strength. The Colombian recording industry understands the genre's great potential as a cultural business and smart economic development. At the international level, the overall response of the market demonstrates this. For this reason, whether or not Colombia's cultural establishment likes it, cumbia will continue its course, helping out and sponsoring the enactment of new forms of Latin American identity, regardless of nationality. In the lists of commercial online music services such as Rhapsody and iTunes, Vives appears next to such contemporary musicians as A. B. Quintanilla and the Kumbia Kings, Celso Piña, Fito Olivares, El Gran Silencio, and Grupo Bryndis, as well as more common staples, such as the bands of Bermúdez and Galán, La Sonora Dinamita, and Corraleros de Majagual. In other words, despite ample disenchantment and many downfalls, cumbia, the orphan child of the Latin American Caribbean (given its scant presence at the official level, Colombia's Atlantic Coast lacks the preeminence to circulate widely its claims of motherhood), has become the only great international genre of Colombian origin (and, at a Latin American level, perhaps its most widespread one), sharing space with cultural production from a number of areas in the hemisphere. Cumbia is an orphan in the sense that, given its strong association with a geographic location (the Colombian Caribbean), its principle of origin—rather than paternal acknowledgment—seems to be the final determination of its musical identity. Quite possibly, the most laudable aspect of its achievement is that it expanded without the support of an established cultural industry (like Argentina's), without an international project of cultural hegemony (the case of Mexico and Brazil), and at the hands of a dysfunctional governmental order and an improvised cultural project. In Colombia and throughout the hemisphere—as well as in other places of the world—the case of cumbia has been a matter of rhythm, cultural circuits, consumerist dynamics, and negotiation of identity, disguised as governmental co-optation and popular resistance. In the future we will see if it continues tenaciously along this course.

Notes

1. For more information, please see the comments regarding this point in the interview with Meza on the website of Afropop Worldwide, the public radio program dedicated to music of African origin: http://www.afropop.org/multi/interview/ID/43/Lisandro+Meza-2003.

2. In terms of musical structure, cumbia has a simple binary meter of 2/2 or 2/4, with a strong syncopated rhythm, and a particular emphasis on the second and fourth beats. Most well-known cumbias are in a minor key. Like Colombian accordion music, traditional cumbia tends to begin with string melodies; later it is accompanied by percussion instruments. In general, there are two types of cumbia groups: the cumbia of the millet reed kind and that of gaitas. The first consists of a *caña de millo* clarinet, a major drum, a llamador drum, and a bass drum. The second consists of female and male gaitas, maracas, a major drum, and a llamador drum, with only

one interpreter of maracas and the male gaita. For a more detailed musical analysis, see Leonardo D'Amico's essay in this volume.

3. The musicologist José Portaccio Fontalvo (1995) alludes to the memories of Posada Gutiérrez in *Colombia y Su Música*, volume 1, but the remaining bibliography appears in citation in Muñoz Vélez (2006).

4. Wade also alludes to recordings by Camacho and Cano in his interview with Afropop Worldwide, available at http://www.afropop.org/multi/interview/ID/114/Peter+Wade+2007.

5. Unlike vallenato, which emerged in the context of a lettered tradition—think of composers like Alejo Durán and Rafael Escalona—cumbia surfaced in opposition to the interior's lettered convention.

6. Chapter 5 of Wade (2000) covers this period in detail, discussing the process.

7. It is important to note that, at this point, porro already enjoyed a certain degree of popularity thanks to gaucho performers like Eugenio Nóbile and Eduardo Armani. A note in *Time* magazine, dated November 6, 1944, available at http://www.time.com/time/magazine/article/0,9171,803444,00.html?iid=chix-sphere, documents the important role of Nóbile as a promoter of the genre. However, with respect to "Santa Marta tiene tren," the piece cited in this note, one can add that Armani recorded the first version of this song for the label Odeón in 1945, making him the author. In Colombia researchers such as Julio Oñate Martínez argue that authorship of the song belongs to Manuel Medina Moscote. On this, please see Edition 202 of *Galería*, the cultural review of the Universidad del Magdalena, at http://revistagaleria.unimagdalena.edu.co/revistagaleria/Lists/EdicionesImpresas/Attachments/10/Edición 2.pdf.

8. Liliana Martínez Polo, "Carlos Vives regresa a la ceremonia de los Premios Grammy Latinos," *El Tiempo*, September 18, 2002.

9. Celeste Fraser Delgado, "King of Colombia," *Miami New Times*, January 11, 2002.

10. For a sample of texts on tropipop, see the blogs in the culture section of *El Tiempo*, the Bogotá newspaper: Azteca64 (2007) and Demacondo (2007), which evinces the degree of rejection produced by the genre in certain sectors of Colombian society. For inventive criticism, see http://www.youtube.com/watch?v=-LP3I7rZ94A.

References

Abadía Morales, Guillermo. 1973. *La música folklórica colombiana.* Bogotá: Universidad Nacional de Colombia.
———. 1983. *Compendio general de folklore colombiano.* Bogotá: Biblioteca Banco Popular.
———. 1991. *Instrumentos musicales: Folklore colombiano.* Bogotá: Biblioteca Banco Popular.
Abello Vives, Alberto. 2002. "Por debajo todas las raíces del árbol están conectadas." *Aguaita,* no. 7.
Abramo, Helena Wendel. 1994. *Cenas Juvenis: Punks e darks no espetáculo urbano.* São Paulo: Editora Página Aberta and Associação Nacional de Pós-Graduação e Pesquisa em Ciências Sociais.
Agencia Española de Cooperación Internacional (AECI) (institucional). *Amazonía: Guía Ilustrada de Flora y Fauna.* Madrid: AECI, 2006.
Aguirre Beltrán, Gonzalo. (1946) 1989. *La población negra de México: Estudio etnohistorico.* Mexico City: Fondo de Cultura Económica.
Akpabot, Samuel Ekpe. 1975. *Ibibio Music in Nigerian Culture.* East Lansing: Michigan State University Press.
Alvarenga, Oneyda. 1947. *Música popular brasileña.* Mexico City: Fondo de Cultura Económica.
Andacht, Fernando. 2000. "A Semiotic Framework for the Social Imaginary." Peirce Gateway, http://www.cspeirce.com/menu/library/aboutcsp/andacht/socimagn.htm.
Anderson, Benedict. 1983. *Imagined Communities.* London: Verso.
———. 1991. *Imagined Communities: Reflections on the Origin and Spread of Nationalism.* Revised 2nd edition. London: Verso.
Andrews, George Reid. 2010. *Blackness in the White Nation: A History of Afro-Uruguay.* Chapel Hill: University of North Carolina Press.
Angeles, Miguel Angel. 2007. "A Mexican Sonidero Shouts Out." Hispanic Marketing and Public Relations, http://www.hispanicmpr.com/resources/articles/a-mexican-sonidero-shouts-out/.
Aparicio, Frances. 1998. *Listening to Salsa: Gender, Latin Popular Music, and Puerto Rican Cultures.* Hanover, N.H.: Wesleyan University Press.
Appadurai, Arjun. 1996. *Modernity at Large: Cultural Dimensions of Globalization.* Minneapolis: University of Minnesota Press.

Aretz, Isabel. 1991. *Historia de la etnomusicología en América Latina*. Caracas: FUNDEF.
Attali, Jacques. 1985. *Noise: The Political Economy of Music*. Minneapolis: University of Minnesota Press.
Averill, Gage. 1997. *A Day for the Hunter, a Day for the Prey: Popular Music and Power in Haiti*. Chicago: University of Chicago Press.
Azteca64. February 5, 2007. "Disonancia: Del tropipop a la tropipeste." *El Tiempo.com* (blog), http://www.eltiempo.com/participacion/blogs/default/un_articulo.php?id_blog=3509446&id_recurso=300000882.
Bailón, Jaime. 2004. "La chicha no muere ni se destruye, sólo se transforma: Vida, historia y milagros de la cumbia peruana." *Íconos* 18 (Ecuador): 53–62.
Bauman, Richard. 1986. *Story, Performance, and Event: Contextual Studies of Oral Narrative*. Cambridge: Cambridge University Press.
Baumgardner, Jennifer, and Amy Richards. 2000. *Manifesta: Young Women, Feminism, and the Future*. New York: Farrar, Straus and Giroux.
Bermúdez, Egberto. 1985. *Los instrumentos musicales en Colombia*. Bogotá: Universidad Nacional de Colombia.
———. 1992. "Música, identidad y creatividad en las culturas afro-americanas: El caso de Colombia." *América Negra: Expedición Humana* (3): 57–68.
———. 1994. "Syncretism, Identity, and Creativity in Afro-Colombian Musical Traditions." In *Music and Black Ethnicity: The Caribbean and South America*, edited by Gerard H. Béhague. Miami: North-South Center.
Bertolotti, Virginia, and Magdalena Coll. 2003. "A Synchronical and Historical View of the TÚ/VOS Option in the Spanish of Montevideo." In *Linguistic Theory and Language Development in Hispanic Languages*, edited by Silvina Montrul and Francisco Ordóñez. Somerville, Mass.: Cascadilla Press.
Betancur Álvarez, Fabio. 1993. *Sin clave y bongó no hay son: Músicas afrocubanas y confluencias musicales de Colombia y Cuba*. Medellín, Colombia: Universidad de Antioquia.
Biaya, T. K. 1993. "Cyombela, the Luba Drummer within an Urban Milieu." In *Drums: The Heartbeat of Africa*, edited by Esther A. Dagan. Montreal: Galerie Amrad African Art Publications.
Blanco, Darío. 2007. "Mundos de frontera: Colombianos en la línea noreste de México y Estados Unidos," *Trayectorias* 26 (Mexico City): 89–106.
Bourdieu, Pierre. 1999. *Sociología y Cultura*. Mexico City: CNCA.
Briggs, Charles L. 2004. "Theorizing Modernity Conspiratorially: Science, Scale, and the Political Economy of Public Discourse in Explanations of a Cholera Epidemic." *American Ethnologist* 31(2): 164–87.
Briggs, Charles L., and Richard Bauman. 1992. "Genre, Intertextuality, and Social Power." *Journal of Linguistic Anthropology* 22: 131–72.
Broughton, Simon, and Mark Ellingham, eds. 2000. *World Music*. Vol. 2: *Latin and North America, Caribbean, India, Asia and Pacific*. London: Rough Guides.
Brown, Roger, and Albert Gilman. 1966. "The Pronouns of Power and Solidarity." In *Style in Language*, edited by Thomas A. Sebeok. Cambridge: MIT Press.

Bullen, Margaret. 1993. "Chicha in the Shanty Towns of Arequipa, Peru." *Popular Music* 12(3): 229–44.

Caetano, Gerardo. 1992. "Identidad Nacional E Imaginario Colectivo en Uruguay: La Síntesis Perdurable Del Centenario." In *Identidad Uruguaya: ¿Mito, Crisis, o Afirmación?*, edited by Hugo Achugar and Gerardo Caetano. Montevideo: Ediciones Trilce.

Caetano, Gerardo, and Milita Alfaro, eds. 1995. *Historia del Uruguay Contemporáneo: Materiales para el Debate*. Montevideo: Fundación de Cultura Universitaria.

Camargo Franco, Jaime E. 1994. *¡Caribe soy!* Medellín: Ediciones Salsa y Cultura.

Cantero, Margarita, and William Fortich. 1991. "Taller folklórico de Córdoba." *Nueva Revista Colombiana de Folclor* 3(11): 117–30.

Carbó Ronderos, Guillermo. 2003. *Musique et danse traditionelles en Colombie: La Tambora*. Paris: L'Harmattan.

Carricaburo, Norma. 1997. *Las Fórmulas de Tratamiento en el Español Actual*. Madrid: Arco Libros.

Carrizosa, Toño. 1997. *La onda grupera: Historia del movimiento grupero*. Mexico City: Edamex.

Cerutti, Mario. 1983. *Burguesía y Capitalismo en Monterrey 1850–1900*. Mexico City: Claves latinoamericanas.

Cerutti, Mario, Isabel Ortega, and Lilia Palacios. 1993. "Grupos económicos en el norte de México: Del estado oligárquico a la globalización." In *La globalización en Nuevo León*, edited by Esthela Gutiérrez. Monterrey: UANL.

Ciria, Alberto. 1983. *Política y Cultura Popular: La Argentina Peronista, 1946–1955*. Buenos Aires: de la Flor.

Clayton, Jace. 2010. "Vampires of Lima." In *What Was the Hipster? A Sociological Investigation*, edited by Mark Greif, Kathleen Ross, and Dayna Tortorici. New York: n+1 Foundation.

Convers, Leonor, and Juan Sebastian Ochoa. 2007. *Gaiteros y tamboleros: Material para abordar el estudio de la música de gaitas de San Jacinto, Bolivar (Colombia)*. Colección Libros de Investigación. (Parts 1 and 2, DVD). Bogotá: Pontificia Universidad Javeriana.

Cornejo Guinassi, Pedro. 1998. *Sobrecarga: Los cortocircuitos de la música pop contemporánea*. Lima: Emedece.

Corona, Ignacio, and Alejandro Madrid. 2008. *Postnational Musical Identities: Cultural Production, Distribution, and Consumption in a Globalized Scenario*. Lanham, Md.: Lexington Books.

Cortina, Regina, and Monica Gendreau, eds. 2003. *Immigrants and Schooling: Mexicans in New York*. New York: Center for Migration Studies.

Cragnolini, Alejandra. 2006. "Articulaciones entre violencia social, significante sonoro y subjetividad: La cumbia villera en Buenos Aires." *Revista Transcultural de Música* 10.

Cragnolini, Alejandra, and Ana Maria Ochoa Gautier. 2001. *Músicas en Transición*. Bogotá: Ministerio De Cultura.

D'Amico, Leonardo. 2002. *Cumbia: La musica afrocolombiana*. Udine, Italy: Nota.

D'Amico, Leonardo, and Andrew Kaye. 2004. *Musica dell'Africa Nera*. Palermo, Italy: L'Epos.

De Aranzadi, Isabela. 2009. *Instrumentos musicales de las etnias de Guinea Ecuatorial*. Madrid: Apadena.

De Gori, Esteban. 2005. "Notas Sociológicas Sobre la Cumbia Villera: Lectura del Drama Social Urbano." *Convergencia* 12(38): 353–72.

De Granda, Germán. 1970. "Cimarronismos, palenques y hablas 'criollas' en Hispanoamerica." *Thesaurus* 25(3): 448–69.

Degregori, Carlos Iván. 1984. "Huayno, Chicha: El nuevo rostro de la música peruana." *Cultura Popular* (CELADEC) 13/14: 187–93.

———. 2000a. *No hay país más diverso: Compendio de antropología peruana*. Lima: Pontificia Universidad Católica del Perú.

———. 2000b. "Panorama de la antropología en el Perú: Del estudio del Otro a la construcción de un Nosotros diverso." In *No hay país más diverso: Compendio de antropología peruana*, edited by Carlos Ivan Degregori. Lima: Pontificia Universidad Católica del Perú.

Deive, Carlos Esteban. 1974. "Glosario de afronegrismos en la toponimía y español hablado de Santo Domingo." *Boletín del Museo del Hombre Dominicano* (5): 17–42.

Del Castillo Mathieu, Nicolás. 1982. *Esclavos negros en Cartagena y sus aportes léxicos*. Bogotá: Instituto Caro y Cuervo.

Demacondo. October 10, 2007. "Em-Ci-Di-Ci: De Juanes, el tropipop y otros demonios." *El Tiempo.com* (blog), http://www.eltiempo.com/participacion/blogs/default/un_articulo.php?id_blog=3720932&id_recurso=350002702.

de Soto, Hernando. 1989. *The Other Path: The Invisible Revolution in the Third World*. New York: Harper and Row.

Dickason, Olive Patricia. 1984. *The Myth of the Savage and the Beginnings of French Colonialism in the Americas*. Edmonton: University of Alberta Press.

Duarte Ayala, Adolfo. 1998. *Músicos y Música popular en Monterrey, 1900–1940*. Monterrey: UANL.

———. 2000. *Desde el Cerro de la Silla*. Monterrey: Herca.

Escalante, Aquiles. 1954. "Notas sobre Palenque de San Basilio." *Divulgaciones etnológicas* 3(5): 207–354.

———. 1964. *El negro en Colombia*. Bogotá: Universidad Nacional de Colombia.

———. (1954) 1979. *El Palenque de San Basilio*. 2nd edition. Barranquilla, Colombia: Mejoras.

———. 1989. "Significado del Lumbalú, ritual funerario del Palenque de San Basilio." *Huellas, Revista de la Universidad del Norte* (Barranquilla) (26): 11–23.

Escobar, Luis Antonio. 1985. *La música en Cartagena de Indias*. Bogotá: Intergráficas.

Fabian, Johannes. 1983. *Time and the Other: How Anthropology Makes Its Object*. New York: Columbia University Press.

Fals Borda, Orlando. 1980. *Historia doble de la costa: Mompox y Loba*. Bogotá: Carlos Valencia Editores.

———. 1986a. *Historia doble de la costa: Resistencia en el San Jorge* (part 3). Bogotá: Carlos Valencia Editores.

———. 1986b. *Historia doble de la costa: Retorno a la tierra* (part 4). Bogotá: Carlos Valencia Editores.

Fernández L'Hoeste, Héctor. 2007. "All Cumbias, the Cumbia: The Latin Americanization of a Tropical Genre." In *Imagining Our Americas: Towards a Transnational Frame*, edited by Sandhya Shukla and Heidi Tinsman. Durham: Duke University Press.

Ferreira, Luis. 2003. *El Movimiento Negro en el Uruguay 1988–1998: Una Versión Posible*. Montevideo: Ediciones Étnicas Mundo Afro.

Fisher, Marv. 1979a. "Discos Melody: Mexico's Surging Independent." *Billboard*, April 29: 71–72.

———. 1979b. "The Multi-Faceted Latin 'Musaic.'" *Billboard*, August 18: 12–13.

Flores, Juan. 2000. *From Bomba to Hip Hop: Puerto Rican Culture and Latino Identity*. New York: Columbia University Press.

Flores Marín, José Antonio. 1987. *La explotación del caucho en el Perú*. Lima: Consejo Nacional de Ciencia y Tecnología.

Fontanella de Weinberg, Beatriz. 1999. "Sistemas Pronominales Usados en el Mundo Hispánico." In *Gramática Descriptiva de la Lengua Española*, edited by Ignacio Bosque and Violeta Desmonte. Madrid: Espasa.

Fortich Díaz, William. 1994. *Con bombos y platillos: Origen del porro, aproximación a las bandas pelayeras*, vol. 3. Montería, Colombia: Domus Libri.

Foster, David William. 1971. "Tú y Vos en 'El Túnel' de Ernesto Sábato." *Hispania* 54(2): 354–55.

Fox, Aaron. 2004. *Real Country: Music and Language in Working-Class Culture*. Durham: Duke University Press.

Franco, Carlos. 1991. *Imágenes De La Sociedad Peruana: La Otra Modernidad*. Lima: Centro de Estudios para el Desarrollo y la Participación.

Friedemann, Nina S. de. 1985. *Carnaval en Barranquilla*. Bogotá: Editorial La Rosa.

Friedemann, Nina S. de, Jeremy Horner, and Benjamín Villegas Jiménez. 1995. *Fiestas: Celebraciones y ritos de Colombia*. Bogotá: Villegas Editores.

Friedrich, Paul. (1966) 1979. "Structural Implications of Russian Pronominal Usage." In *Language, Context, and the Imagination*. Stanford: Stanford University Press.

Frith, Simon. 1996. "Música e identidad." In *Cuestiones de identidad Cultural*, edited by Stuart Hall and Paul du Gay. Buenos Aires: Amorrotu.

Garay, Narciso. 1930. *Tradiciones y cantares de Panamá*. Brussels: Presses de l'Expansion Belge.

García, Hugo. 2008. "Los límites del espacio televisivo transnacional: Multimedios Televisión en Houston, Texas." PhD diss., http://cinco.mty.itesm.mx/investigacion/LimitesTVtransnacional.doc.

Garcia Canclini, Nestor. 1995. *Hybrid Cultures: Strategies for Entering and Leaving Modernity*. Minneapolis: University of Minnesota Press.

Garzón, Lucía. 1987. "Gaitas y tambores de San Jacinto." *Nueva Revista Colombiana de Folclor* 1(2): 73–99.

Gil Olivera, Numas Armando. 2002. *Mochuelos Cantores de los Montes de María la Alta: Adolfo Pacheco y el Compadre Ramón.* Vol. 1. Barranquilla, Colombia: Instituto de Filosofía Julio Enrique Blanco, Universidad del Atlántico.

Goberna, Carlos. 2008. *¡Siga el Baile!* Montevideo: Rumbo Editorial.

Goffman, Erving. 1979. "Footing." *Semiotica* 25: 1–29.

González Henríquez, Adolfo. 1988. "La música costeña colombiana en la tercera década del siglo XIX." *Revista de Música Latino-Americana* 9(2): 187–206.

———. 1989. "Calidad en la vida musical en la radio barranquillera." *Música, Casa de las Américas,* no. 117: 21–35.

Grignon, Claude, and Jean-Claude Passeron. 1989. *Lo culto y lo popular: Miserabilismo y populismo en la sociología y en la literatura.* Buenos Aires: Nueva Visión.

Gutiérrez, David G. 1998. "Ethnic Mexicans and the Transformation of 'American' Social Space: Reflections on Recent History." In *Crossings: Mexican Immigration in Interdisciplinary Perspectives,* edited by Marcelo Suarez-Orozco. Cambridge: Harvard University Press.

Hanks, William F. 1987. "Discourse Genres in a Theory of Practice." *American Ethnologist* 14(4): 668–92.

Hebdige, Dick. (1979) 1991. *Subculture: The Meaning of Style.* London: Routledge.

Henry, Astrid. 2004. *Not My Mother's Sister: Generational Conflict and Third-Wave Feminism.* Bloomington: Indiana University Press.

Hernández-León, Rubén. 2002. "Urban Origin Migration from Mexico to the United States: The Case of the Monterrey Area." PhD diss., State University of New York at Binghamton.

Horton, Christian Dowu. 1999. "The Role of the *Gumbe* in Popular Music and Dance Styles in Sierra Leone." In *Turn Up the Volume! A Celebration of African Music,* edited by Jacqueline Cogdell DjeDje. Los Angeles: UCLA Fowler Museum of Cultural History.

Hurtado Suárez, Wilfredo. 1995a. *Chicha peruana: Música de los nuevos migrantes.* Lima: ECO, Grupo de Investigaciones Económicas.

———. 1995b. "La música chicha en los 90's." *Revista Márgenes: Encuentro y Debate* 7(13/14): 171–87.

Hymes, Dell. (1975) 2004. "Breakthrough into Performance." In *In Vain I Tried to Tell You: Essays in Native American Ethnopoetics.* Lincoln: University of Nebraska Press.

Isuiza Trigoso, Javier. 2006. *Galería de autores y compositors loretanos: Apuntes sobre el folklore amazónico.* Iquitos, Peru: Tierra Nueva Editores.

Izikowitz, Karl Gustav. 1935. *Musical and Other Instruments of the South American Indians.* Gothenburg, Sweden: Wettergren and Kerber.

James, Daniel. 1988. *Resistance and Integration: Peronism and the Argentine Working Class, 1946–1976.* Cambridge: Cambridge University Press.

Jameson, Fredric. 1988. "Cognitive Mapping." In *Marxism and the Interpretation of Culture,* edited by Cary Nelson and Lawrence Grossberg. Urbana: University of Illinois Press.

Johnston, Thomas. 1974. "A Tsonga Initiation." *African Arts* 7(4): 60–62.

Kapchan, Deborah A. 1996. *Gender on the Market: Moroccan Women and the Revoicing of Tradition*. Philadelphia: University of Pennsylvania Press.

Kaplan, Caren. 1996. *Questions of Travel: Postmodern Discourses of Displacement*. Durham: Duke University Press.

Karp, Michelle, and Debbie Stoller. 1999. *The BUST Guide to the New Girl Order*. New York: Penguin.

Kasinitz, Philip, John H. Mollenkopf, Mary C. Waters, and Jennifer Holdaway. 2008. *Inheriting the City: The Children of Immigrants Come of Age*. New York: Russell Sage Foundation / Harvard University Press.

Keenan, Elizabeth K. 2008. "Who Are You Calling 'Lady'?: Femininity, Sexuality, and Third-Wave Feminism." *Journal of Popular Music Studies* 20(4): 378–401.

Kernfield, Barry. 2011. *Pop Song Piracy: Disobedient Music Distribution Since 1929*. Chicago: University of Chicago Press.

Kimmel, Michael S. 2005. *The Gender of Desire: Essays on Male Sexuality*. Albany, N.Y.: State University of New York Press.

Kisner, Diana. 2008. "Fusión y discusión: La cumbia peruana está originando un nuevo debate sobre un viejo tema." *Cosas* (June): 22–25.

Korn, Julio. November 6, 1944. "Music: South American Smash." *Time*, http://www.time.com/time/magazine/article/0,9171,803444,00.html?iid=chix-sphere.

Kulick, Don. 1998. "Anger, Gender, Language Shift, and the Politics of Revelation in a Papua New Guinea Village." In *Language Ideologies: Practice and Theory*, edited by Bambi Schieffelin, Kathryn Woolard, and Paul Kroskrity. New York: Oxford University Press.

Kun, Josh Kun. 2005. *Audiotopia: Music, Race, and America*. Berkeley: University of California Press.

Laclau, Ernesto, and Chantal Mouffe. 1987. "Post-Marxism without Apologies." *New Left Review* 166: 79–106.

Lane, Jill. 2008. "Smoking Habaneras: The Presence of the Racial Past." Working paper, Tepotzlán Institute of Transnational History in Latin America.

Lapesa, Rafael. 1980. *Historia de la Lengua Española*. 8the edition. Madrid: Gredos.

Larroca, Oscar. 2009. "El día que la cumbia villera entró en el MEC." *La Pupila* 2(10): 10–14.

Lemos, Ronaldo, and Oona Castro. 2008. *Tecnobrega: Pará Reinventing the Music Business*. Rio de Janeiro: Aeroplano Editora.

Leyva Arroyo, Carlos. 2005. *Música "chicha," mito e identidad popular: El cantante peruano Chacalón*. Quito: Abya-Yala.

Limón, José. 1994. *Dancing with the Devil: Society and Cultural Poetics in Mexican-American South Texas*. Madison: University of Wisconsin Press.

Lipsitz, George. 1994. *Dangerous Crossroads: Popular Music, Postmodernism, and the Poetics of Place*. New York: Verso.

List, George. 1966. "Ethnomusicology in Colombia." *Ethnomusicology* 10(1): 70–76.

———. 1967. "The Folk Music of the Atlantic Littoral of Colombia: An Introduction." In *Music in the Americas*, edited by G. List and J. Orrego-Salas. Bloomington: Indiana University Press.

———. 1973. "El conjunto de gaitas de Colombia: La herencia de tres culturas." *Revista Musical Chilena* 27(123–24): 43–54.

———. 1980a. "African Influences in the Rhythmic and Metric Organization of Colombian Costeño Folksong and Folk Music." *Revista de Música Latino-Americana* 1(1): 6–17.

———. 1980b. "Colombia: Folk Music." In *New Grove Dictionary of Music and Musicians*, vol. 4, edited by S. Sadie. London: Macmillan.

———. 1983. *Music and Poetry in a Colombian Village: A Tricultural Heritage*. Bloomington: Indiana University Press.

———. 1987. "Two Flutes and a Rattle: The Evolution of an Ensemble." *Musical Quarterly* 75(1): 50–58.

———. 1994. *Música y poesía en un pueblo colombiano*. Bogotá: Patronato Colombiano de Artes y Ciencias.

———. 2001. "Colombia: Traditional Music." In *New Grove Dictionary of Music and Musicians*, vol. 4. London: Macmillan.

Lotero Botero, Amparo. 1989. "El porro pelayero: De las gaitas y tambores a las bandas de viento." *Boletin Cultural y Bibliográfico del Banco de la República* (Bogotá) 26(19).

Lotman, Iuri. 1998. "La memoria de la cultura." In *La semiósfera*, edited by Desiderio Navarro. Madrid: Frónesis.

Lyman, Peter. 1998. "The Fraternal Bond as a Joking Relationship: A Case Study of the Role of Sexist Jokes in Male Group Bonding." In *Men's Lives*, edited by Michael S. Kimmel and Michael A. Messner. Boston: Allyn and Bacon.

Madrid, Alejandro. 2008. *Nor-tec Rifa! Electronic Dance Music from Tijuana to the World*. New York: Oxford University Press.

———. 2011. "Transnational Musical Encounters at the U.S.-Mexico Border: An Introduction." In *Transnational Encounters: Music and Performance at the U.S.-Mexico Border*, edited by Alejandro L. Madrid. New York: Oxford University Press.

Manuel, Peter. 1988. *Popular Musics of the Non-Western World*. New York: Oxford University Press.

———. 1998. "Gender Politics in Caribbean Popular Music: Consumer Perspectives and Academic Interpretation." *Popular Music and Society* 22(2): 11–29.

Martín, Eloísa. 2011. "The History: Trajectory and Consolidation of the Cumbia in the Field of Argentine Music." In *Troubling Gender: Youth and Cumbia in Argentina's Music Scene*, Pablo Vila and Pablo Semán. Philadelphia: Temple University Press.

Martín-Barbero, Jesús, and Zilkia Janer. 2000. "Transformations in the Map: Identities and Culture Industries." *Latin American Perspectives* 27(4): 27–48.

Marulanda Morales, Octavio. 1984. *El folclor de Colombia: Práctica de la identidad cultural*. Bogotá: Artestudio / Gladys Gonzalez Arévalo.

Massone, Manuel, and Mariano De Filippis. 2006. "'Las palmas de todos los negros arriba . . .': Origen, influencias y análisis musical de la cumbia villera." *Revista Latinoamericana de Estudios del Discurso* 6(2): 21–44.

Matos Mar, José. 1984. *Desborde popular y crisis del estado: El nuevo rostro del Perú en la década de 1980*. Lima: Instituto de Estudios Peruanos.

Matos Mar, José, et al. 2004. *Desborde popular y crisis del estado: Veinte años después*. Lima: Fondo Editorial del Congreso del Perú.

Middleton, Richard. 1990. *Studying Popular Music*. Buckingham, U.K.: Open University Press.

Miller, Toby. 2001. "Introducing . . . Cultural Citizenship." *Social Text* 69, 19(4): 1–5.

Miñana Blasco, Carlos. 2000. "Entre el folklore y la etnomusicologia: 60 años de estudio sobre la música popular tradicional en Colombia." *A Contratiempo, Revista de música en la cultura*, no. 11: 36–49.

Mukuna, Kazadi wa. 1979. *Contribuição Bantu na Música Brasileira*. São Paulo: Global Editora.

Muñoz Vélez, Enrique. March 2006. "La cumbia: Trazos y signos de una historia cultural." *Pacarina*.

Ndege, George O. 2007. *Culture and Customs of Mozambique*. Westport, Conn.: Greenwood Press.

Neira, Hugo. 2004. "Del Desborde de Matos Mar a los desbordes: Llave y polladas. Retorno a la cuestión de la anomía." In *Desborde popular y crisis del estado: Veinte años después*, edited by José Matos Mar et al. Lima: Fondo Editorial del Congreso del Perú.

Nieves Oviedo, Jorge. 2008. *De los sonidos del patio a la música mundo: Semiosis nómadas en el Caribe*. Bogotá: Convenio Andrés Bello.

Ocampo López, Javier. 1976. *Música y folclor de Colombia*. Bogotá: Plaza y Janes.

Ochoa, Ana Maria. 1996. "Plotting Musical Territories: Three Studies in Processes of Recontextualization of Musical Folklore in the Andean Region of Colombia." PhD diss., Indiana University.

———. 2003. *Músicas locales en tiempos de globalización: Enciclopedia latinoamericana de sociocultura y comunicación*. Buenos Aires: Grupo Editorial Norma.

Ochoa Gautier, Ana Maria, and Carolina Botero. 2009. "Pensar los géneros musicales desde las nuevas practices de intercambio sonoro." *Revista Acontratiempo, Revista* N13 (May), http://www.bibliotecanacional.gov.co/tools/marco.php?idcategoria=39295.

Olvera, José J. 1991. "Musical Preferences in Cadereyta." BA thesis.

———. 1998. "Al Norte del Corazón: Evoluciones e hibridaciones musicales en el noreste mexicano con sabor a cumbia." In *Actas del III Congreso latinoamericano de la IASPM*. Bogota, http://www.iaspmal.net/es/actas/actas-del-iii-congreso-latinoamericano-iaspm-al-colombia-2000/i-interacciones-entre-lo-global-y-lo-local/al-norte-del-corazon-evoluciones-e-hibridaciones-musicales-del-noreste-mexicano-y-sureste-de-los-estados-unidos-con-sabor-a-cumbia/.

———. 2003. "Origen de la cumbia norteña." Unpublished manuscript.

———. 2005a. *Colombianos en Monterrey: Origen de un gusto musical y su papel en la construcción de una identidad social*. Monterrey: Fondo Estatal para la Cultura y las Artes de Nuevo León.

———. 2005b. *Colombians from Monterrey: Origins of Taste and Its Role in the Construction of Social Identity*. Nuevo León, Mexico: CONARTE.

———. 2008. "Las dimensiones del Sonido: Música, frontera e identidad en el noreste." *Trayectorias*, nos. 10–26 (January–July): 20–30.

———. 2010. "Los caminos de la vida en la Independencia son de migración y diversidad . . . Además de la colombia." In *Colores y ecos de la Colonia Independencia*, edited by Camilo Contreras. Nuevo León, Mexico: COLEF, CONARTE, Municipio de Monterrey.

Olvera, José J., and Helena Simonett. 2005. "Monterrey." In *Continuum Encyclopedia of Popular Music of the World*, vol. 3, edited by Dave Laing, John Shepherd, and David Horn. London: Continuum.

Olvera, José Juan, Benito Torres, Gregorio Cruz, and César Jaime Rodríguez. 1996. *La colombia de Monterrey: Descripción de algunos elementos de la cultura colombiana en la frontera norte*. San Antonio, Tex.: Guadalupe Cultural Arts Center.

Oñate Martínez, Julio C. 2006. "Santa Marta tiene tren." *Galería* (2): 61–63.

Ortiz, Fernando. 1985. *Nuevo catauro de cubanismos*. Havana: Editorial de Ciencias Sociales.

Pacini Hernandez, Deborah. 1992. Review of "Cumbia, cumbia: Tropicalísimo" by Peregoyo y su Combo Vacaná; "Rebelión" by Joe Arroyo; "¡Cantando!" by Diomedes Díaz and Colacho Mendoza; and "Vallenato Dynamos" by the Merino Brothers. *Ethnomusicology* 36(2): 288–96.

———. 1993. "The Picó Phenomenon in Cartagena, Colombia." *America Negra* 6: 69–95.

———. 1995. *Bachata: A Social History of a Dominican Popular Music*. Philadelphia: Temple University Press.

Pajares Cruzado, Gonzalo. 2008. "La cumbia todavía no es valorada por el Perú oficial." *Perú 21* (March 25): 23.

Pardo, María Laura, and María Eugenia Massone, eds. 2006. Número monográfico: La cumbia villera en Argentina. Special issue of *Revista Latinoamericana de Estudios del Discurso* 6(2).

Paredes, Américo. 1979. "The Folk Base of Chicano Literature." Translated by Kathleen Lamb. In *Modern Chicano Writers: A Collection of Critical Essays*, edited by Joseph Sommers and Tomás Rivera-Frausto. Englewood Cliffs, N.J.: Prentice-Hall.

———. 1993. "The Folklore of Groups of Mexican Origin in the United States." In *Folklore and Culture on the Texas-Mexican Border*, edited by Richard Bauman. Austin: CMAS Books, University of Texas Press.

Pásara, Luis. 2004. "Desborde popular y crisis del estado: Veinte años después." In *Desborde popular y crisis del estado: Veinte años después*, edited by José Matos Mar et al. Lima: Fondo Editorial del Congreso del Perú.

Paz, Octavio. 1981. *El laberinto de la soledad*. Mexico City: Fondo de Cultura Económica.

Pedroza, Gabriela. 2006. "La radio comercial en Monterrey, apuntes para caracterizar una región." *Anuario de la Investigación de la Comunicación* 11: 131–50.

Pellicer, Juan, director. 2009. *Historia de la música popular uruguaya.* Documentary in 15 parts. Canal 5–Televisión Nacional de Uruguay.

Peña, Manuel. 1993. *The Texas-Mexican Conjunto: History of a Working Class Music.* Austin: University of Texas Press.

Pérez, Alejandro. 1995. *Historia de la música popular mexicana: Los tropicales años '40.* Second series. Fascículo 4. Mexico City: Promexa.

Poole, Deborah. 1988. "Entre el milagro y la mercancía: Qoyllur Rit'i." *Revista Márgenes: Encuentro y Debate* 6 (December): 101–9.

Portaccio Fontalvo, José. 1995. *Colombia y su música.* Vol. 1: *Canciones y fiestas de las llanuras caribe y pacífica y las islas de San Andrés y Providencia.* Bogotá: Logos Diagramáticos.

Posada Gutiérrez, José Joaquín. 1929. *Memorias histórico-políticas.* Bogotá: Imprenta Nacional.

Pozas, María de los Ángeles. 1993. "Estrategias de globalización y encadenamientos productivos: El caso de Monterrey." In *La globalización en Nuevo León*, edited by Esthela Gutiérrez. Monterrey: UANL.

Pulido, Jorge. 1981. "Rigo Tovar, ídolo semiciego de los marginados." *Contenido* 212: 74–80.

Quijano, Aníbal. 1980. *Lo cholo y el conflicto cultural en el Perú.* Lima: Mosca Azul Editores.

Quispe Lázaro, Arturo. 1994. "La chicha está fermentando . . ." *Revista Quehacer* 87: 82–92.

———. 2000. "Rossy War y la *chicha* amazónica." *Revista Quehacer* 125: 106–11.

———. 2002. "La Tecnocumbia: ¿Integración o discriminación solapada?" *Revista Quehacer* 135: 107–13.

Rentner, Simon. July 21, 2011. "Peter Wade 2007." *Afropop Worldwide*, http://www.afropop.org/multi/interview/ID/114/Peter+Wade+2007.

Revista Cultural. 2008. San Jacinto, Bolivar, Colombia: Corporación Folclórica y Artesanal (CORFOARTE).

Roberts, Helen H. 1926. "Possible Survivals of African Song in Jamaica." *Musical Quarterly* 12(3): 340–58.

Rodríguez Linares, Agusto. N.d. *Charapeando: Compendio de vocablos selváticos.* Iquitos, Peru: Self-published.

Roel Mendizábal, Pedro. 2000. "De Folklore a Culturas Híbridas: Rescatando raíces, redefiniendo fronteras entre nos/otros." In *No hay país más diverso: Compendio de antropología peruana*, edited by Carlos Ivan Degregori. Lima: Pontificia Universidad Católica del Perú.

Romero, Raúl R. 2002. "Popular Music and the Global City: Huayno, Chicha, and Techno-cumbia in Lima." In *From tejano to tango: Latin American Popular Music*, edited by Walter Aaron Clark. New York: Routledge.

———. 2007. *Andinos y tropicales: La cumbia peruana en la ciudad global.* Lima: Instituto de Etnomusicología, Pontificia Universidad Católica del Perú.

Rona, José Pedro. 1967. *Geografía y morfología del voseo.* Porto Alegre: Pontifica Universidad Católica.

Rouse, Roger. 1991. "Mexican Migration and the Social Space of Postmodernism." *Diaspora* 1(1): 8–23.

Rumrrill, Roger. 1983. *Iquitos: Capital de la Amazonia Peruana*. Iquitos, Perú: n.p.

Sachs, Curt. (1933) 1994. *Eine Weltgeschichte des Tanzes*. Berlin: Dietrich Reimer–Ernst Vohsen.

Salazar, Luis Orsí. 1988a. "Apuntes para el estudio de algunos temas clásicos de la música popular amazónica." *Shupihui* 13(47): 415–25.

———. 1988b. "Intento de aproximación a la música amazónica: Introducción al estudio de la música del oriente peruano." *Shupihui* 13(47): 315–20.

Salcedo, José María. 1984. "El Perú informal." *Revista Quehacer* 31: 74–97.

———. 2000. "La misma chicha con distinto tecno." *Revista Quehacer* 125: 92–97.

Samuels, David. 2004. *Putting a Song on Top of It: Expression and Identity on the San Carlos Apache Reservation*. Tucson: University of Arizona Press.

Sandoval, Efrén. 2006. "Movilidad, circulación e intercambio en el espacio social Monterrey, N.L.-San Antonio, Texas." PhD diss., CIESAS.

Sandoval, Pablo. 2000. "Los rostros cambiantes de la ciudad: Cultura urbana y antropología en el Perú." In *No hay país más diverso: Compendio de antropología peruana*, edited by Carlos Iván Degregori. Lima: Pontificia Universidad Católica del Perú.

San Román, Jesús. 1994. *Perfiles históricos de la Amazonía peruana*. Iquitos, Peru: CETA, CAAAP, IIAP.

Santamaría Delgado, Carolina. 2008. "La 'Nueva Música Colombiana': La redefinición de lo nacional bajo las lógicas de la World Music." Unpublished manuscript.

Shafir, Gershon. 1998. "Introduction: The Evolving Traditions of Citizenship." In *The Citizenship Debates: A Reader*, edited by Gershon Shafir. Minneapolis: University of Minnesota Press.

Silverstein, Michael. 1985. "Language and the Culture of Gender: At the Intersection of Structure, Usage, and Ideology." In *Semiotic Mediation*, edited by Elizabeth Mertz and Richard J. Parmentier. Orlando: Academic Press.

———. 2004. "Cultural Concepts and the Language-Culture Nexus." *Current Anthropology* 45(4): 621–52.

Simon, Alissa Rae. 1994. "The Costeño Hip Movement: A Conceptual Framework for Understanding Sexuality in Afro-Colombian Folkloric Music and Dance." MA thesis, University of California, Los Angeles.

Simonett, Helena. 2001. *Banda: Mexican Musical Life across Borders*. Middletown, Conn.: Wesleyan University Press.

———. 2007. "Quest for the Local: Building Musical Ties between Mexico and the U.S." In *Postnational Musical Identities: Cultural Production, Distribution, and Consumption in a Globalized Scenario*, edited by Ignacio Corona and Alejandro L. Madrid. Lanham, Md.: Lexington Books.

Smith, Robert. 1996. "Mexicans in New York: Membership and Incorporation in a New Immigrant Community." In *Latinos in New York*, edited by Gabriel Haslip-Viera and Sherrie L. Baver. Notre Dame, Ind.: University of Notre Dame Press.

———. 2005. *Mexican New York: The Transnational Lives of New Immigrants*. Berkeley: University of California Press.
Sotil, Gabel Daniel. 2000. *Historia panorámica de la amazonía peruana*. Iquitos, Perú: CETA.
Stevenson, Robert. 1971. *Music in Mexico: The Only Complete History of Mexican Music from Aztec to Modern Times*. New York: Thomas Y. Crowell.
Stewart, Kathleen. 1996. *A Space on the Side of the Road: Cultural Poetics in an "Other" America*. Princeton: Princeton University Press.
Stobart, Henry. 2010. "Rampant Reproduction and Digital Democracy: Shifting Landscapes of Music Production and 'Piracy' in Bolivia." *Ethnomusicology Forum* 19(1): 27–56.
Stone, Ruth. 1982. *Let the Inside Be Sweet: The Interpretation of Music Event among the Kpelle of Liberia*. Bloomington: Indiana University Press.
Svampa, Maristella. 2005. *La sociedad excluyente: La Argentina bajo el signo del neoliberalismo*. Buenos Aires: Taurus.
Taylor, Donald. 1968. *The Music of Some Indian Tribes of Colombia*. London: British Institute of Recorded Sound.
Towles, Joseph A. 1993. "Nkumbi Initiation: Ritual and Structure among the Mbo of Zaire." *Annales des Sciences Humaines*, vol. 137. Tervuren, Belgium: Musée Royale de l'Afrique Centrale.
Triana, Gloria. 1987. "El litoral caribe." In *Musica tradicional y popular colombiana*, vols. 5–7. Bogota: Procultura.
Tro Pérez, Rodolfo. 1978. "La maraca en los aborígenes de América." *Revista de la Biblioteca Nacional José Martí* (Cuba), January–April: 153–61.
Turino, Thomas. 1984. "The Urban-Mestizo Charango Tradition in Southern Peru: A Statement of Shifting Identity." *Ethnomusicology* 28(2): 253–70.
———. 1990. "'Somos El Peru' (We Are Peru): Cumbia Andina and the Children of the Andean Migrants in Lima." *Studies in Latin American Popular Culture* 9: 15–37.
———. 1993. *Moving Away from Silence: Music of the Peruvian Altiplano and the Experience of Urban Migration*. Chicago: University of Chicago Press.
———. 1999. "Signs of Imagination, Identity, and Experience: A Peircian Semiotic Theory for Music." *Ethnomusicology* 43(2): 221–55.
———. 2000. *Nationalists, Cosmopolitans, and Popular Music in Zimbabwe*. Chicago: University of Chicago Press.
———. 2008. *Music as Social Life: The Politics of Participation*. Chicago: University of Chicago Press.
Vich, Víctor. 2001. *El discurso de la calle: Los cómicos ambulantes y las tensiones de la modernidad en el Perú*. Lima: Pontificia Universidad Católica del Perú, Universidad del Pacífico, Centro de Investigación, Instituto de Estudios Peruanos.
———. 2002. "Mesa redonda y el incendio de las ciencias sociales." *Revista Quehacer* 134: 104–6.
Vila, Pablo. 2000. "Sistemas clasificatorios y narrativas identitarias en Ciudad Juárez y El Paso." In *Voces de frontera*, edited by V. Zúñiga. Monterrey: UANL.

———. 2001. "Música e identidad: La capacidad interpeladora y narrativa de los sonidos, las letras y las actuaciones musicales." In *Cuadernos de Nación: Músicas en Transición*, edited by Ana María Ochoa and Alejandro Cragnolini. Bogotá: Ministerio de Cultura.

Vila, Pablo, and Pablo Semán. 2006. "La conflictividad de género en la cumbia villera." *Revista Transcultural de Música* 10. Spain: www.sibetrans.com/trans/trans10/indice10.htm.

Vila, Pablo, and Pablo Seman 2011. *Troubling Gender: Youth and Cumbia in Argentina's Music Scene.* Philadelphia: Temple University Press.

Villarejo, Avencio. 2005. *Así es la selva.* Iquitos, Perú: CETA.

Wade, Peter. 1997. *Gente negra, nación mestiza: Dinámicas de las identidades raciales en Colombia.* Bogotá: Siglo del Hombre Editores, Ediciones Uniandes.

———. 1998. "Music, Blackness and National Identity: Three Moments in Colombian History." *Popular Music* 17 (1): 1–19.

———. 2000. *Music, Race and Nation: Música Tropical in Colombia.* Chicago: University of Chicago Press.

Warikoo, Natasha. 2004. "Cosmopolitan Ethnicity: Second-Generation Indo-Caribbean Identities." In *Becoming New Yorkers: Ethnographies of the New Second Generation*, edited by Philip Kasinitz, John H. Mollenkopf, and Mary C. Waters. New York: Russell Sage Foundation.

Warner, Michael. 2002. "Publics and Counterpublics." *Public Culture* 14(1): 49–90.

Waters, Melanie. 2007. "Sexing It Up? Women, Pornography and Third Wave Feminism." In *Third Wave Feminism: A Critical Exploration*, edited by Stacy Gillis, Gillian Howie, and Rebecca Munford. Houndmills, U.K.: Palgrave Macmillan.

Waxer, Lise. October 24, 1997. "Salsa, Chapeta and Rap: Black Sounds and Black Identities in Afrocolombia." Paper presented at the Society for Ethnomusicology, Pittsburgh.

———. 2001. "Colombia: Popular Music." In *New Grove Dictionary of Music and Musicians*, vol. 4, edited by S. Sadie. London: Macmillan.

———. 2002. *The City of Musical Memory: Salsa, Record Grooves, and Popular Culture in Cali, Colombia.* Middletown, Conn.: Wesleyan University Press.

———. 2003. "Salsa, Champeta y Rap: Los sonidos negros y las identidades negras en Afro-Colombia." *Boletín Música*, Casa de las Américas, nos. 11–12: 19–30.

Weinerman, Catalina. 1976. *Sociolingüística de la Forma Pronominal.* Mexico City: Editorial Trillas.

Wetherell, Margaret, and Nigel Edley. 1998. "Gender Practices: Steps in the Analysis of Men and Masculinities." In *Standpoints and Differences*, edited by Karen Henwood, Chris Griffin, and Ann Phoenix. London: Sage.

Wolfe, Alex. July 21, 2011. "Lisandro Mesa-2003." *Afropop Worldwide*, http://www.afropop.org/multi/interview/ID/43/Lisandro+Meza-2003.

Wong, Wan-chi. 2001. "Visual Medium in the Service and Disservice of Education." *Journal of Aesthetic Education* 35(2): 25–37.

Woolard, Kathryn A., and Bambi B. Schieffelin. 1994. "Language Ideology." *Annual Review of Anthropology* 23: 55–82.

Wurtzel, Elizabeth. 1999. *Bitch: In Praise of Difficult Women*. New York: Anchor.
Zapata Olivella, Delia. 1962. "La cumbia: Síntesis musical de la nación colombiana. Reseña histórica y coreográfica." *Revista Colombiana de Folclor* 3(7), second series: 189–200.
———. 1967. "An Introduction to the Folk Dances of Colombia." *Ethnomusicology* 11(1): 91–96.
Zapata Olivella, Manuel. 1967. "Caña de millo, variedades y ejecución." *Revista Colombiana de Folclor* 2(6), second series: 155–58.
Žižek, Slavoj. 1989. *The Sublime Object of Ideology*. London: Verso.

Contributors

Cristian Alarcón is the author of *Si me querés, quereme transa*, a book about the internal war of Peruvian drug dealers in Buenos Aires, and *Cuando me muera quiero que me toquen cumbia* (2003). He is the academic director of the program Narcotráfico, Ciudad y Violencia en América Latina, created by FNPI and the Open Society Institute; the coordinator of the Latin American website of judicial journalism, Cosecha Roja; and the editor of the program on gang chronicles created by the Coalición Centroamericana para la Prevención de la Violencia Juvenil in Guatemala, Honduras, El Salvador, and Nicaragua. He is a professor at the Universidad Nacional de La Plata and has written articles for the Argentine newspapers *Página/12* and *Crítica* and the magazines *Rolling Stone*, *Gatopardo*, *Soho*, *Lateral*, and *Planeta Humano*. Recently he received the Samuel Chavkin Award granted by the North American Congress of Latin America.

Jorge Arévalo Mateus has been the head archivist and curator of the Woody Guthrie Archives since 1995, overseeing the administration, management, and development of the Woody Guthrie Collection. For nearly twenty years, Arévalo has provided consultation services to numerous museums, libraries, archives, and historical organizations, including the Louis Armstrong House and Archives, Queens College; the Alan Lomax Archives at Hunter College, City University of New York; the RAICES Archives of Latin Music at Boy's Harbor, Inc.; and the Center for Traditional Music and Dance. He is currently in residence at Wesleyan University, where he works with the World Music Archives and the Music Department. As a popular music scholar, Arévalo has published numerous essays, articles, and reviews in academic and popular journals, edited volumes, and other publications, such as *New York Archives Magazine*, *Ethnomusicology*, *Journal of Popular Music Studies*, and *Centro, the Journal of Puerto Rican Studies*. In his musical life, he has toured, performed, and recorded with an eclectic variety of artists that include the composers Jeffrey Lohn, Rhys Chatham, Anthony Braxton, Guillermo Gregorio, and Peter Kotik and the choreographers Karole Armitage, Donald Byrd, and Jody Oberfelder.

Leonardo D'Amico is a professor of ethnomusicology at the University of Ferrara and of anthropology of music at the University of Siena. He is an ethnomusicologist with a research specialization in Afro-Colombian music and sub-Saharan Africa. He has written *La música afrocolombiana* (2002) and *Musica dell'Africa Nera* (2004), coauthored with Andrew Kaye, and edited *Folk Music Atlas: Music of Africa* (1997) and

Musica dei Popoli: Viaggio nella musica tradizionale del mondo (2005). He is in charge of the FLOG Centre for Folk Traditions (Florence) as art director of the traditional music festival Musica dei Popoli and of the ethnomusicological film festival Festival del Film Etnomusicale, and is involved in the creation of an array of public programs: festivals, concerts, exhibitions, publications, conferences, audio recordings, multimedia products, and TV programs. He is president of the Italian Committee of International Council of Traditional Music.

Héctor Fernández L'Hoeste is a professor at Georgia State University in Atlanta, where he teaches Latin American culture. He specializes in Latin American cultural studies. His publications include *Narrativas de representación urbana* (1998) *Rockin' Las Americas* (2004), and *Redrawing the Nation* (2009). His essays on Latin American culture, literature, and media have appeared in *Hispania, National Identities, Chasqui, Revista de Estudios Hispánicos*, and *Film Quarterly*. He directs the Center for Latin American and Latino/a Studies at Georgia State University.

Alejandro L. Madrid is an associate professor of ethno/musicology at Cornell University. He is the author of *Music in Mexico: Experiencing Music, Expressing Culture* (2012); *Nor-tec Rifa! Electronic Dance Music from Tijuana to the World* (2008); and *Sounds of the Modern Nation: Music, Culture and Ideas in Post-Revolutionary Mexico* (2008); he is also coeditor (with Ignacio Corona) of *Postnational Musical Identities: Cultural Production, Distribution and Consumption in a Globalized Scenario* (2010), and editor of *Transnational Encounters: Music and Performance at the U.S.-Mexico Border* (2011). A recipient of the Woody Guthrie Book Award from the International Association for the Study of Popular Music, U.S. Branch (2010), the Casa de las Américas Award for Latin American Musicology (2005), the Samuel Claro Valdés Award for Latin American Musicology (2002), and the A-R Editions Award of the American Musicological Society, Midwest Chapter (2001–2), Madrid serves on the advisory boards of the *Boletín Música, Latin American Music Review, Dancecult: Journal of Electronic Dance Music Culture*, and *Trans. Revista Transcultural de Música*, the editorial advisory board for the music collection of Editorial Doble J, and the international advisory board of the Tepoztlán Institute for the Transnational History of the Americas. He is also senior editor of Latin American and Latina/o entries for the new edition of the *Grove Dictionary of American Music*.

Kathryn Metz is the education instructor at the Rock and Roll Hall of Fame and Museum where she teaches K-12 students (on-site and through videoconferencing), adults, and teachers and also co-produces public programs and concerts. She is also a Presidential Fellow at Case Western Reserve University. Kathryn holds her Ph.D. in Ethnomusicology from the University of Texas at Austin. www.rockhall.com/education

José Juan Olvera Gudiño is a cultural sociologist and university professor. He has been working at Universidad Regiomontana, Mexico, for more than fifteen years, where he coordinates the graduate program in communication. His research interests are sociology of music, discourse analysis, and intercultural communication. He is the author of *Colombianos de Monterrey: Origen de un gusto musical y su papel en la construcción de una identidad social* (2006) and has received several grants from the Rockefeller Foundation (1996), Conarte (1998), and CONACYT (2002–4).

Cathy Ragland is a visiting assistant professor of ethnomusicology in the College of Music at the University of North Texas. Her areas of interest and research include music of the Borderlands, Mexico, and the Hispanic Southwest, regional American and country music, and popular music. Research topics include music and migration, globalization and transnational networks, deejay culture, applied ethnomusicology, and cultural policy. She is the author of *Música Norteña: Mexican Migrants Creating a Nation between Nations* (2009) as well as articles and reviews in *Ethnomusicology, Yearbook for Traditional Music, Journal of American Folklore, Free-Reed Journal*, and others. A native of San Antonio, Texas, she has been a music critic and columnist at the *San Antonio Express-News*, the *Seattle Times*, the *Seattle Weekly*, and the *Austin American-Statesman*. She has also been a folklorist and program director at the Center for Traditional Music and Dance in New York, the Texas Folklife Resources in Austin, and the Northwest Folklife Festival in Seattle.

Pablo Semán is a member of the Consejo Nacional de Investigaciones Científicas y Técnicas (CONICET), Argentina. His research deals with issues of religion, music, and literature among popular sectors. He is the author of six books: *Bajo continuo: Exploraciones descentradas en cultura masiva y popular* (2005); *Entre santos y piquetes: Las culturas populares en la Argentina reciente* (2006); *La religiosidad popular: Creencias y vida cotidiana* (2005); *Cumbia: Raza, nación, etnia y género en Latinoamerica* (2011); *Troubling Gender: Youth and Cumbia in Argentina's Music Scene* (2011); and *Youth Identities and Argentine Popular Music: Beyond Tango* (2012). His articles have been published in Argentina, Brazil, Venezuela, France, the United States, and Canada.

Joshua Tucker is an assistant professor of ethnomusicology at Brown University. His research on Andean folkloric and popular music in Peru has been funded by the Wenner-Gren Foundation for Anthropological Research and the Social Sciences and Humanities Research Council of Canada, and has been published in *Ethnomusicology, Popular Music and Society*, and *Cultural Studies*. He is also the author of *Gentlemen Troubadors and Andean Pop Stars* (2013).

Matthew J. Van Hoose is the associate director of the Center for Latin American and Caribbean Studies and a PhD candidate in sociocultural anthropology at Indiana University–Bloomington. His research program related to Uruguayan popular music began in 1999 with the support of a U.S. Fulbright Student Fellowship, which he dedicated to a study of the relationship between candombe drumming and Afro-Uruguayan civil rights activism. Following his Fulbright tenure, he worked in Montevideo as an arts administrator and musical performer and producer. His dissertation research, conducted with support from the Wenner-Gren Foundation, examines tropical music as an arena of contestation over Uruguay's sociospatial relationship to the Latin American region.

Pablo Vila is a professor of sociology at Temple University. His research focuses on the social construction of identities on the U.S.-Mexico border and in Argentina. He has researched issues of national, regional, racial, ethnic, religious, gender, and class identities on the U.S.-Mexico border and has written *Crossing Borders, Reinforcing Borders: Social Categories, Metaphors, and Narrative Identities on the U.S.-Mexico Frontier* (2000); *Border Identifications: Narratives of Religion, Gender, and Class on the U.S.-Mexico Border* (2005); *Identificaciones de región, etnia y nación en la frontera entre México-EU* (2004); *Identidades fronterizas: Narrativas de religión, género y clase en la frontera México-Estados Unidos* (2007); and *Ethnography at the Border* (2003). In his work on identification processes in Argentina, he has researched the way different social actors use popular music to understand who they are and act accordingly. This part of his research has resulted in several articles and the books *Cumbia: Raza, nación, etnia y género en Latinoamérica* (2011); *Troubling Gender: Youth and Cumbia in Argentina's Music Scene* (2011); and *Youth Identities and Argentine Popular Music: Beyond Tango* (2012).

Index

Abakuá, secret society, 35
Acapulco Tropical, 108
Adicción, La, 98
Adrián and the Black Dice, 196
Aéro, 223
Afro-Colombia, 30–31, 34, 45, 50–51, 55, 79, 118n4, 124–25, 136n6; Afro-Colombian music and cumbia, 30, 50, 89; and dance styles, 46n6, 63, 84n11
Afro-Cuban, 37, 146
Age, 12–13, 15–17, 80, 151, 224n2; and cumbia, 97; and gender, 182, 196, 201, 209–10; and music, 50, 66, 76, 84n14, 93, 99; and poverty, 197–98; as an unmarked identity, 17; young people as immigrants, 79–80, 86n23, 93, 121–22, 129, 133, 257
Agustín, El, 138
Aicardi, Rodolfo, 48n27
Alcides, 196
Alejandro, Miguel "Conejito," 196
Amar Azul, 25, 217, 220
Amazon: and cumbia, 16; environment of, 169–70, 186n2, 186n3; indigenousness in, 170–71; and Jesuit missionaries, 170; musical styles of, 23, 148, 161–62, 167, 179–82; pandilla's effect on, 172–79; perception in other nations/regions, 180; performance of Amazonian identity, 23, 169, 177
Amazonian Basin, 12
Amazon River, 180
Anal sex, 201, 204–5
Anderson, Marian, 5
Andes, 10–11, 16, 22, 140–44, 170, 179, 253

Angulo, Moisés, 264
Araújo, Consuelo, 42
Arawak Indians, 35
Argaín, Lucho, 41
Argentina, 4–12, 18, 24–25, 39, 41, 45, 98, 100, 136, 155, 162, 164, 188, 191, 193–99, 201, 204, 210, 216–18, 222, 224n2, 226, 228–29, 232, 236, 241, 245–46, 261; Argentine villera, 12, 26
Arhuacos, 251
Armani, Giorgio, 164
Arnau, Lucas, 264–65
Arrieta, Freddy, 85
Arroyo, Joe, 43
Articulation, 13, 15–17, 78, 100, 115, 211, 239
Asia (nightclub), 161, 163, 171
Atlixco, 121, 130
Atómicos de Monterrey, Los, 92
Audiences of Cumbia, 21
Ayala, Ramón, 92, 103

Bachata, 128, 189
Bailanta, 8, 10, 195, 199, 202, 215, 217, 225n3, 261
Baile de los palos, 47
Bailes cantados, 30, 47n7
Bajo Palabra, 198
Balada, 111, 155
Ballet Nacional de Sonia Osorio, 262
Bambuco, 26, 253; in Colombia, 48n29, 249, 262; and cumbia, 38–39, 253, 265; and socioeconomic class, 16
Banco, El, 30–31, 34, 41, 250
bandas de hojita, 38
Barbès Records, 139
Bareto, 139

Barranquilla, 40, 252–53, 255, 257–58, 263
Barros, José, 250, 256
Batalla de Flores (Battle of Flowers), 31
Bazanta, Sonia, 44
Bella, Agua, 139
Benavides, Iván, 44, 82
Benjamin, Walter, 106, 115
Bermúdez, Luis Eduardo "Lucho," 256
Big Jackal. *See* Chacalón
Billboard, 107, 264
Billo's Caracas Boys, 259
"Black soul." *See* Ethnicity
Black Stars, Los, 260
Bogotá, 2–4, 19, 36, 39, 42, 53, 59–63, 68–69, 73, 79, 81, 83n5, 84n11, 84n14, 85n19, 85n21, 103n1, 253, 255, 257–59, 262, 265
Bola 8, La, 239–40, 242, 247
Bolero, 36, 39, 60, 72, 89–92, 101, 111, 118, 145, 150, 160, 189, 205, 211n6
Boletín Historial, 252
Bolívar, 35, 46n1, 52, 54, 59, 67, 84, 250–51, 256
Bolivia, 25, 187, 213, 216; and immigration, 10, 12
Bonaerense, El, 199, 215
Bonka, 264–65
Bossa, 18, 286
Botero Bar, 139
Bourdieu, Pierre, 4, 7, 102, 210n1
Bravos del Norte, Los, 92, 103n8
Brazil, 12, 18, 32, 119, 162, 170–71, 180–82, 267; and dance, 47; music of, 10, 36
Bronco, 93, 109
Bronx, 130, 137, 261
Brooklyn, 49, 81, 120, 122, 124–25, 130, 137
Brownsville, Texas, 107
Buenos Aires 5, 7–8, 10–12, 24–25, 194–95, 197, 199, 213–25, 259
Bukis, Los, 109, 118n3
Bullerengue, 30, 36, 47, 50–51, 86
BUST magazine, 192

Cabecita negra, 12
Caetano, Adrián, 199

Café Moreno, 264
Café Paris, 254
Calle, Policarpo, 97
Caluda, 126
Camacho y Cano Ángel María, 254
Caminos de la vida, Los, 216
Campuzano, Alberto Sánchez, 25, 213, 216, 218, 224
Caña de millo (cane of millet), 29–30, 33–34, 267n2
Candelié, Henry, 252
Candombe, 47n14, 231, 237–39, 246n5, 288
Cano, 254, 268n4
Capriles, Renato, 259
Cárdenas, Rocío, 253
Caribbean music, 2, 9, 11, 29, 31, 36, 42–43, 46n2, 46n3, 47n7, 111, 145, 163, 189, 194, 212n8, 231, 238, 253–56, 258–59, 261, 263–64, 267
Caribeños, Los, 139, 162–63
Caribs, 251
Carmen de Bolívar, 48n22, 52, 54, 61, 256
Caro, Jorge Arrieta, 62
Carril, Hugo del, 245n3
Cartagena, 32–33, 36, 40–41, 47n8, 52, 55, 79, 83n8, 85n19, 85n21, 249–55
Cartageneros, Los, 194
Cartoneros, 222–23
Casahuamán, Víctor, 150, 167n14
Casino de La Playa, 37
Castellano, Edwin, 62
Catholic Church: and immigration, 122, 170; and music, 30, 32, 63
Caú, Los, 7, 194
Cauca Rivers, 31
Cedrón, Lucho Pérez, 41
Central America, 22, 39, 41, 114, 116, 259, 261
Cerro de la Loma Larga, 95
Cerveza Águila, 64, 84n12
Chacal, 150, 167n13
Chacalón (Big Jackal), 167n13, 167n14; criticisms of, 151, 153; and Grupo Celeste, 150; influence on chicha, 23,

138, 141; and La Nueva Crema, 138, 150–52; and Peruvian Cumbia, 140, 149, 154; singing style, 150; and El Super Grupo, 150–51
Cha-cha-chá, 111
Chamamé, 7, 25, 194, 216
Chapulín, 154
Charanga del Caribe, La, 194
Charapa, 175–77, 182, 185, 186n6
Chávez, Domingo, 92
Chelo y su Conjunto, 111
Chévere, 196
Chicago, 108, 130, 132–33, 136n5; Chicago Pan American Festival, 108–9
Chicha: and academic commentary, 139–40; and cumbia, 42, 138, 161–65, 166n8, 169; developments in and origins of, 22–23, 140, 142, 151, 155; and migrant life, 141; and "the optimistic narrative," 157–61; in Peru, 143, 145–49, 154, 175, 180–81, 261; and violence/crime, 152–53
Chicha Libre, 139, 166n1
Chichódromos, 148
Chile, 12, 41, 45, 108, 171
Chocolate (band), 237
Cholificación, 157
Choreography of cumbia, 55, 203, 208
Chotiz, 88, 91
Chucu-chucu, 44, 249, 260, 264
Chúntaro, 97, 137n7, 216
Cildañez, Mexico, 214
Cinco del Ritmo, Los, 194
Ciudad Nezahualcóyotl, 136n3
Clayton, Jace, 214, 222
Clothing styles: on album covers, 194; and female sexuality, 200, 205–6, 208–9, 211n3; and music, 95, 153, 164
Club del Clan, El, 5
Coahuila, 87–88, 90–92, 95, 100, 103n9
Colombia: and cumbia, 8, 10–12, 22, 25, 30, 32–33, 42–46, 87, 98, 100–102, 133, 140, 145, 166n2, 181, 216–19; Colombian music in Monterrey, 95–97, 104n11; Costeño culture, 29; geography of, 46n1; golden age of coastal music in, 256; indigenous groups of, 34–35; ministry of culture, 81, 248; music of, 6, 9, 18–20, 26–27, 36–37, 39–42, 46n3, 46n6, 47n7, 47n8, 48n20, 49–51, 53–55, 59–63, 75–76, 78, 82n2, 83n3, 84n11, 93, 103n6, 124, 137n8, 146, 231, 248–68; and Peru, 16, 171; and race, 79–80, 86n23
Colombiana de Monterrey, 20, 87, 90, 97, 100–101
Colonia Independencia, 95, 100
Colonization, 185
Combo Camagüey, 236
Combo de las Estrellas, El, 260
Cómicos ambulantes, 159
Commanche, 219
Compadrazgo, 211n4
Complejo, 168
Conjunto Costa Azul, 107–8
Conjunto norteño, 90–91, 93, 95, 99, 101–2
Conquistadores, 143
Contenido magazine, 116
Córdoba, 25, 37–38, 46n1, 48n19, 54, 59, 250
CORFOARTE, 59, 84
Corona Records, 88
Corraleros de Majagual, Los, 9, 41, 43, 91–92, 97, 267
Correa, Daniel, 82n1
Corrido, 88, 91, 95, 101
Cosas magazine, 164–65
Cosmopolitanism, 163; and cumbia, 23–24, 45, 62, 77, 110; and gaita, 52, 80; and migration, 79; and nation, 19, 51, 81, 86n23, 140, 170, 173, 179, 182, 184–85, 263; and region, 169–71
Costa Azul, 106–8, 111–12, 117, 118n7
Costeño, 1–2, 16, 29–31, 37–39, 44–45, 52–55, 59–60, 62–63, 67, 70, 73, 78, 84n11
Criollo, 79, 140–41, 144–46, 151, 154, 157–58, 161, 164, 166n7, 172, 177, 186n3
Crucet, Lia, 196
Cruz, Celia, 109
Cruz, Sebastián, 52, 82n1

Cuarteto Imperial, El, 193
Cuarteto Zupay, El, 6
Cuba: Cuban music, 36–37, 39, 41, 43–44, 48n20, 146, 150, 231; cumbia in, 12; U.S. embargo on, 231
Cucumbis, 47n10
Cugat, Xavier, 37
Cultural capital, 77, 95, 102, 106, 182; and class, 4, 20, 114; and solutions for cultural necessities, 99
Cultural citizenship, 117; and migration, 20; and music, 114–15
Culture industry, 87–88; Mexican culture industry, 93–95; and stigmatization, 97
Cumbia, 10; Argentine, 5, 8, 17; changes to, 83n5, 84n11, 111–13, 148–57, 162–65, 166n8, 181, 213–15, 218, 227–28, 242, 249–67; *cumbia andina*, 142, 145, 154; cumbia colombiana de Monterrey, 97, 101; *cumbia costeña*, 148; *cumbia de exportación*, 41; *cumbia norteña*, 90–93, 99–100, 102, 103n7; *cumbia plancha*, 226–27, 242, 244, 246n5; *cumbia rebajada*, 124; *cumbia santafesina*, 25; *cumbia selvática*, 148; dance, 22, 65, 126, 128, 131, 161, 216, 252; etymology of, 31; as folklore, 82n2; and gender, 16, 201; and geography, 15; and identity, 2, 9, 17, 21, 87, 101; and language, 226, 247, 260–64, 267n2; Los Angeles, 219; lyrics of, 55, 72, 84n11, 85n17, 86n24, 95, 98–99, 109, 138, 142, 148, 151, 154–55, 162, 181, 226–27, 232, 234, 239–40, 242–43, 265; Mexican, 3, 15, 17–18, 87, 123, 125, 133; Monterrey, 95–98; and nation, 17–18, 135, 257; as oral culture, 31, 38; origins and history of, 10–15, 19–27, 31–36, 45, 49, 106, 117, 160, 162, 165, 193–99, 223, 227, 249–67; and reggae, 18, 175, 262; and resistance, 10, 161, 185, 242, 248, 255, 267; Rio de la Plata, 24; and rock music, 43, 145; and salsa, 43; and ska, 97–99; Uruguayan, 26, 226–245, 246n4. See also Chicha; New Jersey; New York; Tecno-cumbia; Tropipop
Cumbia (Colombian)/*cumbia colombiana*, 29, 44, 100, 137n8, 145, 166n2, 181, 217, 248–68; and dance, 29
Cumbia (Peruvian), 12, 16–18, 22–23, 42, 117, 138–67, 171, 173, 213, 246n5; and immigration, 11. See also Chacalón; Immigration; Socioeconomic class
Cumbia elegante, 11, 142; and tecno-cumbia, 163
Cumbia villera, 98–99; and the Argentine economic disaster, 24, 195; changes to, 195, 197; and dance, 189–90, 194–96, 202–4, 206–9, 216; emission of, 190, 199–204, 208; and gender, 8, 16–17, 24–25, 188–212; lyrics of, 189–93; misogyny in, 200, 210; origins and developments of, 25, 98, 189, 193–99, 211n3, 213, 217, 221; as parody, 203, 210; and rap music, 24, 214; relationship to transformations of women's role(s), 200–201, 206, 209; and sex and sexuality, 25, 190–91, 200–210; and shanty towns, 24; and youth, 16. See also Mexico; New Jersey; New York; Socioeconomic class; Symbolic terrorism; Texas
Cumbiamba Eneyé, La, 19, 49–86
Cuna Indians, 251
Currulao, 43, 46n6, 51

Damas Gratis, 98, 196, 198, 208, 214, 220–22
Dance: and cumbia, 12, 22, 25, 29, 31–33, 39, 46n5, 65, 72, 91, 96, 202–3, 230, 243; and identity, 95, 99, 101, 114; and sexuality, 200, 204–10; styles of, 21, 47n10, 84n11, 126–31, 134–37, 161–65, 168, 172, 175, 177, 180–83, 187n11, 194–96, 220, 227, 237, 246n7, 252–55, 261
Dany y la Roka, 198
Danzón, 36, 89, 131
Darién Gap, the, 251
Dávila, Pacho, 82n1

Décimas, 55, 58
Deejay. *See* Sonideros
De Fuego, Los, 217
Del Bohío, Los, 217
Delgado, Enrique, 145
Delgado, Fabián "Fata," 237–38, 241, 246n6
Del Valle Records, 88
Demonios del Mantaro, Los, 145
DEM'Y Records, 91
Derrida, Jacques, 14, 17
Destellos, Los, 139, 145–48, 150
Diablos Rojos, Los, 148
Dialectical images, 106, 115
Dialectical soundings, 106, 115
Diasporic communities: Colombian, 52, 62, 67, 78–80, 83n5, 86n23; "diasporic public sphere," 22, 120, 126; and globalization, 119; Latin American, 15, 20; Mexican, 130; and music, 114, 134; in New Jersey, 53. *See also* Immigration
Díaz, Matilde, 40, 256, 259
DISA Records, 91–92
Disco, 261
Discos Fuentes, 40, 44–45, 82, 255
Discos Melody, 107, 109, 118n2
Discos Sonolux, 40
Discos Tropical, 40–41, 45, 255
Discos Vergara, 258
Discos y Cartuchos de México (DCM), 107
DJ Rapture, 215
DJ Sancocho, 239
DLC, 91
D'León, Oscar, 103n6
Dominican Republic, 47n7
Dorsey, Tommy, 253
Drug cartels, 9, 94
Dulce, El, 154
Durán, Alejandro "Alejo," 43, 268n5
Duarte, Adolfo Ayala, 88

Ecuador, x, 12, 41, 148, 213
Ecos de la Montaña, 258
Ecos, Los, 148, 167n12
Education: and identity, 17, 114; and music, 62, 101–2, 257, 265

Effects of government on music, 59, 94, 97, 137n8, 166n10, 167n15, 248, 266–67
Emisora Atlántico, 36–37, 256
Emisora Atlántico Jazz Band, 37, 256
Emisora Fuentes, 36–37, 40
Encuentro de Danzas folclóricas de la Costa Atlántica, 71
Escalona, Rafael, 42–43, 48n26, 262, 268n5
Escobar, Luis Antonio, 40, 253
Escuela de Bellas Artes, 256
Esperanza in San Fernando, La, 213
Estrada, Ernesto "Fruko," 43
Ethnicity, 6–7, 11–13, 15–18, 79–80, 86n23, 106, 185, 250, 255, 255, 264–65; "black soul," 17, 263; and music, 29, 44–45, 46n3, 47n9, 54–55, 67, 77, 248; and nation, 157
Explosión, 23, 168, 172, 179, 182–83, 185

Fader, The, 215
Falcón Records, 88, 108
Fandango, 30, 37–38
Fanny Lu, 264–65
Fantasma (Ghost), 126–27, 131, 222
Fantástico Bailable, 195, 214
Fantástico TV, 197
Fantástico TV de la Tarde, 197
Faroto, Monte, 251
Farotos, 251
Fashion. *See* Clothing styles
Fatales, Los: formation of, 237–38; and linguistic strategies, 241
Fatales para Niños, 237
Femininity, 203, 205, 207, 210
Feminism, 188–93, 200–201, 203, 205–7, 210n1, 229
Fernández, Pedro, 48n20
Fernández, Toño, 55, 58–59, 66, 68, 72, 84n11
Festival de la Cumbia, 31
Festival de la Leyenda Vallenata, 30, 42, 97
Festivales patronales, 52
Festival Nacional Autóctono de Gaitas, 49, 63

Fiesta Menemista, La (the Menemist party), 195
Flamers, Los, 103n6
Flor de Piedra, 198, 219–21
Flores, Raúl, 182, 187n12, 187n14
Florida, 113
Fonovisa, 118n2
Fonseca, 264–65
Fontalvo, José Portaccio, 251
Fortou, Emilio, 40
Fragmentation, 13, 142, 207; of gender, 200, 207; of identity, 14; of national identity, 134–35
Frómeta, Luis María "Billo," 259
Fronterizos, Los, 6
Fruko y sus Tesos, 43
Fuego Cubano, 194
Fulbe (Fulani), 34
Fujimori, Alberto, 180

Gabriel, Peter, 44
Gaceta Municipal, 252
Gaita corrida, 49–50, 53
Gaitambú, 64, 74, 85n19, 85n21
Gaita music: and cumbia, 51–55, 60, 80; development of, 35–36, 50, 52–58, 66–67, 78–80, 84n11, 252, 262–63; Festival de Gaita in San Jacinto, 30, 59–75, 78–79, 83n8; Festival Nacional de Gaitas, 49; instrumentation of, 83n6, 83n7, 83n9, 85n22, 251, 254; and place, 19–20, 51, 61–65, 75–78, 81, 82n2
Gaiteros, Los, 49–52, 58–59, 64, 77–79, 81, 82n2, 85n21, 85n22, 86n24
Gaiteros de Soplaviento, Los, 85n21
Gaiteros of San Jacinto, 44, 74
Galan, Pacho, 2, 37–39, 48n24, 81, 84n11, 256, 259
Gallegos, José, 85n17
Gangs, 123, 127, 130; and sonideros, 137n9. *See also* Sonideros
Gapun, Papua New Guinea, 230
Garabato-chande, 51
García, Joaquín, 172
García, Manuel Antonio "Toño," 49, 59

García, Rigoberto Tovar, 107
Gardel, Carlos, 257
Garzón, Pedro, 62
Gender, 4, 9, 16–18, 188–90, 192–93, 196, 201, 207, 211n4, 229; and class, 25, 110; in dance, 31, 33, 65, 181–82, 189, 196, 202, 204, 206–7, 209; gender relations, 25, 189, 193, 199; and hegemony, 189, 191, 211n4; and identity, 193; in lyrics, 191, 207–9; in music, 24, 34–35, 50, 72–73, 189, 198–210, 211n5, 212n8, 265; and power relationships, 188–89; women in the popular sectors, 16, 24
Geography: creation of a "sociospatial environment," 2, 125; "diasporic public sphere," 22, 120, 126; and music, 143, 184, 242
Gilda, 196
Girlie, 192
Gladys "la Bomba Tucumana," 196
Globalization, 106, 116, 119, 184, 191
Globe Style, 44
Goenaga, Miguel, 252
Goodman, Benny, 37
Gótica nightclub, 161
Graduados, Los, 260
Grammys, Latin, 44, 49, 64, 65, 82n2
Gran Silencio, El, 267
Gran Combo, 109, 234, 236
Green (band), 196
Grupera/o music: and class, 15, 115; and *conjunto norteño*, 90–91, 93, 95; and cumbia, 93–95; developments of, 92–96, 99–100, 106, 109, 111, 117; and media, 102; and region, 87–90; and tejano music, 87
Grupo Bryndis, 267
Grupo Celeste, 150
Grupo Costumbres del Folklor, 85
Grupo Etnia, 85
Grupo 5, 139, 162–164, 168
Grupo Maigame, 85
Grupo Mallanep, 163
Grupo Néctar, 162
Grupo Son Batuca, 85n19

Grupo San Felipe, 85n19
Grupo Vocal Argentino, El, 6
Guachín, 198
Guajira Peninsula, the, 34, 46n1
Guaracha, 36, 39
Guatemala, 113, 216
Guayacán and Grupo Niche, 43
Guinea, 31–32, 35
Gulf of Urabá, 46n1
Gutiérrez, Alfredo, 41, 97
Guttiérrez, Posada, 251, 252, 268n3

Haley, Bill, 166
Hegemony: and class, 4, 26, 116–17, 142; and dance, 18; and the development of music, 261; and gender, 189, 191, 211n4; and identity, 100, 114; and nation, 258, 266–67; resistance to, 161
Hernández, Juan Nicolás, 49
Hernández, Tomás, 66–67, 69, 82
Hillbilly. See *Chúntaro*
Hispanos, Los, 260
Homology, 13, 159
Honduras, 113
Horóscopo Records, 148
Hotel Nutibara, 259
Houston, x, 89, 91, 94, 96, 100, 103n3, 107
Huanca Hua, Los, 6
Huapango, 88, 101
Huaracina, Pastorita, 145
Huayno, 42, 140, 144, 145
Húmisha, 168, 173–75, 177, 183
Huracanes del Norte, Los, 92
Hybridization, 21, 29, 80, 87, 91, 99, 104n11, 111, 119, 158, 171, 179

Ibero-American Exposition, 253
Ideal Records, 88
Identity, 13, 95, 157, 159; absences, 16–17, 135; articulation of, 11, 13, 15–17, 78, 100, 115, 229; construction of, in Mexico, 15, 125, 130–31, 134–36, 219; and cumbia, 16, 21, 27, 39, 87, 99, 153, 185, 248, 257, 262, 264–67; and dance, 123, 162; and embodiment, 15, 208; essentialism, 15, 191, 260, 264; and ethnicity, 86n23, 185; fragmentation of, 13–14; and gender, 189, 206, 210; and geographic space, 11, 15, 21–22, 53, 102, 114, 119–25, 130, 135, 229; and immigration, 115, 134–35; interpellation, 11, 14–15, 159, 166n3; intersection, 17, 106; and language, 16, 177, 242; marked identities, 17–18; and morality, 17, 100, 141; and music, 29, 45, 54, 77, 79–80, 96, 100–101, 120, 255, 260; narrative identities, 11–15, 53, 100–102, 157–61; and nation, 2–3, 18–19, 23–24, 29, 39–40, 48n29, 60, 78–79, 81, 88, 117–18, 144, 161, 169, 248, 261; and region, 179–80, 185, 257; subject positions, 9, 14, 17, 149, 153, 191, 192. *See also* Gender; Hegemony; Socioeconomic class
IEMPSA, 145, 148
IIAP Seminal, 172
Illegal immigration. *See* Immigration
Illinois, 113
Imagined communities, 79, 106, 230
Immigration: Argentine, 194; and class, 15–16, 116, 151, 158; Colombian, 86n23, 95, 104n11, 255, 257; and cumbia, 18, 25, 113–14, 149–51, 153–55, 169, 180, 214; and identity, 20, 115; illegal, 16, 120–21, 126–27, 133, 135; Latin American diaspora, 15, 20; from/to Mexico, 15–16, 18, 21, 99, 101, 106, 109, 113–14, 120–21, 124, 127, 129–30, 133–34, 136n3, 136n5, 219; Middle Eastern, 46n2; migration status, 15–17; and music instruments, 32; and Peronism, 6, 12; Peruvian, 10–11, 16, 138, 140–42, 144, 148, 153–55, 157–59, 164, 166n3, 170, 175, 185; and remittances, 116; and a sense of community, 119; Uruguayan, 230
Impacto de Montemorelos, 93
Indio, El (band), 198
Indo, El (play), 72–73, 86
Instrumentation and rhythm of cumbia, 31–36, 72, 105, 124, 137n7, 145–46, 151, 222, 254
Intocable, 94

Iquitos, 184–85; cosmopolitan development, 170; indigenous populations of, 171; and music, 23–24, 168–69, 172–73, 179–82, 187n11; rubber boom in, 170–72
Island Records, 44
Itaya River, 170
iTunes, 267

Jacoby, Máximo, 222
Jalisco, 93, 103n8
Jamaica, 32
Jazz, 5, 9, 11, 37, 76, 94, 193, 253–54, 256, 258
Jedientos del Rock, Los, 219
Jerau, 264
Jesuit missionaries, 170
Jones, Nicky, 5
Juaneco y su Combo, 139, 148
Juarez, Cesar. *See* Fantasma

Kamko, 34
Kanatari, 172
Karamelo, 264
Karibe con K, 234, 236–37, 240, 242, 247n8
Karicias, 196
Karina, Ruth, 162, 182
Kirovski brothers, the, 195, 219
Kiss (band), 7, 194
Kogi Indians, 35, 46, 54, 251
Korean War, 144
Kumbala, 126
Kumbia Kings, 117, 267

La Merced market, 122
Land, Jolly, 5
Landero, Andrés, 97
Language, 177, 197, 210n1; and ideology, 25–26, 226–45, 247n13; and nation, 114, 228; and Peronism, 245n3; pronominal meaning, 16, 25–26, 229–30, 233–36, 240, 247; and sexuality, 200–201, 203. *See also* Identity; Uruguay
Lara, Agustín, 90
Lara brothers, 58–59, 72
Larreta, Enrique, 230
Las Vegas, 108, 130

Latin America, 1, 4, 18, 26, 41, 100, 106, 116, 124, 125, 150, 189, 197, 227, 230, 231, 244, 263
Latin American diaspora, 15, 20
Latino, Paco, 180, 187n10
Laure, Mike, 93, 103n8, 111
Laza, Pedro, 38
Leader Records, 195–97
Leales, Los, 217
Lennon, John, 108
Lescano, Pablo, 25, 195, 213, 219; and Colombia, 216; and drug use, 25, 215, 218–24; effect on cumbia music, 198, 214, 222; motorcycle accident, 220
Leticia, Colombia, 180
Lezama, Angel, 130
Libres y Locos, 98
Lima: cumbia in, 140, 183, 216; Iberocentric center of gravity, 22–23; immigration to from the Andes, 22–23, 139–44, 185; and Peruvian identity, 145, 158
List, George, 33, 46n3, 253
Loma Larga, 95, 100
Longoria, Valerio, 92
Loretano, 176, 186n7
Loreto, Peru, 170, 172–73, 175, 180, 183, 186n6
Los Angeles, 108, 123, 130–33, 214, 216, 219
Los Angeles de Charley, 123
Los Caribeños, 139, 162–63
Los Destellos, 139, 145–48, 150
Los Shapis del Perú, 139, 154
Los Socios del Ritmo, 123
Lumbalú, 46n4
Luna Park, 213, 221, 223
Luna Verde, 264
Lyman, Peter, 203
Lyrics. *See under* Cumbia

Macaferri y Asociados, 211n3
Machismo, 151, 202
Machito, 37
Madre de Dios, x, 172
Magdalena River, 29–31, 44–45, 46n1, 47n8, 251, 255

Magenta Records, 195–97, 219
Magia (Magic), 126
Makuna, 85n19
Mala, Yerba, 98
Mala Fama, 198
Malagata, 196
Mambo, 37, 111, 145
Mango Records, 44
Manhattan, 239, 261
Mapalé, 30, 40, 252, 254
Máquina, La, 197
Maracaibo, 103n6
Maravilla, Ricki, 196
María, Angélica, 118n3
Marinera, 173, 175, 183, 186n3
Marioneta, 19–20, 50–53, 58, 61–63, 65, 67–71, 73–74, 76–79, 82, 84n14, 85n22
Márquez, Gabriel García, 44
Martínez, Petrona, 47n7
Martinez, Rodolfo, 246n6
Marullo, Alex, 73–74
Masculinity, 191, 210n1; subaltern masculinities, 189; and symbolic violence, 190; and women, 206, 209–10, 211n4; working-class masculinity, 110
Mass media, 102, 181; and cumbia, 97, 199; explicit sexuality in, 190, 201–2; in Monterrey, 89; in Peru, 145; and tecno-cumbia, 182
Master (sonidero), 126
Matamoros, Tamaulipas, 20, 87–88, 90, 92, 100, 107
Matiolli, Leo, 221
Mauricio y Palo de Agua, 264–65
Maxixe, 36
Medellín, x, 39–40, 84n11, 96, 254–55, 257–60, 262, 265
Media distribution of music, 36–42, 44, 78, 80, 106, 115–17, 125, 154, 162, 185, 196–97, 238, 256, 258
Mejía, Nolasco, 59
Meléndez, Eliécer, 59
Melódicos, Los, 259
Mendoza, Mañe, 59, 70, 72
Menem, Carlos, 8, 195

Mercedes Sosa, 6
Merengue, 2–3, 18, 42–43, 128, 163, 175, 181, 261–62
Mesa, Lizandro, 97
Mestizaje, 12, 45, 52, 60, 157–59, 173
Meta Guacha, 198, 219, 221
Metrópolis, 223
Mexican economic miracle. See Mexican Miracle
Mexican Miracle, 116–17, 118n8; end of, 20, 113
Mexico: cumbia in, 11, 20–21, 87–102, 103n6, 106–9, 111; dances in, 120, 217; and economics, 113–16; identity in, 11, 15; music in, 9–10, 41, 103n2, 218, 221, 261; and the United States, 21–22, 110, 120–31, 133–35, 136n3, 166n1. See also Mexican Miracle
Mexico City, 89, 93, 120, 122–27, 133, 136n3, 137n7, 216, 218
Meza, Jorge, 217
Meza, Lisandro, 217, 251
Michael, Chris, 83n3
Michelsen, Alfonso López, 42
Middleton, Richard, 159
Mier, Los, 93
Migration status. See Immigration
Mike Laure y sus Cometas, 111
Miller, Glenn, 253
Miranda, 213, 223
Mirlos, Los, 148, 216
Mixtec Indians, 121
Molina, Aniceto, 92, 217
Mompox, 30–31, 47n8, 250
Mompox Depression, 31, 45
Monterrey, 20, 108, 216–19; Colombian music from, 95–98; and cumbia, 15, 25, 87–95, 98–99, 102, 103n7, 107, 124, 214; and migration, 100–101; and rap music, 102
Montes de María la Alta region, 52
Montevideo, 232, 241
Montoya, Juan, 90
Morales, Ignacio, 107
Moré, Benny, 37
Moreyra, Jaime, 154

Movida Tropical, La, 196, 199
Murga, 216, 237
Murillo, Emilio, 253
Museo Etnoarqueológico de Montes de María, 61
Música costeña, 37, 148, 150, 154; and the Caribbean Coast, 29; and Colombian salsa, 43
Música duranguense, 123, 136n5
Música gallega, 48n28, 260
Música guapachosa, 108, 118n4
Música tropical, 37, 39, 43–45, 118n4, 142, 195, 199, 247n8, 256, 258, 260; in Argentina, 194; and cumbia, 39, 87, 90, 145, 181, 196–97, 222, 227, 238, 262; and political protest, 8, 232, 246n7; in Uruguay, 232, 234, 236–39, 244, 246n5
Música tropical andina, 142
Musical groups and performers. *See specific groups and performers*
Music festivals: Chicago Pan American Festival, 108–9; Festival de la Cumbia, 31; Festival de la Leyenda Vallenata, 30, 42, 97; Festival Nacional Autóctono de Gaitas, 49, 63; *festivales patronales*, 52; San Juan festival, 186n7; Virgin of Candelaria festivals, 252–53

Naco. *See* Tovar, Rigo
Naco norteño, 137
Nadal, Fidel, 221
NAFTA, 109, 116
Nanay River, 170
Narrative identities. *See* Identity
National Fund for Culture and the Arts of Mexico, 214
National identification processes. *See* Identity
Negros, 8, 11–12, 32, 198
Neoliberal, 8, 106, 116, 179, 184, 195, 197
New Jersey, 21; dances held in, 120, 122; Mexican immigrants to, 123, 124, 126–31, 136n3; music played in, 125
New Orleans, 263
New York: and cumbia, 63, 68, 75; dances and dance halls in, 120–33; and immigration, 62, 79, 136n3; music played in, 21, 51–53, 85n22
Nicaragua, 113
Niceto, 214–15
Nóbile, Eugenio, 268n7
Novarro, Chico, 5
Nueva Colombia, 49, 51, 80–81
Nueva Crema, La, 138, 150–52
Nueva Rosita, 91
Nuevo León, 87–88, 90, 92, 96, 108

Obras Stadium, 7, 194
Ocampo, Ernesto "Teto," 263
Ochoa, Ana María, 49, 53, 82n2
Olivares, Fito, 93, 267
Olivares, Joe, 94
Olivella, Delia Zapata, 46n3, 55, 84n11, 252, 262
Olivella, Manuel, 46n3, 54, 55, 84n11, 252, 262
Onda grupera, 15, 20, 109, 111
Oral sex, 200–202, 205
Orchestral arrangements, 37–38, 91
Oriente peruano (Peruvian Orient), 181
Orozco, Efraín, 193
Orquesta de la Luz, 18
Orquesta de Pedro Movilla, 3
Orquesta Emisora Fuentes, 37, 40
Orquesta La Voz de Barranquilla, 37
Orsí, Luis Alberto Salazar, 172
Ortiz, Fernando, 31, 252
Ospina, Juan, 58, 62, 82n1

Pacharacos, Los, 145
Paisa, 249, 261–62
Paisa cumbia, 262
Palenque de San Basilio, 46n3, 46n4, 47n8, 48n21, 55
Palermo, Mexico, 214
Panama, 12, 35, 46n1, 251
Panchos, Los, 91
Pandilla, 23–24, 168–69; and the Amazon/Amazonian identity, 172–73, 176; and carnival, 174–76; and folklore, 187n9; indigenous roots of, 177; instrumentation and rhythm, 177–78;

lyrics of, 176; as savage, 185–86; and tecno-cumbia, 179, 182–84
Papayeras, 255
Paraguay, 12, 213, 222
Parlanteras, 219
Parra, Catalino, 83n8
Pasión de Sábados, 214
Pastorcillos de Rigo Tovar fan club, 110
Patria Club, 221
Payola, 182
Pedro Laza y sus Pelayeros, 38
Peñalosa, Antonio María, 38
Pérez Prado 37, 48n20
Peronism, 6–8, 12, 17, 245n3; and cumbia, 6–7
Peru, 23, 172–73, 180, 182–83; and colonialism, 170, 184; and conquistadores, 143; and cumbia, 16–17, 22, 25, 42, 45, 139–46, 148–49, 151, 154–55, 157–58, 160–65, 166n8, 213, 216, 246n5, 261; and immigration, 10–11, 16; and the Korean War, 144; and pandilla, 168–69, 175; the Peruvian Andes, 177; and social change, 138, 171, 185
Peruvian Amazon, 23, 168, 173, 181, 186
Peruvian Orient. See *Oriente peruano*
Piaxtla, 121
Piba, la, 198
Pibes Chorros, Los, 98, 196, 198, 219
Piña, Celso, 96–97, 124, 267
Pintos, Carlos "Bocha," 239
Plato, 31
Plebe, La, 226–27
Pocabuy, 250
Pocho la Pantera, 196
Polka, 88, 91, 101
Polo, Juan Fernández "Chuchita," 49
Pop latino, 238–39, 242
Pope John Paul II, 108
Populares de Nueva Rosita, 91
Potencia Latina, 124, 126
Poverty, 6, 11, 22, 24–25, 98–99, 101, 107, 116, 118n6, 148, 150, 154–56, 163–64, 171, 180, 192, 197–98, 222, 226, 232, 238, 240, 242
Principales, 264

Pronominal meaning. See Language
Pro-sex feminism. See Feminism
Psychedelic cumbia, 139
Psychoanalysis, 206
Puebla, 21, 120–22, 124–27, 129–35, 136n3
Puello, Juan Carlos "El Chongo," 57, 65, 79
Puente, Tito, 109
Puerto Rico, 47n7, 103n6, 109, 131

Queens, New York, 49, 120, 122, 125, 130–31
Queens Theater in the Park, 49
Quilmes, Buenos Aires, 217
Quintanilla, A. B., 267
Quispe, Lorenzo Palacios, 22, 138

Rada, Francisco "Pacho," 43, 256
Radio Inca, 148
Radio Loreto, 183
Radio Santa Fe, 258
Ramirez, Arnaldo, Jr., 108
Ramón Ayala y sus Bravos del Norte, 103n8
Rampolla, Alexandra, 201
Ranchera, 2, 18, 36, 93, 111, 145
Rap music: and cumbia, 24, 214, 262. See also Monterrey
Raspa, 249, 260
RCA Victor, 88
Rebaza, Juan, 167n14
Redova, 88, 91
Reggae, 97–99, 221
Reggaetón, 18, 175, 262
Regional identities, 179, 185. See also Identity
Renacimiento, 74
Reyna, Cornelio, 92
Reynosa, 92
Rhapsody, 267
Ricardo Rojas Cultural Center, 222
Rio de la Plata, 24
Ritmo Fantástico, 195
River Plate, 16, 26, 226, 229, 230, 236, 238, 240–41, 246n4, 246n5
Robeson, Paul, 5

Roble, 91–92
Robledo, Margarita, 104n9
Rocha, Department of, 234
Rock en español, 123, 136n5
Rock music, 7, 87, 91–93, 97, 136n5, 262–63; in Argentina, 18, 194; and cumbia, 43, 76, 87, 91–93, 97, 103n8, 111, 123, 139–40, 145, 220–21, 223; in Peru, 166n9, 166n10
Rock nacional, 7, 18, 194
Rodolfo y su Típica, 44
Rodríguez, Adolfo, 85n17
Rodríguez, Camilo, 58, 62, 82n1, 85n17
Rojas Center, 222
Ron Medellín Añejo, 64
Rose, The, 49
Roxy, The, 213, 223

Sabinas Records, 92
Salas, Santiago, 236
Salazar, Fausto, 124
Salazar, Juan, 90, 103n7
Salsa, 18, 43, 45, 67, 75, 103n6, 128, 131, 139, 146, 161, 163, 181, 189, 212n7, 261
Salsa romántica, 155
Samba, 18, 181, 183
San Alejo, 264
San Antonio, x, 89, 91, 96
San Basilio de Palenque, 52, 253
Sandoval, Chris, 91
San Fernando, California, 83n8, 213–14
San Jacinto, 19, 30, 35, 44, 46n3, 49–55, 58–64, 67–70, 74–81, 82n2, 83n3, 83n8, 83n9, 84n12, 85n19, 85n21, 85n22, 86n24, 252
San Juan festival, 186
San Luis Potosí, 95, 100
San Pelayo, 30, 37, 48n19, 52, 54, 84n10
Santa Barbara de los Iquitos, 170
Santa Catarina River, 108
Santafesina cumbia, 217
Santa Isabel de Cholula, 120–22, 124
Santa Marta, x, 43, 262
Santa Rosa, Peru, 180
Saturday Night Fever, 110
Second-wave feminism, 189, 190–91
Selectah, Toy, 124

Selena, 94
Selena y los Dinos, 117
Selvática, 11, 148
September 11, 2001, 133
Septeto Nacional, 37
Serranía, 52, 54, 59, 61–62
Se te ve la tanga, 208–9, 221
Sevilla, 253
Sex: as autonomous from love, 211n5, 212n9; and cumbia villera, 16, 192–93, 200–210; in media, 25, 190; and second-wave feminism, 189–91, 207; and third-wave feminism, 192–93. *See also* Anal sex; Oral sex
Sexteto Habanero, 37, 48n21
Shapis, Los, 23, 42, 140, 155–56, 160
Shapis del Perú, Los: and chicha music, 154–55, 160; and Peruvian cumbia, 42, 139–40, 154
Shipibo tribe, 170, 175
Sin Ánimo de Lucro, 264
Sierra, Silvia, 82n1
Sierra Leone, 32, 35
Sierra Nevada de Santa Marta, 35, 46n1, 54, 251, 265
Sinú River Valley, 37–38
Sipaganboy, 198
Ska, 97–99
Smithsonian Folkways label, 44, 50, 64, 82n2
Socioeconomic class, 26, 264–66; in Argentina, 6–12, 194, 261–62; and chicha, 141, 145, 164, 167n18, 180; in Colombia, 43, 79, 83n5, 254–55, 262; and cumbia, 14, 17, 20, 31, 38, 45, 97, 101, 106, 109, 164, 194–95, 207, 238, 241; and dance, 232; and gender, 13, 16–17; and genres of music, 5; in Lima, 142–43, 148, 150; and migrants, 15–16; and nation, 2–4; in Peru, 155, 158, 161, 167n17, 171; in Uruguay, 237, 140, 242; and vallenato, 43; and villera, 98–99. *See also* Chacalón; Tovar, Rigo
Soledeño Francisco "Pacho" Galán, the, 256

Sombras, 196
Son (music style), 2, 36, 39, 42, 44, 48n21, 150, 181
Son Baracu, 85n19
Sonidera cumbia, 216, 218
Sonidero bailes, 22, 121, 122–23, 125, 133–35
Sonideros, 110, 125, 217–19; and the construction of geographic space, 21–22, 122–28, 130–31, 134–35; deejays, 120, 134; and gangs, 137n9; as immigrants, 114, 133; and the reading of personal dedications, 128–130, 134–136; and September 11, 133; and technology, 132; and travel, 137n8
Sonido, 114, 122, 126–27, 128, 133, 173, 175
Sonolux, 40, 44–45, 48n24, 258
Sonora Dinamita, La, 41, 103n6, 217, 260, 267
Sonora Escándalo, 217
Sonora Matancera, 37, 41, 48n20
Sonorámico, 123, 137n8
Sonora Santanera, 111
Sonora Veracruz, 103n6
Son Sabana, 85n19
Sound system. See *Sonido*
Spain, 144, 213, 264
Spinetta, Dante, 223
Spinetta, Luis Alberto, 223
Splendid (radio station), 195
Subculture, 116–17, 123
Subject positions. See Identity
Sucre, 35, 46n1, 54, 59, 75, 250–51
Super Grupo, El, 150–51
Super Tropi, 217
Symbolic terrorism, 189, 200

Tabatinga, Brazil, 180
Talar de Pacheco, 218
Tamaulipas, 20, 87–88, 90, 92, 100, 103n9, 107
Tango, 18, 36, 145, 194, 217, 257
Taz (DJ), 215
Technobrega, 119, 136n1
Tecno-cumbia: in the Amazon, 23–24, 162, 168, 173, 179–82, 185–86; and chicha, 155; and dance, 187n11; de-Andeanization of, 142; development of, 139, 162–64, 169, 261; and Iquitos, 172, 179; and pandilla, 169, 173, 182–84; and payola, 182; in Peru, 42
Teenagers, Los, 260
Tehauacan, 121
Tejano music, 90; and grupera, 94–95
Tepito, Mexico, 122, 125, 137n8, 218
Texas, 132; Anglo-Saxon sectors of, 88; cumbia in, 94, 103n4, 103n9, 107–8; and Mexico, 87–88, 90–91, 99
Tex-Mex, 42, 90
Third-wave feminism, 192–93
Tijuana, 133
Toada, 162, 180–81
Tok Pisin, 230
Tongo, 163
Totó La Momposina, 44, 262
Tovar, Rigo, 100, 103n8, 106–8, 114; and the Mexican culture industry, 20, 93; musical instrumentation and sound of the music of, 111–18; as a *naco*, 20, 110–11, 116–17, 124, 137n7; and popular success, 108–11; trade unions, 197–98; in the United States, 106, 108, 110, 114
Transnationalism, 51, 53–54, 80–81, 90, 109, 134, 139, 171, 250; and cultural space, 115, 119–20, 122; and cumbia, 15, 18–21, 24, 29, 45, 87, 107, 113–14, 169, 179, 184–85, 224, 227–28, 259–61; and Gaita, 79; and Rigo Tovar, 106, 117
Transnational movement, 119–20, 122, 134
Trío Matamoros, 37
Tropical Caribe, 96
Tropicalísima, 197, 222
Tropical music. See *Música tropical*
Tropihit, 197
Tropipop, 249; and bambuco, 16, 249, 262, 265; and class, 16; and cumbia, 26–27, 264–66; as "inauthentic," 264–65
Tropitango, 25, 194, 213, 216, 218, 221

Tropitango de Pacheco, 213
Trovadores, Los, 6
Tumberos, 199
Tupamaros, Los, 260
United States: cumbia in, 18, 21, 87, 92, 127, 179, 256; immigration from/to, 10, 99, 106–7, 113, 120–21, 214, 219; and Mexico, 15, 22, 89, 108, 120–21, 124–25, 129–30, 132–35; and Nueva Colombia, 51; salsa in, 103. *See also* Tovar, Rigo
Universidad del Atlántico, 256
Univision Records, 118
Un Oso Rojo, 199
Urarina tribe, 170
Uribe, Juan P., 82n1
Urrea, Freddy, 62
Uruguay: language use in, 228–30, 232–44; music in, 16, 232, 246n5, 246n6; politics in, 230; and race, 11, 231, 246n4; as the Switzerland of the Americas, 230, 242. *See also* Cumbia: Uruguayan; *Música tropical*

Vale, Raúl, 182, 187n12, 187n14
Valledupar, x, 30, 42, 97
Vallenato, 1–3, 6, 48n26, 67, 96, 217; in Colombia, 101, 124, 181; and cumbia, 22, 26–27, 41–43, 45, 64, 83n5, 93, 96–97, 133, 219, 262–63, 268n5; and tropipop, 265
Vallenatos de la Cumbia, 96
Valses, 145, 160
Vejarano, Martín, 19, 49–54, 58, 61–63, 65–68, 70, 72, 74–77, 82n1, 83n3, 83n5, 84n14
Velásquez, Alvaro, 43
Vélez, Nazarena, 201
Venezuela, x, 12, 32, 39, 103n6, 259
Victor Studio, 253
Villa, Beto, 91–92
Villareal, Alicia, 93
Villero, 99, 102, 198, 241

Vío, Víctor, 108
Virgin of Candelaria festivals, 32–33, 252–53
Vives, Carlos, 43, 82n2, 262–67; as the "Colombian Elvis," 263
Voz de Antioquia, La, 258–59
Voz de Barranquilla, la, 36–37
Voz de Laboratorios Fuentes, la, 36
Voz de la Víctor, la, 36–37, 258

War, Rossy, 42, 161
Wawancó, Los, 194
Wayúu Indians, 34, 46n1
Weber, Max, 142
Wills and Escobar, 253
WOMAD (World of Music, Arts, and Dance), 44
Working class. *See* Socioeconomic class
World Circuit, 44
World music, 44–45, 81; and authenticity, 53, 80
World Music Network, 44
World Youth Festival, 155

Yagua tribe, 170
Yaipén, Hermanos, 163
Yepes, Dionysio, 49
Yerba Brava, 198, 204
Yerena, Pedro, 90
Youth, 104n10; and music, 14, 62, 95, 97, 99, 103n1, 127, 130, 135, 136, 148–50, 257–58, 263, 265; and sexuality, 25, 190
YouTube, 14, 129, 133
Yuruparí, 46n3

Zacatecas, 95, 100
Zambo, 250
Zegna, Ermenegildo, 164
Zenúes, 251
Žižek (night club), 25, 213, 215
Žižek, Slavoj, 25, 209, 210
Zuleta, Emiliano, 43
Zuluaga, Tulio, 264

www.ingramcontent.com/pod-product-compliance
Lightning Source LLC
Chambersburg PA
CBHW070753230426
43665CB00017B/2341